Sample Essays for the TOEFL Writing Test (TWE)

ToeflEssays.com

Sample Essays for the TOEFL Writing Test (TWE)

ISBN 1-4116-0774-0

ToeflEssays.com

www.toeflessays.com

For more information, please visit www.toeflessays.com or www.lulu.com/toeflessays.

Table of Contents

Topic 1 **Why go to university?**

People attend college for various reasons. Some people consider college as a challenge and others take it as a new experience. In my opinion, I think that people attend college to increase knowledge, meet new people and develop a career. Studying at a college can benefit a person greatly since it augments a person's knowledge, aids in developing a career and gives a chance

5 to meet new people of different backgrounds.

Knowledge is such a powerful tool that possessing it can diminish nearly all life problems. A college or a university is the place where one can gain knowledge and become valuable to the society. An individual can acquire knowledge about a wide variety of subjects. When my brother was in college, he learned about bacteria and viruses. He had learned that at high school a little bit, but in college he studied it in depth. In addition, he also learned how deal with life problems in

10 college.

Developing a career is a very important stage in our life. Most students, after graduating from high schools, go to colleges or universities to be trained and educated. Some major in various subjects while others go for professional degrees. Universities help students in achieving their goals by preparing them for the career they have picked. If I go to a medical school, I know that the school will prepare me well enough for me to become a successful medical doctor.

15 Interacting with new people is always a challenge. A university is a place where people from different backgrounds get opportunities to interact with each other. Information about different cultures, different life styles and certain types of food is shared among students. My father used to study in a university, and he told me about all the different cultural backgrounds of the students there.

A college or a university is the place where dreams can be fulfilled. The subjects such as how to deal with life, how to

20 interact with people and how to become independent are taught and experienced there. A college or a university makes a individual complete and help him/her to lead a successful life.

Topic 1 **Why go to university?**

A university degree often helps a person achieve his goal with more ease. However, do we attend university just in pursuit of a degree? Does a university only provide us nothing beneficial besides a paper-made diploma? As far as I am concerned, we enjoy university

25 education in the following aspects:

Firstly, with the knowledge learned in a university, we will have a deep understanding of our society. It is true that genuine knowledge comes from practice, but it cannot be denied that genuine knowledge tells us how to practice. A systematic study in a college or a university, of course, enables us to realize how the society works and how to cope with certain problems arising from it in a more efficiently, and more skillful way.

30 Second, a university education usually makes it possible that we get hold of a decent job. As a result of the accomplishment of a four-year study, it is not difficult for us to find a good job in most cases. How can we imagine that a graduate majoring in astronomy has to be a vendor in the street! No doubt, he/she should sit in his/her laboratory, doing research on aircraft science before a computer. Obviously, a university education assures him/her a decent job.

Last, but not the least, we can help others much better if we put what we have learned in a university into practice. A

35 university education fortifies our values, enhance our skills, and broaden our horizons. With those, we are more capable of giving a hand to those who are in need of help than ever before.

Knowledge is power. When achieving a degree in a university, we can get a better understanding of the society, find a decent job in an easy way, and help others better. All of those are due to the knowledge learned in a university.

Topic 1 **Why go to university?**

I strongly encourage anyone who asks my opinion to attend university. Entering university is at the same time a so much promising step into a world of opportunities as long as it is accompanied by a strong will and desire for distinction. The quality and diversity of opportunities and the spread spectrum of choices higher education can provide us is the core motive for everyone intending to attend a college. I will try to examine below the specific reasons for entering university according to which I think are the most common viewpoints nowadays.

45 First let us look at what a person can typically gain from a successfully study at a college. It is a diploma and maybe other several formal qualifications. This is by default leading to a more distinct, respected, well-paid profession. Nowadays unemployment crisis is troubling not only the poor countries but the west civilization as well, so that the ease of finding a job may play an important role in the decisions everyone is making.

Another serious reason is that people want to get more educated. It is something simple to say but it relies on the human

50 nature. University provides the next level of education and has all these resources and facilities that may be a constant sparkle for the knowledge craving. Learning is the key to everything that we want to improve. So, higher education helps us widen our understanding capabilities and increase our intellectual ability.

Apart from the points I made above there is also a well known fashion all over the world that is called career preparation. Many people attend college in perspective of making either a career in science and technology or a career in business. It is believed that the ideas, opportunities, qualifications, in-depth knowledge and expertise in science areas often make attending university imperative. Many times a four-year study at a university may only be the beginning of a sequence of moves someone can make in order to accomplish what he thinks best for his career.

Finally, I cannot oversee the fact that many times studying at a university also means living in a city far from home. New
5 responsibilities always appear but they do not become a serious drawback. In contrast, the new sense of freedom and independence a young man can experience or thinks he will is thought of as something of great importance. One thing is for sure though, there is chance for everyone in the community of a university to meet people, make new friends and know individuals of great importance.

Last but not least I wish to say that the purpose of university is to harvest knowledge and to being educated, so it is
10 obvious that everyone can find a reason for attending university.

Topic 1 Why go to university?

University is no longer a fresh word to people nowadays. Since the beginning of this century, more and more youngsters choose to enter university after they have completed the study in high schools rather than to join the army or become an apprentice. Therefore, it is kind of interesting to find out the reason behind.

15 First of all, students can only learn fundamental knowledge during high school while they are able to focus on their own interested majors in universities. This period is the key to knowledge accumulation, which will contribute a lot to the future of an individual. Moreover, university is no doubt the symbol of high education. It offers more than pure knowledge. A degree from a university gives people certain identity that makes them stand out among their competitors. It can be seen from the fact that most international companies will only hire those who have at least a Bachelor's degree in
20 China.

But, as far as I know, sincere dreams might also be the reason for university or college. For instance, in the 60s and 70s, people in China experienced hard times. Many of them had to give up advanced education and take up the burdens of life at their early age. Now, as they became parents or even grandparents, their dream for university education had no doubt realized by their younger family members. Those young people, as reported, often study very hard in order to fulfill the
25 expectations of two generations.

There is no doubt that university can be the turning point of one's future, because higher education will provide people with not only knowledge prepared for their careers, but also the fulfillment of their life goals. Meanwhile, the society has improved its strength to sponsor higher education. Compared with the past, people now attend universities also because they are able to secure various scholarships and supports from different channels. A very good example is that many
30 Chinese students are now studying in the U. S. Their incentive for application should be attributed to not only to their own performance but also the comprehensive education frameworks in the U. S.

Broadly speaking, people who study in universities have their hopes: to fulfill themselves. At the same time, our society generously provides such an environment for people to achieve such goals. Therefore, when we see more and more fresh smiles on the campus of universities, let us just wish them a promising future.

Topic 2 Are parents best teachers?

Obviously, the first teachers we have in our lives in most cases are our parents. They teach us to walk, to speak, and to have good manners before we reach "the real world. " More than even the professional teachers that we have at school, parents are generally the most involved in the development and education of children.

Almost for sure our parents are the best teachers at the beginning of our lives, which actually corresponds to the parents'
40 role in nature. Parents are most committed and involved in teaching their children; they have a kind of instinct to sacrifice a part of themselves for the betterment of their children. They love us and have great patience while passing down their knowledge to us. They wish us a success and thus will not teach us bad things. And of course, implicit learning occurs when children unconsciously copy some of their parents' habits and styles of behavior.

During the second stage of child development, adolescence, parents can still be in the best position to offer advice even
45 though the children might not accept it. In this case, perhaps the child's friends would be the best teachers. Adolescents are notoriously rebellious in many cultures and may automatically reject any advice from their parents. My first marriage for instance, was solely a matter of doing the opposite when my parents tried to intrude in offering their advice. So in such matters, parents should be much more flexible and be rather the partners with their children. So we can see that being a teacher of growing child become more and more complicated case as the time passes and many parents are simply
50 not able to meet the increased demands.

On the other hand, I would say that parents are not professional teachers and they tend to be very biased by their love of their children. So wishing good things and an easy life may prevent children from maturation. In any case, parents usually can present only one viewpoint of the world, while good teaching should be based on different attitudes. Thus, when children go to school and have a great diversity of teachers, they learn much more than their parents could probably give
55 them. Furthermore, once our parents get older, they become more conservative and cannot always be objective in regard

ToeflEssays.com

to modern trends and fashions. Thus we need to take their advice with caution during that period. However, some kind of intuition that I believe shared between relatives about what everybody needs and great love that exists in families still makes our parents very good teachers and advisers at any time.

In conclusion, while parents are not the ideal teachers, and well-rounded children will generally need a great diversity of
5   teachers in their lives in order to have a more accurate view of the world, parents are generally the most committed of all teachers and have the greatest emotional investment in their children and their future.

Topic 2 **Are parents best teachers?**

Our entire education system is based on what we accumulate each day of our life. In spite of the fact that school teachers are those who give us lots of information in a variety of fields, our parents are still the best teachers; they start their educational process as soon as we were
10   born and never stop teaching us.

In the initial years of our life, our parents are involved in guiding us, in modulating our personality and making us understand the differences between right and wrong. When I was five, my parents bought me a dog; they taught me how to take care of him, feed him, play with him and bath him. Thus, I learned that we all have responsibilities.

Even if parents are not specialized in education, their role in teaching the children to be aware of the need of improving
15   their knowledge at school is tremendous. Our parents are not supposed to teach us Math, Chemistry or Biology, but they are very much involved in giving us lessons about being independent, strong and confident in ourselves. As my mother said to me, "fight your own battles because I will not be always able to protect you."

Teenagers have to be informed about all the negative effects that can occur if using drugs, drinking alcohol, or smoking. Regarding this issue, parents have to cooperate with school teachers to make children aware of those possible risks.

20   I believe that parents are the best teachers because their lessons last forever. My parents are old now. Even when I am a grown up person, I consider that they can still give me very good advices when I need them, based on their life experience. My parents have the most important roll in my education during my life and I will always be grateful for everything they have taught me.   *role*

Topic 2 **Are parents best teachers?**

Throughout all the years in my life, I was influenced by my parents in many fashions, from the way of thinking to the trifle everyday habits. No doubt, we inherit the gene from our parents and get basic knowledge and norms from them. What we learned from our parents in the early years will be encoded in our mind and be reflected in nearly every aspect of our behaviors. But in terms teaching, I do not think it's our parents who are the best teachers.

As is known to all, a child will be better trained with a systematic education. However, except those parents who are
30   schoolteachers themselves, few parents grasp the systematic way of teaching. On the one hand, children can only learn a large scope of knowledge step by step from formal education at schools. On the other hand, the parents can only teach their children sporadic knowledge. It is obvious that the young will be better equipped through formal education in classroom.

From the emotional angle, the bond between child and parents are so tight that the parents cannot give a more objective
35   instruction than a schoolteacher can. Some parents tend to spare their children from hard working and, to the extreme, some even spoil their children to do everything they want. All these are resulted from parents' love toward children. But from an objective angle, hardworking is sometimes a necessary step toward success. Parents should not be blamed for loving their children but such love may become obstacle for objective instruction.

With the coming of the knowledge economic, we may find that our parents' knowledge is becoming obsolete. In a
40   changing world, the young are always the first to fashion the news ideas and technology. The elderly, however, are always not used to such rapid changes. Thus, conflicts are inevitable between parents and their children. Accordingly, the young are no longer willing to commit to their parents ideas. To catch the tide of such changes, it is of the best interest for the young to learn from the open world instead of from the obsolete knowledge of their parents.

All this is not to say that to learn from parents is useless. In fact, even in the rapidly changing world, the scope of parents'
45   knowledge still has great influence on their children, especially on young children. But for the young to get the most needed knowledge, they should not solely rely on what they learned from their parents.

Topic 2 **Are parents best teachers?**

Nowadays, some may hold the opinion that parents are the best teachers. But others have a negative attitude. As far as I am concerned, I agree with this statement because, obviously, the first teachers we have in our lives in most cases are our parents. They teach us how to walk,
50   how to speak, and what are good manners and bad manners before we reach the real world. Therefore, parents are the people who influence their children most, and children will carry on qualities of their parents. More than even the professional teachers that we have at school, parents are generally the most involved in the development and education of children. The reasons are presented below.

One of the primary reasons is that our parents are the teachers at the beginning of our lives, which actually corresponds to the parents' role in nature. First, parents are most committed and involved in teaching their children and have a kind of instinct to sacrifice a part of themselves for the betterment of their children. Second, they love their children and have great patience while passing down their knowledge to us. They wish us to become success and thus will not teacher us bad
5   things. Surely, children will unconsciously copy some of their parents' habits and styles of behavior. Besides, parents will become their first role models.

There is also a more subtle point we must consider. During the second stage of child development, adolescence, parents can still be in the best position to offer advices even though the children might not accept it. In this case, perhaps the child's friends would be the best teachers. Adolescents are notoriously rebellious in many cultures and may automatically
10   reject and advice from their parents. In such matters, parents should be much more flexible and rather be friends with their children. However, many parents simply are not able to meet the increased demands, being teachers of their growing children.

What is more, I would say that parents are not professional teachers and they tend to be very biased by their love of their children. As a result, wishing good things and an easy life may prevent children from maturation. Frequently, parents
15   usually present only one viewpoint of the world, while good teaching should be based on different attitudes. For this reason, children may learn probably more if they have a great diversity of teachers other than the parents. Furthermore, technology develops very quickly; and parents may not always be objective in regard to modern trends and give children proper advices. However, I believe that the care and love among family members still makes our parents very good teachers and advisers at any time.

20   Taking into account of all these factors, we may reach the conclusion that parents may not be the ideal teachers, but they are obviously the most committed of all teachers. Although well- rounded children will generally need a great diversity of teachers, parents can provide them the greatest emotional support in their lives without a substitute.

Topic 2 **Are parents best teachers?**

Are parents are best teachers? Different people will give different responses to this question from their own characters, emotional concerns and even educational backgrounds. However, when it comes to me, I believe that parents are our best teachers for the following reasons.

In the first place, parents are the people who are closest to us and who understand our real needs best. From infancy on, our parents have witnessed every step in both our physical and mental development. They share every hint of happiness or unhappiness with us and they even know what a little gesture of us might indicate. Based on such a deep understanding, our parents will teach us what we are interested in and what we are not. For instance, they can often buy books on our
30   favored topics such as sea animals and astronomical objects. Little by little, we can mature our minds and broaden our horizons in our favorite fields. (Or are we prospective artists, scientists, teachers, or even businesspeople? Our parents might tell that at our early ages. Consequently, they will give us specific encouragement and abundant resources in our favored fields. Sometimes, our parents can even point out a direction to our future professional goals. Will other people do that for us based on such a solid understanding of us?)

35   In the second place, our experienced parents are our best teachers of today's complicated society. From our teachers at school, we can learn sophisticated knowledge. But how can our teachers tell us how to communicate with others, how to deal with strangers, how to behave in different occasions, and how to make important decisions of our daily life? Only our parents, who will spend their whole life loving us, caring us will tell us how to steer our own boats in the ocean of life without selfish consideration.

40   Admittedly, our friends and school teachers could provide us with valuable advice now and then, and maybe it will be easier for us to follow their suggestions. Their effects on us cannot be neglected or replaced by our parents. And parents might spoil their children or even interfere with children's privacy because of love. To be honest, the roles of these two kinds of people cannot be replaced by each other. However, it seems to me that only our parents, who will spend their whole life with us, will be our best teachers, not only for now but also for our whole life.

45   All in all, if all the factors are contemplated, we can easily reach a conclusion that, parents are not only our first teachers but also our best teachers. Let's be carefully aware of this point and take better care of our parents to repay their efforts to teach us.

Topic 2 **Are parents best teachers?**

Parents are the most committed, the most influential, and almost the best teachers any child can have. The amount of time a child interacts with parents makes them the most influential force in a child's life. The child gets to learn the most basics of things like walking, speaking and interacting with others. It is under the protections of parents that a child learns to behave in society and to comfort him or herself.

Although parents are the most influential teachers in their children's life, they may not be regarded as the best teachers. Parents generally provide a biased view of the world; they always favor their child, and thus they cannot provide a
55   complete panoramic view of the society. Also parents may set a bad example for their child by abusing and fighting

amongst themselves. Psychologists and recent crime charts have proved that young outlaws generally come from disrespectful families, and have grown up in extreme environments.

A child interacts with many kinds of teachers at schools and colleges. Although these teachers, being professionals, have limited time to devote to a child, they provide a complete and diverse view to their students. They provide unbiased guidance to a child.

During the years of adolescence, children tend to be aggressive and non-conforming to others' views. So the parents need to act like friends rather than teachers to get their experiences through to their children. Eventually, it is the parents who provide an environment for a child to develop and mature, and thus have the capacity to be the best teachers to their child. What is important is to provide an unbiased view to their child, to motivate independent thinking and actuate timely maturation.

Topic 3 Has the ease of cooking improved life?

People work hard to fulfill their principal necessities, and food is the one thing that is really important to their survival. Although sometimes belied by other things that seem important, food is the core objective that drives all people to work. But the outcome of the efforts of these people is not a direct supply of food; rather it is in the form of money. Thus these people use the money they obtain to prepare their food.

In old days, preparing food was cumbersome and time-consuming work for those who do it solely for eating purposes. This kind of preparing food in due tie could not comply with the kind of life people lead today. The use of technological advancement makes preparing food practical even for the clumsiest person. This helps a great deal for those who work against time to make their living. It also avoids the waste of considerable amount of money from hiring a cook.

The development in the preparation of food is highly effective for those people who have no know how of it. A person who does not know how to prepare his/her own food would go to a restaurant or some other place where food is served everyday. But with the advanced food preservation technology, now he is free, completely independent of restaurants and other places. He can prepare his own food and enjoy the feeling of "home, sweet home".

For people at work, life has just become easy for them. They will not have to worry all day long about what they are going to prepare for their supper. They can fully concentrate on their jobs, and work with a mind full of peace.

In general this new way of preparing food has helped those who are concerned about their daily meals -- almost everyone. Not only that, it would enlighten those who are frustrated with their jobs just because of the worry of that tiresome work -- preparing food.

Topic 3 Has the ease of cooking improved life?

Food has always been the one of the greatest wants of humankind. It has influenced almost every step that humankind has taken. The search for food is the essence of life. Therefore if food is easier to get and prepare it is a real boon to humankind.

Food is the most important of the three basic amenities of life (water, food and shelter). Though it can be argued that water is the sustenance for any life form, food is more important because if you do not have water you will surely die. But if you are left with a scarcity of food it will lead to a very sickly and torturous life. Nutritious food is very essential for life, food has been the cause of many a battle. Thus if food was easier to prepare it will take away from the mind of the humankind a great burden.

Though the preparation of food becoming easier is considered a great blessing for humankind. The sudden rise in processed and canned food and all the junk food that one gets over the counter is not totally a boon. People who are so busy that they are not able to spend time to prepare their food, develop a liking for these ready-to-eat junk food. Though it might be thought of as a great way to save time, this is a shortsighted idea that could actually lead to a world of harm. Because one must understand that even though junk food saves us a lot of time, the nutritional value of the food is not so good. In reality the preservatives used in these foods are often found to be toxic in nature. Hence it defeats the purpose it is supposed to serve i.e., to provide nutritional value.

Moreover since people do not take time to prepare food, the art of cooking is slowly vanishing. Actually cooking is a good way of releasing pressure that builds up from our professional commitments. Cooking can easily provide relief from all the tensions that prevail in our life. In the past family weekend get together was considered to be a good time to know each other and they used to spend time cooking food for the entire family. They used to exchange recipes and it was a way of rewinding after the hard weeklong labor. Thus this junk food has denied the human kind of one of humankind's oldest arts. It could even be termed as a retrograde step in human culture.

Therefore I believe though the processed food has made the preparation of food much easier, it is not a good step for mankind.

Topic 3 Ease of cooking

Recent technological advancements have changed the way people live radically. They have also made food easier to prepare - fast foods and preserved foods are everywhere. The days when cooking of food was a major errand of the day have long become the past. Nowadays it's only a matter of minutes to cook food. However this improvement does not come without a price.

The most important loss we suffer due to these fast foods is quality. These fast foods are lower in nutritional value and contain less minerals and vitamins. Further they have high calories that result in weight gain, and that in turn leads to heart
5 diseases and other problems. Further, they have added flavors, colors and preservatives that are not always very helpful to our health.

These preserved food have also taken away the natural taste and benefits of fresh foods from our lives. We now depend upon artificial flavorings to make a fish taste like a fish. However we cannot get the natural taste of fresh foods from preserved foods.

10 We have lost the fun of cooking because of these fast foods. Cooking used to be an art and people enjoyed cooking and the satisfactions they got by cooking a tasty meal. Further, cooking is the time when family members gathered and enjoyed their time together. However with less time devoted to cooking, the chances for such meals are now rare.

All these illustrations point out that although fast foods and preserved foods are unavoidable in today's busy world, we must not totally neglect the advantages of fresh foods. We must sometimes take time with our families to prepare a
15 delicious meal and enjoy it together with the ones we love the most.

| *Topic 4* **Experience is the best teacher** | Books are considered to be the source of all knowledge, but all that one learns through a book is only of theoretical nature in the form of ideas and concepts. It is essential to utilize them in a real environment and experience the knowledge that is learned from books. |

Learning is nothing but understanding the world around us. Books, no doubt are a great source of knowledge as it gives
20 us an idea about a particular subject in detail. But all that one could learn from it is limited to the level of knowing how a certain phenomenon occurs, or how a certain concept works. The knowledge gained through books alone cannot help anyone, because what one learns through the books should be put in to use to harvest the benefits. For instance, a person who wants to learn driving can go through various manuals and guides that teach people how to drive, but all this knowledge is useful only when you are actually driving the car on the roads. It would be an utter waste of time if one just
25 reads the books and does not use them for practical purpose.

Learning through experience is always a lot different from learning through books. Let us consider the same example of a person wanting to learn to drive: even if he goes through every book that is available on driving, still it cannot qualify him as an expert driver. This is because of the fact that books about driving can only teach people traffic rules and provide solutions on how to handle certain situations. The situations faced by a driver could be totally different from what he had
30 learnt from a book. Sometimes we find that the real environment is quite different from the one perceived by us through reading books. This is the very reason why, even in educational institutions, all theoretical classes are followed by practical sessions.

Learning through experience can also be more effective than learning through books because one does not envision everything on his own, but is given a chance to experience the reality. The art of driving can be enjoyed only when we are
35 behind the wheels and not when reading it in books. Moreover, any book is actually an account of past experiences, i.e. it is based on the experiences of people who tried to develop a new idea. The books are their experiences, telling us what they already have tried. Thus from their experiences we can correct ourselves and thus save valuable time and resources. It helps us to concentrate on their failures and to correct them, but they alone cannot teach us everything we need to know. The knowledge learned through books alone cannot help us to face all the exigencies that we would face in real life
40 situations; we have to practice on our own.

Books are like a guiding light in one's pursuit for knowledge. But it is left to everyone of us to experience it first hand and learn new things for the betterment of their lives. So the notion "experience is the best teacher" is perfectly true.

| *Topic 4* **Are books more important than experience?** | It is true that "Not everything that is learned is contained in books." A person can learn a lot and retain what he learns through experience. In my opinion life's valuable lessons are learnt from experience and so the knowledge gained from experience is more important. |

Books are a great source of information. A person in his lifetime cannot experience everything, but by reading a book on a particular subject he can gain knowledge over that subject in less time. There are books available on any subject that one needs. However experience seems more important to me.

Suppose a person living in the United States wants to learn about India. He has two options: he could visit India and learn
50 about the people and places there or he could just pick up a book about India and read it. The first option will be expensive and time consuming, but at the same time it gives one first hand information and a sense of satisfaction while the second option is less expensive and saves time.

A person can gain knowledge and learn many valuable lessons through his/her own practical experiences and also the experiences of others. The knowledge learnt from experience is very likely to be retained in our memory for a long period

ToeflEssays.com

of time. The conclusions that we draw from what we learn would be from our practical experience instead of accepting the conclusion drawn in the book by the author.

So in my opinion knowledge can be gained both by reading books and by experience but the knowledge gained through experience is more important.

Topic 4 **Are books more important than experience?**

Nowadays, most people appreciate learning at school, where a number of books are the source of knowledge. However, from my point of view, learning from experience is much more important than learning from books since our real lives concern more about knowledge from experience than knowledge from books.

10 Firstly, knowledge obtained from books is more abstract. As we enthusiastically study in classroom, we have learned several mathematic equations, or a number of science theories. Of course, they all are necessary for some professional occupations, such as scientist, engineer, and doctor, but not for all careers.

In addition, knowledge from books is rather logical and exact. The result of a matter is always follow-concerned theories. For example, a person who has learned science can know how long that an apple falls to the ground takes. Certainly, the answer can be obtained by using Newton's formula.

15 Nevertheless, I think that the most significant lessons cannot be taught; they have to be experienced. No one can teach us how we can get along with others well when we have to change to a new society. Books cannot teach us how to adjust behavior to satisfy others, and think optimistically when we confront a trouble.

In contrast to books, knowledge from experience is adjustable; it does not depend on any theory or equation. A solution from experience is always depending on the situation and other factors influencing the problem. This is because living
20 experience is so fine and complex that cannot be determined by theories or equations.

In conclusion, although both books and experience can give us a variety of knowledge, in my view, the knowledge from experience is more important. The reason is that in everyday life we must face with a lot of situations, either extremely hard or easy to cope with, that cannot be handle by just knowledge from books.

Topic 4 **Not everything that is learned is contained in books**

Learning, as the name indicates has lot many meanings as to which source one would choose to understand things of his own interest. Books have always been an inevitable part of one's life as they have the ability to make people aware of the different things happening in our world. It is said that not everything that is learned is contained in books. This is in fact true because books can offer us knowledge regarding the things that have happened and sometimes the ways to deal with a situation that one can encounter in his life. I would appreciate the fact
30 that the knowledge gained from experience is much more important than that we receive from books. I would like to further illustrate my reasons as follows

Everyone would admit the fact that knowledge gained from experience is one that remains in our mind forever. It is correctly said, "Experience is the teacher of man." Being a science student, I have gone through different books where we come across different reactions and experiments, where the results will be shown in the form of diagrams or may be
35 expressed in a simple language. Unless we conduct that experiment we will not know the problems or the difficulties we will have to overcome during the experiments. Textbook knowledge is merely a description of facts and outcomes, whereas the same knowledge when gained through experience teaches us a lot, right from the start till the end and its a journey through the various aspects of one process which one might not be aware of and might not be described in the books.

40 During my undergraduate years I had only knowledge from books and I used to wonder how the experiments are designed and how they are carried out. But, during my post graduate days I had to do a two month nutritional trial on fishes where I had to cope up with everything like procuring tubs and fishes, arranging aeration facilities, preparation of food for the fishes, daily water exchange, samplings, analysis and so on. Now, I am confident of carrying out similar works and the experience that I have gained will remain with me as long as I live. When similar instances occur, we will have
45 more self-confidence and when such aspects are passed on to our juniors, they would also feel happy and confident.

Needless to say books are also very important. What I have mentioned is from my viewpoint as a science student. There are many different subjects where the conduct of work is tough and in such circumstances we gain information from books. Some aspects would be time consuming and tedious and performing such a work with a limited period of time would not be feasible. In such cases, books definitely open a person's eye towards various aspects and give him first hand
50 information about what he wants to know.

A person who has learned from experience never forgets what has happened and if it was proved a bad thing then he would certainly try to avoid that situation in the future. If something good has happened then he will put his best to further improve it; that in turn will enhance his skill and boost his self-esteem. Knowledge gained by experience can be passed over to others who also are supposed to face the same situation and that helps the person to be aware of what he intends to do. He can even avoid those factors that can affect his performance.

In fact I would rather say that knowledge gained from experience lingers in our minds forever and that boosts our confidence when taking up a similar task. On the other hand, the fact that books are knowledge providers cannot be ignored, because books provide us with lot more information about the different things that are very difficult to be
5   experienced. Hence it can be concluded that knowledge gained from books is second hand knowledge whereas knowledge that are gained from experience is firsthand and it takes a person through the different hidden intricacies of the task and makes him learn the knowledge in a practical manner.

Topic 4 **Are books more important than experience?**

To my opinion, books and real experience are two completely different sources of knowledge. It is really difficult to determine which of the two to be of much greater importance, because normally knowledge gained from experience complements that acquired from books, but not substitutes it. Comparing the features of the two sources, I would stress the following points of differences.

First, the knowledge gained from books is, to a certain extent, of abstract nature. Books are normally the collections of facts and general rules. Books give us the most complete overview of a subject in a more or less structured manner,
15   covering all known details and exceptions. In some way, books are concentrations of knowledge and experiences of many generations of people, given in a concise and comprehensive way. Obtaining such knowledge just from the personal experience would take an immense amount of time or even would not be possible at all. The practical experience, gives us not general knowledge, but particular skills. Without these particular skills, all the knowledge gained from books might be just a useless collection of facts and rules. The best example of the importance of practical experience that comes to my
20   mind is learning a foreign language. One can learn a lot of vocabulary and grammar rules, memorize many exceptions, but without actual applying of all this knowledge in real life conversations, writing letters and listening to real speeches, one can hardly be proficient in the language. The importance of having practical skills is also proved by the fact that most employers appreciate working experience above all grades and diplomas.

Another point of contrast between books and experience is that for some subject, such as economy of sociology, a book
25   may represent a point of view of its author or authors. The conclusions given in the book might be out of date, or might be biased by the personal attitude of the authors. In this case, practical experience helps to build up personal perspective on the matter, to bring the matter up to date.

On the psychological grounds, learning from experience is much more efficient than reading books. Reading books is in most cases a passive action, which can be done without much effort. Despite the fact that there are people who can
30   memorize thousands of papers, for a normal person, such work does not result in a deep, comprehensive knowledge base. On the contrary, doing things in practice, people have to overcome various difficulties, get through unknown areas, and pay attention to small details. The reward for these efforts is much more comprehensive and profound knowledge.

Summarizing the said above I want to admit that both books and practice is important in the process of learning. While none of the two can be considered as absolute substitute for the other, I would place the practical experience in a little bit
35   advance position in terms of importance.

Topic 4 **Are books more important than experience?**

We gain our knowledge about the world and our life from two sources: from experience and from books. These two resources are both important, but which of them is more important?

Knowledge from books forms a very important part of our knowledge structure. In schools and colleges, we learn knowledge that is fundamental to our future career. We learn knowledge
40   from books in order to make our contributions to this society in the future. A student learns mathematic equations and other scientific knowledge and become a scientist or engineer. We will be illiterate and ignorant without learning knowledge from books. Moreover, we acquire knowledge about life and the world by reading books, magazines and newspapers. This is also very important, as we cannot experience everything all by ourselves. Therefore books are a very important source of knowledge.

45   On the other hand, we cannot learn everything from books. "Experience is the best teacher" is an old cliché but I agree with it. The most important, and sometimes the hardest lessons we learn in life come from our participation in situations. We learn how to get along with others or how to gain self-respect from our experience, not from books. We cannot learn emotional feelings, such as love and care, through books; they come from our real life experience. Knowledge from experience is also a very important supplement to knowledge from books.

50   Needless to say both learning sources, books and experience, are very important to us. But in my opinion knowledge from experience is more important, because without knowledge from experience, it is impossible to get a real understanding of knowledge from books, and how to apply this knowledge to real world situations.

Topic 5 **A factory in your community**

I strongly oppose to the plan that a large factory be built near my community. My arguments for this point are listed as follows.

The first and foremost reason lies in the virtually inevitable pollution that a large factory is bound to bring about. Considering the limit of the present technology, hardly any kind of factory is able to secure its mass production without the slightest pollution to the environment. Once a factory enters my community, and embarking on its continuous activities, even a tiny element of pollution will by all odds accumulate to a dangerous degree that will eventually cause a
5 serious damage to the environment of my community. To think of the exhaust gas or water and the noise given off by a factory will help you fully understand this idea. Cities have already suffered from those nightmares of modern industry that shows no signs of ceasing to emerge. No one would like to behold the air of his or her community is no longer clean, or to find his or her community totally removed of hush.

Besides pollution, which is to some extent an invisible but deadly threat to my community, there is an immediate problem
10 that a large factory will force to confront with: it will occupy a large area near or of my community, which should be more likely exploited as a public site that benefit all residents in the community. For example provided a suitable area is available, it is more worth a gymnasium that will enhance the standard of health of every resident in the community, than a big factory leading to disgusting noise and suffocating gas.

Perhaps, some people would like to vote for such a plan of building a factory simply on an economical ground that a large
15 factory will probably stimulate a prosperous future of the area around. But unfortunately, history has witnessed numerous counterexamples. Many factories neither attain an economical success nor left the environment intact. So I doubt this declaration.

Taking into account all these factors, I find the disadvantages weigh much heavier than the possible advantages. Therefore I strongly disagree the establishment of a large factory near my community.

Topic 5 Should a factory be built in your community?

As the company has announced to build a factory right here in our community, I am so eager to say a few words toward this issue. I really think that if the plan is carried out in the near feature finally, there will be much more disadvantages than advantages to be brought to the quality life of our social community.

Of course, during these years' high unemployment rate, introducing of such a large factory will consume unemployed
25 workforce in some respects. A family may increase their income by taking account of its new employed father during or after the construction of the factory, local government can increase its tax income and retail dealers of our community may sell a little more because of the increasing of population that may be the result of the new build factory. However, all these benefits may seem to be so small when compared with all those disadvantages the new build factory may lead to.

The most hateful thing is that you may not able to smell the fresh air in the sunny Sunday mornings because this huge
30 industrial monster will probably deliver a great deal of waste fume and waste materials every day, far more than the amount you can imagine. And far more disappointed than this, those rumbling, non-stopping stream lines in the factory can make noises loud enough to bereave people of our tranquil town out of sweat dreams.

And you will no doubt feel uncomfortable to drive your family to the camping place because maybe the establishment of the new factory will bring more than 20% increases in population as well 30% increases in using of private cars and trucks,
35 imaging how could it be in the street in rush hours, or even in the holidays. So, you can see clearly that increasing in population is not always good news for a small community like ours.

Basic food prices may probably rise and public transportation will burden more, which usually means poor services, public schools and community facilities which once made us feel so convenient living in this small town may get harder and harder to be attended or utilized as the increasing of population, upon all those disadvantages, why should we give
40 applauses to the announcement of the company?

Topic 6 What would you change about your hometown?

Today, everything seems to change in split seconds. But, there is something that still lacks among every soul that resides in my hometown. And, I think you have got what I meant, cleanliness. These ideas of cleanliness in my opinion are divided into two types: external and internal cleanliness.

I was born in Kuala Lumpur and have lived here all my life. The city that I see today is way too advanced and developed compared to when I was in primary school. Kuala Lumpur is well known for its magnificent and the most luxurious airport in the world. But, what is the use of having all these advancements when the sense of cleanliness among the citizens is still below average. In example, I have actually witnessed a man spitting on a beautiful pavement when there was a dustbin right next to him.

50 Apart from what I have mentioned above, I would like to emphasize on internal cleanliness. Most people in Malaysia treat foreigners with good respect and hospitality. But, there are some people who would take advantage of these foreigners. For instance, shop owners raise the price of goods when foreigners visit their shops. I have actually witnessed a cab driver bargaining the ride fare with a foreign lady who was extremely tired after a daylong shopping with her young kids. I am trying to wonder, what has happened to the moral and the culture of our fellow Asians that we used to be so proud of?

I understand that the government has taken lots of steps to improve the state of cleanliness within fellow Malaysians. I just hope that these steps were more comprehensive. We should cultivate the sense of cleanliness among each and every citizen in order to promise success to the planned manifesto. Last but not least, every citizen should willingly contribute to the efforts of maintaining cleanliness in their surroundings. We should not be self-centered when it comes to the matter
5   of cleanliness because cleanliness ensures a healthy living. Think your deeds of maintaining cleanliness as a charity and start it from the steps of your home. At the end of the day, you will experience self-satisfaction towards your contribution to your hometown, as a wise person once said, "The greatest gift of charity is to give what is in your heart."

Topic 6 What would you change about your hometown?

I am from Arroz e Feijao, a small town in the northeast of Brazil. If I can change one thing about my home town, I would like to build a factory here. Building a factory in there will bring a lot of advantages and disadvantages, but I believe that Arroz e Feijao will mostly benefit from the building of a new factory because it is largely populated by poor people and the factory would bring many benefits to this small town. However, of course, a factory has disadvantages as well.

As you know, factories usually bring pollution. If this factory is not managed very effectively and efficiently according to
15   specific rules, it's prone to polluting the local air and water. What's more, factories usually make noise. Beside clean drinkable water and fresh air, an ideal community should be quiet. If the factory cannot maintain this standard to the community, it will not last long. A factory that is too noisy or pollutes too much will eventually be relocated to a new area.

On the other hand, a factory could bring a lot of benefits to the community. So I would support the plan to build a factory to my community for all the reasons I will describe below.

20   First of all, the construction of a factory will surely improve the local infrastructure. To run smoothly, the factory will have to have a steady, reliable supply of water and electricity. Some old pipes will be changed, and some facilities will be renovated. The residents' living standard get improved as a result of these widespread changes, an important benefit in Arroz e Feijao, where many people do not have access to clean water.

Secondly, to make sure the shipping of materials and products and the employees' commute more convenient, the local
25   roads will have to be rebuilt and broadened, resulting in improved public transportation. The town's residents can take a public bus to go shopping or go to work. As a result, air pollution and fuel consumption might be reduced.

Most important, a factory's establishment will bring up a lot of employment opportunities for the community. A factory needs experts from various fields. The residents can take just a few minutes to go to the factory to work. So, the local residents can benefits from this factory.

30   Generally speaking, I would like to build a factory near my community if I have a chance. If the factory can be managed successfully, the factory and the local residents can have benefit mutually.

Topic 6 What would you change about your hometown?

If I could change one important thing about my hometown, it would be air pollution problem, and I will give the following reasons to explain why I want to solve the problem.

The first and most important reason is that I hope that my hometown can become a beautiful city. As an old industrial city, my hometown has made a great deal of contribution for the country's economic development. At a result, the natural environment of the city has been badly damaged. The forest has disappeared; the mountains have become bald, and the most awful thing is that the air quality becomes more and more worsen. People seldom see the blue sky during most time of year.

40   Another reason why I want to change my hometown's air pollution situation is that the city's development needs clean and tidy environment to attract investors. Nowadays people have come to know that the city's environment, which is so called "software facility of the city", plays an important role in the city's future. For example, due to the fact that the environment of the city is very poor, many local students who pursue their study out of the city would rather find themselves a job in other cities than coming back to their hometown after they graduated.

45   In addition, nowadays people have paid more and more attention to their health. If the air pollution problem cannot be solved as quickly as possible, people's requirement for a healthy body will never be realized.

In my mind, changing air pollution will apparently be my first choice if I can change one important thing about my hometown. Fortunately people in my hometown are gradually aware of the serious problem and start doing something about it.

Topic 7 How do movies or TV affect people?

"Reel life is based on real life," they say. But how far it is true is left to the judgment of the individual's intelligence. The impact that movies and television have on our lives can never be over-emphasized.

Nowadays television and movies are the only sources to keep in pace with the latest trend in

the global environment. Every part of our lifestyle is somehow influenced by what we see in the television or in movies. The advent of the motion picture has been one of the greatest influences of the cultural activities of the humankind. It does not require great intelligence to ascertain this fact. If we just give a glance to see hanging or posted on the walls are the photos of our favorite celebrities from the tinsel world, mounted on the table are things from our favorite T. V. show,
5 the music blaring out of the system of the latest excuses for musical excellence, in your wardrobe are outfits last seen on our favorite stars, the hair cream, shampoo, paste, and what not, the list is endless. This does not stop with just what we wear and own it also extends to the way we behave in our peer group.

Some time back, my friend and I were at the cafeteria near our college when were suddenly mobbed by a group of students who were dressed up as people straight out from prehistoric age. They were carrying contraptions that resembled
10 like weapons for a battlefield, which made us wonder whether they were struck in a time warp. And what followed actually bemused us completely, the group started speaking to each other in a very laboriously slow manner in a language which sounded nothing of this world. My friend and I were not able to understand a single word of it, we left that day with a really confused mind and were in the same state for quite some time. But it all ended on the day we decided to watch the movie "Lord of the Rings" Peter Jackson's adaptation of J. R. K. Tolkiem's novel of early 1900s. We understood the
15 costumes and the weapons were the film's souvenir collectibles, and the language they spoke was that of the elves originally created by the great author.

Thus we see people talking about 'molecular disintegrators', 'laser swords', 'elves', 'hobbits' etc., and also tend to act and perform like what they have seen in movies and television. We also see that big FMCG companies bringing in newer products inline with the latest movies. There are several institutions, which glorify such attitude. Those who dare to ignore
20 are considered archaic and become the butt of all jokes. This can be easily acknowledged by the fact the elves language has already been recognized as part an official curriculum in a British university.

Thus the line between real and reel life is fast becoming a blurred one. The whole behavior and cultural activity of the human race is left to the mercy of the next big moviemaker.

| *Topic 7* **How do movies or TV affect people?** | Movies are popular because people are great watchers. They like to watch other peoples' lives. They like to live vicariously. By going to movies, we can escape our own lives, share other people's emotions, and imagine ourselves as someone else. |

Many of our lives are not as adventurous or glamorous as the lives in movies. We do not battle evil all day long and then go back to our luxurious penthouse apartment. We just go to school, do our homework, eat, talk to our friends, and sleep. We need a little excitement in our lives and we find excitement at the movies.

30 Humans are very emotional people. We all like to cry and laugh. Fortunately, there is not much to cry about in my life so I like to go to sad movies where my heartstrings can be tugged. I also like to go to comedies so that I can laugh. I tend to cry and laugh more in a dark movie theater than I do in broad daylight.

Now I am a student, but I know someday I will be a scientist or a politician or a famous model. When I go to the movies, I can see my role models. I see how they act, what they wear, how they talk. I can prepare myself for the day when I will
35 be like them.

Even though my life is quiet, I can go to the movies and watch someone else's life. I can share their emotions and their everyday life. I wonder if they would like to share mine.

| *Topic 7* **How do movies or TV affect people?** | Every human being tends to take some time off from his or her chores for relaxation. There is no doubt that movies and television play a major role in get tiredness and boredom away from us. Though primarily intended for entertainment, these media do influence the behaviors of human beings. I would like to discuss the effect of the media on the demographic divisions of children, teenagers and the adults. |

No doubt that children are the most fascinated and fond of watching movies and television. Though parents are temporarily relieved from baby-sitting their children who are indulgent in watching television, they are certainly worried
45 about the influence of this media. Today's movies are filled with violence. Heroism is being portrayed as the capacity to destruct (the enemies). This easily influences children. The fondness of children to watch WWF wrestling on television bears testimony to it. This proclivity towards violence tends to show up at schools, where they start to bully their classmates.

While teenagers tend to show some maturity over the issue of violence, there are separate gamut of factors in the media
50 that influence them. Teenage is the important period during which one choices his career and subsequently his direction of life. This media greatly influence the choice of ones career. Today's rock concerts and music televisions create an impression that becoming a rock star or a video jockey is the best profession in the world. Numerous teenagers are drawn into this whirlpool and it becomes too late when they come to realize the reality in life.

Adults watch this media mainly for entertainment and to relax themselves. However they too are relieved from being bitten by the media bug. The constantly running television advertisements have a negative bearing on the adults. The ostentatiously displayed by a Porsche car driving by the hero in our favorite films inadvertently propels our instinct to go for a similar car. Seldom do we think about the aftereffects and get entangled in the spider web. We tend to sink our ship by the exorbitant interest rate, mortgage and the overflowing credit card bills. Once overloaded with these, we tend to

5   become peevish losing our natural gregarious behavior.

Hence I feel that the media has an influence on each one of in what ever above said categories we are in. While there are also many things which positively influence people's mind, I have purposefully chose to deal with negative aspects as understanding these problems instigates us to seek a suitable solution. We as a parent, a teacher and a good friend can help some of our friends who need help to get themselves out of these problems.

Topic 8 **Has TV destroyed communication?**

I do strongly support the statement that television has destroyed communication among friends and family. This I support with the following reasons.

First let me describe the role of television today. Nowadays people spend a tremendous amount of time in front of the television. Thus communication among friends and family has

become much more difficult in the 21st century.

15   Because television always keeps you up to date, gives you a good laugh and a lot of handy tips for life, people do not need their friends and family members anymore to support them in achieving their goals.

Sadly enough the likelihood of becoming addicted to television nowadays is tremendously high. Once you start to communicate less with your friends and family members because you prefer to watch television you will get lonelier and lonelier. In this case people will start to replace their own family members and friends with talk shows and comedies. In

20   some dramatic situations people believe they are a part of the families shown on TV and therefore entirely lose their feeling for reality.

Last but not least I wish to say that I consider the television as a very useful information tool nevertheless it should be used like everything within some borders.

Topic 8 **Has TV destroyed communication?**

Nowadays, television plays an important role in people's life. It is the main information source and its popularity is still growing.

Every day many new technological inventions are introduced. Almost all activities at home have already been mechanized. We use machines for everything. For example, we use

microwave ovens to prepare food more quickly than we used to do it before; we order food, books and anything else we need just by clicking on a few buttons on the computer keyboard. Also we use mobile phones to be always in touch with

30   our family, friends and the rest of the world.

This is the good side of using technology. A few centuries ago people used to read newspapers and find out everything that had happened all over the world. Today newspapers are almost completely replaced by a newly invented gadget. This innovation is called television. It has been the most popular information "supplier" since its invention.

Every evening family members sit in front of the TV set and watch programs such as talking shows, news, and movies for

35   hours, sometimes without even saying a word to each other. Instead of sitting around the dining table and telling each other about what happened earlier that day they sit on the sofa and gaze at the TV screen.

Is that right? Apparently, it is not. Everybody has to think for himself whether he and his family want to become 'couch potatoes' or they should continue to communicate with each other and avoid using television and all other technological achievements so much. We should ask ourselves whether we want to lead such a life with no real contact with other

40   human beings. Is it really worth it?

Topic 8 **Has TV destroyed communication?**

What do you usually do to relax yourself and have some fun after a whole day's work? How do you spend most of your spare time with a lowest cost of both money and energy? Most of us will give the same answer: watching TV. As promoted by the development of modern science and technology, television programs today attract a vaster group of audiences by tremendously

45   enriched contents and a 24-hour rolling schedule than ever before. The fact that television

seems to control our choice of leisure and entertainment has recently brought a problem to focus: whether has television destroyed communication among friends and family? Those who agree with the statement insist that such lack of communication should attribute to television. However, I hold just an opposite point of view and I will demonstrate my opinion as followed.

50   First of all, the advantages of television will speak for itself. As known to all, what we find in television is not only some enjoyment or recreation to kill time but also an important source of knowledge and information. Imagine how television makes us familiar with the miracle creatures in the deep ocean that is unavailable otherwise. Undoubtedly television is an indispensable channel for us to learn the world outside.

As far as the interpersonal communication is concerned, television also plays a key role in improving, but destroying like someone thinks, the relationship and understanding among friends and family. A good case in the point is that television often focuses the attention of public by broadcasting current events, social news and popular teleplays. It is always easy to find interesting topics with friends and colleagues if you have watched the same TV program lately and want to share your
5 ideas about it. Besides, in my own family, my parents and I enjoy the time when we are sitting together and watching tele-films. Because it is the moment for us to feel and enjoy the peacefulness and happiness of family life.

I do not deny that there may be some cases that people are so addicted to television or some other habits that he/she will probably ignore communication with friends and family. Yet it is the wrong attitude of the person him/herself that results the problem but television. Thus, for the reasons above, I shall say: television, like many other important inventions of
10 human beings, benefits our life with both enjoyment and knowledge.

Topic 8 **Has TV destroyed communication?**

Has television destroyed communication among friends and family? Different people will give different responses to this question from their own characters, emotional concerns and even educational backgrounds. However, when it comes to me, television has severely affected our contact with our friends and family for the following reasons.

15 In the first place, watching television will obviously take up our leisure time that can be otherwise spent staying with our friends and family. In fact, the television has provided us with a variety of shows, which can easily catch our eyes. An example is that, a very hot television play will eat much of our free time magically! Many people will admit that the glamour of television is irresistible! So, how about talking with our old friends? Let us watch another hot television soap opera instead! Without television, we will obviously have more time to share with friends, namely, playing tennis,
20 swimming, playing football etc. These activities are all good entertainment and improve our physical fitness as well! Do you expect getting in a good shape or having floppy muscles when sitting in front of television?

In the second place, programs on televisions have some negative effects on us in terms of violence, illusion and even brain malfunctions. People who are infected with long exposure to television will indulge themselves in a world full of illusionary love, violence or even pessimistic views of life. How can those people have good time with their friends or
25 other family members? Without television we will have more chances to realize this world realistically, cherishing people who are loving me, paying more attention to social problems and leading an optimistic life! From this point of view, television seems to be the source of all these tragedies!

Admittedly, television is obviously a tool for us to broaden our horizon and entertain ourselves. And such positive effects of television should not be neglected. However, it seems to me that the disadvantages brought by television have
30 outweighed its advantages.

All in all, if all the factors are contemplated, we can easily reach a conclusion that television has destroyed our communication with our friends and family and is not as effective as we might expect. Let us give up tonight's soap opera and pay a visit to our old friends instead.

Topic 9 **A small town vs. a big city**

I grew up in a small town and then moved to a big city, therefore I have experienced the good and bad sides of both. I never thought that I would like living in a big city, but I was proved wrong. After ten years of living in one, I can't imagine ever living in a small town again.

Small towns and big cities both have some problems in terms of transportation, but in different ways. In a small town, you have to own a car to ensure a comfortable living. You can't get around without one because there isn't any kind of public transportation. Big cities generally have heavy traffic and expensive parking, but then you have a choice of taking
40 public transportation. It's not free, but it's often cheaper than driving when you consider gas and insurance. Especially if you don't have a car, you're better off living in a city.

I love the excitement of big cities. Small towns have a slow pace. Large cities mean you have to adapt to a variety of situations, like finding a new route to work or trying a new restaurant. I enjoy that challenge very much. Another aspect of the excitement of city living is the variety of cultural activities available. There is a wide assortment of theatres, music and
45 dance performances available in big cities. These things are rare in small towns.

The final thing I like about large cities is the diversity of the people. The United States is made up of people of different races, religions, abilities, and interests. However, you seldom find such a variety of people in a small US town. Living in an area where everyone is just like me would quickly make me bored.

Of course, security is a concern, and that's one area where small towns are superior to big cities. Still, I would rather be a
50 bit more cautious and live in a large city than to feel secure but bored in a small town.

Topic 9 **A small town vs. a big city**

In English, there is a well-known fairy story about a poor country boy, Dick Whittington, who goes to London because he believes that the streets of that city are "paved with gold." The story is a tale of "from rags to riches." Dick eventually becomes the Lord Mayor of London.
Like the hero of that story, I always find wonder and adventure in cities.

Cities contain a great assortment of people. Whenever I walk around a shopping precinct at midday on a weekend, I am fascinated by all the different types of people hurrying around the shops. Sometimes, I just sit on a public bench and simply watch the variegated streams of shoppers. Today, in the age of globetrotting transport and communications, city life is more mixed than it has ever been. Capital cities are not cosmopolitan, and eager to attract foreign trade and currency.
5 There is a contemporary English joke that tells, "You can never find an Englishman in London."

Whether rightly or wrongly, governments and local authorities usually build public amenities in the big cities. Money is invested in transport, libraries, parks and museums. Often, countries will compete with each other for the best "show-case" building. Malaysia has built a skyscraper that is taller than is anything in New York. In large countries, region will compete against region: New York against Chicago, Shanghai against Hong Kong and Beijing.

10 All of this is good for the citizen. The magic of the Dick Whittington story is rekindled in me when I enter a library in a magnificent building. If a person is at university studying art or music, a large city usually offers galleries and public performances. Even as a teenager, I appreciated the worth of living in a city because two or three times a year there was a rock concert by a favorite band.

Architecture is the urban landscape. If a person has an appreciation of architecture, a city can be as visually exciting as the
15 Himalayas. A modern metropolis is a mountain range of height, light and solidness. And then there are the old buildings: the quaint, unspoiled side street or shops and homes from a distant age. If a person lived all of his life in one large city, he would continue to discover its architectural secrets into his old age.

Man is a 'social animal'. He talks, mixes and creates. Cities offer the libraries, universities and cafe bars for him to meet others of his kind.

Topic 9 **A small town vs. a big city** | Where shall we live? Some may choose to live in big cities, while other like the natural and quiet surroundings in the countryside. As far as I am concerned, I would like to live in a big city because living in a big city has more advantages than living in the countryside.

To begin with, the city is the symbol of human civilization and there are a many facilities for living, recreation and health care. Therefore, living there is more convenient than living in the countryside. For example, we can find a plenty of malls
25 around our neighborhood, where we can buy everyday necessities at a low price. Furthermore, people concern more about their health and safety than other things in their lives. In big cities, medical facilities and emergency services are easily accessible than in the countryside. Big cities also have convenient transportation and utility systems. They also offer faster Internet connections. These all make our life easier in big cities.

In addition, we can take part in a variety of events in big cities. Human being likes to live together and need to interact
30 with each other. In a big city, the population density is high therefore there are always plenty of social activities, sports events and concerts. There are more recreational places in big cities, such as opera houses, movie theatres, clubs, and swimming pools. You will have many kinds of entertainment in big cities, and meet many people. In countryside, however, the life may be dull and quite, and you may only have a few neighbors. Living alone with few activities can easily cause mental diseases.

35 Some may argue that the pollution in cities makes people sick. However, with automobiles and modern highways we can easily take a break to expose to fresh air in the countryside and sunshine on the beach.

In conclusion, I strongly hold that living in big cities is much better than living in the countryside because of the advanced facilities and social activities in cities. Moreover, the autos and highways enable us to enjoy the natural and quiet surroundings in the countryside.

Topic 9 **A small town vs. a big city** | The environment where a person grows up and lives molds his personality to a greater degree. He becomes a part of the culture of that community where he lives and the ideals, the line of thinking, the way people dress, the way they speak, the types of food they like, all of these are influential and somehow makes the person what he is. Taking this into consideration, I would prefer living in a big city.

I would like to be aware of a lot of things. I would like to be up to date as to the current technologies that would help
45 lighten up activities of daily living, such as the Internet, washing machines, microwave ovens, cable television and the like. I would like to experience the benefits of living in the era where high technology is the trend and make total use of it. I would like to be exposed to things that would make me an achieving professional in order to succeed in life. It is not that I belittle those who would prefer to stay in a little town. I think they have the advantage of having a peaceful life, free of noise, air, and water pollution, live abundantly with fresh fruits, vegetables, milk and meat.

50 Also, the intimacy of having a small community far outweighs the crowded city. But they are deprived of what is new or if it comes to them, like television, people in the city are using far more advanced tools and gadgets, such as palm top computers or watching through their cell phones already. For example, it is very difficult for electricity to reach far fetched places and so how can they make use of the Internet over there. Nowadays, it is very easy to travel publicly, especially with the metro rail train in the city. In a matter of minutes, you are already in your destination without the hassles of traffic.

But in a small town, one has to walk by feet or if they become lucky, some improvised moving carts made of plywood are the means of their transportation.

5 I would not prefer living in a situation where I think I would not grow as a person; where if ever I would learn things, those are still way behind those of the urban people. I want diversity. I want an evolving environment. I want to be at pace with the challenges of the place I am living at and not stay drowned in the stunted growth I may have if I choose to stay in a little town.

Topic 9 **Country and City**

10 People are always wondering whether the country or the city is the ideal place to live. If there is one preference-which I take leave to make a conclusion-then it is the country rather than the city that provides people with optimal living conditions. There widespread testimonies for it and the primary ones are listed as follows.

The foremost reason for dwelling in the countryside is the soothing and comfortable life provided by the pastoral view. Hardly anyone could resist the clean atmosphere, the friendly neighbors, the closeness to nature and the gentle pace of living. Those who have enjoyed the first cock crow in the morning, the twittering of birds in the tress and the breathtaking sight of the rising sun would go into rapture at only mere mention of the idyllic life. Relaxed and suburban dwellers are 15 able to hold a more positive attitude for life and achieve more accomplishment.

Oppositely, the obvious things brought about by noisy and flashy city life are more pressure and forever-lasting anxiety, agonizing and torching people's mind day in and day out. Another subtle explanation rests on the fact that country habitants are fortunate enough to enjoy the cozy and pleasant ambience of the family without exhausting social life. How satisfactory and refreshing it must be to have dinner together with your loved ones in the spacious and pastoral 20 surroundings after a frustrating day! Furthermore, nothing can be compared with the joy of watching heart warming TV programs, playing convivial games and sleeping in the tranquil and relaxing atmosphere.

On the contrary, it would be far more difficult to acquire such pleasure for those urbanites. Consecutive and excessive recreations not only thrift money but also deteriorate people's health, which is the last thing one would like to encounter. Naturally, it is possibly to reckless to assert that nothing beneficial combines with city life since several accompanying 25 merits also come along with it. Living in the metropolis means having more accesses to various people involved in multiple attractive cultures. Living in the metropolis also provides plentiful opportunities, both in career and studies.

Nevertheless, the fact that city life makes it more convenient to purchase a job does not prevent us from concluding that country life is more enjoyable as well as healthful and placing a certain amount of reliance on the notion that country life is always the sensible choice.

Topic 10 **The importance of hard work**

That hard work is a key to success is a well-known adage. Parents, teachers as well as others guide a child to work hard so that he can achieve good scores. Though a little bit of luck plays a positive role but I believe that hard work is the key to success. In fact if only luck is to be considered, no one would work but just wait till their luck shines up.

But this is not the case. Today we see that technology has improved to such an extent that a person can have a lunch in 35 Paris and a dinner in New York on the same day. There lies great contributions from people like the Wright brothers and Henry Ford to invent these means of transportation, which were the result of their hard-work and great efforts. If these people had waited for the D-day probably we could still have been using fire and wood to cook instead of using electrical ovens, and the globalization would not have taken effect.

A person can excel in his career due to hard work. If he sits at home, no one would offer him a job unless he initiates the 40 job searching process. Also if you are working in a company you will be promoted only because of working hard; luck does not lie in the picture.

A student stands out first only if he studies hard. Many students after the graduation say that probably they were not lucky enough to get good marks, or the evaluators must have marked their papers strictly. But again these are merely reasons that can't be given preference.

45 Today science has developed so much that hand shaking can be virtually done between any two countries. This is due to the tremendous amount of researches accomplished by scientists. All achievements in science and technology are because of hard work contributed by people in different fields.

Thus a young individual has the potential to do something and crave in reaching a particular acme. Whether your luck prevails or not condition being hard work and efforts, which will pick you up wherever you are.

Topic 10 **Luck and hard work**

There is a humorous saying in English "The grass is always greener on the other side of the valley." The saying is used ironically to point out that there is a temptation in us all to insist that others are more fortunate than we are. This is nowhere more true than on the question of luck and hard work. When faced with the "bad times", we often find comfort in the idea that we are special in our degree of misfortune. I feel that such an attitude is negative, and that it can bring only further misfortune.

Many famously successful people have begun from small origins. Mao was the son of a (modestly prosperous) peasant; the explorer Captain Cook was so poor that, as a child, he had to work by day and study by night; many of the affluent Americans of today are the children of the poor immigrants of yesterday. Beethoven, it should be remembered, became
5   deaf before the end of his career. There are many, many more people who have also made genuine, though Jess spectacular, successes against the odds.

Within his own terms, a person who is born into poverty in India is a great success if he manages to own a house in later life. Poverty cannot be reduced by merely complaining and blaming others: no matter how guilty other people are, each individual must reach out to success for himself. Indeed, some economists believe that the world operates by what they
10   call "the rule of the jungle." They believe that in economics a person always attempts to gain profit from his neighbor: that given the chance the poor man would quickly make himself rich by trading to his own advantage.

Also, it is presumptuous to judge another according to his or her apparent fortune. No man can ever truly understand the sufferings of his neighbor. A man who appears comfortably rich may have suffered elsewhere in his life - through the death of a loved one, for example. Retired businessmen have often worked long hours in their youth. Surely, it must be
15   wiser to respect achievement than to deny that anyone has achieved good in the world.

To rely on notions of luck - to believe that life is a kind of lottery - is an attempt to escape reality. Paradoxically, the only time a person can claim that luck is more important than work is when he reflects on his own success. Because of that modesty, the great man then becomes even greater.

Topic 10 **Does luck has anything to do with success?**	Some people believed that they achieved success by their own ability, whereas other people believed that they did it by luck. As for me, I would like to side with the former people. I am willing to discuss it by proposing two main reasons.

First, As for the genuine meaning of the term 'success', luck is not the dominant aspect to gain success. What is success? I like to say that success is a great integration of a good motivation, a good procedure, and a good result. That is, success means not only the self-realization or economic abundance, but also enduring endeavor or
25   firm belief. Being a rich man or powerful man without hard work is never a 'success'.

Second, for the social cohesion, I support the former point of view. If we acknowledge that a person who becomes a rich man due to luck as a successful man, we would lose the moral principle that makes our community safe and harmonious. That is because most people are willing to buy lottery or play gambling instead of work hard. 'No pain, No gain' is not fallacy.

30   As for me, I would like to live in a society where there is no luck for success. I believe that hard labor and great endeavor rather than luck is the origin of human happiness and success.

Topic 11 **Sports or library?**	When it comes to the issue of the arrangement of the university budget, some people suggest that universities should spend more money on their libraries rather than on student's sports activities, while others maintain the opposite view. As far as I am concerned, the former point

35   carries more weight. I take this view on account of the following reasons.

First of all, libraries are the places that maintain records of traditional theories, which are priceless treasure of human being. To keep these important materials, a lot of special devices have to be purchased. For example, a vacuum chamber that is used to keep a book printed hundreds of years ago may cost a fortune and constant budget has to be applied for its maintenance.

40   Second point to take into account is that libraries need more money to meet the need of the increasing development of technology. With the exponential leaps of the information technology in the recent years, massive amount of information can be easily and instantaneously obtained through computers and the Internet. Libraries also have to purchase such equipment, which may be very expensive, to meet the student's acquirements.

Last not least, the quality and quantity of the library indicate the level of a university. Therefore, if one university wants to
45   achieve a better recognition, it must spent more money to improve the overall situation of its libraries.

Just as the English proverb goes, "a coin has two sides" those who take the opposite view are partly reasonable that more sports activities and better physical conditions will greatly promote student's health. But with the factors I outlined, I still believe that applying more budget on university libraries is much more important than sports equipment.

Topic 11 **Sports or library?**	I disagree strongly with the idea that the same amount of money should go to university sports activities as to university libraries. Although playing sports is a wonderful way to learn about teamwork, strategy and reaching your goals, it should not be the principal focus of a

university education.

Students need the most up-to-date library facilities available to get the best education. Many of those facilities are very expensive to buy and maintain. These include computerized programs and access to Internet research databases that students can use to find information all around the world. If a university is only offering its students resources of a decade ago, it's depriving those students of a tremendous amount of information.

5 Even the book and magazine budget of universities has gone up tremendously in the last decade. More is being published on every subject, and every university wants to have this information available to its students.

It also costs money for universities to keep their libraries open. Students need to have access to all the libraries` research tools as much of the time as possible. Because students are young and can stay up all night studying, many universities are starting to leave their libraries open all night during exam periods. This costs money, because the staff has to be paid extra to be there. It also costs money to run the building (electricity, heat) during that time.

10 Students at universities are only going to benefit from their education if they can get to all the tools they need to learn. Sports are secondary to the resources that students need from university libraries. For this reason, libraries should always be better funded than sports activities.

Topic 12 **Why people go to museums?**	As a tour guide for a Japanese woman in the city of Beijing three years ago, I was amazed that she would be interested in the Chinese Culture and History Museum, which even Chinese pupils does not like to visit. Museum in my eyes used to be a really boring place, which could only display items that are dull and motionless. I thought Museums were dead. Until after I traveled to some places myself did I start to realize the life of museums.

A place consists mainly of its past and present in terms of time. When you are visiting one place, the existing scenery, streets and buildings give you chances to understand its present easily. But when it comes to the past of a place, things are 20 different. With time going by, the past is always staying in the past. Sometimes with the new constructions, a place's past can even be burnt into ashes.

In most cases, museums preserve part of the original appearance of a certain place and present plenty of information in terms of objects and pictures that one cannot obtain from the present. Only when information from the present and that from the past are combined could one obtain a relatively integrate image of the place. That is why the Japanese woman 25 insisted that she visit the Culture and History Museum in Beijing. Like most of other cities, Skyscrapers, glass walls and the modern street scenes are all over the place in this city. The red and gray walls, the palaces and small courtyards, which were typical scenes in the past, can only be found in the vintage photographs in the museum. Thus, visiting museums is a very effective way to understand a place's past, therefore one can get a whole picture of a place that one visits.

Topic 12 **Why people go to museums?**	It is an interesting phenomenon that, when traveling to new places they have never been to before, many people choose to visit museums. Why museums are people's common choice? Based on my personal experience and according to my observations, I think this is because museums tell people a lot about the culture of those places and provide them with entertainment.

It is easy to find out many ways to obtain knowledge about the culture of the place where people visit for the first time. 35 You can go to a theater, a church or a nightclub. Another option is to sit in the park and watch the people around you. Among various options, visiting museums might be the most efficient way. Museums show you the history and art and those things that the locals think important, some of the exhibits might be unique in the world. On the other hand, the museums themselves are part of the landscape of a place. Many museums are designed and built based on the historical and artistic characteristics of the places where the museums are located in. The Forbidden City Museum is the most 40 favorite tourist site because not only it contains a large variety of historical treasures and art works but also it is the representative of the Chinese history and the highest achievement of Chinese ancient architecture. As a result, people are willing to choose museums as their first destination to understand culture of the place that they visit.

Museums also give people entertainment. Even if you are not interested in art or history, there is always something to catch your attention. Many museums now have what they call "interactive" exhibits. The "interactive" activities were 45 originally designed to keep children occupied while their parents were looking at the exhibits. However, the interesting thing is that adults are keen to these activities as well as their children. It is fascinating to create your own work of painting at an art museum or to design an appearance of a robot by yourself in a science museum. People can be really pleased through performing the "interactive" works in museums, as well as gaining related knowledge.

Both local people and visitors welcome museums because museums are an essential part of our life. They reflect our 50 history, our art, our values, our creations and our dreams. No matter who you are and what you like, somewhere there is a museum that will amaze and interest you.

Topic 13 **Eat out or eat at home?**	Nowadays, some people like to eat at home and prepare food by themselves, but others prefer to eat out side in restaurants or at food stands. As far as I am concerned, I prefer to eat at home.

Of course there are some advantages to eat out. Firstly, restaurants offer a more comfortable environment to eat and the food there tastes more delicious than home-cooked meals. In addition, eating at restaurants is a good way of getting together with friends. People also do not need to worry about washing dishes and cleaning. For people who are too busy to cook, eating out is certainly an ideal choice. Furthermore, for people do not know how to cook and do not have some
5 one to cook for them, eat out seems to be the only choice.

However, I prefer to cook and eat and home. The main reason is that at home, family members can prepare their meals and enjoying their food together, which can enhance their relationships. Family members can talk, make jokes and exchange feelings on current affairs with each other while preparing a meal. Parents have a chance to communicate with their kids and keep track of what they are thinking and doing; while children can learn to help with some household tasks
10 and develop intimacy with their parents. Image that you and your brothers and sisters help your mother to cook on a weekend, and enjoy the food later on, and you feel everything is so nice.

Another reason is that eating at home can save money. The same amount of money that you spend on a meal in a restaurant can buy a lot more foods from a supermarket. You can use the money saved to buy a new cloth, or attend a concert.

15 General speaking, eating out side is comfortable and convenient, but eating at home has more benefits. I prefer to eat at home.

Topic 14 **Should university students be required to attend classes?**	The extent to what level of efficiency modern education system could perform in teaching students is always a hot topic. Among many developing suggestions that could improve learning efficiency, the necessity of attending class has been argued frequently in recent years. When it comes to whether giving students freedom of attending class as an optional choice or not, tradition has it that class is a firm part of the school life. Nevertheless, in my part, I prefer having the rights as individuals to make our own decisions about attending a class.

I believe that studying out of class does certainly save our time and make learning more comfortable. Take e-learning at home as an example: students may learn at home via "visual classes", which are powered by computer and the Internet
25 installed at home instead of pens & paper and white board in a classroom. Being connected with professors in different locations, learners do not need to battle rash-hour traffic for going to campus. Indeed, students could do their research at home or even at a vacation hotel. With modern technology, people could choose to learn any topic no matter what they are doing - drinking, eating or even listening music, at anywhere and any time. Therefore, studying without a real class attending requirement will save our time, and offer a comfortable learning environment.

30 Another advantage of making class an optional choice is that people could customize their learning process according to their own interests and capabilities. While classic class leverages learning speed and depth to satisfy every student in the class as a whole, learning out of class means self-control. Students choose to attend one class because its topic is just suitable for his study plan, and discard another class because he had learned it in advance during the weekend at home. He may then accelerate his studying speed and go on to the further topics that interest him.

35 Admittedly, attending class at regular time has its own advantages. Students in a real class may be regulated by a teacher to concentrate on their study. Teachers, who are well trained, could also give learners professional guides and interesting demos. Moreover, some special programs such as physical exercises and experiments may only be conducted at real classes.

All in all, from what I have been discussed above, I suggest granting students rights of making their own decisions for attending classes. To make classes optional in universities will certainly bring advantages for learning and benefit the whole
40 society.

Topic 14 **Should university students be required to attend classes?**	Should university students be required to attend classes? There are two different opinions. Some people claim that attending classes is a must to students. Other people, however, argue that it should be up to the students to decide whether they need to go or not. As far as I am concerned, no matter whether students like it or not, they must attend classes.

Students who do not like to go to classes have their reasons. The main one is, they can learn knowledge by themselves. If they were asked to attend the class in which the professor teaches something they already have known, it would be a pain. By not attending class, students can control their time more freely and are likely not to waste time.

Although I agree that there are maybe one or two advantages of not attending classes, I insist that the advantages of
50 attending classes far overweigh that of not attending. In the first place, professors can teach students a lot of things that are not written in the books, such as the way of thinking. In the dictionary, a university is defined to be a place where teachers lecture what they know to students. Books normally offer just concentrated knowledge. How the authors developed their ideas and reached their conclusions is usually not written in the books. How to answer these questions? Go to the classes. The professors will not only teach you knowledge, but also teach you methodologies and answer your
55 questions, face to face.

In the second place, students will benefit from seminars and group discussions with their classmates when they attend classes. It is a society that emphasizes on the importance of communication and listening to other people's opinions and ideas. It is very important to share your ideas and knowledge with other people. In a class, the professor often gives some topics for students to discuss. In the discussions, a student will be surprised that he/she can get so many fresh thoughts 5 and ideas from his/her fellow students.

In conclusion, I believe that students should attend classes not only because professors can teach you knowledge and methods, but also because students can learn from each other in the classes. In short, one must attend classes if one chooses to attend university.

Topic 14 Should university students be required to attend classes?

Some people may believe that going to classes should be optional, but I really disagree with them about it. I do not understand how a university student can expect to learn much knowledge if he doesn't attend classes. Although self-study is a good way to acquire knowledge, students, I believe, need to be in class.

In classes students receive the benefit of the teacher's knowledge. A teacher does more than just going over the material in the textbooks; she draws her students into discussions that may 15 lead further understanding of the teaching material. She not only teaches acknowledge and theories, but also presents opposing opinions that help students think and absorb what they have learned. Additionally, she may invite guest speakers to give her students extra information from another prospect, or play some documentary films on certain subject.

Besides teaching knowledge, a teacher impart her students the right method of study. In that way, the students can understand how to study efficiently, how to find information from proper resources, and how to apply what they have 20 learned into practice. In other word, if there is no teacher to lead them to the right way, the students may go into a roundabout and waste lots of time.

The last reason for attending classes is that going to classes can train students to be more responsible and have good sense of teamwork. In classes, the students may be given some group assignments. To achieve assignments, they can know what is their respective responsibility and how to cooperate with others. Meanwhile, they can learn from each other because 25 each student has his strong points, different background and experience.

In short, going to classes give students more knowledge, help them to become more responsible, cooperative and thoughtful. I believe that attending classes cannot be optional, but should be a essential part of university education.

Topic 15 What are the qualities of a good neighbor?

When I think about my childhood years, I my first friends come to my mind, those who were the first people besides my family I got to know, who became my friends and grew up with me. Most of them were classmates, relatives and of course, neighbors. Neighbors are those people who share the street, block and fences with us. Their existence has always been taken for granted, and they haven't been given the importance or attention that they deserve.

For some people, neighbors can mean "troublesome" or "annoyance." For others, neighbors are considered as relatives, and they enjoy having a good and close relationship with their neighbors. Of course, the opinions depend on personality 35 of individuals, culture, type of housing (house or apartment), place (a big city, a small town, or the country) among others. But both points of view may come to an agreement when determining "what makes a good neighbor?"

In the first place, a good neighbor should be considerate. Knowing that you should treat others the way you expect to be treated is a quality that makes people respect boundaries (physical, social and emotional). For instance, a neighbor who can tell when the noise of his stereo makes may bother the people next door, and is able to turn it down taking into 40 consideration of his neighbors' needs.

In the second place, being sympathetic is another characteristic that a neighbor should have. Putting yourself in someone else's shoes makes you understand better the feelings of somebody who is in trouble, and consequently, offer appropriate help. An example could be a situation where you know that your neighbor divorced recently and is going through a hard time. Maybe you will be more understanding when you see her in a bad mood, and avoid an unnecessary conflict, because 45 you can see the way she feels.

Finally, good manners and a polite way to address your neighbors can polish even the toughest relationship. When a neighbor is rude, even if we excuse him or her by saying, "that's the way he/she is", we feel a little rejected. A nice smile or a "Hello" helps a lot to start a friendly conversation, and to avoid misunderstandings such as "He never speaks to me, so he must be mad at me or something." Manners do help to start friendships.

50 There are so many more characteristics that we could list, and there are many ways we could make a more accurate picture of the perfect neighbor we all want to have. But I guess the best way to "edify" our neighbors is by being good neighbors ourselves. We cannot demand others to do something for us that we cannot offer to do for them. We should stop complaining about what our neighbor always does that bothers us; we'd better start analyzing what we are doing to make the relationships with "the people next door" flourish. Let us start setting the example.

Topic 15 What are the qualities of a good neighbor?

Human beings are social animals. It is therefore their instinct to live together. This factor has contributed towards civilization that gave rise to splendid cities and towns. However the basic unit of all these grand cities, and for that matter any human settlement is a neighborhood. Since we are social animals, we have to interact with each other and develop social relationship. In this regard, it is imperative to develop warm convivial relationship with our neighbors. For this purpose, it is also very important to have good neighbors as neighbors play a very important role in one's life.

There are many attributes of a good neighbor. First of all, a good neighbor should be a responsible person, mindful of others' rights, which include privacy, peace and security. A good neighbor must therefore avoid unnecessary intrusions into his or her neighbors' personal matters. Also, a good neighbor must avoid practices that are likely to disturb the peace
10 of his or her neighbors, like creating noise, organizing congregations at odd hours, indulging in altercations with them that are likely to cause tension in the neighborhood.

Secondly, a good neighbor must be caring towards others and be ready to help them in time of need. This is especially true when there is a emergency, like a fire, an earthquake or other calamities. In such a situation, neighbors are the first ones who can provide help to those unfortunate ones who have been struck with the adversity, and must do so in a
15 selfless manner. Also there may be instances when one may have to leave his or her family, especially children at home due to unavoidable circumstances. In such a situation a good neighbor is required to take care of their needs and help them in all ways possible.

There may be cases where there are neighbors who are not financially well off. In such cases a good neighbor is required to be helpful towards the unfortunate ones in all possible ways, like sharing one's food with them, or providing them with
20 gifts.

It is said that one has the liberty to choose friends but one may not have the luxury to choose neighbors. Having good neighbors is thus a blessing and one must value good neighbors, while trying to be good neighbors towards them.

Topic 15 What are the qualities of a good neighbor?

Neighbors are the people who live near us, and their behavior influences our daily life. Good neighbors can make us feel comfortable and give us many help, and everyone will benefit from a good relationship among neighbors. In my point of view, these are three conspicuous aspects of the qualities of a good neighbor.

One of the most important characteristics of good neighbors is that they have a good living habit and are friendly to others. A person with bad habit will affect your daily life. For example, children are most likely to be influenced by bad neighbors and carry on bad habits. On the other hand, being friendly is also an important nature of good neighbors. If
30 neighbors are unfriendly, they are hard to approach and difficult to get along with.

Another important aspect of good neighbors is that they should be willing to help others. In our daily life, emergency situations may happen, and we may encounter difficulties that cannot be resolved by ourselves. At this time, the quickest help we can get is probably from our neighbors. To some degree, neighbors are as important as relatives to us, because they could provide the immediate help. In the same way, a neighbor who likes to help others will get help in return. Help
35 each others can form a friendly and harmonious relationship among the neighbors.

All in all, a good neighbor is someone who has a good living habit, is friendly and is willing to help others. Taking into account of all these factors, we may reach the conclusion that a good relationship among neighbors need the maintenance from us.

Topic 15 What are the qualities of a good neighbor?

Speaking of the word 'neighbor', it arouses different responses among people. Some people may frown upon it, others might nod their heads at it with their whole-hearted smile on their faces. No matter which category you belong to, as a person, especially as a person who has to live next to a neighbor, the concern on the qualities of a good neighbor is always a popular issue to bring about and to desire for. In my opinion, a good neighbor must be a friendly person, while at the same time, a person who is willing to offer help to you when you need the most.

45 As an important and fundamental quality of a good neighbor, she or he must be kind and nice. Neighbors are those persons we meet in every day life when we go in and out of the building. They are usually the people we meet at the very beginning of the day, and whom again we will encounter at the end of the day. A nice and sincere smile on their faces, or a simple 'hello' as a warm greeting on the way, may bring us a joyful mood for a start of a day. In a very same way, a caring 'how was your day?' on your way home might be treated as a big comfort on your tiredness at the end of your working day.
50 As nice neighbors, they have provided us a very cordial living environment through their care and friendship.

Other than that, being able to help you out when it is necessary is also considered as a significant trait of a good neighbor. Through our entire lives, there are numerous difficulties or troublesome situations that we have to deal with. When those particular moments come into life, the first person come into our mind is often our best friend or one of the relatives. However, most of the time, they cannot be the real person who we can rely on at those hard times. We will soon realize
55 they are either too far away or they are unavailable right now. We all have once had these similar experiences. Then here is

the moment where good neighbors should begin to play their helpful roles so that we can immediately turn to them for help and useful advice for dealing and solving the emergency, and so that we do not have to lose our minds in trying to find everyone's phone number.

These are the precious and indispensable qualities of good neighbors. They are friendly and nice, and they will always be there ready for you when you need someone's help. Living with such a neighbor, you may start to sway at your old image of neighbor, and you may no longer frown upon that topic at the time we talk about it.

Topic 15 Qualities of a good neighbor

It seems, among so many qualities such as reliability, honesty, helpfulness, and patience, very difficult to prefer one to another because each of them has its unique advantages. Yet that does not mean that they are of the same weight to me. To be frank, I would prefer reliability and helpfulness.

Why I vote for reliability? I stand behind it because I can trust my neighbors only if they are reliable people. That makes me feel safe to associate with them. Imagine if your neighbor is not reliable, will you put your worries to rest to let your neighbor look after your children even when she offers to do so? Do you dare leave your key to your neighbor when she says she will keep it for you? Will you lend your car to her when your neighbor promises that she will return it within two hours? Obviously, reliability is not only a quality of a good neighbor, but also a quality of a good person, and it is the foundation of a good relationship.

Being helpful is another quality that I have chosen to illustrate here. A neighbor should be kind and helpful, because they live close to you, and you never know when you might need help. For example, when you go for a vocation, your neighbor can help you water the plants, and pick up the mail. It is always good when you know that if something happens, your neighbor is there to help.

Of course, other qualities such as honesty and patience are also important to some extent, but everybody has his or her own preferences. I chose reliability and helpfulness as the qualities of a good neighbor because reliability helps us develop a good relationship and helpfulness keeps the relationship remaining for a long time.

Topic 16 Should a new restaurant be built in your neighborhood?

What do you think if there will be a restaurant built near your neighborhood? People may have different opinions. Some people will be against it because of too much noise, potential pollution, etc. Other people, however, will welcome it very much. As far as I am concerned, I like to have a restaurant built in my neighborhood.

In the first place, a restaurant will make my daily life more convenient. As we know, cooking is a very important thing in people's life and it is also very time-consuming. When I come home from work and feel tired, I normally want to eat out. If a restaurant is very far away from my house, I have to give up that idea because I do not want to waste my time and energy on the road. As a result, I have to cook myself. What a pain! If there is a restaurant nearby, it will make a difference. What I need to do is to take a leisure walk to the restaurant, sit down, make an order, enjoy my dinner and then, the most important thing, and leave without cleaning the mess.

In the second place, I have another good place to meet my friends. Sometimes, meeting friends at home is tedious, especially meeting some friends that I am not very familiar with. If there is a restaurant nearby, I can invite them to go to the restaurant. While drinking and eating, we will have more topics to talk about. And the beautiful environment of the restaurant will make the talk more pleasant.

In addition, I can make more friends in the restaurant. A restaurant the best place to meet new people if you are not shy. If the restaurant is just within walking distance of my home, I will be there more frequently and have more chances to know more people.

In conclusion, I will support the plan of building a restaurant near my home not only because a restaurant can make my life more convenient, but also because it can be a ideal place to meet friends.

Topic 16 New restaurant

A new restaurant in my neighborhood would be the most exciting event for me. I personally have positive feelings towards this proposal and also believe that the people of my neighborhood shall also feel excited about such an event.

Life in the fast lane today has turned out to be so hectic and tedious to us that at times we feel exhausted and therefore unwilling to prepare our food. We also feel a strong urge towards a change in the type and flavor of food that we eat. A new restaurant at such times near by shall make a difference to our lives.

In occasions of happiness, get-togethers and enjoyment, having a restaurant nearby is always a convenience for people here. For example, the restaurant can be a convenient place to hold a wedding reception, or a birthday ceremony.

A new restaurant shall certainly add lots of enthusiasms and excitements to people here and people who have the greatest amount of enjoyment would be the younger people. They can relax in a new environment with the experience of a new atmosphere and people around and most of all, tasting something new. On the other hand, a new restaurant in our neighborhood gives hope to young people who would like to make money through a part time or full time job.

In conclusion, a new restaurant will bring convenience to our community. So I personally welcome such a plan.

Topic 17 **Do you learn better by yourself or with a teacher?**

Some people prefer to learn by themselves. They think they can learn better in this way because they have more freedom, independence, and pressure in their self-study. There is some truth in their way, but they fail to see the many advantage of learning with a teacher. Especially, when you learn something more complicated, it is always best to have a teacher. My arguments for this point are listed as follows.

First, a teacher can act as a guide to lead you to success. When you grope for knowledge, you need help and advice. A teacher, who treats you as if you were his own child, will give you a hand when you encounter
10 difficulties; he will render his advice when you are in a dilemma. Without a guide, you would be searching in darkness without a torch to light the way for you.

What is more, a teacher exerts real pressure on you. If you study by yourself, you must be strong-minded enough to keep on. You may become indolent for lack of a strong will. Studying under the guidance of a teacher, however, you will feel there is always someone to supervise you. The teacher may assign you some books to read or some homework to do. You
15 must complete the assignments, or you will not pass the course. You are urged to go no by your teacher.

Last but not least, studying with a teacher will receive the benefit of the teacher's knowledge. In class, the best teachers do more than just go over the material in the textbook. They teach students how to learn, how to absorb information and then apply what you have learned to other situations. They guide all of you on classroom to develop discussion of the material and provide extra materials to broaden the scope of the topic. Without the help of teacher, it is nearly impossible
20 to get these skills just by reading the textbook yourself.

In short, I prefer go to class, studying with teacher to guide and urge me. I choose to learn in a big family----my school. If I was obliged to learn by myself without a teacher or classmates, I would feel very sad and lonely. There would be no fun, no pressure, and no motivation. I could not learn well in such dull and depressing circumstances.

Topic 17 **Do you learn better by yourself or with a teacher?**

Learning is a lifelong theme of every person. How brilliant your achievement will be to some degree depends on whether you can learn anything efficiently or not. Some people prefer to learn by themselves. They think that they can learn better in this way because they have more freedom, independence, and less pressure in their self-paced study. There is some truth in it, but they fail to see the many advantages of learning with a teacher. As far as I am concerned, I would like to learn with a teacher.

30 Firstly, when you are a beginner to a new subject, a teacher is able to provide you with a lot of fundamental knowledge, which is ready to become a solid basis for your later knowledge system. As we all know, entering a brand new area of knowledge usually demands sharp altering of minds and a gradual accumulation of new information. Without a teacher as a guide, you could still march along this road but at the cost of large amount of time and unpleasant experience. However, equipped with a certain amount of basic knowledge, which resembles a map, you will easily steer clear the obstacles
35 barring on the beginning of your long journey. And that knowledge is what a teacher will help you gain without troubles.

Secondly, The storage of concrete knowledge is one matter, while understanding how to learn a certain subject of knowledge is another. As many students confess, it usually takes them quite a long time to find a way of learning suitable to a special subject. Again, a competent teacher is the key to this problem. The teacher will equip the students with some insightful views over the whole subject and much rewarding experience in overcoming difficulties of the subject. For
40 example, a teacher of a Computer Programming Language will certainly let you know lots of rules in programming that is probably hard to accumulate by yourself.

Some people may argue that to learn with a teacher will lose some kind of freedom. For instance, heavy load of assignments will eat up too much time. But a good teacher will take control over such assignment so that the load is only sufficient for students to strengthen what they have learned. It seems that this turns out to be another advantage of a
45 teacher.

In short, I prefer go to class, studying with teacher to guide and urge me. I choose to learn in a big family - my school. If I was obliged to learn by myself without a teacher or classmates, I would feel very sad and lonely. There would be no fun, no pressure, and no motivation. I could not learn well in such dull and depressing circumstances.

Topic 18 **Important qualities of a good supervisor**

Though everyone will work in different places such as a company, a college or university, a factory and so on, I think there are the same standards judging a good supervisor in several aspects.

Firstly, a good supervisor treats his/her staff fairly. He knows how to balance the workload. He will not let some members of his staff do many things while others only do a few things. If he gives you a task, he will tell you in advance. Moreover, he will not ask you complete a project in a few days that actually needs half a month to do. A poor supervisor never considers his employee's feelings. A poor supervisor is usually not a good planer, so he is very nervous when a project comes to its deadline, and he will use his fault to punish his staff. A supervisor like this would certainly not benefit the company.

5 Secondly, a good supervisor praises or criticizes in a straightforward way. If you do very well, he will praise you, and encourage you to do better. If you have made a mistake, he will criticize you face to face, and he will not complain to your co-workers. He will also analyze how to improve your work and point out the ways to do thing right. Furthermore, he will encourage you and trust that you will do well next time.

Thirdly, a good supervisor cares for his staff. He is aware of your feelings and emotions. When you are sick, he will send
10 you flowers or visit you, or he will arrange other members of staff to see you if he is busy. He treats his staff like family members. He is gentle and cheerful. Smile often appears on his face when he greets you. On the contrary, a poor supervisor often pretends to be serious. He never understands what his subordinates are thinking. His staff will never have a good mood when he is present at work.

Finally, a good supervisor must set a good example to his staff. He must work hard, and has a strong sense of
15 responsibility about his company. He must understand the operation of the company, and can do every staff's job in his department when necessary. That way he will win respect from his stuff and his spirit can motivate them.

In short, a good supervisor treats his workers fairly, cares for their feelings, treat them as family members, and set a good example for them.

Topic 18 **Important qualities of a good supervisor**

When asked what are the important qualities of a supervisor, different people hold different perspectives, due to their different experiences. After pondering this question on many occasions, I sum up three vital qualities that a supervisor or a boss should possess.

In my understanding, the most essential trait of a boss is that he or she should be able to do
what is required of his or her subordinates. As an English proverb says," Example is better than precept." If a boss wants the employees to be hardworking, he or she should be diligent himself or herself. The dean of my department, for
25 example, is a very conscientious man. He is never late in the morning and never leaves earlier than the rest of the staff. By setting himself as a good example, he teaches us what is a right attitude to work.

Another crucial feature of a boss is communication skills. The duty of a boss is to give instructions and directions to his or her employees. If the purpose and the means are not clearly explained, people may feel at loss as to what to do. Again, our dean is an expert in explaining a task. He usually not only lets us know what and how we should do, he also stirs up
30 our interest and enthusiasm in the job to be done.

The last but not the least vital feature of a boss is that he or she should be an understanding or considerate person. If an employee made a mistake, the boss should not rush to criticize him or her. Instead, the boss should first figure out the reasons behind the wrong deed. By saying that, I do not mean that a boss should always be lenient. What I mean is that a boss should consider himself or herself equal to the employ as a human being. In that case, both parties can reach an
35 understanding on the basis of mutual respect.

In short, a supervisor should be a person who is self-disciplined, expressive and considerate and who does not deem him or herself a superior being to others.

Topic 19 **Highways or public transportation?**

Transportation is among the most important factors affecting the living conditions of people in the society. A prosper transportation system has different components, among which the roles of public transportation facilities, highways and roads are prominent. But if a government finds itself in the stage of defining its priorities in transportation, should it place higher importance on public transportation facilities, or should it prefer to invest more on
highways and roads? There are many advantages in investing on roads and highways, however these advantages cannot surpass the advantages of investing on public transportation systems.

45 The most important advantages of investment on roads and highways include higher potential for the transportation of goods, reduction in costs pertaining to problems caused by low-quality roads, and notable effect on the thriving of the whole region and country. If a government invests on roads and highways, the quality and quantity of roads and highways will increase, so that the potential of the region for transportation of goods will be improved which will result in booming of the economy and higher income for the government. Furthermore, problems such as accidents, and gradual damages
50 to vehicles that are caused by low-quality roads and highways will be reduced. So, the roads and highways will be safer and fewer damages will be caused on drivers. Finally, a country with vast number of high-quality roads and highways is more apt to prosperity. Because there will be more opportunities for the people of the country to have access to various resources. If the system is organized and managed well, it can lead to greater development.

However there are also many advantages in investment on public transportation facilities. A well-designed and managed

public transportation system can eliminate traffic congestions in cities. Less traffic problem means the less air and noise pollutions, and can provide society with more physically and mentally healthy people. In addition, prosperous public transportation can save lots of our valuable time that otherwise is usually wasted in heavy traffic. Prosperous public transportation can also lower the huge amount of costs consumed on private vehicles including fuel, service and
5 insurance costs. This saved money due to a good public transportation system can compensate the money spent on public transportation facilities. Finally, public transportation will increase people's contact with each other, while private cars may to some extent isolate them from the society.

In conclusion, although there are many advantages in investing on roads and highways, there are more advantages in investing on public transportation. So, government should consider public transportation as its first priority in any
10 transportation investments.

Topic 19 **Highways or public transportation?**	In this modern society, governments always confront the dilemma whether spending more money on improving roads and highways or on improving public transportation. This problem is a much-debated one in that it affects everybody in his or her daily life. Personally speaking, I would be one of those who argue that governments should spend more money on improving public transportation.

15

Though it is quite rational for average people to choose roads and highways because of the obvious reason that a better road condition could suspend more vehicles and accelerate the speed of them. A close scrutiny of the potential benefits of choosing roads and highways would reveal how flimsy it is to stick to the propensity. A better road condition would bring with it more vehicles, thus a much more crowded traffic. Have you ever been caught in a traffic jam? Then how
20 could just spending more money on improving roads and highways do?

Besides, putting the discussion in a wider context, a further reason why I advocate the later lies in the fact that improvement of road condition would stimulate more people to use cars and hence more energy would be used and more pollution would be exposed. This would be the last thing that everyone would like to see. But if we choose to improve public transportation, a quite different result could be. This can be demonstrated by the undeniable fact of our city. We
25 have greatly improved the bus network and reduced the parking places since several years ago. Now more and more people shift from cars to buses and other public transportation, and an azure sky can be highly savored again.

Finally, frankly speaking, there is also a more practical reason why I choose to improve public transportations. Public transportation encourages a sense of community. People who travel to work together all the time get to know each other better while cars isolate us from neighbors. An improvement in public transportation would make it fit more people's
30 schedules and more people would choose to take public transportation to enjoy communicating with each other.

When taking into account all these merits and drawbacks I have numerated, we may safely arrived at the conclusion that we should put more money and concerns more about public transportation. We would experience more convenience when traveling as well as an appreciable nature environment.

Topic 20 **Should children grow up in the countryside or in a city?**	There are advantages and disadvantages for a child to grow up in the country or in a city. It's hard to say which is better. Growing up in the country means a certain degree of isolation. You're in a small town or on a farm with few people. In addition, the people you meet everyday tend to be just like you. Most have the same background with you, and go to the same schools with you. In the city, people you meet are all different. People come from different culture backgrounds.

40 City people tend to come from a lot of different places and move around a lot. So, there is not a sense of community in the city like what you have in the country. People in the city can live in the same apartment building for twenty years even without getting to know each other. In the country, however, everybody knows everybody. A child can get lost or hurt in the city and have no one to turn to. In the country, everyone is a neighbor, and people feel connected to each other.

A child growing up in the city has a lot of interesting and exciting places to visit. He or she can go to a zoo, museums, art
45 galleries and concerts. There are a lot of restaurants with different kinds of cuisines. It's easy to see new movies that come out. Children in the country don't have a lot of these activities to go to.

To my opinion, a childhood in the city is better because it prepares a child more for what real life is like.

Topic 20 **Should children grow up in the countryside or in a city?**	Where is a better place for children to grow up, the countryside or the big city? The answer to this question differs from individual to individual. As far as I am concerned, it is better for children to grow up in a big city.
	Some people argue that the countryside is an ideal place for children to grow up. For one thing, it is less polluted than the city. The air is fresh in the countryside. The sky is bluer and the water is clearer. Living in such a place is good to the children's health. For another, as children

like playing, only the countryside can offer them a big playground. They can run everywhere, play games in the fields, swim in the river. On the contrary, the city cannot provide such places for children. They can only stay at home and watch TV.

Although I do agree that growing up in the countryside has one or more advantages, I insist that it is far better to choose the city as the right place for children. To begin with, living in the city can broaden children's horizons. They can meet a
5 lot of people and hear a lot of things that will never happen in the countryside.

In addition, a city means more chance to receive better education. In most countries, it is no doubt that the level of education in the city is higher than that of the country. As a result, children can meet better teachers and receive high quality of education in the city.

Last but not least, children can also develop many hobbies in the city. They can learn to play the piano, painting, and
10 dancing, to name a few, which are impossible in the country.

In conclusion, I believe that it is better for children to grow up in the city not only because it can broaden their horizons, but also because they can receive better education and have a chance to develop many hobbies there.

Topic 20 **Should children grow up in the countryside or in a city?**

I think that it is better for children to grow up in a big city because living there and getting use to it will prepare them for the real life. Living in the countryside, for instance, in small towns or villages may prevent children from fitting into the society.

As a child born in the countryside (in a small town) I thought life is wonderful and people are always kind as they were in my hometown. When I grew up and I had to think about my further education. The best alternative was to go to study in a language school in a big city fifty kilometers away from my town. The school I chose was a leading institution in the whole country. It was a great
20 opportunity for me to meet new people and to get better education.

I arrived for the school opening day. Everything was absolutely perfect. I met my new classmates and they were great. In a few weeks I understood that life was not as ideal as I thought it was. Students in the school were competing with each other for being the first in everything. It was strange for me and I was drowning in the puddle of cruelty and selfishness. My grades were not as good as these of the other students in my class and at the end of the first semester the headmaster
25 informed me that if I did not improve my grades during the second semester I would be suspended from school.

The idea of being suspended was an unacceptable one. I could not let it happen. I became like my class-fellows - brutal and egotistical. The fight for the first places in the school's rank list was merciless. At the end of the academic year I was ranked number 5 (five) of one thousand students in the school.

Today I am at eleventh grade and I am still one of the best disciples in the school. I realize that now I can afford dreaming.
30 For example, now I want to get a university degree in the United States and I have real chances to be admitted.

However, before I came out from my hometown I did not even think of such fundamental things. It was just an issue regarding the geniuses, not me. But now I can say that I am ready to face the challenges of real life and no difficulties can deter me because this big city taught me how to overcome obstacles and to be one of the best.

Topic 20 **Should children grow up in the countryside or in a city?**

Nowadays, technological development is directed to such people-crowded places such as big cities, resulting in significant differences of lifestyles between people living in the town and in the countryside. It is said that big cities are no longer suitable for bringing up children. In my point of view, I strongly agree that children should grow up in the countryside. Being close to nature, children in the countryside are likely to improve both physical and mental behaviors better than those who are in the city. In the rural areas, children are endowed with real nature
40 that affects to the development of children.

First, fresh air in the countryside provides children with good health. Research has it that more and more children in the town nowadays are exposed to allergy on account of pollution from both vehicles and factories. On the other hand, children living far away from any high technologies are liable to be much healthier. Polluted air is a main cause to destroy the health of everybody, especially children.

45 Another benefit of living in the countryside is that a majority of children spend their free time wisely. After coming back from school or during vacations, most of the city-dwelling children waste their time by watching TV or playing video games. Big cities have limited areas and hardly furnish people in the communities with public places for relaxing such as park and playgrounds. Therefore children in the cities are limited to conducting useless or even harmful activities. In contrast, rural children devote their leisure time playing with others in large open fields or helping their parents look after
50 their cattle. As a result, not only be rural children so strong from everyday exercise, but they also spend their time in a meaningful way by helping their parents do some work.

Finally, children in the countryside may become more considerate man than those who are in the big city. In the cities, there are very high rate of rivalry.

Topic 21 Why are people living longer?

It is a common phenomenon and an indisputable fact that people are living longer now. There are many reasons of this phenomenon. Generally speaking, it is due to the better living conditions people enjoy, the improved medical treatment people receive, and the healthier lifestyle people adopt.

5   With the development of science and technology, people's living conditions have been improved considerably. They have foods sufficient enough to keep them alive, clothes warm enough to protect them against cold, and houses strong enough to shelter them from danger. Hunger, cold, and danger no longer threaten the lives of the human beings. When facing with nature disasters, people can use all available means to survive.

To human beings, diseases may well be another killer. They took away lives of a large number of people, some being very
10   young. But things are quite different today. The quality of medical care has been improved. Doctors know more now about what causes diseases and how to cure them. Many diseases that were used to be incurable can be cured now. Patients who get timely and effective treatments may recover in a couple of months, or even weeks. It is estimated that today's deaths are mostly caused by unexpected accidents.

In ancient times, people did not care much about their way of living for lack of knowledge and shortage of daily
15   necessities. Now, thanks to the progress men has made and the civilization men has built, the present-day people can afford time, money, and energy to consider their living habits and lifestyles. They are eagerly seeking healthier ways of life to live longer, such as giving up smoking, doing physical exercise, and eating low-fat foods such as vegetables and fruits, which are now available year-round.

It is announced by scientists and doctors that human life expectancy will be extended to over 150 years. Men and women
20   of longevity, say 100 years old, are increasing in number. Senior citizens already dominate many cities in developed countries. Although it may present some problems, living longer is a blessing to human beings.

Topic 21 Why are people living longer?

With the development of human society, people are living longer now. Many factors interact together to enable a longer life. There are three most important causes: the quality of food has been greatly improved; people could have access to medical services; more and more people realize that regular sports benefit their health.

The improving quality of our food is the most important factor of the longer life. We could have not only enough food as we want, but also more healthier food. When we preparing food, we no longer consider the cost, but pay more attention to the nutritious value of the food. With the development of transportation systems, inland people now could also enjoy seafood and tropical fruit.

30   Furthermore, governments are paying more and more money on medical establishments. Citizens could have access to medical services more easily. Because of the convenient medical service, more illnesses could be detected at an earlier stage. Also, many illnesses that had been considered fatal could be cured today. The better detection and cure enable people's longer life.

Last but not least, people care more for their own health. Every morning you could see people doing sports outside. More
35   and more people have realized the saying "life is in motion." Regular sports build up a strong body. Naturally, people with stronger body could resist more diseases.

To sum up, the development of our society ensures that people have longer life. People now enjoy better food and better medical services, and they spend more time on sports and exercises to build up stronger bodies. As we could predict, people are going to live even longer in the future.

Topic 22 Important qualities of a co-worker

We spend more time with our co-workers during weekdays than we do with our family. Thus, it's important for our co-workers to be the people we can get along with. In my opinion, there are certain characteristics that all good co-workers have in common. They are cooperative, considerate and humorous.

We no longer observe now a time that worships individual merits with great enthusiasm. Everyone should cooperate with
45   each other. Teamwork is curial to a business. A good co-worker is willing to contribute to the office community and not too stubborn to accept advice. He realizes the fact that if one's work is left not done in time, it may hold up everyone else.

Besides, a good co-worker is very considerate. He may change his own schedule to accommodate another's emergency. He may be a sympathetic listener, comforting others when they are miserable.

What is more, a good co-worker should have a sense of humor. His positive attitude may create a pleasant environment.
50   When we are under the great stress of work, what we need most is not a delicious meal but merely a few good jokes to relax our nerve cells.

What I have listed is not the complete set of characters of a good co-worker, however, we can feel how comfortable it is to get along with a good co-worker. Being a good co-worker is not difficult but really very necessary. Such experience of being a good co-worker will definitely contribute to other aspects of life such as friendship and a healthy lifestyle.

Topic 23 **Should teenagers work while they are students?**

In some countries, teenagers have jobs while they are still students. After thinking about it from several aspects, I do not believe it is a good idea. The reasons are presented below.

Part-time jobs may affect students' academic studies. Working several hours a day consumes a lot of time and one might be too exhausted to study. The main purpose of school life for teenagers is to learn scientific knowledge and techniques in preparation for their future. It is generally suggested that in order to master what they have learned at school, students must spend at least 3 hours each day on their homework. It would be impossible for a student to work part-time while maintaining a high standard of academic learning. As a result, they may find it hard to adjust to what the school and
10 society expects from them as well as what their employers expect them to perform on the job.

Another reason why I do not approve teenagers to work part-time is that working while studying will deprive their time of sleep and will do harm to their health. Teenagers are in the process of building up their body. They need time to do exercises and engage in other activities, and they also need plenty of rest. If they work, they may sacrifice their time for sleep, club activities, exercise, and recreation. Sometimes, teenagers have jobs that consume more strength than they can
15 afford. This will be definitely harmful to their health.

Finally, working part-time and making extra money may contribute to their bad habits. Teenagers are not mature enough to spend money wisely. However with part-time jobs they make money that allow them to spend whatever way they like, such as playing electronic games, smoking, drinking, and even gambling.

Based on the above discussion, I do not think it is a good idea for teenagers to work while they are still students.
20 Compared with their whole lifetime, school life is a short period. Teenagers should value their school life and make full use of the time. Only by working hard during school life can they find their proper jobs in their future life.

Topic 24 **The advantages about living in my city**

It is almost always the case that a person who has been living in a rural area for a while confronts certain conveniences and inconveniences of living in a city. One convenience is the number and diversity of stores and shops available in a short distance in a city. A big inconvenience is the traffic congestion that takes place in many places.

One big thing I remind my foreign friend who is planning to move to my city is that there is cultural diversity, or even conflicts. My friend is an international student from Japan who is living in a small town in California. As a foreigner, he confronts with cultures of local people everyday. On the other hand he realizes that there are few stores and restaurants that are native to his culture. It is very normal that such a person gets homesick and starts missing people and foodstuffs
30 from his own country. Moving to a big city will satisfy such needs of him because there are many stores, restaurants, and supermarkets that are run by Japanese companies so he will less likely to be homesick any more.

However, there is one big inconvenience about living in a city, which is traffic. Especially people who drive often feel stressed on the streets that are always packed with cars lining up in the streets. It is always difficult to find parking spots either in the parking lots or on the street. Furthermore, apartments do not always provide sufficient parking spots to their
35 residents. A lot of people who live in city feel less convenient to keep cars and choose to use public transportation. However, unfortunately, the public transportation system is not perfectly great around my neighborhood.

My city satisfies and dissatisfies my foreign friend who drives. The availability of stores and shops that are native to his country soothes his dissatisfaction about being surrounded by different cultures. However, on the other hand, traffic jam that is always the problem in big cities gives new stress that he is currently free from. It is a matter of balance between the
40 two features that he needs to settle in.

Topic 25 **Does the neighborhood need a new shopping center?**

There are both advantages and disadvantages of establishing a shopping mall in our neighborhood. I am worried about the traffic and how it will affect our community. However, I believe it will benefit local businesses and increase appreciations for our local area. Overall, I think it is a good idea.

For those that I am worried about, traffic congestion and parking problem are obvious. First of all, traffic congestion is always a concern when building something new. Our streets are narrow, with parking on both sides. A shopping center will certainly bring more traffic than ever before, and heavy traffic means big congestion. At the same time, parking is also a problem in this area. There are few garages attached to houses. Most of residents depend on finding spaces on the street for parking. If a shopping mall is built, we must compete with
50 customers and patrons for those parking spaces. Furthermore, if the shopping center offers valet parking service, it would be even worse because valet parking works in terms to grab every possible space available in street.

On the other hand, building up a shopping center will give this neighborhood more opportunities and benefits. Residents in this area could certainly take the job that shopping center offers. People would earn more money and spend on other businesses, such as entertainment and education, which are operating in our neighborhood or adjacent communities. As a result, not only local businesses but also inter-community businesses are boosted up and a prodigious amount of fortune will be accumulated to our neighborhood. A shopping center can also attract people to visit our community. When they drive to the shopping center, they will see what a nice place this area is to live. Therefore, we would have an increasing number of residents in the next couple of years. It is very important to introduce new population because we have lost 5 many residents to suburbs during recent years.

In a short, there are several details to consider when planning a shopping center. In my part, I support to have a new shopping center in my community because its advantages outweigh disadvantages.

Topic 26 Should a new movie theater be built in your neighborhood?

There will be a hectic debate about whether to build a new movie theater near our region or not. Building a new movie theater will cause some problems such as traffic jams, noises, pollution, but based on the specific case and environment near our community, my point of view is to bolster the scheme.

Living in a small town far from the prosperous city, people in our community always complain about the boring life during the weekends. If we wish to entertain ourselves with some new movies, we have to drive all the way to a theater far away. Although digital cable and satellite TVs are available, they cannot 15 totally replace the enjoyment that a movie theater brings. So it is not surprising that many people including me support the plan.

Besides, a new movie theater will provide more career opportunities. The theater has to employ people to work in it. In the meantime, some new restaurants and shopping centers will be built around the theater for people to eat and shop before or after they see movies. All those new commercial facilities will offer more job opportunities to people hunting 20 for jobs during the economic depression.

The final aspect that makes the choice reasonable is that a new movie theater can encourage people to go outside rather than watching senseless TV programs all night. People will meet each other, and exchange information and ideas. People can use the new movie theater as a place to communicate and socialize with each other.

From what we have been discussed above, we may safely draw the conclusion that it is positive to build a new movie 25 theater in our neighborhood.

Topic 27 Should people do things that they do not like?

When it comes to the topic should people sometimes do things that they do not enjoy doing, optimistic and pessimistic people have different attitudes toward this topic. For me, a person who likes changes a little, I would prefer to do some different things sometimes even if I do not like them. There are many reasons why I should sometimes do things they do not enjoy doing.

The first reason is that I could get more experiences from the things I am doing, no matter I enjoy it or not. There are pros and cons for every experience. What I learned from doing something I dislike is to conquer the similar situation and take the advantage of good changes I may encounter again in the future. In addition, I will see such a disagreeable thing as diversity to my routine life.

35 Secondly, many things which I do not enjoying doing can actually do well to me. For example, I do not like to sweat because it makes me uncomfortable with those sticky clothes and bad smell. But for exercise, the activity will cause me to sweat, surely keep me in good shape and benefit my health. Besides, I feel happy whenever I see my figure become more slender. Moreover, Overcoming displeased things gives me a sense of achievement.

All in all, it is not bad for me to do something I do not enjoy doing. Therefore, I agree that people should sometimes do 40 things that they do not enjoy doing.

Topic 27 Should people do things that they do not like?

Should people sometimes do things that they do not enjoy doing? Many people strongly oppose this idea, while others insist that although people naturally favor doing what they enjoy doing, under certain circumstances people may well be advised to act against their interests and it would benefit people in many ways. Personally, I would side with the latter.

For one thing, it usually takes quite some time for people to discover their interest. My personal experience serves as a typical example. From my childhood, I learned a lot of time to discover my interest. I tried to play an electronic organ, draw oil paintings, and even learn ballet. Superficially, it seems to be a sound solution to find out what my interest is, but when carefully weighing in the mind, I find that it has wasted me plenty of time. A scrutiny of these arguments would reveal how unnecessary they are.

50 For another, many things that people instinctively hate to do will actually benefit them in the long run. A basketball star's personal experience is a good example. He likes running when he was a child. When he was in high school, he joined the track and field team. By a chance, he met a basketball coach and was asked if he wanted to become an occupational basketball player. Although he was not interested in playing basketball, nevertheless, his parents told him that doing

something he hated to do might change his whole life in a good way. By taking the advice of his parents, he went to the basketball team and now he turned out be extremely successes! For another example, we are not always interested to move to different places. In fact, we will have more opportunities of improving our lives by moving around. As President Kennedy pointed out," Change is the law of life, and those who look only to the past or the present are certain to miss

5   the future."

Still some people might list other reasons to explain why people should do some things that they do not enjoy doing. However I assume the points I have discussed in the above analysis are the most relevant!

Topic 28 **Has the media paid too much attention to celebrities?**

In this global information age where newspapers or magazines are always handy and TV has already turned so many people into couch tomatoes, few people concern about what these mass media has brought to us; we just accept it anyway. While I think the current focus on personal lives of famous people by these media requires further consideration.

Admittedly, it is reasonable for those media to continuously pay great attention to celebrities, the present fierce competition of the various media, the hard-to-pleased audiences' taste, the bombastic effect of coverage of these shining figures. No surprise sometimes that we feel we just know more than those

15   famous people than themselves.

However, the consequence of such intense coverage on public figures' personal lives not only violate those being-focused on a certain level, but also do harm to us being-informed in some ways. Firstly, the privacy of those celebrities is ineluctably encroached from time to time. Sometimes the result is sad - do not forget the tragedy of Princess Diana. Secondly, our attention is certainly being diverted by such tide of craziness about celebrities. What about those viewers

20   who want to see something about ordinary people' lives? How can mass media not concern more about those people suffering from pain and poverty?

Furthermore, one of the significant results of the current fad on famous figures is that their behavior is so influential while at the same time the media have little guarantee to ensure what the say and do will not mislead the mass public and even cause more problems. For example, if a famous figure is being asked about his or her point of view in a field he or

25   she is not quite acquainted, the words presented to the audience may be misleading. This is especially harmful to those young people who are more likely to watch those programs of their idols, and also are mostly vulnerable to influential but harmful sayings.

In a sense, I don not quite appreciate the coverage of people in the center of spotlight, maybe once the mass media turn a little bit from their current focus to other aspects of the society, they may find out that the world is wonderful all the same.

Topic 28 **Has the media paid too much attention to celebrities?**

With the prosperity of both science and culture, people are accustomed with an abundant supply of information. Modern media, such as television, newspapers magazines, reinforce our accesses to news and information of all kinds, the most prevalent t of which are those about public figures and celebrities. Now there is a growing awareness that media now pay too much attention to the personal lives of famous people. As far as I am concerned, I cannot agree more with the statement and my point of view is well founded.

Nowhere in the history has the condition been more visible that reports about famous people, like music stars, movie actors/actresses and sports figures are easily available and unusually in details. When we turn on the TV, we may be led to the new apartment of a fashion star; when we glance at the paper, we may see dim pictures of an actress and her new boyfriend; especially when we get online, it is almost impossible for us to get ride of the latest affairs of a talented football

40   player. It seems that the personal lives of public figures weigh much more important than the contributions they make to the society. All those absurd attention paid to their privacy is a waste of resources and degradation of public interest.

Another equally important aspect is that most of reports on lives of famous people are always focused on brilliant achievements and extravagant enjoyment, which overstate the gorgeous part and understate the painstaking part. Therefore, young people are often biased and tend to pursue such kinds of lives but with little endeavor. In addition, since

45   the teenage are inclined to adore their idols with such a passion that mass of negative news and information of popular figures may even twist some youths' view of life.

Besides, public attention excessively paid to individual privacy of celebrities not only deteriorate social morality, but also derive the regularity and peacefulness of daily lives from those figures. Furthermore, tragedies are sparked in some extreme cases. One of the most well known examples is the death of Princess Diana of Britain.

50   Certainly I do not deny that some decent habits or features of the famous individuals add to his/her attraction and help to characterize him/her better. But our interests and curiosities should be properly controlled. All I want to assert here is a rational attitude to public figures and respect for individuals.

Topic 28 **Has the media paid too much attention to celebrities?**

Some people feel that television, newspapers, magazines, and other media pay too much attention to the personal lives of famous people such as public figures and celebrities, although others have different opinion about that. As far as I am concerned, I fully agree with that. Safe to say, more than 70% lights are focused on those famous people and all kinds of stars. This is because common people like to watch, to know about and to become famous guys.

Let us look at the television first, when you turn on the television, there are more than 60 channels in United States, but almost all channels are either talking about celebrities, movie stars, or showing some TV soap programs in which some movie star is in it. There are daily programs such as "E-Talk", "Access Hollywood", and "Entertainment Tonight" which concentrate on lives of famous stars. You can tell from their names. Not to mention there 10 are a lot of awards such as Oscar award, Emmy award, Gold Globe, and so on. They are all about famous people. For the program of talking show, such as the Opera Show, or the Larry King Show, most guests that are invited to these programs are celebrities or politicians. And people love to watch that.

As for magazines or newspapers, it is the same situation. The first front page, second page and Headline are very often about famous people in different areas, even sometimes discussing the private life of famous people. It looks like if there 15 are no celebrity photos on the front page, the subscription will decrease. People love to read stories about these stars or celebrities.

Especially, there are so many photographers who want to take pictures of these famous people's private life. They do not care how this will invade those people's privacy, because they know these photos of celebrities may help them get rich. Think about how Princess Diana died in 1997. Nobody can say that it has nothing to do with those paparazzis. The fact 20 that people love to know everything about Dianna, one of the most famous celebrities in the world, killed the princess.

In conclusion, TV, newspapers and magazines need these celebrities to attract people's eyeballs. Otherwise, they cannot survive. And the average people seem to enjoy these personal lives of famous people or celebrities. So it is quite normal for media to pay so much attention to these big guys in the world.

Topic 29 **Has human harmed the Earth or made it a better place?**

The Earth 'our home' is a planet with a wide range of inhabitants. This diversity helps to maintain the balance of the life cycle on the Earth. We humans have a key role to play in maintaining this ecological system. But today, even amidst the huge cry from environmentalists, we seldom recognize the importance of the environment. Some of the changes on the Earth like deforestation are a result of industrial and automobile emissions and nuclear activities. They bear testimony to our negligence towards the environment.

30 Right from our school education we have been taught about the key role played by the forests in maintaining the ecological balance. Forests attribute to release of oxygen and absorb the toxic carbon dioxide exhaled by the humans. Thus the forests act as the natural recycling agents balancing the life on this planet. Deforestation has been taking place for many reasons like manufacture of paper from wood pulp and timber, and for inhabitation by humans. If this trend continues there is no doubt that in the years to come the Earth will become a dry planet.

35 If deforestation is plundering the gift of God, the pollution of environment by automobile and nuclear emissions is a man made menace. Metropolitan cities have been so congested that we are getting used to everyday traffic snarls. Though there has been a worldwide awareness in controlling the automobile emissions in terms of imposing the emission norms on the automobile manufacturers, there is still much left to be done. One step could be to impose the law, to get the vehicle owners check their vehicles for emission norms, once in six months and obtain a valid test certificate.

40 No one can deny the fact that nuclear emissions are more vulnerable to damage the environment than any thing else. But we are always at the threat of a nuke war, despite the strong efforts of the international organizations like UN. It is a pity that most of the governing nations of the Un are the major threats with nuclear weapons.

Not but not least, the knowledge and the responsibility of safeguarding the environment is seldom seen in the individuals. The fact that all of us have been taught about the importance of environment in our education system makes no 45 difference. The governments should organize more effective campaigns to educate everyone across all demographic levels. Only a socially responsible citizen can make a difference towards the environment our descendents have to live in.

Though I feel that with all above references, we humans damage the earth, I feel that I have dealt superficially some of the solutions that help to make the earth a better place to live. Let us hope that in the coming years future generations become socially responsible in safeguarding the earth. After all, we have just one planet (right now!) to live in.

Topic 29 **Has human harmed the Earth or made it a better place?**

Some people believe that the Earth is being harmed by human activity. Others feel that human activity makes the Earth a better place to live. In my opinion, human activity is damaging the Earth. There are many reasons for my perspective as follows.

First, human activity causes many kinds of animals and plants to disappear. Today many species of living beings died out or near died out. We only can see some animals in the zoo because in nature they have disappeared. Human beings have been using their brains and machines to remake nature for many thousands of years. We use the habitats of animals and plants. We eat their food and eat them as food. Because animals and plants cannot grow fast to satisfy human beings, we cannot see them today. If some animals are dangerous to us, we kill them with our weapons. If meats of some animals are delicious, we eat them. No animals can copy with human 5   being.

Secondly, human beings cause pollution to the Earth. I remember when I was young; I drank water from the river and stream. Today we can only drink bottled water bought from the market, because natural water is polluted by human activities. Air in some countries is polluted very badly, so many people died of lung cancer. I saw some reports that says in London people could not see each other clearly in a short distance in the morning because of much smoke and fog.

10   Finally, population on the Earth exacerbate rapidly. Human beings need more food and shelters because of increased population. More food and houses mean more needs from the Earth. Thus people need to cut more trees to build houses. People need to plant more vegetables and feed more cattle, so they demand more lands from the nature. Thus people are destroying more forests and natural lands. The living beings are losing their habitats.

Take into account of all factors I think the earth is being harmed by human activity. Today we cannot breathe fresh air 15   and drink natural water. We have not enough places to live. We worry about our health because of pollution.

Topic 29 **Has human harmed the Earth or made it a better place?**

When it comes to what human activity made the Earth, tradition has human activity that damaged the Earth. Nevertheless, although human activity has caused some damage to the earth, our Earth has certainly been turned into a much more beautiful world than it was centuries ago.

First of all, due to the development of human productivity made possible by science and technology, we now enjoy living conditions that our ancestors could never dreamed of. Nowadays, we use machine to plant crops, use synthetic fodder to feed livestock, use water conservancy project to generate electric power and so on. In term of substantive level, no other reasons in my decision is more crucial than the one above.

25   Furthermore, the use of machines has greatly improved our working conditions, enabling us to enjoy more leisure and entertainment. Tape recorder's invention serves as a typical example. They are small and have well sound quality. We can take it everywhere with us and the tape recorder has a valuable argument that it enabled me to listen to my favorite music wherever I want in a variety of different formats.

Of course, it should be admitted that human activity has resulted in the environmental crisis, which I believe we could 30   overcome with the help of science and technology. The majority holds the opinion that human activity carries lots of pollution, which made the air quality worse, and endangered species increases everyday. On the surface, these seem to be terrible. However, people are taking a fresh look at it that they can be improved sooner because of science and technology development.

In short, human activity makes the Earth develop. It is difficult to imagine how the world will be without human activity. 35   Similarly, a person who does not use machine in peacetime that cannot get anything done. Therefore, after pondering this question on many occasions, I believe that human activity makes the Earth better and beautiful and a great place to live!

Topic 29 **Has human harmed the Earth or made it a better place?**

People have learned how to turn wild natural areas to farm land, how to exploit minerals to adapt their needs, how to build roads and houses to expand their territories. People continuously improve their knowledge and develop technologies to improve their lives. It is undeniable that these activities of human beings make their lives better than ever before. Nevertheless, those activities also cause side-effects to the Earth because of pollution, deforestation, and exaggerated natural resource exploitation.

Nowadays, pollution becomes one of the most concerned problems. Because of the increasingly expanded factories, the industrialized areas, the burning of population etc, too much pollutant spills out everyday. Consequently, all of these 45   things cause bad effect to the Earth. The purity of atmosphere is reduced seriously, the Earth is continuously warmed up, and ozone layer is holed.

Additionally, forest is asking for help in desperation. For last few decades, the forest areas have been reduced to 50 percent because of human deforestation. Green forestland of the Earth can be compared to the lungs of human. How healthy you are if their your lungs are trespassed. I am sure that you will get more difficult with aspiration; as a result, your 50   health will be affect badly. From this example, we can infer that how serious problem our Earth has to face with. I wonder how long it can endure.

Researchers show that the natural means is limited, but today, they are exploited so increasingly to adapt infinite human needs that someday, all mineral can be ended up. Because of serious pollution, alarming deforestation and progressive mineral exploitation, the ecosystem becomes unbalance. Consequently a lot natural calamities happen each year such as flood, hurricanes. A lot wild living creatures are exposed to narrow place of shelter and lacking foods. For these reasons, the Earth will become unhealthy.

In conclusion, the human beings harm the Earth. Human beings as well as their dear planet, the Earth, have been badly suffered by what caused by humans themselves. I hope that humans are soon aware of those problems so that they can have suitable policies in order to not only improve their lives but also keep and maintain the Earth fresh and green.

Topic 29 Has human harmed the Earth or made it a better place?

Although the quality of life has improved over the past decades due to new technological advances but the damages made to the earth weigh more. Damages include increase in pollution and change in climatic patterns. Irreversible damage to earth can include depletion of natural resources.

As the technology advances more factories are built. These factories dispose waste material into natural water, which could be harmful to aquatic life. Emissions from the factories and automobiles pollute the air, which we breathe. Nuclear waste and radiation from power plants are harmful to our health.

There can be drastic changes in the climatic pattern due to the increase in the carbon dioxide released into the atmosphere, which is the main cause of global warming. Global warming would increase the temperature of earth and make it inhospitable. We are cutting more and more trees for furniture's, and wood. Trees purify the atmosphere by absorbing the carbon dioxide from the atmosphere and releasing the oxygen. Furthermore, the roots of tree hold the soil and prevent floods.

Resources of petroleum, oil, and minerals are not endless. There is shortage of water all over the world. Once depleted of these resources, our life would be difficult. Killing elephants for their teeth, and other species for their furs disrupt the food chain. For example killing of carnivorous animals would cause increase in the number of herbivores, which would consume more plants. We also depend on plants for food so there can be shortage of vegetables and cereals for us.

We should preserve the earth and respect all its valuable resources. Pollution and climatic changes can make earth inhospitable. Our future would not be good without sustainable development.

Topic 30 Should a high school be built in your community?

I oppose having a new high school built in my neighborhood. Although I know there's a real need for a new facility, I have to say that I don't want one built so close to me. I think it would cause a lot of problems.

First of all, there are very few teenagers in this neighborhood, or in our suburban subdivision, for that matter. Most of the residents here are either retired or are just starting out with young children. This means that the kids coming to the new high school wouldn't be walking to school. They would come on buses or would be driving to the school. Either way, this would mean a lot more traffic on our streets.

In addition to the traffic on school days, there also would be traffic whenever there was a sporting event, such as a basketball or football game, or activities at the school. Would there be enough parking in the school lot for everyone attending those events? Probably not. Consequently, those extra cars would end up parking in our neighborhood.

My neighbors and I would also be upset about the loss of the park, which is the site that's been selected for the high school. Mothers with young children gather there every morning for their kids to play together. People my age like to take a walk after dinner. On weekends, that park is a place for picnics and relaxation. We'd be sorry to lose our neighborhood park.

I also have some concerns about all those young people being in our neighborhood. Would there be problems with drugs or fights? Could the school district guarantee us that security would be apriority? These are concerns that I don't think can be addressed sufficiently for me to support a new high school in my neighborhood.

Topic 31 Do you prefer to stay at one place or move around?

Staying in one place or moving in search of another place? Some people prefer to living in one place because they enjoy a harmonious relation with their neighbors and environments. While others prefer to moving from one place to another because of various reasons, a better job, house, community, or even climate. Looking back to my education and looking forward to my future career, I have been and will be moving a number of times. But considering my personality, I would rather live in one place when I am old.

For a student, a good education opportunity is the most important concern. Students leave their homes for good university education. Different schools have different teaching styles. It is very common for students to choose among different schools to find a most suitable one. I did pursue my bachelor's degree far from my hometown, and I am pursuing my master degree at another university, and would like to pursue a ph. D abroad.

Career development is another important issue. In order to have a strong experience and to get a fulfilling job, people would work in a number of companies. In different companies, we could experience different cultures and ways of doing things. The variety of people and culture will do much good to our future career development.

However, frankly speaking, I am not an aggressive person. I would rather enjoy my live in a stable pace. When I am old and without the pressure to struggle for a better job, I would prepare to stay in a peaceful and quiet place, where I could chat with my old friends everyday.

5 Taking into account all these factors, I would like to present myself such a solution: To try a number of places for better education and job opportunities when I am young; to stay in a peaceful place to enjoy live with my wife when I am old.

Topic 31 **Moving vs. staying at one place**

Living in one place all your life may seem very convenient. For my part, I am inclined to believe that not everyone is born in the place that is best for him/her, and thus one should take the chance and move to a place that is more suitable. For me at least, in this particular time of my development I find it better to stay in a place for a while, and then move on, to another place. However, as I would grow old I do believe my opinions in this matter will modify.

When I had decided for a career in art history, in a way, I had also chosen for a life on the road. I had always seen myself traveling from one place to another, organizing an exhibition here and there, and moving from one university to the next.
15 In the five years before I started my undergraduate education I had been enrolled in four universities in three different countries. At a first glance, such a way of living seems really appealing. It is always exciting to see new places, and meet new people.

Also the idea of moving in order to find a more interesting and challenging job seems to be quite legitimate. However, one needs to consider that not everyone moves during his/her life because he/she wants to, but on the contrary because
20 he/she have to. There are people that are running away from their pasts, or for one reason or another they simply cannot stay in the place of their choice. Moreover, moving from here to there have disadvantages even for those who enjoy moving. Family and friends are often left behind. Most likely, they miss the places that they have left. A piece of our soul remains in every place we spend a considerable amount of time. And what are we left with in the end? Probably with nothing more than the pain of being away from so many relatives, friends, and places we love.

25 Best thing to do, in my opinion, is travel all around the world, see as many places and cultures, make friends, but always keep a special place to return to, even if this place is not the one where you were born.

Topic 31 **Is it better to move around than to stay in one place?**

With the development of the transportation system and some residence facilities, the world is getting smaller and smaller, and people are not restricted to live in only one area. In addition, since there are different places with diverse cultures, living standards, education environment and others, people are inclined to move from one place to another. Is it better to move around than stay in one place? I believe there are no uniform answers, but in my opinion, I do agree with the claim that to move around is better than to stay in one place.

Most people's growth comes with the transfers in their life. As for me, when I was young I lived in a small county. Because the school in there was not suitable to me, I transferred from my little county to a city to get a better education. As soon
35 as I got to the city, I was amazed that the world was so different here compared with my hometown. If I were still living in my hometown, it was impossible for me to make the wildest guess at what the real world looked like. The first transfer has made me to imagine my own life and urge me to go further. With confidence, I went into a university that is located in a different city so that I have to come into another world. Compared with my living city, the new one is more complicated in which there are different people, more convenient transportation system, and more competitive environment. I love all
40 of this very much. By communicating with different students and teachers, I have learned much from them, and the experience will benefit me throughout my life and influence my lifestyle. Now I am in a graduate school and I will never regret my choice of leaving my hometown because the transfer has given me a splendid life.

Also, like us students, there are many adults transferring their work place in order to seize better opportunities. No matter in industry, in agriculture or in service, workers have rights to choose the companies that they work for. Many of them
45 work from place to place and then they accumulate precious experience and skills to excel others.

People not only move within their own country, but also go abroad to get education, work or live. We can see that many students want to go to foreign countries to further their education, and that many parents send their little sons or daughters to foreign countries to study. After all, diverse circumstances give persons new experiences and broaden their views, and even help them get more comprehensive understanding of the world, the society and life itself.

50 However, some people may say that if people move around, they will spend money, time and energy. It is right to say that it takes one person some time to get use to his or her new environment, new personal relationship, work efficiency and stability of the society and family. I have to admit that people should make extensive plans before changing their places and may not move aimlessly and frequently.

Topic 32 **Do you spend money or save them?**

Some people say that it is better to enjoy your money as soon as you earn it while others prefer to save the money for later. It's a difficult choice faced by lots of people because of the different attitudes they hold towards money. As far as I am concerned, I vote for the former choice, which is that it is better for one to enjoy his or her money as soon as it is earned. Spending money as soon as possible is my preference because of three reasons as follows.

First, we can observe easily in the modern society that the dominant philosophy nowadays is 'enjoy your life when you are still young'. Most young adults like to work for a period of time and then go on for a trip to visit some places they have never been to. Those trips not only helps them to keep in shape but also provides them different kinds of knowledge and new perspective in looking at their environment. Other people spend the money for their leisure, which helps them to

10 relax and go back to work with enough energy.

In the old days, it is said that people who save money in a bank understand the philosophy of thrift. Actually, economists say that in the modern world saving money in a bank is the quickest way to lose it. Moreover, none of the rich people became rich by getting interests from the bank. Living in a constantly changing world, we should adjust ourselves to accept the new ways of investing our money to different areas in order to get the most of it. That is probably the reason

15 why most of the people nowadays put their money into business to get a better payback.

The third obvious reason why I prefer spending money rather than saving them is that it is part of the contribution for the economic growth in our country. If nobody has the needs to buy stuff from others and the market, nobody will think about how to produce useful products and sell them to make the most profits. Some countries continue to lower the interests in order to force people to spend their money and therefore benefit the society as well as the people themselves.

20 In this broad view, I prefer spending money rather than saving them.

In conclusion, I prefer spending money because it benefits ourselves as well as people around us. It's also important for kids to know how to save money as a sense of thrift. Nevertheless, spending money is still the best way to make our lives enjoyable and worthwhile.

Topic 32 **Do you spend money or save them?**

When I am economically independent, I will choose to enjoy the money I earn instead of saving it for some time in the future. Life is a process of consuming; and we are growing old day after day. So why not taking advantage of being young to enjoy yourself fully, deeply and truly with money - which really can give you many things although we say that money cannot buy all?

No one would deny that we are all in pursuit of happiness. And this happiness should belong to today but not tomorrow.

30 Imagine a person, who saves all he can save in the hope of living better in his later life or making use of the money when necessary, suddenly dies from a traffic accident one morning, leaving all his savings without enjoying a pit of them. Since no one will know what will happen in the next second, we had better enjoy what we own now, thus at least nothing regrettable left in our life if something does overtake us. Money is just what can provide us most of the enjoyments. In this highly commercial world, nothing can be done without money - seeing movies, watching a game, eating at a fancy

35 restaurant, and so on. Money itself indeed cannot give us happiness, but at least it can offer us such opportunities to seek happiness in certain aspect.

For the young, youth is such a valuable period that none of us should leave something regrettable in this golden age. Ascetic-like life is not I want to lead. I am a person who thinks material things the most important because I like commodities of famous brand, I like eating in expensive restaurants instead of snack bars, I want to traveling all over the

40 world, things for which money is indispensable. I earn money to fulfill what I look forward to but not put aside to prepare for something that may happen.

Furthermore, in view of the nowadays economy situation, governments in all countries encourage people to consume but not save. Economy in many countries is down and down, the most distinctive indication of which is the poor consumption. If every person saves instead consuming, how could the situation be better? Enjoying what you earn cannot

45 only bring you your own happiness but also contribute to the economy of your country, why not?

In one word, I myself choose to spend what I learn and enjoy in time but not save my money for some time in the future. And I believe that is better both for you and for the society. So, never hesitate, buy what you want to buy if you have enough money, and enjoy yourself as much as you like.

Topic 33 **Jewelry or concert?**

Depending on personal experience, personality type and emotional, we find that some people hold the idea of enjoying a concert if a gift of money has been received, but others choose to buy a piece of jewelry and that is also my point. My arguments for this point are listed as follows.

The main reason for a piece of jewelry I like is that it has a great value of collection. With the resistance of fading, erosion and alteration, jewelry is probably the first durable ornaments humans possessed. In addition, owing to rareness,

55 costly jewelry is regarded as particular merchandise and left behind to the offspring. Furthermore, its value will not

depreciate like paper currency because of turbulent society and economy. According to the three points above, we can reach the investment value of choosing a piece of jewelry.

Another reason can be seen by every one is that jewelry can make people pretty, and always symbolizes something. For example, through the centuries, rings have perpetuated the talismanic role of the diamond. In the Middle Ages and
5 Renaissance period, every ring that was set with a precious stone was not so much a piece of jewelry, but an amulet that conveyed the magic powers of the stone upon the wearer. On the other hand, "A diamond is forever" is internationally known to men and women of all ages and may very well mean something different for everyone. Aside from its status as the ultimate symbol of love, diamonds have been around for millions of years, thus in their own right symbolizing, "forever." So, it is a good present that you buy a piece of jewelry for your love.

10 Admittedly, listening to a concert also has advantages, but the influence is short-lived. So, taking into account of all the factors that I have discussed in the above analysis, I believe that it is more advisable to buy a piece of jewelry rather than a ticket to a concert.

Topic 33 **A piece of jewelry vs. a concert**	People make money for living first and then use the money for other things that lead them to a happy and healthy life, such as buying something they like, watching a movie, or eating a big meal. In my opinion, if I have received a gift of money, I would like to buy a ticket to a concert.

For me, music is always attractive. When I have completed a whole day's study or finished the discussion on some academic problems, my spirit will be eager to relax for a while. When people want to relax, it is a wonderful thing to go to a concert: the music playing on the concert is the best thing to set your mind free. If you spend the money to listen to a
20 concert, you will fell that the cost is valuable.

In addition, you can attend the concert with your friends. It is a good chance to build up the relationship between your friends and you. People are always busy with their work and study, losing many occasions of communicating with each other, a splendid concert and link us together. The music, the conductor and all the musicians on the concert can offer us a common topic; we can discuss those things together.

25 Furthermore, listening to a concert let me learn more about music and all kinds of instruments, it also culture the appreciatory ability. To think that I spend the money to buy a piece of jewelry, I can acquire nothing but being a little bit beautiful at one of my friend's birthday parties. In that case, I just fell that the money has gone.

Money, even a little money, can make your life more valuable, for this reason, I prefer to buy a ticket to a concert than to a piece of jewelry.

Topic 33 **A piece of jewelry vs. a concert**	Some people believe that attending a concert may enrich their cultural experiences, whereas others may agree that jewelry can be permanent and perpetual, therefore a good item to invest. As far as I am concerned, I prefer the latter point of view to the former. I would like to substantiate my conclusion from the following perspectives.

First of all, buying a piece of jewelry is an excellent investment. Once you buy the jewelry, its price tends to be higher and
35 higher due to the limited number of precious gems. Besides, you can sell it for liquidity, when you are financially in trouble. Conversely, you cannot keep a ticket to preserve its value or resell it for money. If you believe "save it for rainy days", you must invest in jewelry other than a concert ticket.

What's more, jewelry symbolizes perpetuity. You must have heard of the famous commercial slogan from De Beers: "Diamond is forever". A piece of jewelry is always a good item to memorize some important days, such as a wedding
40 anniversary. In addition, you can win the heart of the girl you appreciate at the critical moment by buying her a diamond ring! That is exactly the way I used to conquer my current wife.

Finally, a piece of jewelry, like a bracelet or an ear ring, cannot only deliver you fashionable aroma but also provide you with a luster of elegance. You may wear luxurious jewelry when you attend your friend's wedding party. Likewise, you can put it on for more formal social activities. Wearing suitable and decent jewelry may distinguish you from the others,
45 thereby making you feel more self-confident. In general, you will look totally different with the jewelry.

Admittedly, it might be true that attending a concert may satisfy your taste or edify your cultural sense. However, purchasing a piece of jewelry turns out to be more practical and helpful for most of people according to the above reasons. Consequently, I agree that if I have money I will buy the jewelry rather than a concert ticket.

Topic 34 **Should business hire employees for their entire lives?**	In the modern society, people are taking a fresh look at whether companies should offer employees job security for their entire lives, since many businesses are now realizing that job security make employees less motivated to work and this leads to less profit for the company. Even though job security also has its own merits, it is becoming a conspicuous obstacle to develop businesses. Consequently, after pondering this question on many occasions, I believe

that offering job for entire life is not a wiser choice for the development of a company and the society. My arguments for this view are based on the following points.

The main reason is that job security has an obvious disadvantage to motivate employees' work attitudes. Further, it leads to decreased productivity for companies. Workers who are certain that they can never lose their jobs tend to work less
5   efficiently. Many government workers are so indolent that it can take them days and months to complete a task that should only take a few days to finish. Moreover, it is not uncommon to walk into a government office and see employees filing their nails, making personal calls on the office's telephone, or surfing the Interment for fun.

The above reason is but one of many factors, in addition to, for the employees, there is a growing awareness that job security is not absolutely beneficial. With improvement of the society, workers are more eager to choose a better job,
10   because a new job means a higher salary as well as challenges. Even some career consultants are starting to recommend that employees should find new jobs every three to five years.

Admittedly, job security has its own advantages, as a proverb says, "Everything has two sides." The most extreme manifestation is the fact that employee represents an investment because of the number of hours of training required and the company will continue to have a return on this investment. However, we have no complete evidence to agree that
15   businesses should hire employee for their entire lives.

Generally speaking, taking into account of all these factors, I do strongly disagree that companies should offer their employees jobs for entire life. Job security was regarded as an outmoded way of conducting businesses. Nevertheless, the temporary professional jobs are proving to be the most effective way to raise the standard of living of a country.

Topic 34 **Should business hire employees for their entire lives?**

Whether businesses should hire employees for their entire lives is relatively a subject of discussion as hiring employees for the lifetime increases the level of commitment and an undying loyalty and gives the feeling of security to employees whereas hiring new employees brings fresh blood into an organization.

I personally believe that businesses should hire new employees from time to time as this process brings new ideas, new expertise, new motivation, new energy, new technology, new
25   beliefs, new culture, motivated spirit and other similar features which is very necessary for an individual and organization growth.

The inculcation and stirring of fresh blood in an organization keeps the company/organization/business going towards achieving more sales and more profits as new employees are better motivated to take new challenges with a positive attitude and proactive approach. They embrace new culture and offer their values, they bring potential ideas for the
30   internal and as well as the external employees. Rejuvenating new employees helps the company from many perspectives as after certain period of time old employees becomes less contributing because of the same monotonous work, same environment, same relationships and no new challenges and risks to take on.

If you look at all the new multinationals i.e. Microsoft, HCL, HP, etc., they are achieving stunning annual growth and profits because their policy is to bring the best in an organization and keep hiring new employees. Employees are the back
35   bone of every organization and pumping fresh blood to it after certain period becomes evitable for growth.

My advice to all will be to adopt a policy to inculcate fresh employees from time to time and investing time and money on them to help them deliver their best and also to retain some amount of old employees because it is said "OLD IS GOLD" to get the ship going through hard times and conquers at last.

Topic 34 **Should business hire employees for their entire lives?**

Should business hire employees for their entire lives? My answer is no. A business has the responsibility to take care of the right and interests of its employees; therefore it should keep them as long as it can. But it is not realistic that a business can hire its employees for their entire lives.

Firstly, on the business side, in order to survive and thrive, a business, like a human body, needs to constantly bring in new ideas and fresh minds into the corporation, and eliminate
45   those positions that are not needed any longer. Although this might sound cruel, but it is for the survival of the business. If the business itself cannot continue, every employee will lose his/her job. People generally think big companies like IBM or Wal-Mart are the kind of place where people can keep their jobs forever, but these days we often hear about the news that these companies also lay off hundreds and thousands of people due to economic depressions.

Secondly, on the employee side, securing a lifetime job in one company is always not good for his personal advancement.
50   He tends to be satisfied with his current job, and make no plans for the future career advancement. This is harmful for both the company and himself. In fact, it is those hop around among different companies who can get a big increase in terms of salary and benefits, and bring new experiences and skills to their new employees.

In conclusion, I believe it is not a good idea to hire employees for their entire lives. It is both harmful to business and its employees, and therefore, also harmful to the society.

Topic 35 A live performance vs. television broadcast

I do not agree with the statement that attending a live performance such as a play, concert or sport event is more enjoyable than watching the same event on TV, because there are many disadvantages in attending a real performance.

Firstly, there is too much trouble in attending a real performance. You have to buy tickets, sometimes stand in a long queue; you have to plan the trip and set out a few hours before the show started. After arrival at the theatre or stadium, you will have great trouble finding a parking place. During a sport event, your personal safety might be jeopardized: the sports funs might get too excited about the event, and become a mob. Many people might have heard the news that a girl was killed by a puck during a hockey game. If you take public transport or a taxi home after the show, you might find it very difficult to catch a bus or find a cab.

Secondly, the seating arrangement can greatly affect the comfort of watching the show. If your seat is far from the stage or playground, you cannot even see the show clearly. People's heads and cheers will distract you from viewing the show, and in the end you do not even know whom you have seen in a play, or who wins in a sports event!

Thirdly, there is no flexibility in a real show. After you have been through so much trouble and eventually start to enjoy the show, you might find that you are quite disappointed about the show after all. Unlike watching TV programs, you neither simply change channels nor leave the theatre in the middle of a concert or play. You might spend a lot of money to suffer from a show that you do not like.

On the contrary, watching TV at home, where you can make yourself a cup of coffee, sit back comfortably and relax, watch the show closely, and enjoy the realistic image and sound from your SONY home-theatre system. Besides, you can watch programs whatever you like, and go to bed right when the show has ended.

Although many people enjoy the excitement of watch a real show, I think nothing is more convenient and comfortable than watch TV at home.

Topic 35 A live performance vs. television broadcast

Some people like to attend a live performance while others think that watching the same event on television is more enjoyable. To me, I choose watching an event on television because it is easier and not limited and you have choices and can know more details of the event.

Watching an event is easier than attending it. You need only a TV set in your room. You do not have to buy a ticket or drive to the place where the event is performed. You can drink some coffee or tea when you want. But if you attend a concert or a play, you have no freedom to drink or do something else. In addition, at home, you do not need to worry about the traffic jam and being late for the event, so you have a light mood to enjoy the event.

The other advantage of watching an event on television is that you can enjoy it at any time and you can choose what you like from many channels. But if you attend a real event and find you have no interest on it, you would regret that you have wasted the time and money. Watching it on television can avoid it. If you are interested in the play, you can stay on it; if you are bored, you can change the channel to find some programs that are interesting.

Watching an event on television has another advantage in that you can get more details of the event from the interpretation. You can understand the background, the present situation and such information of the event. But if you attend it, you cannot get this information.

I choose watching an event on television. I think it is more enjoyable than attending a live performance.

Topic 35 A live performance vs. television broadcast

To many people, attending a live performance, such as a melodrama, a concert, or a sporting event is so incredibly attractive that they will go all out to get a ticket, regardless of the expense or the difficulty involved. But why not enjoy the performance on television while you can comfortably lie in your sofa or couch with popcorn at hand? That is because attending a live performance provides you with far more enjoyment than watch it on TV.

In a live performance, you will feel that you are in the company of many friends who are indulged in the same interest, who can share your sorrow or pleasure or excitement. This kind of resonance at heart is so rarely sensed in our daily life that this one reason itself is sufficient enough for many people to attend a live performance. While watching it on TV, we certainly find it hard to feel the emotion sharing, and our loneliness is hardly mitigated.

Furthermore, attending a live performance gives you a sense of participation that cannot be replaced by watching on TV. Live performance is an interaction between the audience and the performers, and both parts of the performance decide whether it will be a wonderful one. In this way, you may lament or laugh, may sob or smile as you are so influenced by the misfortune or happiness of the characters. You may fall into the indescribable intoxication while listen to a favorite piece of music. And correspondingly, the performers will receive the response of their audience and act accordingly. So the final success of the performance results also from the participation and interaction of the audience, of which you are a member.

With these foregone advantages, we may say that attending the live performance is definitely much more enjoyable than TV watching.

Topic 36 **Which transportation vehicle has changed people's lives?**

The ancient Chinese people dreamed of flying to a place thousands of miles away within minutes by utilizing the force of a special wind. In many ancient mythologies, deity heroes who had the magic power of traveling a long distance in minutes were highly admired by the common people on earth.

The invention of airplane, which I think is probably one of the greatest achievements of mankind, has helped people fulfill such dreams. In the past, it was a very difficult and daunting task for a person to go far away. Confucius, the great ancient Chinese scholar, once said that a
10 man should not travel a long distance while his parents were still alive. By this, he not only stressed the importance of interpersonal relations among family members but also indicated the difficulties and the time spent on going far way. In ancient books, we can find numerous descriptions of the hardness and risks travelers often faced, not to mention the long time they had to spend on the road.

However, the invention of modern transportation means, airplane in particular, has greatly transformed people's way of
15 traveling. Now, they can easily go within hours to places thousands of miles away, a distance which people would have taken several months to go in the previous time. Besides, airplanes make traveling much safer and comfort. Sheltered from sunlight, rain, hot or freezing temperatures, people can now fly in the air and avoid being exposed to bad climates and strong winds. Another advantage of airplanes is that they can transport people as well as goods swiftly to other places. For instance, airplanes play an important role in sending rescue teams and goods to an area damaged by an earthquake, as a
20 result of which the lives of thousands of people are saved. Now, in the global anti-terrorist war, military forces can be dispatched and deployed in a short time to areas where an terrorist attack occurred.

Airplanes have undoubtedly changed people's lives. The earth has become "smaller" now because of the convenient exchanges of people and commodities made possible by airplanes. We can accomplish many things that could never have been done by the ancient people.

Topic 36 **Which transportation vehicle has changed people's lives?**

An airplane is a form of transportation that has changed people's lives. Thanks to the plane, our lives are now faster, more exciting, and more convenient that before.

You cannot deny that a plane is fast. For example, the Concorde flies at supersonic speed. A businessman can leave Paris at 11 a.m. in the morning and arrive in New York at 8 a.m. the same morning in time for a day's work. Many business people in Europe will fly to London for a noon meeting and then return home to Rome or Madrid for dinner.

It is always exciting to take a plane trip. When you take a trip by plane, you know that you might cross many time zones, many oceans, and many countries. When you get off the plane, you could be in a place that speaks a different language. A plane is like a magician's trick. You get in a box and you come out somewhere totally different.

35 Nothing can beat the convenience of a plane. In the old days, it might take you days to do what the plane can do it an hour. Boats, for example, only leave on certain days of the week and take a long time to get to their destination. Planes give you the option to leave several times a day and get you to your destination quickly.

Although other forms of transportation may be more comfortable, none has changed the way we do business and live our lives more than the plane. Thanks to the speed, excitement, and convenience of the planes, our lives are richer.

Topic 37 **Is progress always good?**

Is progress always good? Scientific progress brings us many conveniences and advanced machines, such as computers, automobiles, and so on. Progress seems to have made life simpler and more comfortable. But if we analyze it carefully, we will find that progress is not always good.

Modern industry brings us many conveniences. But at the same time, some problems emerge. For example, "the green-
45 house effect" is a very serious problem that scientists try to solve. It increases the earth's temperature, causes icebergs to melt and the ocean level to become higher and higher. Maybe someday the oceans will swallow some big cities nearby them.

Progress enhances the efficiency of industrial production, but it also brings us another serious problem -pollution. Pollution in some countries is so serious that ecological balance is damaged and many animals and plants lose their living
50 environment and become extinct eventually. The air is polluted and it is not suitable for people. The water is also polluted and people are facing deficiency of drinking water.

Progress makes the pace of life faster and faster because of the application of computers and automatic machines. People have to work faster than before and it makes them nervous. More and more physical and psychological problems disturb people's life. Many people do not have time for recreation.

From the above statements, it can be concluded that progress is not always good. It has its own negative influences on our life. Let hope those problems can be solved by more progress.

Topic 37 **Is progress always good?**

With the evolution of civilization over the past several thousand years, man has made tremendous progress in all aspects of human society. While enjoying all the convenience and happiness brought about by this progress, we cannot deny that it has also caused severe problems. Scientific advance is always praised and extolled by many as the most essential cause of social development.

10 However, we shall not forget that on the other hand, major scientific inventions and technical advancement sometimes also form big threats to human society. The two world wars happened during the past century witnessed the blood shedding battles that cost millions of lives. Weapons made with modern technology have brought about such large casualties and devastations that could never been done by people in the previous time. Environmental problems have attracted more and more attention of the people around the world. With the development of modern industry and farming, global environment has kept deteriorating. Scientific researches indicate that the green house effect has

15 contributed to the warming of the earth.

We live in a much worse surrounding than our ancestors: polluted air and water, extreme high temperatures in summer, etc. which are all harmful to our health. The world now is undergoing a globalization process that has caused divided opinions among different people. I think we should be highly aware of some of the problems it may cause. For instance, globalization would eliminate the differences between different people. The languages and unique customs of some ethnic

20 nations are on the verge of extinction.

What a world would be if we see people everywhere speak the same language, wear similar clothes, live in houses of the similar styles, and use the same brand of products? We do benefit a lot from the progress of human civilization, but we must pay closer attention and be highly alert of the problems it brings about. Progress is not always good if we neglect its side effects.

Topic 38 **Is learning about the past useful?**

It is often argued that spending much time on studying history is unreasonable, since the information people obtain lacks the practical implementation. However, after careful thought, I have come to disagree with it. I believe that history provides valuable sources for understanding different people and societies, predicting future trends and building a person's identity. History generates past experiences and formulates the steps of development. It

30 provides us with numerous examples of "cause-effect" events, which help to understand different social mechanisms.

Everything that is happening today stems from the past and will have direct effect on the future. Being aware of our history helps to avoid old mistakes and make right decisions. The majority of all the political conflicts have a long history, for instance the Middle East or Russia-Chechnya tensions. A closer study of their deeper reasons and the measures taken beforehand can prove to be invaluable in finding the right solution today. It can save thousands of lives.

35 At the same time, studying history of our own country or region builds up our identity, gives us a feeling of belonging to a certain group of people. Therefore, if we face a problem of communicating with a person of other culture, the basic knowledge of his history can prove absolutely necessary for a successful and productive interaction.

To sum up, I strongly believe that it is highly beneficial for modern people to posses a good knowledge of the history, because it assures a profound understanding of social mechanisms, helps to avoid many mistakes and promotes a better

40 communication between different nations.

Topic 38 **Is learning about the past useful?**

Every country, every nation, even every person has its own past, present and future. Events from our past reflect on our present. Events from our present will reflect on our future. The time-line is unbreakable. Therefore no one should live only for today isolated from the past or without any connections to the future.

45 Every one of us is a member of the society. Living without learning about our history is the same as building a house without foundations. Furthermore, everyone is strongly connected with his past even when he does not comprehend it thoroughly sometimes.

Our life is a result of a series of events from our past. Our success today is a consequence of hard work or some victory in the past. Our present failure is maybe a result of not taking our chances in time or not making a proper decision in the

50 past. I truly believe that everyone makes his own destiny and fate has nothing to do with it.

In my opinion, learning about the past is of great importance to all of us. Even if we are completely devoured by our present existence we should look back to the past as carefully as we can. Thus we can avoid our previous mistakes or to find an easier way to success. In this case history is our best teacher. And if we learn the lessons of the past we will make progress much faster in the present.

We have made our history step-by-step and day-by-day. Those of us who live only in the present and only for today are like trees without roots-so easily 'fragile' in a stormy day. The past is the base on which countries; nations and communities build their present. That is why I think learning about the past has really no value because learning about our history is invaluable. So let us take a look back to learn a little more about ourselves.

Topic 39 **Can new technologies help students?**

"With the help of technology students nowadays can learn more information and learn it more quickly." I agree with this statement. Technology has helped a student cross national boundaries, open up new views and increase the speed at which he imbibes information.

New technology in the form of Internet has helped breach the limitations of a country's frontiers. A student sitting in a small town of India can access the latest course material released by MIT on his topic of interest. He can gain access to the latest info that his happening in physics and thus improve his existing warehouse of knowledge. He can browse through the previous papers in physics and dwell deeper and deeper in his specialized study. And how long does this all take? A click of a mouse. Compare this with searching through the mazes of his small hometown library, only to find some outdated articles and consuming a great part of his daily activity.

Technology has helped open up many new avenues that previously were considered impossible. Take for example the simple LCD projectors. They give a visual feel of the subject that the student is studying helping him to learn not only quickly but also effectively. Or for that matter video conferencing. A student can ask questions and clear his lingering doubts when he interacts with a professor considered as the authority in his field.

An overlooked aspect of technology is the transportation. With rapid advances in transportation, a student in Japan does not think twice before signing up for a program in the US. Would this have been possible 100 years back? Certainly not.

In concluding I would like to say that technology has played a major role not only in increasing the speed at which students learn but also in bringing a radical change in the way they learn it.

Topic 39 **Can new technologies help students?**

The information technology is developing so rapidly that nearly all families in Hong Kong have at least one computer. Not only can students surf on the net and search for information at home, but they can also use computers at schools, at cyber centers and even in certain fast food restaurants. No doubt, the convenience in accessing information on the Internet helps students to learn more knowledge and learn it more quickly.

In the past, students can only learn from traditional books. In addition to the school curriculum, students might be able to learn from the extra-curricular books. They can go to the library and search for information. But this is much inconvenient than just sitting in front of the computer and learning things from websites from all over the world. In comparison, the information from the traditional books is so limited. By surfing on the net, students can get a wider horizon about any kind of information and have a deep understanding on each field.

On the other hand, students can never have such a quick way to search for information that they required. In a library, students might have to spend a whole hour in searching for a single book with relevant information. Yet, with a computer, students can search for an entire page of links with a search engine such as Yahoo. The whole process involves just few clicks and several seconds. Moreover, information from books in library might be outdated. On the net, students can learn the first-handed information. With the help of technology, students can get information much quicker.

However, searching on the net for information has its disadvantages too. It is difficult to ensure the information is accurate or not, as the publishing of website do not have the controlling policies as that of publishing books. Yet, in general, it is still true that information technology help students to learn more and learn more quickly.

Topic 40 **Never, never give up**

Continuous exertion may sound very exhausting and thus, it is understandable even if some people suggest it should be better to give up sometimes. It is true at some points because the human race is not almighty creature. However I would say it is not about giving up, but just changing a goal. Recognizing life events as a sequence, I think even when giving up something, it is just adjusting the goal to more reachable level and processes for previous goals always play a role in reaching next goal.

In the first place, I would like to emphasize that this is not only about the youth becoming competent, but also about all the people making their own lives more comfortable and enjoyable. For instance, both following examples I present can be seen as continuous exertion: a young person trying to become a professional musician and a person on the verge of death exercising hands in order to move them better than the previous day. If their goals are too high for them, the young person may have to change it to be working in a related field such as becoming a commentator, a voice trainer or so, and the dying person may have to change it to exercise fingers instead of hands. That is, people naturally keep trying in any case until the last minute they accept death.

Furthermore, there are also two advantages of indomitable attitudes. Firstly, some different approaches to a goal are necessary, other than blind efforts. Such a contrivance activates brain and makes human beings more alive. I do not think it is exaggerative to say.

Secondly, this attitude is also important when trying to achieve something extraordinary, because chances and right ideas do not always lie all together. Other chances and ideas never show up if it is given up. Totally different idea or better chances sometimes appear after groping in the dark.

From what I have been discussing above, there is no doubt about favorable influences of continuous exertion. Whether agree or disagree with the statement of this topic, people keep trying by nature and it does make us alive. When I have no energy left to keep trying, I simply keep it on my mind so as not to miss any possibilities. In other words, it is possible to keep trying even when feeling like giving up. Thus, I strongly believe that we should never give up.

Topic 40 **Never, never give up**

My English teacher always want us to remember Churchill's famous speech near the end of Second World War "Never, never give up. " This brought people in many countries extremely strong courage in front of blood and death and helped them overcome the most serious difficulties in the human history.

"Never, never give up because I can always see the coast and it brings me courage all the time." This is what the girl who swam across the English Channel successfully answered when the reporter asked what had made her reached her goal. She said that she chose a very sunny day to make sure that she can see her hope and just went for it. To be able to see the goal helps us a lot when we feel frustrated somewhere and even almost lose our confidence. In the long term to success, hope is our belief and it can make us be very strong when we face great difficulties and even want to quit. Some people failed simply because they lost their sight of their "coast" although they are very qualified and capable.

Never, never give up and always give yourself a second chance. We may fail sometimes but it absolutely does not mean that we will fail very time. Thomas Edison, one of the most famous inventors in the 20th century, tried more than one thousand times before he found out that tungsten was the right material for the electric bulb, and so as most of the great scientists in many fields. When the Curie couple faced failures they never gave up and always told themselves to stick to what they were doing. It's not likely to achieve a great success by the first try. The real success is always based on a great deal of failure.

Psychologists tell us that the influence of what we strongly hold in mind is so important to our career. First we have to make sure that our goal is achievable and practical then just go for it no matter how difficult it is and we will never lose our passion and will always be positive. The characters in The Lord of the Rings have thousands of chances to turn back. However they kept going because they were holding on to something -- There is some good in the world that worth fighting for. "Never, never give up" is always the secret to success.

Topic 40 **Never, never give up**

To me personally the expression "never, never give up" sounds pretty optimistic, but not terribly encouraging anyway. No matter how good this nice piece of advice is, it would not always be easy to do exactly what it tells you, that is, to brace up and to keep your head above water no matter what happens. I am not sure it is worth discussing whether this happy-go-lucky motto is in the right or in the wrong. I simply believe that for different people placed in different situations it may mean totally different things.

It goes without saying that for some this expression may sound like their personal life slogan. In my view, category of people has the whole life planned out for them in advance. They are very likely to have a set of short-term and long-term goals and to do their best to achieve them all. They would work hard, try many different ways to get to their aim and finally, they would most certainly succeed. Which at first may seem to be a fairly natural run of things. Their second favorite expression may be at first you failed, try, and try again. This is what they do and this is something they are good at. Sometimes it may also seem that they are just awfully stubborn and even stupid, not being able to see that some of their goals are just beyond them. But they still prefer to try to work for their so-called goals, regardless. No one wants to be a loser.

At the same time, I have the impression that once in a while? And quite good once in a while it is? it might be useful to be able to face up the facts and realize that some of your goals are too much of a job for you. I don't think it means being pessimistic, by no means. This can be called realism though. If you have already tried to do some particular task a hundred of times and it still didn't get you anywhere, what's the use of trying? Wouldn't it be more reasonable to admit the hard truth, rather than to go on with the same senseless grind for ages? I believe that this capacity to admit your own failure is a highly important, but incredibly difficult thing to do.

Anyway, I suppose that giving up is not a part of the human nature. Because if it were, the rate of suicide will be incredibly high, because as I understand that is the greatest giving up ever. But well, things don't happen this way. So, if you don't succeed, you try again because first of all you don't have much choice left. If you failed the second time and the third time and then over and again. You just realize that you failed. And even if you did fail, what are you left with? You just have to put up with that and start getting by it. It's the easiest way, after all. The one many people go for.

Topic 41 **Should we save land for endangered animals?**

In the past, there have been many endangered animals. Now they are extinct. Does it matter? Has our environment been affected by their absence? Has the quality of our own life been changed? The answer to these questions is "Yes. "

It does matter if we destroy an endangered species habitat to develop more farmland, housing or industrial parks. There is a delicate balance of nature. If one small part is removed, it will affect all the other parts. For example, if certain trees are cut down, bats will have no place to roost. If they cannot roost, they cannot breed. If there are no bats, there will be no animal, or bird to eat certain insects that plague our crops.

Our environment has been affected by the absence of certain animals. Certain flowers are pollinated by butterflies that migrate from Canada to Mexico. Some of the breeding grounds of these butterflies were destroyed. Now these flowers are disappearing from certain areas. We will no longer be able to enjoy their beauty.

The quality of our life has been changed. America used to be covered with giant trees. Now we have to visit them in one small park. Rainforests around the world are being cut down to make room for humans. We will never be able to see or study this fragile ecosystem.

I would encourage us humans to look for other alternatives for our farmlands, housing, and industries. We have alternatives; the animals do not.

Topic 41 **Should we save land for endangered animals?**

Human beings tend to put their needs in the first place all the time. It is obvious, that we all need shelter, food and clothing to survive. For some people possession of mentioned above things is not enough and they start to build houses and industrial institutions all over the world. In my view, this way we put the wild life of our planet in jeopardy. I definitely do not agree with the statement that our need for farmland, hosing and industry is more important than lives of endangered animals.

We all know that industry provides not only necessary things for people, but also destroys our environment. Of course, every person in the world needs such things as food, clothes and home. People already has built abundance of mega polices, small towns and villages with all kinds of industrial institutions. Human's activity influences our environment dramatically every single day. For example, people cut forests, throw garbage into the ocean and create pollution all the time. Many species of animals are already endangered because of our poisonous activities. Do we need to destroy our picturesque world even more, or it is time to stop now? I believe that people should decrease the development of industry, hosing and farms where there are wild forests and animals.

Also, I would say that everything in the nature is connected so strongly that by killing one kind of animals and destroying one type of wild plant, we can destroy many other species. As an example, Panda bears eat only bamboo trees and leaves. If people cut bamboo forests where Panda live, they would disappear too, because of the luck of their favorite food.

Et the end, I would say that the land should be saved for wild and endangered animals. People should start thinking not only about their goods, but also about saving our planet.

Topic 42 **What is a very important skill a person should learn?**

Success has been an issue broadly discussed and defined by different approaches. Some say that being successful means being wealthy. Others associate success with popularity and power. A third approach would relate success with social and emotional well-being. So we come to the questions: "When can be someone considered successful?" and "What skills make success easier to achieve?"

In order to answer the second question, we should have a point of view about what success is. I consider that someone is really successful when that person is able to handle and enjoy social relationships. A leader can be powerful and recognized, but if he is unable to enjoy his leadership and feels lonely because he cannot establish a deep friendship, can we really say such leader is successful? On the other hand, a wealthy person may have all the possessions money can buy, but again, what if he cannot manage a marriage or a friendship? This person is likely to feel lonely and unsatisfied.

Developing social abilities may be a very helpful skill for a person to learn, in order to be successful in the social-emotional side of his or her life. One ability to develop could be effective and assertive communication. Many misunderstandings and conflicts can be prevented if we express our ideas clearly and respectfully, and if we learn to ask for clarification when we feel threatened or offended by something someone told us. Another ability could be learning to handle teamwork. We need to learn to work with others at work, at home, at school, in our community. Getting into an agreement with our parents, children, coworkers and friends is a situation that can become hard to handle sometimes. Dealing with teamwork can be really helpful. Finally we could add the ability to deal with conflicts with others and conflicts with our own wishes or decisions. We will always find obstacles in our paths; it can be quite useful to know how to overcome them.

In my opinion, I would define success as being able to enjoy what you have, what you do and who you deal with everyday. And to achieve success, you should have skills that help you handle relationships with your peers. We are social creatures; we need each other to succeed, and to enjoy our success.

Topic 42 **What is a very important skill a person should learn?**

"It is never too late to learn" is an English proverb meaning that people should never stop learning all his life. In other words, life is a process of constant learning, which enables an individual to make continuous progress to perfect him or her as a human being. Therefore, I deem the ability to learn is the most important skill of a person in the world today to achieve any accomplishments.

10　We are living in an era of knowledge explosion. There are too many skills to be grasped by a single individual within a comparatively short period of time. Skills considered necessary nowadays include English, computer, driving, etc. It is not very likely for a fresh college graduate to be proficient in all these skills. The most possible occurrence is that a person first chooses his field of profession and then starts to master those required skills in his field. Thus, I argue that the ability to learn new skills is more essential than the skills themselves.

　Another reason for my avocation for the learning ability is that if a person is capable of acquiring new knowledge soon,
15　he must be a smart, trainable and adaptable person who is what the rapidly developed society needs. In a society fraught with new difficulties and problems, a quick-witted person, when faced with them, will come up with solutions more easily than those who only know "the skills." That is why I believe the capacity to acquire knowledge carries more weight than "the knowledge" itself.

　In short, in a time teeming with many unprecedented events, the problem-solving ability or new knowledge-acquiring skill
20　is the most crucial one necessary for a person who wants to be successful.

Topic 42 **What is a very important skill a person should learn?**

Two years ago, if you ask a person what do they think is the most important skill to be successful in the world, you will get a variety of answers. If you ask a person who is about my age the same question, presumably, eight out of ten will give the same answer as mine - the computer skill is the most important skill a person should learn.

　Why I think computer skill is the most important skill? First, computer skills such as operating a word processing software package or typing are convenient and efficient. For example, I am writing this essay by using a computer. If I do not have computer skill, I cannot make a composition as quickly as possible; maybe I can only write on paper. Another example is that many colleges is offering online classes for student to choose from, which means the students can study in the comfort of their homes and acquire their knowledge by means of using
30　computers at home.

　Secondly, computers are an important tool for teaching and communicating between teachers and students. Recently, school teachers have an increasingly demand on students to turning in their papers or school works, and the teachers can score on line. If the teacher has a assignment, they just send an e-mail to the students. In addition, many young people use computers to communicate with each other. They use online chat rooms, ICQs and messengers. They even play online
35　games through the Internet. Therefore computer skills are important for students to communicate with their teachers and fellow students.

　Last but not least, computer skill helps a person to find a good job after they graduate. As we open newspapers and search for a good job, we can find that computer skill is a required skill for nearly every job. Indeed, whether you work as a receptionist, salesperson, warehouse manager and office clerk, you have to operate a computer and therefore computer
40　skills is absolutely necessary for these jobs and most others.

　Although there are many other important skills for a person to succeed in today's world, judging from what I have mentioned above, I think my point of view is solid and sound. Having computer skills is one of the most important things in today's world.

Topic 42 **What is a very important skill a person should learn?**

Nowadays people say that we have stepped into "The Information Age", therefore computer skills are one of the most important skills in today's society. Being able to operate a computer is an advanced technique and can increase one's work efficiency and simplify many works.

　Using a computer can help people do many complex works. You can calculate a very complex arithmetic problem. Many arithmetic problems in engineering are too complex to work out by hands. A computer can do these works conveniently and easily. You can also look for some
50　references from a foreign country from a computer if you login in the Internet. You can save your documents in some discs on a computer no matter how large they are and you do not need to take a lot of paper.

　Using a computer can increase your work efficiency. With its help, you can book plane tickets and hotel rooms for a business trip. You can easily compile your files in a shorter time and retrieve them whenever you need. If you are an engineer, you can control machines automatically with the help of a computer. The products are more precise than those controlled by hands and the product efficiency is higher. You can save a lot of time to consider other things and this is important for your success.

If you can operate a computer, you can sit down in your own home and control distant work. All you need to do is pressing some keys. With the help of a computer, your work can be simplified. You also can use a computer to
5   communicate with your friends by e-mails and it is quicker and safer than ordinary means.

There are many other skills a person should learn to be successful, but I think that being able to operating a computer is the most important.

Topic 42 What is a very important skill a person should learn?

Upon the question that what is the very important skill a person should learn in the world today, different people have different opinions. In my point of view, I prefer to think that communication is the most important skill for almost every person. There are many reasons to support my view.

Firstly, communication is a bridge between people. Nobody is omnipotent; people depend on one another in their daily lives. We all hope we can be become the person who masters every
skills and can complete every kind of work by ourselves. However the real world tells us that this just is a dream.
15   Therefore, people are interdependent; no one can say that he does not need other people's help. The society requires cooperation among people. Communication is the link. Communication is the first step of successful cooperation among people. By communication, we exchange thoughts and information, and get other people understand our needs and ideas. For example, in a company, big or small, a manager always has to communicate with his boss, colleagues and subordinates.

Secondly, communication can help us keep friendship and make new friends. Friends need to communicate to each other,
20   so that they know each other's needs and feelings. Indeed, one of the most important qualities of a friend is communication and understanding. If you are a good communicator, it is very easy for you to keep your friendship and make new friends. If you do not communicate with your friends, you will not only feel lonely, but also can eventually loss your friends.

From all above, I think that communication is the most important skill for people to survive in this society. I hope
25   everybody works hard to get the skill.

Topic 43 Why are people attracted to a dangerous sport?

Have you experienced the fear of bungee jumping? Have you ever enjoyed the excitement of car racing? Nowadays, more and more people are attracted to such dangerous activities, especially the young people. Wondering why? After thinking about the lifestyle of those people, the reason goes as follows.

30   While the world is becoming more and more competitive, the tasks on each person's shoulders become heavier and heavier. People's everyday activities are very intense. The best way to relax and get relieved is to go in for dangerous activities, because while you are doing something dangerous, you have to concentrate on it, and you cannot think about anything else. Hence you relieved all the unhappiness and the troubles you had in the daily work.

In addition, to take risks and try out new things is one of human being's basic instincts. People always like to do
35   something new, especially when something is popular as well. According to some statistics, the dangerous activities are becoming extremely popular among young people. If you do not try some dangerous activities, people will think that you are a coward and you are afraid of doing it. So it is reasonable enough for them to do dangerous sports to show their braveness.

However, I do not like dangerous activities and I believe the phenomenon that people are attracted to dangerous activities
40   is just a whim. After realizing countless disadvantages of them, people will reconsider about them. Some safer activities to help people to get relieved will be developed afterwards.

Topic 43 Why are people attracted to a dangerous sport?

I think some people get attracted to dangerous sports or other dangerous activities for diverse reasons. There are many dangerous sports or activities, but for the purpose of this discussion, I will just mention a few of them. These are: Car racing, Bull fighting, Skiing, Horse racing and Mountain climbing. Some people are attracted to dangerous sports/activities based on the following reasons I will present in the next three paragraphs.

First, some people engage in dangerous sports/activities for recreational purposes. Often, they derive pleasure from such activities, and they believe it's fun. For example, horse racing is dangerous, accidental fall from the horse back during the race could lead to death or serious injury. Nevertheless the fun and excitement of horse riding cannot be replaced by
50   other sports/activities.

Second, some people get attracted to dangerous sports/activities for economic reason. Some earn their living through their participation in dangerous sports/activities. For example, there are two famous mountain climbers in my country that earn a lot of money through this dangerous activity 'mountain climbing'. Unfortunately, one of them can no longer participate in the activity because of his predicament. He missed his step and fell from the peak of the mountain and broke his spinal cord.

Lastly, some people are attracted to dangerous sports to get attention from the people or to prove that they are brave. Such people may engage in bull fighting, they want to show people that are fearless and can face any challenge that might
5 seem inevitable.

In conclusion, people have different reasons for engaging in dangerous sports/ activities .I believe with the above mentioned reasons you can see why some people are attracted to dangerous sports.

| *Topic 44* **Travel with a companion vs. travel alone** | Traveling is a favorite recreation for many people, especially for young students. It can enable us not only to accumulate our knowledge about history, culture, geography and local tradition, but also to edify our minds and spirits greatly. However, upon the question, which is better, traveling alone or together with several friends, people seem to have different opinions. As far as I am concerned, I like to travel with friends. |

When traveling to other places, the most important thing for us to consider is safety. In China, many famous scenery spots with Buddhist temples or shrines are situated in deep mountains or remote areas. Travelers sometimes have to go on a
15 tiring and even dangerous road before they can arrive at these places: crossing rivers with rapid currents, climbing high mountains, walking along a narrow path on deep cliffs etc. If a person travels with others, he may receive aids or lend a hand to his companion in time of needs. Several years ago, I traveled with some other people to Wuyi Mountain, a famous scenery spot in Fujian Province. When climbing a high cliff, one of the people slipped, but he was grasped by hand almost instantaneously by a man at his side. If he had traveled there alone, he would have fallen down the high cliff and injured
20 himself.

Another reason why I prefer to travel with others is that we can ease the feeling of loneliness and nostalgia by talking with each other. When traveling to far away and unfamiliar places, we may easily fall into a low spirit and have strong nostalgic feeling. There are numerous ancient Chinese literary works, poems or essays etc., which describe such feeling on road. A man sat in an empty hub, facing a small lamp, seeing the dumping rain outside the window, etc., all constitute a typical
25 picture of a lonely traveler. But if at this time, the traveler had a companion to chat with him, his sad feeling would be much lessened.

In a higher sense, life is like a traveling, most of us need someone to accompany us to go through the road. I think those who have to live alone are unfortunate ones in human society.

| *Topic 45* **Getting up early vs. staying up late** | Some people prefer to get up early in the morning to start the day's work; while other people like to get up later in the day to work until late at night. Which option do you prefer? I would choose to get up early in the morning. This view is based on the following reasons. |

By getting up early in the morning you can enjoy a lot of good things that the nature offers. You can breath fresh air, smell aroma of flowers, listen the birds singing in the morning. What a beautiful world! In the meantime, these can refresh our brains and quickly get ready for the day's work. We can immediately concentrate on the
35 work, and solve the problems with great efficiency. For example, when I was in senior middle school, I got up early in the morning everyday to go over my lessons and prepare for the courses that I would have that day. I found it was so efficient and I memorized my study material so deeply. On the contrary, people who get up late and go to bed late tend to leave all the day's work to the night, and tend to go to bed until the finish the day's work. This is not a good living habit and also not an efficiently way of working.

40 Another reason why I would like to get up early to start a day's work is because I believe that it is good for our health. The body's cycle follows the nature: when the sun rises, it is time to get up; when the moon rises, it is time to go to bed. Besides, by getting up early we can have time to do some exercises such as jogging, hiking and swimming, which will benefit our health. Many statistics show that most people who live a long life get up early and go to bed early. While getting up late and go to bed late violates human biology and therefore will do harm to the health. And people who get up
45 late never got a chance to do morning exercises.

In a word, getting up early in the morning to start a day's work is a smart choice for people; it can benefit both people's work and health.

| *Topic 45* **Getting up early vs. staying up late** | Some people prefer to get up early in the morning and start the day's work. Others, however, prefer to get up later in the day and work until late at night. As far as I am concerned, getting up early is a good habit because it is good for health, and it is easy for people to take care of everyday work. |

In the first place, everyone knows that getting up early is a very good habit for our health. You can enjoy the fresh air in the early morning, and also you can get a good night's sleep during the quiet midnight. Moreover, if you get up early, before go to work, you still have enough time to do some exercises, such as walking, running and riding the bike. Without doubt, all of the exercises can help your to stay healthy.

In the second place, it is easy to take care of everyday work if people get up early. For example, if everyone in the family gets up early, the wife will have enough time to prepare the breakfast for the whole family, the children will have enough time to catch the school bus, the husband will never forget to change his dirty shirt. Everything is in order.

5 Admittedly, some people who work until midnight and get up later in the day claim that working in the midnight is more efficient for them and they can concentrate on their work without distraction. However, the advantages of getting up early carry more weight than those of getting up late.

To sum up, from what I have discussed above, we can safely draw the conclusion that getting up early can benefit us not only because it is good for our health but also it is easy for us to take care of everyday work. Therefore, I prefer to get up 10 early in the morning and start the day's work.

Topic 45 **Getting up early vs. staying up late**

Meng Haoran, an ancient Chinese poet, wrote in one of his poems his happy feeling when wakened by the chirping of birds in a spring morning. It seems that he did not get up early and waked "naturally" after a sound sleep. What kind of timetable a person should follow depends on the character and habit of him and even on the job he does. I think it is important to
15 arrange our life in such a way as to ensure high efficiency of our work and good to our health. Some people prefer to work until late at night because they feel that they can concentrate their mind in a quiet environment when others are in sleep.

For instance, many writers like to write at night. It is said that a famous French writer who lived in a small house on a hill at seaside was accustomed to working so late at night that the lamplight from the window was perceived by the sea
20 crewmen as a signal leading their ships into the harbor. In China, people are encouraged to follow a regular living habit, which requires early sleep and early rise. For a long time in the past, China has been a traditional agricultural society, in which people lived a life that progressed slowly with the change of time.

As an old Chinese saying goes, "a man should get up early so as to clean the house to prepare for the day's work." Even today, we can see many old people do exercise early in the morning in parks or open areas of cities. However, with the
25 rapid social and economical development, people are now forced to some extend to abandon such a living style based on the progress of the time.

Nowadays, we are living in a fast changing society, sometimes we have to following a rhythm or timetable according to the need of our work instead of our own will. But however we arrange our life, we should try to take into account of our own conditions in order to do our work well.

Topic 46 **Important qualities of a good son or daughter**

It is commonly known that parents expect to see their children behaving decently and respectfully. It is extremely important for parents to provide to their kids a clear explanation of what is bad and what is good. Hence, by having parents' support and advices, children could achieve the important qualities that later their parents could be proud of. In my opinion, the basic qualities of a being a good son or daughter have been remaining the same over years.

35 The most important quality, I think, is that we should respect our parents. It was our parents who brought us into the world and brought us up. They provided us food and clothes, and send us to schools to be educated. They tried their bests to make our life happy and comfortable. Accordingly, it was our responsibility to respect our parents, including their efforts and opinions. We should not spend too much money on useless items because the money comes from parents' hard work. At the same time, we must listen to the right advices from parents and don't act according to our own wishes
40 and desires despite the objection of our parents.

The second quality for a good son or daughter is that we should take care for our parents when they become old. Nowadays we have already attended the university, usually far away from parents. So we should keep in touch with them by telephone, letter and e-mail, not making them feel lonely. We may talk about their life at home, such as their work and their health. In fact every time when I give a call to my parents, I may feel that the call bring them happiness. The reason is
45 that not only can they know that I am doing well, but also they know that their son cares about his parents.

A good son or daughter should have many merits. From my point of view, respecting the parents and caring for them are the most important for everyone. What's more, these values cannot be changed with the development of the society because they are the fundamental qualities of a good son or daughter.

Topic 46 **Important qualities of a good son or daughter**

In Chinese culture, a person who is filial and obedient to his parents is regarded as a good son. Confucianism, an ideology that had great effect on the Chinese society, stresses the importance of harmonious interpersonal relations between family members, particularly that between parents and children. Judgment on a man is often based on his attitude toward his parents.

Confucian classics contain many principles regarding the "right" conducts people should have to handle the relation with their parents. For instance, people in the past were required to pay respects to their parents everyday in the morning. Children should follow whatever orders or instructions their parents issued. A person who was most respectful to his parents was highly praised and often set up as a model in the society.

5   The ancient Chinese thought that there was a connection between the relations within the family and political institutions of the country. They extended the formula of administering a family to social and political affairs. In other words, the Chinese people ran the country on the principles based on family life. The emperor was respected by his subjects as a father was by his children. An official faithful to his lord was often compared to a son filial to his father.

However, China has undergone great changes over the past century. Influenced by western thoughts, the Chinese people
10   have revised and transformed many traditional ideologies and ways of thinking. Parents have no longer had absolute authority over their children. Now young people may stand on an equal relation with their parents and they stress more personal freedom and independence. But the traditional ideology remains to be very influential, a good son who is respectful to and takes cares of his parents is considered by others as one of high moral character.

Topic 47 **A large company vs. a small company**	Some people show special interest in working for a big company, while other are more willing to work for small ones. Of course, every individual has his own opinion about the strengths and weakness when it comes to serving in a big firm or a small one; for me, my choice is definitely to work for a big company.

Now let's use the analysis of "SWOT", which was always employed in the field of economics to get the problem solved. Here, S stands for "strengths", W for "weakness", O for "opportunities" and T for "target".

20   Working for a big company will have many advantages for your development in your career, because a big company usually provides more competitions and it demands its employees to be self-educated at the very beginning of becoming one member of the group, or he or she will be dismissed without hesitation. For as a big company, there is always a pool of talents waiting for a position to be filled.

Besides, in a big company, you will deal with different kinds of people, who are from different provinces or even different
25   countries, having various education, thus you will be inevitably influenced by "multi-culture", which is of great importance to a person with the hope of tailoring himself to be an international talent.

Finally, in a big company you will be given more opportunities to be charged up either at home or abroad and be endowed with more chances to contact with more elites in the specific field.

When speaking of the weaknesses, every thing is a double-edged sword. Working for a big company, there might be little
30   chances for many people to stick out due to the bulk of talents, but compared with the strengths and the opportunities mentioned above, it can be ignored.

When it comes to the target, you, as a member of a big company, will be more likely to motorize your target because of the plentiful resources including material resources, as well as human resources.

All that I have said above boils down to the conclusion that if you are a person who craves for competitions and desires
35   to be an international or inter-provincial talent, you should choose the big firms for your future development.

Topic 47 **A large company vs. a small company**	Each year, millions of students graduate from schools and join the army of people seeking for jobs. Many of them aim at getting a position in a large and outstanding company that often means higher income on average and good fame. Walking in and out the high buildings in downtown areas and wearing professional clothes and attires, those lucky people working in

40 big companies are admired by others. They are often referred as "white collars" or even "golden collars" that rank high in the society.

A large company offers many advantages that are helpful to a person's career development. I am now working in a company that is one of the largest ones in China and ranks among Fortune top 500. Our office building is located at the most prosperous downtown area in the city. Staff members of our company have higher income than those of many
45   other companies. In recently years, our company is aiming at proceeding into the world market and has established business connections around the world, which provides us with opportunities to work abroad. In short, working in a large company may enable us to gain valuable experience and have broader views in a competitive environment.

But not everyone is suited to work in large companies. For those who like to work independently and enjoy more personal freedom, a small company may be a good choice. People in a large company may feel stable and be less likely to be
50   dismissed, but they are also subjected to many restrictions imposed by the regulations of the company. A small company may require their employees to do more comprehensive works and give them more free choices.

In business, stagnation equals retrogression. Wherever we work, large or small company, it is essential to work hard to make progress. In a fast changing society, if we always stay where we are, we will face the risk of being surpassed by others.

Topic 48 **Why people work?**

When talking about working, some people always complain a lot about it. They regard working as affliction that means hardship, vapidity and low earnings. They may even dream that they can also live a happy life without working. But as we all know, that won't come true. Everyone needs to work for many different reasons. I believe the three most common reasons are to
5 acquire knowledge, to seek fame and to enjoy life.

In the first place, we work to practice our skills and we have to learn many aspects of knowledge to solve the problems and to overcome difficulties. So working makes us skillful and effortless. The experiences we learn from working are the most important wealth. They are the major sources of wisdom. If we don't work, how can we improve our intelligence and then how can we expect a wonderful life?

10 In the second place, we work to realize our value by producing large amount of goods and serving others. A farmer is not a farmer until he plant corps, a teacher is not a teacher until she teach classes. They all have their responsibilities and they also win our respects because of their contributions to the society. That's the meaning of life, which gives us courage and confidence to exert our powers to build a happy home.

In addition, we work to keep us healthy. We can communicate with each other during work. Meanwhile, we are helped and
15 encouraged. We have to work to relieve our pressure. When you do something you are very competent to, you will view it as a kind of entertainment. You even find joy from them. If we don't work, we will become torpid and fat.

In conclusion, I believe that working is a tool by which we can make a key to the gate of knowledge; it is a road that leads to tomorrow, and it is a prescription that can keep us fit. All in all, working provides us so much that I love work.

Topic 48 **Why people work?**

At the outside, it might seem obvious that jobs are just to earn our daily bread. But as we explore the facts beyond the selection of job, there are myriad of factors that go together in selecting a job. Earning money might be a priority because no one likes to live in penury, but it is not the only determining factor. I feel that the selection of a job based on remuneration might be a priority for entry-level aspirants who are in searching for their first job. But once people climb up the corporate ladder there are other factors one looks for. Going by my own experience I would say job satisfaction, recognition in society and realization of a
25 long dream or vision will become the deciding factors as we progress.

With the information technology (which is the most human resource dependent industry) growing at an exorbitant rate, Human resource managers have a tough time to understand what is really needed to retain the cream of talents in their organization. Recent studies show that job satisfaction and recognition are the prime factors that matter to the best talents, of course not to mention a competitive compensation package.

30 Every man has a vision, and continuous progress in the realization of their vision give a great feeling of satisfaction and moral boosting. I believe that without this vision we would never have our soldiers sleeplessly safeguarding our country. 'Serve with honor' is the mantra which keeps them going strong. It is the same sense of responsibility and pride in serving the humankind that propels the doctors to serve the people without looking at their watches.

Every job is important and has their pros and cons. But it is still our social stigma to weigh a person based on their
35 profession .It is this stigma which instigates the people to be finicky in the selection of a job when it comes to social recognition. Even in a social gathering the treatment given to a so-called executive is totally contrast to that of an ordinary low profile truck driver. Yes, people love to be recognized and it does matter to have a job worthy of it.

There is a never-ending list to follow in addition to what is said above, like flexible working timings, Profit sharing policies, free insurance, and others that lure the aspirant to take up the job. But, in my view I would priorities that job satisfaction
40 and sense of recognition are the prime factors in a person choosing to retire (of course only after serving their life time) from a company.

Topic 48 **Reasons for work**

Though people work primarily to earn money, there are some other reasons that they work: enjoyment, honor, assistance to others, etc. For some people, to work is to produce something to enjoy themselves and others. Musicians compose songs and melodies that give pleasure to
45 listeners. Writers create novels and stories that arise deep emotions in readers. Painters produce beautiful artistic works that appeal very much to the people who see them.

But on the other hand, these people, musicians, writers, and painters, are often beside themselves with joy in their work. Some people work for honor. Military men devoted to battles to safeguard the freedom and dignity of themselves and their nations. In human history, many people would rather sacrifice their lives than submit to foreign rules. Sports people
50 contest with each other for the honor of championship. To get a gold medal in the Olympic games is a dream cherished by many athletes around world. There still some other people who work to help others. It is the responsibilities and duties of doctors and nurses to relieve the pains and strains of their patients.

Wherever an accident occurred, we can see the relief team rescue and give assistance to the people in need. Teachers, who often referred as "the engineers of human souls", work to help students not only in their study but also in their moral progress. No wonder that teachers are highly respected in a civilized society. Socrates, the ancient Greek scholar, once said to his disciples, "I eat to work while others work to eat." Most people work to get money for a living, but money is not the sole reason for many to work.

Topic 49 **Face-to-face communication vs. emails or phone calls**

Many people hold the view that face-to-face communication is better than other types of communication, such as letters, e-mail, or telephone calls. As far as I am concerned, I do not agree with that view. There are many reasons that support my point of view, and I would explore a few of the most important ones here.

The main reason is that people live and work with a fast pace nowadays. They are busy with everything. However, they also need to communicate with their friends or relatives. The result is that they have no time to set an appointment. This situation is very common. The best solution is to communicate by letters, e-mails or telephone calls. We could write letters or e-mails in our leisure time and send them out immediately or call somebody and talk for a few minutes. These things would not take up a long time and can be scheduled quite easily.

15 Another reason is that it is too time and money-consuming for two friends that live far away from each other to schedule a face-to-face meeting. In this situation, using letters, e-mail or telephone calls will be a better way. People by this means could communicate with each other conveniently no matter how far they apart. Take one of my friends for example, he communicates with one of his friend in Germany by using emails.

Furthermore, I believe that sometimes people will find it difficult to communicate face-to-face. They need to talk about something that is hard for them to confronting each other. At this time, letters, e-mail or telephone calls are better ways of
20 interaction.

Given the factors I outlined above, we may reach the conclusion that communication by letters, e-mails, or telephone calls is better than face-to-face communication.

Topic 49 **Face-to-face communication vs. emails or phone calls**

Since the beginning of time the most important method of communication has been the face-to-face communication. In fact for a long time, face-to-face communication was the only method used. As time progressed new methods came along with the use of letters, telephone calls, and emails. Even with these improvements in communication, nothing has been able to replace the face-to-face method.

One reason that face-to-face communication is better than newer methods is that it allows one person to see the facial expressions of another. When a person is talking about good news
30 they usually smile and their eyes light up. Or when a person is having a serious conversation, their eyebrows are usually lower and they keep a straight face on while talking. Without these facial expressions it can be tricky to figure out a person's meaning behind what he says.

Another reason why face-to-face communication is important is that you can tell whether the person is telling the truth or not. When people communicate over the phone or through an email it is impossible to tell when a person is lying. But
35 when it comes to personal communication it is not as easy to get away with a lie. Many people in business prefer this face-to-face method because it helps them to figure out if the person speaking is honest enough to go into business with.

When it comes to face-to-face communication there is one more reason why it is better than other methods of communication. When a person is expressing feelings of love or sympathy, no other method of communication will express them perfectly. When a person is showing his/her love for someone, he/she must do it face-to-face so that the
40 other party can see how much he/she mean what he/she says. Also when it comes to expressing sympathy for someone, using any other types of communication is just not enough. By calling someone or emailing him/her to express sympathy, it just shows that you do not have the time or care enough to go over and say it in person.

For the reasons listed above, face-to-face communication will always be better than other types of communication. But while face-to-face communication is better, newer methods cannot be ignored. These methods have helped to carry
45 communication over through long distances around the world; thereby expanding the world we live in and bring everyone closer together. Through the use of letters, telephone calls and emails, a person living in New York can now communicate with his/her loved one as far away as South Africa.

Topic 49 **Face-to-face communication vs. emails or phone calls**

With the rapid growth of high technology, computer, telephone and other communication tools have become more and more important in our daily life, so what people have gradually ignored face-to-face communication.

If I were asked whether face-to-face communication is better than other forms of communications, such as email, phone calls or letters, I would choose email and phone calls. Here I am going to enumerate some reasons to support my choice.

The main reason is that communication by telephone or by e-mail is more convenient. There is no need to make appointment with friends before meetings; all you need is just to remember their phone numbers or email addresses. Wherever you are and whenever it will be, communication is as easy as face-to-face talking. Moreover, it is more efficient for people to communicate.

5 Another important reason is that the way people connect by email can make more friends. I have many friends on the Internet and we communicate with each other regularly, so I have gained more information and knowledge in many other fields.

Last but not least, indirect communication such as emails and phone calls can avoid direct confrontation and embarrassment. Sometimes we may not feel comfortable to borrow something or ask for a favor from our friends,
10 because we are afraid of being rejected. At this time, an email or a phone call can be more convenient and can avoid embarrassment.

If all these factors are contemplated, the advantages of communication through email or telephone carry more weight than those of face-to-face communication.

Topic 50 Doing same things vs. trying new things

I have to say that keep doing the same thing all the time is boring, and I certainly do not like being bored. In the real world, there are uncountable things for you to do; so, why not try them when you still have the chance?

There will be no future if no one tries new things no more. Human beings would not have gone this far without trying new things. Our ancestors had done so much in doing so: they made tools for hunting, created communication languages and introduced many other techniques that we are still using today. All of these were
20 new to them, and they tried the new instead of doing the old. Without their hard trying, we would still eat raw meat even at this time.

Some people may say, "I do not like to try new things because, sometimes, they could be risky." I cannot deny that. However, there is nothing that never has a risk. You may get hurt even when you keep staying at the same spot, and when that happens, you are probably going to get more pain. The reason is simple: if you failed in the domain that you are not
25 familiar with, you may not get too depressed because you knew it was new to you, and you can gather some thoughts, and then, try it again; on the other hand, if you did not do well in the area that you are good at, then, there is a great chance that you would lose your confidence because it was not as good as you thought it would be.

Thus, if you come to think of it, trying new things is not as bad as it sounds. Moreover, those risks hidden in the process of trying new things are often worth to take. Once you tried them out and got them right, the rewards you are about to
30 get are often surprisingly good. That try new things, legal and harmless, is always good. Even if you failed or got hurt, as long as you are still ok, you have gained some experiences out of trying them. The whole world out there is for you to explore. Therefore, you should do so to make your life valuable. Concerning the topic, I prefer to try new things and take risks.

Topic 50 Doing same things vs. trying new things

When asked about the approaches to life, many people have the idea that change and new experiences bring us a meaningful life. However, others take the view that staying the same and not changing the usual habits is the better way of the life. In fact both approaches have its advantages and disadvantages, which are listed as follows.

Some people believe change and new experiences provide us a meaningful life because when we adapt to the change and new environments, we must face the difficulties and try our bests to overcome them. This process not only builds our
40 personality, but also gives us an exciting and meaningful life. What's more, the change around us improves our spirit of adaptation and independence. They benefit us in competing for survival in the society. Let us suppose we always stay the same and do not change the environment. Then if someday we have to step into another environment, how can we adapt to it?

On the other hand, people who hold an opposite view consider that sticking to the usual habits is the better way to life.
45 They point out that the longer you keep the same habits, the more adaptive you are and you may live comfortably. They point out that usual changes make you acquaint with nothing, and then it is impossible for you to have a happy life. In order to see this point clearly, they give us a good example: If you change your environment every month, you have to always change your habits and customs. Then how can you live happily?

As far as I am concerned, the advantages of change carry more weight than those of staying the same because I need to
50 improve my adaptation. Only in this way, can I survive in the society.

Topic 50 Doing same things vs. trying new things

Without Christopher Columbus's global navigation five hundred years ago, we can never know the existence of the American continent. Without the first brave man who tasted the poisonous "love apples" which are called tomatoes today, we can never have the delicious tomato & pea soup on our dinner table. And to a person, without jumping into the water, he can never become an excellent swimmer. So, when it comes to doing only what you already do well or trying new things and taking risks, I appreciate more the latter one.

While, the idea of doing what you have already been good at is without advantages. Probably, the most reasonable benefit of this behavior is that, one can make sure to be successful and never lose face. Success is important. For example, if you
5   are an employee of a large competitive company, are you reluctant to drop every precious promotion opportunity to show your failure to your department manager? Or will you be tolerant to losing a job because of an unintentionally tiny error? The answer is possibly not. And doing the things one has already done well can also become a protection to a sensitive self-esteem. This may account for why a considerable number of people seldom speak a foreign language to the native speakers.

10 Nonetheless, pound for pound, I reckon that trying new things has more advantageous. First of all, there is no doubt that this is a sufficient way to perfect one a lot. It is just the failure that points out where he is inadequate and not developing well. And it is also the experience of failure that teaches him where to avoid making the same mistake as before.

Second, a little forward step always leads to a meaningful important discovery. In science, physicists insist on researching to explore the unknown mysterious substance cosmos and chemists seek out new useful materials through the results of
15 millions of thousands of chemistry experiments. To some extent, we can say that stop exploring stop progressing.

Although there may be tremendous risks and masses of difficulties waiting us on the exploring way, we can really not stop our forward step. Given the factors I have outlined, I believe that a person who is full filled with the courage to try something he doesn't do well is more likely to overdo himself and enjoy a more and more colorful world.

Topic 50 **Doing same things vs. trying new things**

Doing something already done well is really easy for almost everyone, it's reasonable to choose this other than try new things and take risks. But for me, I firmly stick to do something I haven't done before, for these sorts of things can really prove my ability, give me more experiences, and make my life full of fun and excitement.

First, choosing a different thing to do needs a person's courage. When we come to a completely new thing, almost everyone will feel hard to start, which is common but it strengthen our wills and determinations. In fact, the beginning of
25 a task is a real challenge for everyone, and its importance may directly bring about the result. At this very moment, courage is the thing we really need, but it is also the thing we do not always possess. To conquer the difficulties along with the risks will certainly bring you courage and pride that you never have before.

Second, the things you have already done successfully are of less interest and excitement than that of the new thing. Here's a simple example. Getting the right answer of one plus one, compared to working out an untaught new math
30 problem, which means more to you? Definitely it is the latter! Or you may rather stay at a certain level without try to achieve any higher and being outstanding.

Lastly, to the human being, standing at the side of the society's evolution, the whole world needs new things to be invented, new areas to be explored, new ways to be tried out, and all these are the right things to make progress and build a better tomorrow.

35 I chose to try new things, and I will continue to make my new days in the future.

Topic 51 **Taking risks vs. planning**

Once upon time, a man pleaded a piece of land from a tribe chief. The chief gave the man a pole and told him that if he could insert the pole in a place from which he could come back before the sunset, the land between tribe station and the pole would belong to him. The man
was so greedy that he exhausted to death on the way back. From this story we can see that although the man had his goal
40 and action, he had no plan. A good plan is essential for success. It can quantify the task and make it possible for a man to arrange his time effectively.

First, by means of planning a man quantifies his task. He divides his final target into several periodic ones. Thus, he could average the pressure and see his progress during each period. A good plan encourages a man to fulfill his destination positively rather than passively. Actually, all successful people have their careful plans. For example, an excellent student
45 must have a study schedule that include how to learn new knowledge and how to review old contents; an outstanding businessman needs a rational marketing plan that defines the best avenues to reach his target customers and then assigns a reasonable budget to his efforts. If one could execute his periodic target successfully every time, he could easily achieve his ultimate target. More significantly, during this process a man will acquire a lot of qualities that are essential to success.

Secondly, the advantage of good planning is that one can dispose his time and energy more effectively. It occurs very
50 often in life that one should do a lot of things simultaneously. To take care of his children, to work, to spend enough time with his family and friends, only by a careful planning can a man accomplish his several targets in a short time.

Let us come back to the former story. If the man were a coward he would always fear that he could not come back before the sunset. The answer must be that he got much less than what he could have. Therefore success, to some extent, needs risk. But I think a careful plan is more important because it changes success into a routine and it helps a man use his time more effectively.

Topic 51 **Taking risks vs. planning**

According to the words of Salustius "One is a creator of his own fate." Some people believe that success in life always comes unexpectedly and that's why it is only due to taking risks or chances. On the other hand, others are more inclined to planning their own lives. In my opinion, planning is the better approach for one who strives for success in life because it gives him an assurance in his future success and makes it possible for one to use his time more efficiently and to be more cautious regarding the difficulties that may appear on the way to success.

Success in life comes from careful planning and hard-working. To plan means to pursue some aim and to be confident that it will come some time inevitably. In this way, one acquires a bigger faith in his own abilities and become more urgent in pursuing that aim.

Another important priority of planning is that one can predict some of the difficulties that may arise during his work and in this way he can be better prepared for them. For instance if one desires to gain a better assignment within his office he must clarify his aim and plan everything in advance before taking great pains in pursuing it.

Other advantage of planning is that one can dispose of his time in the most appropriate way in order to fulfill everything that is related to his views of success. It occurs very often in life that one should do a lot of things concomitantly - to look after his children, to work, to spend enough time with his dears and relatives, to find time for rest, etc. Thus only careful planning can make it possible for one to complete many tasks in a short time.

Of course, both careful planning and mere taking risks have their strong and weak points but the former is more likely since it gives one more confidence in future success in his work, it helps one to overcome every impediment more easily and use his time in full value.

Topic 51 **Taking risks vs. planning**

Every day, new businesses are created. Some of these businesses will succeed, but many will fall by the wayside. Some ventures may be on shaky ground at the start, but with perseverance and careful planning, they will prevail in the end. Hopefully a careful plan will not lead to a surprise but rather an expected result and success.

There is a tide in the affairs of men
Which, taken at the flood, leads on the fortune
Omitted, all the voyage of their life
Is bound in shadows and in miseries.
----By Shakespeare

Admittedly, chance can sometimes help a man to succeed. But on the other hand, not everyone will have such luck. How can a businessman who succeeds by taking risks sustain his dealing with his business when he is suddenly out of luck? Most likely, their company will be out of business if they have not made an all-rounded plan.

Nevertheless, chance favors a prepared mind. The opportunity is equal to all the people. The key to success is not waiting for a chance, but seizing it. Obviously, careful planning will guide a man definitely, from which, he cannot only find a destination and prevent him from aimlessness, but also assist him to grip the chances on his way to success. For instance, an entrepreneur should understand the power of a cautious plan which may help him define his business concepts, estimate costs, predict sales, control risks, and even increase the chances of succeeding. The plan may tell him what he should do and how to do it. Going into business without a plan is just like having an expedition in the extensive ocean without a compass.

In the second place, a comprehensive plan is also a reliable backup. Although the original plan is followed, suffering may come for some unpredictable occasions. In that way, a well-considered plan that mentions all the possibilities can be very helpful.

From what has been discussed above, chances and taking risks may be unavoidable, but success results primarily from careful planning. A comprehensive schedule, similar to a guide in explorations, is a necessity for achievement.

Topic 51 **Careful planning**

Gorge Barton, the famous American general in the Second World War, was well-known for his bold plan and his ability to grasp chances to strike the enemy in an unexpected way. However, few people know that Barton was also very careful with the battle plans, taking into consideration all the details and making preparation for any sort of accidents. I think in a modern society success often comes from taking risks or chances, but careful planning is vital for us to attain our goals.

No matter what good ideas or big ambition we have, we need to make careful plans in which every step is to be considered. Otherwise, these ideas or ambition will remain "something in the air" which may never be realized. In China, a person who likes to take risks and is hasty in making his decisions is often criticized by others as one who is bold and immature. From early childhood, we are encouraged to take careful considerations before doing any thing important.

Confucius, the ancient Chinese scholar, told his disciples that he would think it over for many times before making any decision. However, on the other hand, in today's fast changing world, we should try to find new ways and come up with new ideas in our work. If we are contented with what we have and always follow the same routine everyday, we may face the risk of being surpassed by others.

5 As an old Chinese saying goes, "a wise man should have a careful mind as well as a bold spirit." In order to achieve success, we should not be afraid of taking risks and try to grasp chances, but at the same time our efforts must be based on careful planning.

Topic 52 **What change would make to your hometown?**

Teenagers nowadays live in an environment that is exposed to high technology. This includes the prevalent access to the Internet, the use of special gadgets such as the cellular phone, palm top computers, electrical organizers, and the like, all of which makes communicating with each other so much easier. Aside from this, youngsters like to hang out in clubs where they can dance the night away and listen to the their favorite music being played by a live band. This is the missing link in my hometown province, Balayan, Batangas.

Though Batangas is just a four-hour drive away from the capital city of the Philippines, which is Manila, it is still
15 considered a far province. With that, the technology and the places where young people like could hang out are very scant. Being a province where the culture is very much tight and conservative, the old natives of the land do not like their children being influenced by what they connote as "urban living." They would still like to have the peacefulness and the early ways of girls being timid, shy and quiet type and boys being courteous and gentlemen in nature. Therefore, any deviation from these norms would appear to them as major acts of disrespect, whereby it would reach a point that elder
20 people disgrace and disown any of their younger relatives who try to lead a life likened to that of city people. I think open-mindedness should solve this problem. It is just a matter of acceptance that it is not really too bad and that it does have some benefits as well.

Take for instance, going to clubs and parties develops camaraderie and meeting people increases ones circle of friends. No man is an island. One will never know that the person he may meet today would help him out in the future. With this, I
25 think a nice club with a live band, nice food and drinks would be a place to be for teenagers to hang out every night. As a compromise, it should not open until the wee hours of the morning, so the elders would not see it as so much as detriment to their children. Putting up Internet cafes would also be good. Having Internet connections helps province-based people to keep abreast with current events in the city or even international news. In this manner, they would not get bored. They would have a lot of topics to surf about in the Internet. Mobile telecommunication companies could also
30 extend their services into to far-off provinces in order for every cellular phone to have a signal wherever a user may be. Loss of signal in certain places hinders teens from going to the provinces since they know they will have a hard time with communication.

Overall, it all boils down to two things-fun and entertainment. A certain place, which is not only limited to my hometown, should develop itself into becoming more appealing to the youth of today by bringing in things that could keep up with
35 their level of thinking, with the way they do things and counteract their very short attention span.

Topic 52 **What change would make to your hometown?**

Everything in the universe is in constant change. And everything needs continual improvement if the ever changing and increasing demands of humankind are to be met. If I were ever given the chance to change one important thing about my hometown, it would be the Internet service. Needless to say that nothing generally revolutionized the way we live as the Internet in the past decade. Thus, an improvement in this vital service would mean an even more, unheard betterment to the people in my hometown.

It is said that information is power. True saying indeed! I can envision how everything in my hometown could improve dramatically if the Internet service in it were made free, fast and staying out there like electricity, telephone or water all the time. One thing, a fast free and reliable Internet service could improve the way people work in my hometown. With this
45 service people in my hometown do not need to commute to a far place to do their job. This in turn would mean less traffic jams, spacious work place, more time for family and recreation and so on.

The way people learn would be another important thing that a fast, free and reliable Internet service could be useful for my hometown. People will have the chance to go through tremendous amount of information resources in a very small amount of time. This assures a more fulfilled life for my hometown people.

50 Since its advent, Internet touched every part of our life. It in a dazzling way improved the way we do business, learn and communicate. A change in Internet service implies good way of living for every one in my hometown.

Topic 53 **Is money important for a job?**

These days, someone may hold the opinion that the most important aspect of a job is the money a person earns. It sounds like true, because with a lot of money, one can live a better life materially. Admittedly, no one can deny the important role money plays in his daily life. But, when you take other aspects of a job into consideration, such as the precious skills and experiences one gains from that job, the prospect of the job and the social status, you may doubt: Is money the most important? Isn't this attitude too narrow? As far as I am concerned, I don't agree with the statement, I doubt whether it can bear much analysis.

5　We live in a big society that is composed of people from all walks of life. Different jobs have different functions in this society. For example, the function of cleaners is to keep the city clean and tidy; the function of soldiers is to maintain the safety and peace of the society. Maybe they earn less money than those businessmen, but they still work heart and soul on their duties. I believe it is the contributions they make to society that makes them work that hard!

Now, let's take a close look at the scientists. Some of them spend their whole lives inventing new things, exploring the mysterious things and innovating new technology. The scientists, such as Edison, Einstein and Madam Curie, will be
10　shining like the stars in everyone's heart! We can say, it is the spirits they have, contributions they have made to all human beings, great findings and inventions they have left to us that makes them giants! Thanks to them, the society is developing faster and faster. Can we say what they do is for the sake of money?

Furthermore, if everyone in this society worked only for money, what can it turn out to be? Severe competitions may make people become cold-blooded, force them to use illegal means in order to make profit, or even commit some crimes.
15　For their own benefits, no one would like to help others in the same industry. And the relationships among people might become estranged. To conclude, I think money cannot be the most important aspect of a job. Money is not everything! As a saying goes: Money can buy a house but cannot buy a family, money can buy blood but cannot buy one's life, money can buy a wife but cannot buy true love." So, don't stress too much on the money one earns. In fact there are other highlights of a job waiting for you to feel, to find.

| *Topic 53* **Is money the most important aspect of a job?** | Most people have some sort of bias against money, thinking that everything linked to money, no matter what the thing is, is evil. If money is really evil in itself, it must follow that money should never be a consideration in choosing a job. The validity of this argument, however, is seldom questioned. Only when we notice that money is merely a means of exchange and does not lead to any moral judgment in itself, we can then study the issue impartially. |

25　The crux of the issue here is why we should take any job at all. Surely there are many reasons for taking a job, such as for professional respect, for the passion to serve the society, for some kind of social status---and, for money. In very rare cases do people ever choose their jobs for merely one of these reasons. Most of the times people work because they want to achieve a number of their personal goals. The most important aspect of their jobs will hence vary from person to person. Of course it is perfectly possible that a person may choose a job largely because of the
30　generous pay that the employer offers. Everyone has to get enough money to survive. Hence if a person is currently living in a miserable condition and, out of his desperate desire for money, he accepts a job offer, the most important aspect of his job is most probably the money. And there is nothing morally wrong with that. The demand for money should surely prevail in this case.

However the need for certain minimum level of salary is only one of the considerations that people make when choosing
35　jobs. It is hence also possible that the person is already rather rich even without a job, but he chooses to work to make himself happier. The pleasures of his career life may emerge from his passion for the profession or the social recognition he may get thereby, but no matter why he feels happy after taking the job, in this case money may only play an insignificant role, if any, in his job.

What have now been presented can actually be seen as the two extreme ends of the issue. Most likely is still that a person
40　works both for his basic needs and for the pleasure specifically derived from the career life. Whether money will come out as the single most important determinant is hence dependent on the various possible cases, or more particularly, on the importance of the wages to his living standard. It is therefore rather ridiculous to give a general yes-or-no response to this question and it takes person judicious considerations before he decides to take a job.

| *Topic 54* **Should one judge a person by external appearances?** | What do you feel when a handsome gentleman or a beautiful lady passes by? Then how about a fat short person wearing a dirty shirt? You feel differently? Yes, most people do. It's very common for people to judge a person by external appearance, because it's easy and direct, and it's instinctive. Appearance is a very important aspect of a person and reflects one's personalities. Sometimes you can tell the person's characteristics from his appearance. However, in most cases, you cannot tell exactly what the person is like just from the external |

50　appearance, and ethically, we should not judge a person just by one glance at his external appearance.

"Beauty and beast" and "Snow white and seven dwarves" are two stories that are almost known by everyone. Although there are fables, there are deep meanings inside them. What you can learn from them is that people that are not so good-looking can be very good people internally. And actually there are tons of examples in reality. Napoleon is a very short guy, but he was one of the most famous people in the history. Theodore Roosevelt, former US president during World War II,
55　is handicapped; but he is one of the most successful presidents in American history. So how can you tell about the people from their external appearance?

Moreover, there are other undeniable facts that show that a beautiful person may be rotten inside. There are many prostitutes on the busy streets. It's obviously that they are very beautiful, but are they really righteous people? A beautiful appearance is a good thing, but a righteous heart is more valuable. Finally, as we can see, it's out of question that we should not judge people just from their external appearance. The most important standard is their internal personality.

Topic
54 Appearance

Lincoln, one of the greatest American presidents, was said to be very bad looking. Once when his rival accused him to be a "two sided" person, Lincoln replied by saying to the audience, "If I had another face, would I wear this one?" Now what we remember about Lincoln is his character, his deeds, his contribution to the country, no one would care about what he looked like.

I agree with the title statement because a person's inner quality is much more important than his external appearances.
10 Whether a person looks good or bad cannot be decided by himself. A man's external appearances are born and generally cannot be changed. But everyone can improve his inner quality by his own efforts. By reading books, learning from others and working hard, we can make progress and achieve success. It was said that Napoleon was very short, but he was respected and admired by people as an outstanding military and political leader. It is the dream of every man to have a pretty wife, yet it is also widely acknowledged that a beautiful woman does not necessarily equal a good wife.

15 Many men would rather choose a woman with a common face than a good-looking one. Because they know that the virtue of a woman is more important than her outer appearance. A great deal of couples who go hand in hand for their life attribute their happy marriage to loving the other's inner quality instead of loving a pretty face. In business, a boss would never judge his employees by their external appearances; instead what he concerns would be their capability, their assiduity, and their performance. A person with bad appearances but good performance will more likely be promoted than
20 another one with good appearances but bad performance.

Above all, if a person has good appearances, he should not rely on them because he will unlikely achieve success if he does not work hard. However, on the other hand, if he looks bad, he should not feel depressed because he can make others respect him through his own efforts.

Topic 55 Should one make an important decision alone?

Decision-making is a common phenomenon each one of us undergoes in our daily life. Its magnitude varies from trivial issues like choice of a daily wardrobe to making a crucial corporate decision involving millions of dollars. A decision may have its implications ranging from a single person to the entire universe. Hence it is very important to making a correct decision. But I have a mixed feeling when it comes to the choice of making a decision collectively or as a single person. I feel that the decision making process cannot have its hard
30 and fast rules but has to be tailor made to suit a situation. Hence a decision may have to be personally made or in consultation with others as demanded by the situation.

I would like to analyze the decision-making methodology in its two ramifications, one involving personal interests and the other for common issues involving business, political or environmental significance.

Every person is different and has the rights to make his own destiny. It is this quality of uniqueness which makes the
35 mankind so special. We are the best judges when it comes to making personal decisions, for no one can understand a person better than himself. There are many things in life such as selection of a life partner, or choosing a career that are specific to the taste and likings of an individual. It is always useful to hear the opinion of our well-wishers regarding the deciding issue. However the individual should take final decision after carefully weighing all options. It not only gives us the self-confidence, but also institutes the responsibility in us to live by our decision.

40 Things are quite different when it comes to decision making involving business, political or environmental issues. The decision made in these cases has serious consequences than that of the personal issues. It puts at stake the wealth, safety and future of many others directly or indirectly involved in these issues. It is here the concept of teamwork, Special knowledge etc come into picture.

When taking decision on a business activity, it is always better to have a brainstorming session of all the involved persons
45 to discuss about the issue. It gives the best possible decision after carefully analyzing all the possibilities, with the concurrence of the team. Also all the members involved in the decision-making are clear about their individual roles in contributing to the success of the decision.

There are some cases, where expert knowledge and experiences required in taking the decisions. In such cases one can resort to the help of the experts or the consulting agencies for the correct solutions. The decision suggested by the
50 consultants can be expected to be more suitable, since most decisions suggested by the experts/consultants are either by scientific methods or based on a reliable statistical data of the past. Consultants are available in almost all fields such as engineering, finance, law, insurance etc to name a few.

Also when it comes to taking decisions that are of international importance, the governing bodies such as the United Nations Organization insist on a Veto for decision-making. This method of decision-making ensures that the decisions
55 are in the interests of the member countries.

Hence going by the above decisions, one can take the liberty to chose by self when it comes to personal issues. However when it involves decisions beyond the individual, one should always be a part of the decision making team constructively facilitating the decision, which lies in the best interests of everyone involved.

Topic 55 Decision Napoleon once said that an ordinary military commander would perform better than two excellent ones. By this he meant that a military commander should exercise his power independently and make his decisions without the interference from others, which could ensure high efficiency in military operations. Napoleon is a genius and his words might be true in military struggles. However, for most people, it is essential for them to consult other people before they make any important decision.

10 Young people need to seek advice from elder ones in the matters of their life and careers. Sometimes the opinions of the old people are so valuable that it plays a very important role in helping young people make decisions. Each year, millions of young students attend a national entrance examination for higher education. When deciding on the subjects and schools, the students often receive opinions from their parents, teachers, friends or those who took part in the examination in the previous years. When running the government, officials need to consult experts and the masses before they make any important decisions. "A wise ruler should gather opinions from all sides", this is an epigram held by 15 generations of Chinese rulers in the past. In the seventies and eighties of the last century, some local governments in east China constructed many chemical plants to facilitate the development of the economy, without hearing the opinions of environmental experts.

As a result, the wastes and gases discharged from these plants have brought about serious pollutions to the local environment. As an old Chinese saying is, "three cobblers with their wits combined equals Zhuge Liang, the master 20 mind." A person may benefit a lot from the opinions of experienced people: he can avoid the similar mistakes and learn valuable lessons. The successful people are often those who are able to utilize the opinions of others.

Topic 56 Arts or environment? In my opinion, a company should give money to protect the environment. Although art is one of the best forms of recreation that can touch the soul with its myriad forms, and can calm emotions, the present situation calls for protecting the environment. We all are aware of the 25 harmful damages that human race has inflicted on earth. It is time for us to rectify these damages before it is too late and humans are completely wiped out from the face of the earth. Only if human exist, will art forms exist, as they are directly proportional to each other.

Humans are considered the most intelligent of all species primarily due to their very developed and complex brain. But they are also the most selfish of all creatures. We have done a lot of damages to the environment due to our selfish 30 reasons to live comfortably and luxuriously. Deforestation has happened on a large scale to build urban and rural dwellings. Forests, once upon a time, occupied about 60% of the earth's surface. But today they are just confined to a few places. Active deforestation has lead to the loss of habitat for a number of species of flora and fauna. This has lead to the extinction of a variety of animals leading to an imbalance in the ecosystem.

The other issue of concern is the depleting ozone layer above Antarctica. This is also a direst result of human interference. 35 In order to make our lives more comfortable, refrigerators and air conditioners using chlorofluorocarbons or CFC's as they are commonly referred to be produced in huge quantities. The damaging effects of these chemicals are visible on the ozone layer. Due to its damage, harmful UV rays of the sun can reach the earth surface causing skin cancers and other ailments.

In view of the above concerns, the organization should promote the protection of our environment by donating funds 40 generously and organizing campaigns. In fact all the industrial organization should come together and put in sincere efforts to undo the harmful actions that we have done. This is only possible by creating mass awareness among the general public .For this the company must help with both its technical and financial support.

In conclusion, I think the company should choose to protect the environment for the above reasons. Art is of no use if mankind dies. Our future is dark if we do not take steps to protect our environment.

Topic 56 Arts or environment? Frankly speaking, both arts and environment are important to human being. However, if I were the CEO of a company, I would rather give the money to protect the environment than to support the arts. Because environment protection is quite urgent and matters the future of our globe, while arts is a continuous process to improve the quality of life.

First of all, environment protection is very urgent. Global warming is becoming more and more serious. Many spices are 50 dying, the ice in South Pole is melting, and many rivers are being contaminated. Now it is time for us to do something to save our earth and our own future.

Secondly, environment protection is very important for all, including human being, plants, animals and the Earth. When I was a little boy, I often played in the river that is located beside my village. The water was so clean that we could just drink it directly. There were also many kinds of fishes in the river. It was such a beautiful place that I often played for a whole day. Now things are totally different, the water became brown in color due to pollution from factories, very few fishes can live there. Those small children can never enjoy the fun that I once did.

Thirdly, the art is a continuous process to improve the quality of life, which is not as urgent as environment protection. In addition, there are many ways by which funds can be raised for arts, such as exhibitions and auctions of artistic works. 5 Environment protection needs money more urgently than arts do.

Although both arts and the environment are important, I prefer to give the money to support environment protection, due to the three reasons mentioned above.

| *Topic 57* **Serious movies vs. entertaining movies** | In this busy world filled with hectic activities, it is up to a human being to take some time away for relaxation. Relaxation helps to quell away the tiredness and rejuvenate our spirits .One of the prime ways of relaxation is watching movies. The ubiquitous movie theatres in each city can witness the fact that watching movies is the main form of entertainment for people. However, how people make the choices on the movie? Well I feel most people have a proclivity towards an entertaining movie may it be on an action, love or a comedy, rather than |

a serious one.

15 People's inclination towards entertaining movies can be strengthened by analyzing the factors behind why people watch movies. Most people visit cinema halls only for relaxation and naturally tend to choose a light subject. It is most common for youngsters to use cinema halls as meeting places and they make watching a movie a part of their weekend holiday plan. That is the reason why all the box office hit movies fall in the entertainment category, whether thrill or action. More over, children are always fascinated by entertaining and fun cartoon movies. Children play the deciding factor in pulling their 20 busy parents to the cinema halls, even if their parents have an inclination towards serious subjects.

However, I would like to see beyond public acceptance of a particular movie, whether it a serious movie or an entertaining one. Filmmaking has been functioning as an industry by itself. I would also like to analyze which movie, whether serious or entertaining will help to boost the growth of the movie industry. As discussed, the main reason of success of an entertaining movie is the wide range of audience who can accept the movie and enjoy it. Hence making an entertaining 25 movie imposes a lesser risk on the capital invested in the making of a movie. However film producers hesitate to spend more on a serious subject with the trepidation over the chances of the movie not making a good performance. This limitation of budget on the serious movies can be witnessed by lack of luster in these films.

The fact that the movies handling a lighter subject make a good business does not necessarily go against making movies with no themes or thought provocation. A message or a subject, when it goes hand in hand with entertainment or 30 amusement is well received invariably by people. Also there are many other avenues to address serious problems, such as books, campaigns, advertisements etc. However I feel that watching movies is the best way to enjoy action and entertainment. It helps to bring out the exact feelings as conceived by the director. Some of our favorite films tend to linger in our memories for ever and just a little thought about the film unleash the entire sequence of actions in the films drawing us back into its virtual world.

35 Hence there is no doubt that given a choice I would prefer to watch an entertaining movie rather than a serious one. I am unable to discuss much in detail, for I am running out of time and my friends are already waiting for me. We are going to watch 'Lord of the Rings' by Jack Peterson.

| *Topic 57* **Serious movies vs. entertaining movies** | It makes me sensitively to think of Hollywood place where movies were first made before World War I. In those days, Hollywood movie was like a magnet, drawing ambitious young men and women form all over the world. |
| | Up till now, there is nothing that can substitute the position of movies that is the most efficient way to relax us. I prefer movies designed to make the audience think. As far as I know, most movies are supposed to be made from the source material that mirrors a part of the |

social events. That means there is another methods to force us to think about what we have done for our country, what is 45 our responsibility in the society and so on. In fact what kind of information we need can be gain from different medias including television, the Internet, radio, newspapers, especially from some movies.

Tracing back to my childhood, I like watching the first work directed by Alfred Hitchcock, *Rebecca*. So young though I was, it did make me sunk into contemplation. Not only did the plot make me a little confused, but also it really told me the truth that whoever is right or wrong, no one can live in the shadowy place and everyone must live his or her own live, 50 enjoy the sunshine belonging to their own.

A movie worthy thinking about should conquer everything, including one's heart, which never fade with time going by, even be possible to change our lives.

Here I can not help siding with the other view, however it does not mean that we should totally ignore it, this is not a matter of making an "either-or" judgment. What we want to clarify here is what is primary and what is secondary.

If permits, a movie primarily designed to make audience think add some amusement and entertainment, just like tasting a cup of cappuccino.

Topic 57 Serious movies vs. entertaining movies.

This is a very flexible topic to argue upon. Both sides have their own pros and cons. But I would like to argue on the fact that the movies are to amuse and entertain the audience rather than fomenting their emotions and causing them to think. In the following paragraph, I have supported my argument with some examples.

Think of a person who has been working the entire day. When he returns home, he will be completely exhausted and will start feeling that he leads a very hectic life. At that situation, if
10 he watches a movie that is full of lively pranks and jokes, he will be revitalized like a battery that is being recharged. This is what everyone wants, especially when they are dejected and doomed.

On the other hand, when a person watches a movie that is very serious and emotional, it will only increase his tiredness. He will be having a lot of thoughts in his mind, like, what to do next? What is my first job when I go to work tomorrow? What are my assignments tomorrow? What is my account balance? Among all these numerous things, when he watches a movie that contains serious dialects, he will start thinking about those things. This is not the thing that should have come
15 to his mind.

Moreover, a movie can be made to convey a subject in an entertaining way rather than in serious ways. This will do more good for children too. We would have seen many kids who will be imitating their favorable characters. For example, the American kids are greatly moved by the cartoon character called the `Barney`, after seeing which they try to talk in the same accent and style. So a child can be molded through their favorite character. The movies can be made to convey a
20 good moral through their famous stars, which will inculcate a deep emotion in them in the right way. On the contrary, when a serious movie is played to the children, they are left confused and soporific, and they will neglect it even when there is a good moral in it.

Hence, I conclude that, the movies that are filled with amusement and entertainment will be appreciated by most of the people of all categories. After all, movies are a virtual world were impractical things can be put into practicality and
25 ideology.

Topic 58 Can business do anything they want to make a profit?

Nowadays, Merchants tend to strive for remaining in existence by all means due to the extensive competition and burdensome pressures. However, I am always amazed when I hear that it is necessary for businessman to do anything possible to make a profit. It may be as highly laudable and exemplary a thing as it is held to be by those who are addicted to money.

Apparently, I strongly object to it due to various factors that weigh heavily against the notion. The foremost reason is that merchants would be rewarded by nothing but distrust and even hatred from the customers if they hardly care about anything but money. It is widely known that nothing can be compared with the good reputation of a company, which attracts more upright and loyal customers. Suppose we are facing the dilemma of which brand of shampoo to purchase. It is of no surprise if you decide to take the one produced
35 by P&G or other reputable large companies. As a result, what assures the buyers most is the credit of the service suppliers?

Another subtle explanation for my point of view rests on the fact that various appalling results would in some cases, be caused by the immoral and even illegal businesses. It is decent to make profits and receive the repayment of diligent work and continuous efforts. Nevertheless, producing unqualified or even deleterious commodities, which possibly lead to detriments of people's health or security, is never the sensible method to operate a company. What impressed me most is
40 the tragedy happened several months ago in some part of China. Hundreds of infants died because of the nonnutritive milk powders produced by some merchantmen without ethics. Therefore, it is never too rigid to denounce the immoral and irresponsible behavior. The third point I would like to mention is that the merchants themselves would not be reassured to enjoy the property acquired in improper ways.

In most cases, it is the essential satisfaction of benefiting the public, rather than the material items, which inspires people
45 profoundly. What a pleasant thing it would be to receive repayment of your diligent work and continuous efforts! On the contrary, few people would go into rapture even if they possess a mass of wealth earned through indecent ways. Thus, only by obeying commercial disciplines could a businessman obtain supreme success and maximum pleasure.

Taking into all the reasons above into account, it is barely too arbitrary to conclude that only by descent and good Intentioned business activities could a company achieve respectable and decent success.

Topic 58 Can business do anything they want to make a profit?

Can businesses do anything they want to make a profit? That is a complex and controversial issue. Some people think that businesses should do anything they can to make a profit, while other people believe that businesses should be honest while making a profit, not only for themselves but also for the community. I agree with the latter point of view and in the following paragraphs I will try to explain my position more clearly.

First of all, I truly believe that one of the foremost important qualities of a successful business is honesty. Businesses should be honest because it can help to expand a client base and maintains a long-lasting partnership. No one wants to conduct business with a dishonest company.

5 Secondly, not every business is ethical. For example, computer games are a very successful business, but they often impact children's behavior, and increase the cases of violence on the playground. Another example is companies like McDonald's that sell fast food to children. According to the Canadian Pediatric Society, a quarter of the children living in North America are now obese, a rate that tripled between 1981 and 1996. Therefore, some businesses can destroy our health, with only one goal in mind, and that is to increase profit. I believe it is an unacceptable situation and steps must be taken to make drastic changes.

10 Thirdly, businesses should be beneficial to the community, because the profit they make comes from the community to begin with. A percentage of the profit should be returned to the community. Businesses should support and encourage the construction of playgrounds, schools and parks.

Given the reasons discussed above, the conclusion, which may be intertwined at the beginning of the discussion and thus become more persuasive, may be safely reached that businesses should not only do what they can to make a profit, but 15 also support and develop the community, with integrity and honor.

Topic 58 **Can business do anything they want to make a profit?**	It is claimed that the only aim of business is to make a profit. Moreover, it is thought that running a business without making benefits makes no sense. Actually, from an economic point of view, the statement "businesses should do anything they can to make a profit" is thoroughly true. However, from a moralistic and legal point of view that statement seems not quite well sustained.

I consider that to make a profit means that a person deals with business to be as flexible as possible. It means to put new technologies in application or to explore new scientific areas. Furthermore, to invest in individual improvement of the employees' professional skills and to be awake of the global market tendencies are things absolutely necessary for the modern management of business.

25 Unfortunately, business is not a quite fair game. It is well-known that sometimes businesses have their own "dark" sides such as tax evading, illicit trade or disloyal competition. In addition to this, many employers make their employees get overworked without any extra payment.

Another point worth mentioning is that businesses do not care enough about the environment and they frequently pollute it. Laws in most countries prosecute these actions, although some businesses keep breaking it without any punishment.

30 I consider that businessmen sometimes forget about utter limits in their ambitions to make a profit. Generally speaking, I do agree that businesses should do anything they can to make a profit but do not forget that anything does not mean everything.

If I ran my own business I would do it in a way that would neither ruin my name nor corrupt my conscience.

Topic 59 **What's your hurry?**	Life is short. Haste makes waste. What's your hurry? These three sayings characterize the way I manage my day-to-day chores. I don't want to rush through things; I prefer to take my time.

Life is short. You never know what may happen tomorrow so it is important to enjoy today. Of course, some people will say that's why it is important to cram a lot into a day. But then, how would you possibly have time to enjoy all of those experiences. By doing a few things slowly and doing them well, you can savor the experience.

Haste makes waste. We are not machines. We can't rush through things mechanically. If we do, we might forget something; 40 we might take shortcuts. By taking our time, we can do a chore carefully, completely, and correctly.

What's your hurry? Where's the fire? I don't see any need to rush to the next experience. There's still a lot to see and learn from the chores around you. Taking care of your baby brother for instance can be very rewarding. You could simply keep him near you while you watch TV and write a letter and talk on the phone. Or you could devote your whole attention to him and observe his reactions to his environment. You can observe carefully, if you are trying to do four things at the 45 same time.

To twist a common saying, "Don't just do something, sit there!" Take life easy and savor each minute. Life is shorter than you think.

Topic 59 **Get things done**	People are different in many aspects. Some people are always in a hurry to go places and get things done as fast as they can, while others prefer to take their time and live a life at a slower pace. Either way is good, but I choose the first style due to two reasons: extra time and more

chances to do other things.

In the first place, my personality makes me do things fast and go to places in a hurry. I always keep one thing in mind: if I save some time, I could do more things. From my experiences, I used to finish all my homework after classes in order to have more of my own time at home. I will read novels or I will do extra exercise for Math or English. I find it is better to my study, and my life will be more interesting. This is the major reason that I prefer to get things done fast.

In the second place, I have many experiences that let me understand that the faster pace, the better effects. For a long time, I feel secure at a faster pace, since it will leave me a chance to go over my work and correct my mistakes. I think it is useful in many cases especially when writing a test. And even when I am going to see a movie, I prefer to get there earlier for a better seat. There are many examples in daily life that show the advantages of getting things done fast.

Of course, for those who prefer to take their time, they will have some good reasons too. But I like to live life at a faster pace. It is not only because of my personality, but it also because of my experiences.

| Topic 60 **Are games important to adults?** | Some people think that games should play an important role in the life of everyone including adults; others think that games should be left for children. There are many arguments for and against both positions, but in my opinion everyone should have a hobby and playing games is good. |

One of the most cited reasons against playing games in adulthood is the lack of time. Most games are very time-consuming, and to play games most adults have to sacrifice time they spend with their family. I have a friend who was fascinated by recreating great historical events especially battles. He spent all his free time on studying old uniforms and rules of conduct. Even on work he searched for information about ancient wars on the Internet. His productivity declined sharply. As soon as his boss found out about his passion, he was fired.

On the other hand, many games are good for entertainment in spare time. For example, it's much better to play in role-playing game, than spend time watching numerous soap operas on TV. Some games are very good for people's health, for example followers of Tolkien spend a lot of time learning how to use swords and bows.

Some games are very good at improving brainpower. For example many experts agree that chess, reversi and other intellectual games enhance thinking and concentration. Also a person who actively play chess stand less chance to get Alzheimer's disease comparing to average people.

Also it is easy to bridge a generation gap by playing games. Games help to bring people together. Many families I know that like to play games are very well-knit families. Parents spend much more time together with children if they have similar interests.

Adults should not spend all their time thinking of and playing games, they should balance time they spend at work and with their families. If they have children, sharing their interest with their children is extremely recommended. In conclusion, I want to say that playing games is a very good hobby for adults.

| Topic 60 **Are games important to adults?** | Playing games has always been thought to be important to the development of well-balanced and creative children; however, what part, if any, it should play in the lives of adults has never been researched that deeply. I believe that playing games is every bit as important for adults as for children. Not only is taking time out to play games with our children and other adults valuable to building interpersonal relationships but is also a wonderful way to release built up |

tension.

There's nothing my husband enjoys more after a hard day of work than to come home and play a game of Chess with someone. This enables him to unwind from the day's activities and to discuss the highs and lows of the day in a non-threatening, kick back environment. A close friend received one of my most memorable wedding gifts, a Backgammon set. I asked him why in the world he had given us such a gift. He replied that he felt that an important aspect of marriage was for a couple to never quit playing games together. Over the years, as I have come to purchase and play, with other couples & coworkers, many games like: Monopoly, Chutes & Ladders, Mastermind, Dweebs, Geeks, & Weirdos, etc. I can reflect on the integral part they have played in our weekends and our "shut-off the T. V. and do something more stimulating" weeks. They have enriched my life and made it more interesting. Sadly, many adults forget that games even exist and have put them away in the cupboards, forgotten until the grandchildren come over.

All too often, adults get so caught up in working to pay the bills and keeping up with the "Joneses'" that they neglect to harness the fun in life; the fun that can be the reward of enjoying a relaxing game with another person. It has been said that "man is that he might have joy" but all too often we skate through life without much of it. Playing games allows us to: relax, learn something new and stimulating, interact with people on a different more comfortable level, and to enjoy non-threatening competition. For these reasons, adults should place a higher priority on playing games in their lives.

| Topic 60 **Are games important to adults?** | The young of most mammals, including humans, likes to play. Scientists claim that with lions, for example, play fighting prepares the cubs for their future life as a hunter and killer. The question is whether games teach humans about life. Many people believe that games accustom |

the player to life-skills such as perseverance and competitiveness.

However, I disagree with the title statement because I consider games to be mainly for children. In childhood, we do not have responsibility for the world. The child is always eager to grow up - to become a year older or to reach the legal age of an adult. Children find happiness in games by pretending to be an adult in the real world. The problem is that games are
5   optional; they contain too much happiness and too little hardship to ever be real. An adult, by contrast, finds meaning in his life by accepting that there are greater things in the world than his own happiness.

One of the dangers of games is that some people attempt to translate the rules of a game onto reality. The modern example of this problem is television and computer games. People in the West are now growing concerns that children and teenagers occasionally imitate violence that they see on the screen. Death is fun on a computer game; and unstable
10   teenagers who kill people in computer games can forget the value of life. American films are often accused of making violence glamorous.

This is not to say that games did not deceive people before the invention of television and the microchip. Success as a sports-star can lead a player to self-importance. If a football player is made captain of his team and receives praise from the local press, he might be tempted to assume that he is the boss in other areas of his life, such as within friendships.
15   Also, he might be surprised to find that sport is simply not important.

Finally, gambling should also be mentioned as a dangerous game. Although gambling and the acceptance of luck are acceptable features of many cultures, a selfish gambler can neglect his financial duties towards his family. Eventually, gambling can become a drug that destroys life.

To an extent, life for most people is precarious enough to include some degree of winning and losing, and of adventure.
20   Also, an unexpected opportunity or lucky find is one of the joys of life. But sooner or later we have to settle down and face the grind of adult life.

Topic 61 **Should parents make decisions for their teenage children?**	The issue of whether parents or other adult relatives should make important decisions for their teenage children arouses much controversy among people with different perspectives and backgrounds. Some people believe the statement is legitimate, because children are not mature and have not enough experiences to determine the optimal choice. On the other hand, people claim that no body can control other's life even their parents. People should be responsible for their own behaviors and determine their lives. As far as I am concerned, I would like to refute

the former and support the latter. In the following discussing, I would like to address some evidence to substantiate my point of view.

30   In the first place, the most important reason for me to choose this position is that old teenagers have their own thoughts and ideas. The fact that the thoughts of children are not perfect and logical dose not mean their parents have right to eliminate their decision without considering the children's intentions. In the era of rapid social and technological changes leading to increasing life complexity and psychological displacement, the good decision in parents' time would be out of data.

35   In the second place, the job of parents is not to make decision for their children, but to help them to choose. In this period of 15 to 18 year-old children, they are always radical. If their parents make decisions instead of themselves, they will not obey these decisions. Parents had better told their kids about their opinions, worries and experiences as friends. Give much more room for their kids to think and decide. Respect and believe their kids will choose the better one and will face the result directly.

40   In sum, considering the aforementioned reasons I support the statement that older teenagers had better make decisions by themselves. Admittedly, our parents are our best and most early teacher. They would give us more important advices to help us choose the best decision.

Topic 61 **Should parents make decisions for their teenage children?**	First of all, it is not easy to define if people at the age of 15 to 18 are adults or children because they are physically grown up and intelligent enough to carry out general work like adults do in a company, while a lot of them are under their parents' control. I believe that they should be able to make important decisions by themselves, no matter how hard for them.

Needless to say, the recognition of age and maturity is not universally identical. There were some times that 15 to 18 years old were recognized as adults and supposed to think and act independently. It was usual for women at the age of 15 to get married in my grandmother's generation in Japan. Even in
50   the present days, it is still a common thing in some developing countries. Thus, I guess it depends on whether the community is wealthy enough for 15 to 18 year-old children to be children or not. Women in my grandmother's generation needed to get married as soon as possible and have about 10 children in order to get enough labor forces for their family business and have them taking care of their parents and grandparents. In those days, children must have grown up with prediction of earlier age they had been supposed to become independent.

These days, women in developed countries do not need to have so many children anymore and they can go on to higher education, by comparison with early times. It has enabled mothers to get a job as well as fathers in order to make their family wealthier and keep their children beside them longer. As children are not expected to be important labor forces for their family anymore, it may not really matter if they are mature enough to make important decisions. Then how do
5   children predict themselves to be independent at the age of 15 to 18 in such a situation?

I strongly believe that this phenomenon has made today's adults more immature and immoral. I could not believe that a lot of 20 year-old Japanese people attended the ceremony for Coming of Age Day with their parents this year. Unless adults stop treating young people like children, future adults will become even more immature. They still need parents' and other adults' advice to make important decisions but I cannot agree with the title statement: parents or other adult
10   relatives should make important decisions for their older teenage children. I would say that it is no more than spoiling children.

Topic 62 **What do you want most in a friend?**	A lot of characteristics make a good friend. However, in my opinion, having a friend who is intelligent can do you good in many ways.

An intelligent friend can share your problems and help you solve them properly. You are overwhelmed with stuff? He can show you the order to finish them on schedule. You are having problems with someone? Tell him and he will find out the appropriate way to satisfy you and the other friend of yours. Let's imagine you were stuck in an elevator for instance. You could be very upset and unable to get out of it. The situation could change dramatically if you had an intelligent friend beside. He could calm you down and quickly find the way to rescue you.

20   An intelligent friend is also a good example for you to learn from. In fact, you can get a lot of interesting and invaluable things from this knowledgeable friend. You can better yourself by learning his unique way of thinking and handling things. My friend is very intelligent, not only in his study, but also in his everyday life. He can solve problems in the way that I can never think of. Having him my close friend for ages, I have learnt a lot of things from him that may help me much in my life. He taught me the way of finding and solving problems, and even changing unchangeable situations in some intelligent
25   ways.

Indeed, having an intelligent friend can give you the motivation to keep on trying to be equal to him. This makes you become competitive, or emulative in some positive ways. You may have a thought: "Why could he do that but couldn't I ?" And you will try your best in order not to be inferior to your friend. You then will change your old and conservative way of thinking and doing things, becoming open-minded to grasp new things and develop your true potentials.

30   All of these fabulous things an intelligent friend brings to you can be a stable basis for a long-lasting friendship. However, friendship requires a thorough and mutual understanding. So, you, yourself, also play an important part to make it last forever, with whoever friends you have.

Topic 62 **What do you want most in a friend?**	Almost every person in the world needs friends. Different people hold different opinions in choosing friends. Some consider intelligence as the most important characteristics in their friends; others regard a sense of humor as the most significant personality. As far as I am concerned, reliability, which means faith, confidence and trust, is of vital importance. The reasons go as follows.

Firstly, based on reliability, friendship can be lasting. On the one hand, when your friends are faithful, you would love to get in close touch with them. For instance, you could reveal your secrets to them without worry about being betrayed, and
40   tell them your pleasure so as to double the joys. On the other hand, when you are loyal to your friends, they would also like to keep relationship between each other. Undoubtedly, you will be frequently invited to friends' get-togethers and discussions, in which your opinions will be fully taken into consideration since your friends respect you and know your suggestion does good not only to yourself but also to them as well. Thus, willing of both your friends and you to continue the formed friendship will lead to your perpetual friendship.

45   What's more, reliability makes real friendship more solid and deeper. Take borrowing money as example, it is almost completely sure that, probably besides your family, people you ask for money are your most reliable friends. You turn to them because you trust their sincerity to give you help, and, at the same time, they exert themselves to meet your need because they are confident of your attitude to your friendship, to be more specific, your promise to return money. Friendship between those friends and you, thereby, gets further development and finally becomes really invaluable
50   friendship just in coincide with the old saying- a friend in need is a friend indeed.

In conclusion, reliability can be a norm to exam the real friendship and motivate people to deepen their friendship. When I choose my friends, reliability is the foremost factor to be considered. Not only should my friends be reliable to our friendship, but also I should too.

Topic 62 **What do you want most in a friend?**

What is the most important quality in a friend? Is it intelligent, humorous, or reliable? As far as I am concerned, I think it is reliable. Among countless factors that influence the choice, these are three conspicuous aspects as follows.

To me, reliability is the most important quality of a friend. A friend is person whom we know, like, and trust. We may know and like a person who is intelligent, or who has a sense of humor, but we cannot call him a friend unless he is also faithful and trustworthy. Perhaps we all know the famous novel by Victor Hugo, *Notre-Dame de Paris*, and wish that we had a friend like Quasimodo. Although he is ugly, the man has a kind heart and a very loyal nature. He seems dedicated to anyone who will show him true kindness. Even if someone we know who does not have a sense of humor, or does not intelligent enough, he can still be our friend because he is the one who we can trust.

Another reason is that a friend must be a person whom we can depend on. He is willing to listen to us, give us supports, and lend a helping hand to us when we are in need. "A friend in need is a friend indeed. " A friend is a person whom we can trust our feelings and inner thoughts with, and do not fear that he will betray us. It is hard to imagine that anyone will share his thoughts with a person who afterwards will spread the content of their conversation to everyone else in the world.

Of course, intelligent and humorous are also important qualities of a friend. A friend who is mentally acute can give us sound judgment and rationality when we face problems; a friend who is funny can give us an enjoyable time, and add spice to our life. But for me, I still think that the most important quality of a friend is being reliable.

Topic 62 **Friends**

Friends are as precious as priceless treasures sent by angels. Every individual are longing for sincere and congenial friends. Among various virtues that contribute to an ideal friend, I believe that it is honesty that I value most.

The foremost reason for an honest friend is that I can always count on him whenever I am involved in some trouble. As the saying goes? A friend in need is a friend indeed? Come what may, the loyal friend always gives me a feeling of security and warmth. What is more, it is my sincere friend that inspires me and shows me the courage to carry on. Some so-called friend may draw back in the case of a serious adversity while the honest friend would reach out his hands to me, unconditionally and sincerely.

Another subtle explanation is that an honest friend always laudable and exemplary. It is a great honor and fortune to own such a convincingly honorable friend and, definitely, following his step as an honest person is never too excessive a thing to do. Honesty is, most of us believe, the indispensable part of a person's valuable traits/peculiarity. Never can a person achieve many accomplishments nor have a high prestige without the conspicuous sparkling quality: honesty. There are numerous instances closely fit the notion, just like the American president George Washington. His bravery to be honest was acknowledged by the story readers and it was of no accident that he later became one of the greatest American presidents.

In addition, the third reason I would like to mention is that a truthful companion points out my shortcomings and it is definitely a tremendous help for me. Unaware of the innate defects, I am apt to make the same mistake again and again unconsciously. Friends, some of who are more or less sophisticated and artful, are reluctant to rectify my mistakes in fear of irritating or offending me. Things would be completely different if I am fortunate enough to have a truthful friend. By his hearty advice, I am persuaded to go the right way; by his pertinent blame, I am able to be free form making repeated mistakes; by his good intentional warning, I am alert to the conceivable danger.

All in all, it would not be too hasty to determine that honesty is the enormously significant virtue of friends. A genuine friend is, without doubt, always a great helper, a responsible teacher and furthermore, an instructive advisor.

Topic 63 **Are difficult experiences valuable lessons for the future?**

Some people argue that most experiences in our lives that seemed difficult at the time, can later become valuable experiences. I cannot agree with them more. There are numerous reasons why I hold confidence on this opinion, and I would explore only a few primary ones here.

Difficulties are beneficial to our personal growth. In the course of our life, we are going to face numerous difficulties and obstacles, and each difficulty will help us grow up, and become a valuable lesson for the future. A toddler fells off the ground for many times before he knows how to walk, and a child learns how to swim after he drinks water in the swimming pool. In addition, only after we experienced failures, we know the value of success. We will never appreciate anything that comes so easy. Difficulties can make us feel stronger and be more confident for the future obstacles.

Furthermore, difficulties in our work can help us gain more experience and knowledge. Most of the times we can gain knowledge and experiences faster through experiencing difficulties in our life and trying to find a solutions to the perplexities that we face. There is a famous saying, "no pain, no gain." For example, when we take on a new job that we do not have much experience in, the first few weeks can be extremely painful and we may feel enormous pressure and

difficulties. And we will try our best to adjust, to learn and to think, how to do this job better. The more difficulties we feel, the harder we try to acquire the skills and knowledge to overcome it. Learning and this stage is extremely efficient and our problem-solving skills well increase. After we overcome more and more problems, we can become an experienced worker in this field and will be able to take on more challenges. We will never fear that we will face the same kind of
5   problem again. This means that we have accumulated valuable experiences for the future.

In a word, a difficult experience is a gift that life gives us. We should appreciate it and take it as a precious opportunity to gain knowledge and experience about our study, work and life.

Topic 63 Are difficult experiences valuable lessons for the future?

No one in the world can escape some kind of difficulties for perhaps they are given by fate and they will accompany us for a whole life. Success is one of the most important life goals for everyone, but every mature human being has to admit that success will be a blank dream without difficulties.

From childhood, my parents and teachers told me that there is no flat and paved road for me and I have to explore the road by myself. I do not know what are waiting for me in the unknown future, but what I know is that if I withdraw without courage to face difficulties, I
15   will never reach my success. Every time when I met difficulties, I always felt upset and sometimes I felt so hopeless that I think the world is closing the door on me; but looking back afterwards, my life experience always tells me that what I felt at that time was wrong. Life consists of all kinds of difficulties and these difficulties are the most useful lessons given by life.

We bring about most of the difficulties by ourselves. It's a rule that making mistakes will result in difficulties, and by
20   dealing with difficulties we will reduce mistakes. I think that is a process of making progress. At the same time, difficulties can teach us how to face life and help us to gain courage. Once you have courage and deal with all difficulties with a healthy mood, you will really know what life is like and to some extend, you have achieve a kind of success.

All in all, difficult is the best teacher for us.

Topic 63 Are difficult experiences valuable lessons for the future?

Life experiences definitely come in many different forms and shapes. They can be really sweet and really painful just as well. There is an opinion that sooner or later all of the above mentioned experiences would turn into valuable lessons of some kind.

I think it is a little naive and somewhat childish approach. This is the way people want it to be, not the way it actually happens in real life. I am convinced that, unless some supernatural powers interfere, no experiences will start turning into anything of value. It seems to me that some efforts must be applied, because experience is not the sort of things that can come naturally, so to speak. To give an obvious example, if a student flunks his or her examinations one day, and gets into big trouble with the faculty and the dean put together, how likely is this student to do well on the exams next term? It remains to be seen, unless the student in question had given the whole thing some thought and decided to do everything possible not to get in such a jam over again. I suppose that if he hadn't done that, he would simply repeat the whole mess once
35   more.

Quite naturally, things don't work out this way all the time. There are people who do learn from their mistakes. The bad part about this very peculiar kind of learning is that it always hurts, one way or another. If one has the habit of learning only after some first-hand experience, he will most certainly suffer from it. I personally can tell from my own experience that it's way more reasonable to stay on the safe side and avoid unpleasant experiences. Because when you have to deal
40   with some of them you rarely think about all of the good things that can come with it some time in the remote future. What you really think about in such moments is how uncomfortable, upsetting and painful the whole experience is and how much it hurts to go through it.

Still I have to admit that it can do you some good later on. But it's necessary to work on the difficult experiences that happen to you once in a while, if you really want them to turn into valuable lessons in the future. Gain is how we learn,
45   said C.S. Lewis. That's the way things go. But not always, unfortunately. Sometimes people happen to die if the pain is too big. And therefore they don't learn anything anymore.

Topic 64 Self-employed vs. employed

My friends and I always talk about our jobs. Whether to work for ourselves, own a business or work for an employer is one of the hot topics we discuss. Some prefer to work for themselves or own a business. While others prefer to work for an employer. As far as I am concerned, I would like to work for myself. My arguments for this point are listed as follows.

First of all, perhaps one disadvantage to work for others is that we could not plan our time freely. We have to work from 8 to 5 according to the employer's schedule. No matter what the weather is like and no matter whether it is necessary, we have to go to our office on time. We have no choice but to obey the rules set by the employer. Suppose we work for ourselves, we could decide our own timetable. We could find the best time for us to work and improve the work efficiency.

Another reason for my inclination for working for ourselves is that we earn what we deserve. Our wages would be very clear to us. We know what we should earn. That's fair and we would work harder to get better result. However, when we work for others, the boss decides what we earn. It often occurs that we get less than we could earn.

5   In addition, working for ourselves, we try our best in our work to reach our goal, thus we would be faster to succeed in life. If we work for others, the enthusiasm to work may not be so high. I heard many enterprisers who work for themselves succeed earlier than people of the same age.

In a word, in spite of the fact that there may be a couple of disadvantages to work for ourselves, I feel that the advantages are more obvious, that is we could plan our time for work more freely, earn the amount of money that we deserve and get early success in life. Taking into account of all these factors, I would choose to work for myself.

Topic 64 **Self-employed vs. employed**

Although the idea of owning a business is an exciting and admirable one, it is not always a realistic option, especially for a new graduate like me. On the contrary, I would like to work for someone else after my graduation. The reasons for my view go as follows.

The most obvious reason is that I can learn plenty of practical business and administrative knowledge as an employee. If I were given the opportunity to work at an outstanding company such as Mckinsey &
15   Company or IBM, I certainly would absorb its first hand management skills accumulated for years. I would also benefit greatly from its various valuable training programs. With the help like that I can avoid many unnecessary trials and failures that may be involved in my own business path.

Another positive aspect of working for someone else lies in the development of my broader social contact network. As I just step into adult society, I am still timid and lack of communication skills. Working for others will offer me
20   opportunities to get access to all kinds of clients, customers, and employers. Undoubtedly, adequate exposure to them will teach me how to communicate with one another, how to deal with socializing problems, and how to establish my own personal social network.

Moreover, working for an employer, to some extent, can build up nice personalities that are essential for my future career. As we all understand, management knowledge itself does not lead to success without a combination of broad social
25   network and nice personality. Working with colleague helps me to cultivate nice dispositions-cooperative, responsible, caring for others, outgoing, etc.

All in all, working for an employer suits my situation perfectly. Therefore, from what has been discussed above, I would rather choose to be an employee and prepare myself in all fields, if possible, for my future self-employed.

Topic 65 **Should a city preserve or destroy its historic buildings?**

The issue here is whether old, historic buildings in a city should be preserved or replaced by modern buildings. In my opinion, buildings of historical value should definitely be protected rather than destroyed. I base my point of view on following reasons.

Firstly, each historical building is precious property of human being. Like an antic, the value of an old building cannot be measured by money. We will lose those valuable historical buildings permanently if we don't preserve them. Once a historical building is destroyed, we can never
35   restore it; even if it is restored to its original look, the new building is only a fake replica; the historical value will never come back to us.

Secondly, a historic building always represents history and has educational functions. Each one of them can tell us a story. For example, some buildings are evidences of foreign invasion, others are signs of various religions existed in past decades. People nowadays can always obtain historic or cultural information through visiting these old buildings and sites.
40   Although we can learn the past from books, pictures and by visiting museums, nothing can compare with the actual historical buildings themselves, which can bring vivid educational material to us.

Thirdly, historical buildings are a symbol of a city and a valuable tourist resource; therefore a city cannot go without historical buildings. Beijing is represented by the Forbidden City, the Summer Palace, which are all historical relics. It is hard to imagine that someday the City of Beijing decides that all these buildings should be destroyed and modern
45   buildings be built on their sites. Because those historical relics and buildings are too important to the city and can generate profound tourist income. A city will benefit more by protecting its historic buildings than by replacing them with modern buildings.

For all reasons given above, I will strongly suggest a city municipal should preserve the old, historic buildings.

Topic 65 **Should a city preserve or destroy its historic buildings?**

Every culture has its special features. Buildings, as symbol of architectural heritage, are an important part of the history of any country or city. Moreover, they could help us find the answers of many questions about the historical development of our society. Therefore, I truly believe that every city-administration should try to preserve the old, historic buildings.

All over the world many buildings are preserved in their authentic appearances. Furthermore, many of them have unique constructions and are really beautiful and impressive. In my opinion, the destruction of such remarkable pieces of architecture and their replacement with modern buildings can be called 'barbarity'. Therefore, a lot of old buildings belonging to the historical heritage of the world are protected by UNESCO.

5　It is a fact that cities, which have their old, historic buildings, are favorite places for holiday and tourism. The reason is that these cities keep their special atmosphere and could offer us a magnificent journey through their cultural and architectural history.

The only reasonable argument to destroy some historic buildings and replace them with modern ones, is when there is a risk of self-destruction, which could endanger human lives. But again the safety standard can be achieved by renovation or restoration of old buildings.

10　In conclusion I would say that preserving old, historic buildings could be considered as a sign of our respect and regard to the previous generations. I am aware that it is an expensive initiative. But who can evaluate the worth the historic buildings have, for those who will come after us. And I would dare to ask – who gives us the right to destroy what the centuries have kept for us? And I would answer `Nobody`!

Topic 66 **Are classmates a more important influence to a child?**

I strongly agree that classmates are more influential to a child's success at school than parents. This I support with the following reasons.

A child spends so much time with his classmates at school. They study together, play together, and write exams together. Psychologists agree that during their first years at school, children are more influenced by their classmates on their emotional and mental growth.

20　In addition, a child has nothing to hide with his classmates in terms of academic performance. For instance, a child who does a bad job in a math exam will be revealed on his grades; a child who wins the first prize in oral debate contest will be rewarded before the whole group of students. So his classmates know both his good and bad sides. However, It is easier for a child to conceal something to his parents while describing his conduct at school--often limit to those good points.

Finally, classmates are of similar age with a child. They share so many interests in common. So a child is more attracted by
25　his classmates' activities. If he is in a group of children who are interested in creative activities, he will more likely to think of inventing something. So classmates are very helpful in a child's success at school.

From the above discussed, I agree that classmates will influence a child more in his success because they spend more time together, they understand him better than his parents, and they have so much common interests together.

Topic 66 **Are classmates a more important influence to a child?**

Children's success at school depends on a lot of factors, excellent classmates, qualified teachers, good parenting and so on. Among all the factors, classmates play an important role in determining children's success.

First, classmates are a great help in the academic studies of our children. Children spend most of their time at school with their classmates, sharing learning experiences among each other. No only are they competitors, but also they are learning pals as well. When someone face
35　difficulties in the learning process, he can seek immediate help from his classmates especially when teachers are not available at that moment. In some cases when courses relating to language teaching demand that students practice speaking in groups, cooperative classmates will be a great assistance to achieving the goal of effective learning.

Second, children acquire communication skills during their encounter with their classmates. Children who are able to
40　establish good relationships with their classmates are more likely to achieve in their future career. Since a classroom consists of a group of people including teachers and students, they are just like a small society. If children can deal with everything appropriately with their schoolmates at school, they are more likely to keep good terms with their colleagues in the future workplace. A Good relation with others is part of their success.

Finally, children have also obtained a great deal of life experience from their classmates. Being of the same age, children
45　are easier to communicate with their generation than with their parents. As a result, they learn more from their counterparts than from their parents.

From those reasons, we can safely conclude that classmates are too important a factor to ignore and they are a more important influence than parents on children' success at school.

Topic 67 **What kind of workers to hire?**

When it comes to whether an employer should hire workers with less experiences and lower pay, or to hire experienced workers with a higher salary, since there are always advantages and disadvantages of the two, and there are always different situations, my personal option is that
different strategy should be applied for different situations.

For situations where basic and simple jobs which requires less training, and cutting down cost is vital for the survival of the business, I would prefer to hire someone who has less experience and willing to work under a lower pay. For example, a factory should hire more inexperienced laborers to work on the part of the plant where less skill but more physical strength is needed; and a restaurant owner should hire a cheaper kitchen hand rather than more chefs to cut down the cost of operation.

5 On the other hand, for situations when more knowledge and skills is crucial for a job, I would tend to hire someone who is more experienced and would rather pay more salary. Training an inexperienced person for an advanced position can cost a great deal of money, and a mistake an inexperienced makes sometimes can bring disaster to a company. Therefore an experienced personnel is a valuable asset for a business. Sometimes the value cannot be measured by money. A company may lost millions of dollars of revenue when some important positions are vacant and it has to look for
10 someone who is qualified or take a lot of time to train a new person.

In conclusion, when we decide whether to hire a inexperienced, cheaper worker or an experienced, but more expensive worker, it is always depend on the nature of the business and the position, the amount of training required, and of course, the employers' personal preferences.

Topic
67 **Inexperienced, cheap workers or experienced workers?**

To hire an inexperienced worker at a lower salary or an experienced worker at a higher salary, this is an interesting question for an employer. As far as I am concerned, a good employer will choose the latter without hesitation, because he knows an experienced worker deserves what he is paid.

Qualified workers play the most important role in any business. The directors controls the business, the managers operate the business, whereas, it is nobody else but the workers who are expected and responsible to produce qualified products. Without those products the business will be a castle in the air. Thus qualified workers are indispensable for an employer.

What makes a qualified worker? Undoubtedly, experience is one of the most valued merits. Experience means quality and efficiency; both of which guarantee a well-run business. It is true that the employer has to pay more for an experienced worker, but what such a worker brings to the employer is much more than he is paid.

25 Admittedly, no one is born to be an experienced worker. A rookie is inevitably a rookie at his debut, and he needs opportunity to obtain the required experiences. Hence there must be some employers who are willing to provider them with such opportunities.

In a word, for an employer, it is profitable to hire an experienced worker at a higher salary than to an inexperienced one at a lower salary. However, some wise employer may want to hire inexperienced workers with potential.

Topic 68 **Is daily homework necessary?**

It is commonly known that students could increase their values of knowledge by absorbing all necessary information given by their teachers during the lessons and by practicing and analyzing a broad variety of assignments, known also as homework. I firmly support the necessity to assign as much homework as possible since students could improve and understand given lessons more effectively.

35 Every year, frustrated and upset students complain about having too much homework assigned by their teachers. It is understandable that unwillingness to do their homework could be resulted due to many temptations attracting young students in every day life. After intensive learning provided at schools, students usually want to relax and enjoy watching interesting movies, playing video games and spending the leisure time with their friends. Hence, doing assigned homework is usually postponed for later time or ignored at all. This tendency of not doing homework could result in poor and
40 negative students' results on later tests and would probably destroy the willingness and important habits to study at home.

As far as I am concerned, daily homework should be assigned within different numbers of exercises according to the overall interest and enthusiasm demonstrated by students during the lessons. An enormous amount of homework should not be given if most students tended to be discomforted by not understanding given lessons. In this case, teachers should focus on providing more accurate and elaborate explanations of their lessons unless the students are showing potential
45 interests for getting further information. Hence, students, who are completely satisfied and fascinated by provided learning materials, could polish and improve the gained knowledge at home by doing their homework enthusiastically and effectively.

Finally, I would like to say that daily homework could give students the opportunity to improve and enhance their knowledge gained during the school time. Also, students' results of daily homework could show many teachers whether
50 their learning materials were well introduced and explained. Moreover, it could be interpreted as an important source of information for teachers to make the crucial decisions of whether to begin new learning objectives or revise previously discussed lessons by assigning more homework.

Topic 68 **Is daily homework necessary?**

There's much controversy about the necessity of daily homework for students. Some say homework is necessary since only practice makes perfect, while others disagree because they believe a student should have the freedom to study whatever in whatever forms just as he/she likes to.

5   In my opinion, daily homework is necessary for students. First, a teacher could assign homework as a measure for the students to study. A student needs guidance from a teacher because he/she does not have an overall understanding of the knowledge he is going to study from the teacher. This means, at the beginning, a student could not well plan his/her study, just as a kid who is for the first time in a swimming pool could do nothing but to play with water. A teacher could make a good study plan for him/her, so that he/she could learn efficiently.

10   Secondly, even when a student has already understand what he/she should do in order to master some skill or knowledge, he/she is still unwilling to do this for the lack of motivation. Hey, do not tell me that you have never been lazy at all when you were young. Some homework could function as a task for the student to perform which is helpful to motivate him/her.

Thirdly, homework is an important form of feedback for a teacher to understand the effectively of his/her teacher. As I
15   have mentioned before, a teacher makes a study plan for the students; but does it really work? or does it work for all the students? It's not difficult to know this only if the teacher pays some attention to the homework of the students. Then he/she may be able to find if there's some problems in his/her teaching, and make corresponding adjustment of his/her teaching, either for all the students or for a single one. Without some feedback, it is impossible for the teacher to do this. A test is also a good form of feedback, but obviously one or two tests are not enough, and sometimes this kind of
20   feedback just comes to late.

However, This conclusion might be misleading that one may believe all forms of homework are necessary. Actually, only proper amount of homework in proper forms is acceptable; some homework may not only fail to help the students, but on contrary bore them, so much so that they may lose their innate interest to study. "Proper" homework, in my opinion, should vary in its forms; it might be some extensive reading, a paper, or even just a game, as well as other ordinary
25   exercises. And it should leave enough freedom to the students so that they could do things they really like to do with self-motivation, rather than unwillingness. We should always remember that homework is something for us to guide the students, rather than drive them. Only if a teacher keeps this in his/her mind, the homework could be of most help to the students.

Topic 68 **Is daily homework necessary?**

Most students in this world struggle daily with their homework. Many teachers believe that daily homework is the key to education and school success. I agree with this opinion. Here are my reasons.

First, daily homework can reinforce the knowledge students learned at school. A student cannot concentrate every minute, and remember everything that a teacher taught in class. Daily homework is the best way for students to review what he learned during the day, study on the problems that he does not understand, and prepare for
35   the next day's work.

Second, daily homework is the bases of success in exams. This is especially true for those students who are not so bright, and the only way to succeed at school is doing homework each day. Whenever the homework flags, the class behavior dips, the learning is muddled, and the grades take a nosedive. No matter what the ability of a student is, daily homework is the key to students' school success.

40   Third, daily homework can help students develop good learning habits. Learning is not always an enjoyable experience and students always need to spend hard time on it. Daily homework can form a kind of habit of learning for students. Once a habit is formed, learning is not such a painful thing and a student can find it more and more interesting. Obviously this will greatly benefit to a student.

In conclusion, daily homework is crucial to students' success. Life requires us to keep learning in order to catch on with
45   this fast pacing society. A good learning habit and method that we developed when we are students can benefit us for the rest of our life.

Topic 69 **What subject will you study?**

If I could study a subject that I have never had the opportunity to study, I would choose computer programming, because computer programming is so vital in today's society.

Firstly, computer programming is important to our daily life. With the advance of technology, we are practically facing an information age; every piece of information today is stored in the information highway, which consists of computers and networks as hardware, operating systems and software. Without software installed in these systems, the computers are like bodies without soul, and will not be able to function at all. Only with programming languages, information can be retrieved and stored into the information highway. Whether we hook up a phone line or television cable, book a ticket, travel to a foreign country, apply for a passport, an operator will
55   immediately check our information from the computer network. If the computer systems are down, we cannot go

anywhere or do anything. We can safely say that computer programming languages are ubiquitous in our daily life.

Secondly, computer programming is important to technological success. With the skill of computer programming, scientists can write programs to monitor their scientific research and experiments, to analyze the trend of technological development, and to forecast the future. Computer programs can simulate a scientific experiment in a much cost-effective

5 and timely manner, thus can save scientists a lot of time and money, therefore it can greatly expedite the pace of the development of technology. For example, a civil engineer can use a modeling program to simulate the water flow of an urban area; when there is a storm, he can quickly know which parts of the city have the danger of being under the water and dispatch his crew to that area to prevent the disaster.

Last but not least, computer programming techniques can help us earn higher salaries in our future jobs. Since computer

10 programming is important to our society and daily life, programmers can usually have a higher salary than other professionals. Many people have shifted to computer programming from other careers during the economic boom, and even when the economy is going low at the moment, programmers and computer engineers can still live a better life than others.

From all above, I can safely draw a conclusion that if I have a chance to study, I would not hesitate to choose computer

15 programming.

Topic 69 **What subject will you study?**	If I could study a subject that I have never had opportunity to study, I would choose to study how to use the Internet. There are a lot of advantages that the Internet can bring to us. For example, it can get us informed timely, expose us to a lot of chances of knowing other peoples and their cultures, and help us obtain the materials for our studies conveniently. If I know how

20 to use it, I can take the advantages of it.

The Internet can get me informed timely. There is always a lot of news on the Internet that is broadcasting 24 hours everyday and updating timely. I can read the headlines, the financial news, the sports news, and the weather reports every time when I connect my phone modem with my computer. From reading the news on the Internet, I can know everything happening around me. It is very important for me to deal with my daily life with this information. It gives me a lot of

25 chance to know different people. I can know what they are thinking about and how they are living their lives. The World Wide Web includes every country's information. I can travel internationally on the net without going out of my house. That is helpful since people in the world should understand each other to make sure that we could live together peacefully.

The Internet gives me the convenience of getting almost any useful materials for my study. I can just type a few letters and click the search engine to get them. I can do them in the early morning in my pajama while having my breakfast at the

30 same time. Nothing could be more convenient than the Internet in doing research work like this.

In short, if I could choose one subject to study, I would definitely choose to study the Internet for its timely updating news and its convenience. I would also like to travel to new worlds and meet other different peoples. That will be really helpful for me to live a life successfully.

Topic 69 **What subject will you study?**	There are so many subjects that I wanted to take while I have a student but I never had the opportunity to. The most, I wish I would have taken a course in cultural management. Most likely, one day I will follow my desire and enroll probably in a MA program in cultural management.

Why pursue a cultural management program? Firstly, a program as such is relevant for my future career as an art historian. It would be essential for my intellectual development to learn how to organize effectively an exhibition, a cultural study

40 trip, or any other type of cultural activity.

Moreover, a MA in cultural management would provide me with the theoretical and practical skill I will need in order to contribute substantially to the Romanian cultural development. My country needs cultural managers, but they hardly exist. There are no schools to teach cultural management, and one can hardly find a person to have a proper training in this particular type of management.

45 On the personal level, I strongly believe that such a course would be of great benefit to me. Like any other management class it will help me organize myself better, and thus gain much time and much confidence in myself.

Overall, a cultural management program would be quite beneficial form my personal and academic development. I know that by studying this field not only I would improve my life, but also I will be able to contribute to the revival of my country's culture development. This is why I would choose to study cultural management.

Topic 70 **Have automobiles improved life?**	I support the statement that automobiles have caused serious problems. While automobiles have brought us many conveniences, they surely have brought us many undesirable consequences, of which three can be singled out: traffic congestion, air pollution, and highway accidents.

Automobiles have congested city streets. The problem is more obvious when the masses of motor vehicles enter or leave cities at peak traffic hours. The constantly growing number of automobiles throughout the world has made the congestion problem worse and worse because planners and engineers simply cannot find a solution to keep up with the increasing volume of traffic growth. The widespread use of automobiles for business travel has also led in many cities to a
5 decline in public-transit systems, which result in more and more use of private cars, and exacerbate the congestion problems.

Air pollution is another program caused by the automobile. Automobile exhausts commonly contribute half the atmospheric pollutants in large cities and even more in cities where atmospheric and topographic conditions cause the smog formation. Although many cities require the installation of catalytic converters and other controls on motor vehicles
10 to restrict the emission of pollutants, the concentration of many thousands of motor vehicles in large cities has given the problem a new dimension.

Highway accidents create a distressing toll of fatalities and injuries wherever there is widespread use of automobiles. Each year there are hundreds of thousands of motor vehicle fatalities worldwide and about 50,000 in the United States alone. The social and economic costs of such accidents are enormous. Efforts to improve highway safety have been successful in
15 most countries, but a reduction in the ratio of fatalities and injuries per distance traveled is often offset by increases in numbers of accidents because of the ever-growing use of motor vehicles.

In short, automobile has brought us more bane than boon. We should take public transportation whenever possible, and reduce the number of cars running in urban streets.

Topic 70 **Have automobiles improved life?**

Since the first automobile was introduced to our life, we can notice that there are a lot of changes happened around us. As a modern transportation, it not only brings convenience to our daily life, but also enhances the efficiency.

One of advantages of using automobiles is that it can give the users much more convenience compared with other transportations, such as bikes or buss. For me, I like to go to the supermarket once per week and normally buy many foods at one time. Can you imagine that I need to carry a lot of foodstuff and maybe take a crowded
25 bus to reach home? How inconvenient it is! Suppose that I have a car, and then I will feel very easy because what I need to do is to put all my stuff at the back of the car. I can go back with nice music and happy mood for the shopping.

On the other hand, automobiles can save our time and energy. Driving the automobile, we can go wherever we want to go. We can decide the destination and reach there faster than other transportation means. Assuming that a train takes about two hours to reach Suzhou from Shanghai, but a car only needs about one hour. We can use the saved one hour to enjoy
30 the views or do anything that we want. After all, time means a lot to modern people. It can mean money to businessmen, knowledge to school students and profit to companies. By means of cutting time with the help of automobiles, we can increase the efficiency of our society.

Of course, I must admit that automobiles bring a lot of problems such as traffic jam and air pollution. But these outcomes cannot be avoided during the development of a society. I believe we will have a better solution to solve all these
35 problems.

Generally speaking, I would like to say automobiles have improved modern life through providing more convenience to people and increasing efficiency. We should encourage the society to support the automobile industry and develop different kinds of automobiles to meet various needs.

Topic 70 **Have automobiles improved life?**

When Henry Ford manufactured the first automobile, he didn't realize how he would affect our life. Now expanding road systems and thousands of automobiles are playing an important role in our society. But every thing has two aspects. Some people think that the automobile has improved modern life. Others think that the automobile has caused serious problems.

The automobile has a very close relation with industrialization. It is a part of industry itself. Industrialization is a symbol of a modern society. Automobiles carry all kinds of goods and people from one place to another. They function as
45 human's blood. Without automobiles our country would return to a completely agricultural society. No one likes to live without modern conveniences such as electricity, cars and so on. It is sure that the automobile brings convenience.

But automobiles also bring some troubles. Each year many people are injured in traffic accidents. Another serious problem is pollution. Thousands running automobiles emit poisonous smokes. Their motors and sirens give out deafening sound. All these are harmful to our environment.

50 How can we deal with it? Stop using automobiles? It is not realistic. We should design better automobiles. It gives off less gas and runs more quietly. We should build wider roads and obey traffic rules. All problems are cause by human beings. We certainly can resolve them by ourselves.

Topic 70 **Have automobiles improved life?**	It is a well-established fact that automobiles have contributed to the modern life in a favorable way. Automobiles improved different aspects of the human life, but, on the other face of the coin, cars have their crucial impacts upon our life. It is our turn to minimize these defects and galvanize other favorable sides. Hereinafter, I will present and analyze this issue and provide a personal perspective.

The automobile is considered amongst the most beneficial inventions that ever existed. These means of transportation provide unprecedented mobility, flexibility, and privacy. Cars have abridged the travel time among distant locations and provided a self-scheduled means of transportation. A car user is not obliged to obey any predetermined departure and arrival schedules, barring engine check and fuel filling.

10   Moreover, the car represents an elastic means of freight transportation. Automobiles allowed more goods and products to reach remote areas or locations that lie far from public transient system. Also, this rendered products less prices based on less transportation cost as well as more pervasiveness.

Admittedly, services like mail and tourism benefited intimately from the automobiles. Taxi added to the diversity of flexible and on-order mean of transportation. Also, special services like home delivery could have been too slow or even
15   not existing without cars. Adds to the favor that many are interested in racing or rallies that represent car-based sports.

On the other side of the fence, automobiles contributed to the aggravating environmental conflicts. Car exhausts that contain compounds like carbon monoxide dioxide, nitrous and sulphoric ions threaten the public health as well as the environment. Phenomena like acidic rains and green house effect more or less are correlated to automobiles exhausts. Moreover, automobiles are considered expensive mean of transportation, especially with their close relation to roads and
20   asphalt industry.

Another disadvantage is the intruding of some new habits like car captivity. It was found that some persons are biased to car usage even if it is more expensive, slower, or liable for traffic problems. Car captivity is considered intimately related to obesity and heart diseases. Moreover, increasing car ownership introduced traffic conflicts like congestions and delays. Imprudent driving habits leads the way for fatal car accidents, and it is extremely impressive to know that accidents
25   victims exceeds the number of second war casualties.

Ultimately, automobile, like all successful facilities in our life is double-bladed weapon. Alleviating automobiles disadvantages like producing cleaner fuel, unleaded petroleum, natural gas as a fuel, or even electrically driven engines as well as improving the public transportation system should absorb these impairments. We must also anneal the merits by introducing articulate traffic control systems, improving the quality of pavements and other favorable aspects.

Topic 70 **Have automobiles improved life?**	Although automobiles have improved our modern life in some way for its speed, convenience, and capacity of carrying freights, we have had to pay the price for it. Now, as more and more automobiles have been putting into use, the problems that the automobile has caused are seemed to be more and more serious accordingly. These problems, in my mind, like the accidents, the air pollution, the damage of the ozone layers should be given more attention

35   than anytime before.

There are a lot of problems that has been caused by the automobile. It kills hundreds of thousands of people and disables many more every year. It drinks up our precious fossil fuels that cannot be replaced. New roads for the automobile also eat up our precious farmlands while many children are starving all around the world. These problems are really serious and disturbing many of us.

40   The most serious problem caused by the automobile is air pollution. It is said that it emits millions of tons of harmful gas into the air everyday. The dirty air harms our human beings health badly. It can cause a variety of diseases such as plumbism, insomnia, mental disability and even certain kinds of cancer. That is really terrible.

Air pollution caused by the automobile can give rise to even more serious consequences. One thing, it will destroy the ozone layer that protect the lives on the earth from the hurt of the strong and direct ultraviolet rays. Much more
45   ultraviolet can also destroy the fragile ecosystem on the earth. It is just the life circle in which we survive. Another thing is that the air pollution caused by the automobile can lead to the global warming. If the weather is getting warmer and warmer, the icebergs scattered in both of the two poles of the earth will be melted, which will cause the sea level rising and flooding all the cities and villages along the seashores. The lost of the lives and property will be countless. That is really a tremendous disaster.

50   I do not mean to deny the fact that the automobile has improved our modern life in many ways. It acts a vital role in our social life. It also supports our industries. It is indispensable in our modern life. We cannot imagine how we can live a modern life without the automobile. However, the problems it has caused today, such as the lives and properties lost, the dirty air and the consequences of the pollution, seems to be more dangerous and obvious than anytime. Therefore, it will never over do to emphasize the seriousness of these problems and urge the governments and other responsible
55   organizations to solve them.

Topic 71 *A high-paying job vs. quality spare time*

Some people may prefer to have a lower-paying job as long as the job asks for shorter working hours so they can have more free time spending with their friends and family. However, I would rather be given a higher-paying job with longer hours, even if I would have little time with my friends and family. I do not much care about the free time nowadays; I really care about money. Besides, all my friends and my family members are usually busy working. Furthermore, if I do not earn a lot of money, I cannot spend my free time with my friends and family happily.

I really care about money because my budget is too tight nowadays. I am so poor a student. The tuition is high, but I have to pay for it. I also have to pay my rentals of room and pay the board. I have to pay the transportation fares, the books, the clothes and a lot of daily supplies. All these seem to be a heavy financial burden to me. So, I have to look for a job that
10 could offer me a higher salary.

My friends and my family members are all very busy all day long. Some of them are busy working; others are busy studying. They are usually having little free time to spend with friends and family, including me. If I were given a shorter hours job and more free time, I could not meet them anyway.

Besides, even if my friends and I have managed to find out some leisure time to spend together, if I have not enough
15 money, where the fun will be? Any meeting or party costs a fortune, even the simplest picnic. If we have no money to spend for our gathering, we have to just sit over there and chat. We will feel boring soon. Knowing this, I am eager for a higher-paying job so that I can get the money ready for the meetings in the future.

For all these reasons, I would like to have a higher-paying job to support myself and earn enough money to meet my busy friends and family sometime later. Although this job cannot offer me more time to spend with my friends and family now,
20 I believe that I will compensate it after I have become some kind of millionaire in the future.

Topic 71 *A high-paying job vs. quality spare time*

Between a high-paying job with long hours and a lower-paying job with shorter hours, I will definitely choose a high-paying job with long hours, although I might have little time to spend with my family and friends.

Firstly, money can help my dreams come true. I need a lot of money to do many things. I want
25 to buy a huge house with a garden and a swimming pool. I also want to have an expensive car. Maybe my relatives need my financial assistance. Especially, I hope my family can have a kind of comfortable life. My children can go to a famous private university to get excellent education. If I have no money, all of my dreams cannot come true.

In addition, to me, making a lot of money is a sign of success. I think that no one respects a poor man in today's society. From newspaper to television, almost all media focus on wealthy people instead of the poor. I cannot let the others
30 consider me an incompetent man.

Of course, making this choice means that I have to pay a price. Perhaps, I cannot spend too much time with my family and friends. But I never regret my decision because I believe that both my family and my friends can understand me. For my family, I think they should know whom I do this for. For my friends, they will think how success I am and they will proud of me.

35 In conclusion, money is so important to me that I must choose a high-paying job regardless of the consequences it will cause.

Topic 72 *Does grades encourage students to learn?*

A lot of people claim that marks in tests encourage students to learn. I agree with this statement, because examinations are a good way for a student to review what he/she has learned; test scores are a standard measurement for students' learning ability and knowledge level; and the test system can benefit students' future.

First of all, tests are important for students' learning. Attending classes is not enough for students to learn the subjects no matter how carefully they listen to what the teachers say. They need examinations to review the lessons. In most cases, grades or marks are the only means by which teachers measure students' learning ability and learning progress. Grades encourage students to study for examinations, and it is a good system for students to learn.

45 Secondly, test scores are a standard measurement for students' learning ability and knowledge level. Most people would agree with this, therefore universities all over the world take test results as a standard measurement to give admission to new students, to offer fellowships, and to decide whether to grant a student graduation. High school teachers use test results as a means to evaluate the effects of teaching, and students' learning progress. By test scores, teachers also know each individual student's ability to learn.

50 Thirdly, test results can stimulate a student to work hard on his courses. The testing mechanism encourages students to work hard in order to achieve a better result; they will devote more time on study, and develop a "never give up" spirit. This will not only benefit their study, but also teach them a truth, that everyone needs constant learning and hard working in order to be useful to this society. Students who have developed such learning habit and never give up nature will not only have good performance at schools, but can also superior to others in other aspects; for example, such natures are

important factors even after finishing schools. I believe most students understand the importance of these qualities and impacts on their life; therefore they know how important it is to work hard and try to achieve a better score.

In conclusion, marks can stimulate student to learn, and good marks can give them advantages in going to a good university and finding a good job. Therefore I strongly support the statement that marks can encourage students to learn.

Topic 72 **Does grades encourage students to learn?**

In many schools, teachers evaluate students by their grades. Many people think that it is unfair and one-sided to evaluate students by grades and will discourage students to learn. I believe, however, grades encourage students to learn. The reasons can be analyzed as follows.

To begin with, using grades as a standard to evaluate students can give students a pressure to learn. No stress, no motivation. In order to pass or get high grades, students must study hard. They must read more books,
10 do their homework carefully. Pressure helps them learn more knowledge. The worries that they will not pass simultaneously force and encourage students to learn.

Grades can encourage students to compete with each other. The modern society is full of competition. Students can learn the concept of competition through grades. At the same time, they can develop the spirit of competition. To compete with others and obtain good results, students must work hard to get high grades. Competing for grades at schools can
15 make students more adaptable to the society.

Grades can also give students confidence and feeling of success. When they get high grades through hard work, students may think that they gained a great achievement. The feeling of success will encourage students to study harder and harder. At the same time, the success achieved at schools encourages students to succeed in society.

From the above analyses, it is not difficult to get the conclusion that grades encourage students to learn. Grades give
20 students the pressure and make them compete with each other so that they must study and work hard to succeed.

Topic 72 **Does grades encourage students to learn?**

Almost in every modern society, grades play an import role in assessing students' academic ability. There are all kinds of tests to winnow out weak students. Knowledge itself is so complicate and vast, each one of the test usually cannot cover every aspect of it. So I wonder whether grades can really encourage students to learn.

25 The basic reason why I disapprove of the title statement lies in the belief that grades usually do not have positive impact on student who is strong or weak alike. Take the example of a student who has high grades: if Tom gets good grades in the class, normally he will feel conceited. This situation certainly will not lead him into finding some blind spots or weak points in his study. And he will not realize that may be just his photographic memory helps him a lot or this kind of test suits him well. Let us look at another example: suppose Johnny is so not good at memorization, but he works very hard.
30 Unfortunately, he got poor grades in tests that facilitate memorization. One can foresee what harm will bring to him due to the poor grades. In these cases, grades play a negative role in encouraging students to learn.

Most important of all, the grades are usually a convenient way of assessing a student's academic ability. But it is by no means a scientific one. Teachers cannot determine from the grades whether the student is hardworking (diligent) or out of cram. Given tests to all students regardless of their individual characters and traits, is just like forcing everyone to wear
35 shoes of the same size. The Famous educationist Confucius said two thousands years ago: "teaching students in accordance with their aptitude." Our world is a colorful world, so should our educational system be.

Grades, especially poor grades will frustrate potentially successful students to learn. It will give them a false impression that their intelligence may be inferior to other students. The worst thing about poor grades is that it may have repercussions in an underachiever's heart when all his fellow students and teacher have long forgotten. In fact, the
40 potential talent of a student will be strangled by those poor grades - a real pity to the student and the society.

Last but not the least, there is some advantages in taking grades as a tool to evaluate students' academic performance. As in my humble opinion, they should be combining with other scientific methods to encourage students to gain knowledge but not solely focus their energy on how to achieve high scores. After all, it is the knowledge that it is power, not the grades.

Topic 73 **Has computer made life easier?**

Computers are involved in our world form sorted trash to satellite control, making our life easy, convenient and efficient. Obviously, it's a great revolution of human being. It's odd that some consider that computers make life more complex and stressful. I suppose computers will become a necessity, like food and water to the mankind.

Computers have changed people's life style, in a way that we can concentrate on scientific research rather than wasting
50 time on data analyzing and calculating, for computers are much more efficient in dealing with these strenuous jobs. Many activities could not be run in their present form without computers. Examples are the banking systems, and the weather forecasting systems. How is it possible to deal with data-switching between banks and clients simultaneously and accurately without computers? As we known, weather forecasting requires multiprocessing data from the meteorological

satellites and simulating the weather change, which are easy jobs for computers.

Although the knowledge of computer is not easy to acquired, especially at early stage, the IT industry has been making the computer operation system more friendly and at the same time more powerful. Therefore, using computers to handle problems is not the specialties of computer majors only. Even children can use computers to do their homework. We can
5 now benefit a lot from computers in our day-to-day life.

One of the concerns is that computers may cause some troubles when we rely too much on them, such as various computer viruses and the Y2K problem. Nevertheless, computer experts will surely solve these problems and improve the computer technology. In this sense, the computer technology has much potential to develop.

After all, the computer is one of the most important inventions in the twentieth century. It has formed a new era in our
10 life, and it affects culture, industry, science, education and other areas. Computerization is a trend nowadays, and computers are being used in many areas. Computers like any other technology hold the key to increased productivity, which will benefit all of us.

Topic 74 **Is it better to travel with a tour guide?**

Traveling is one of the most widely enjoyed recreations. The tourist business is becoming increasingly important for many countries' economies and provides a great variety of products and services. People are different and so are their preferences when it comes to spending a vacation traveling to interesting and exotic places. One of the first choices one should make when planning a trip is whether it would be individual or with a group let by a tour guide. If it were up to me, I would go to an excursion as a part of a tourist group.

First of all, a common problem of people traveling abroad is the unfamiliar language of the country they are visiting. This
20 is a major inconvenience as it could hamper their communication and prevent them from learning valuable things about the place. That's why I think that a tour guide, who in most cases knows at least two languages, would be needed. This is a professional whose job includes guidance and help. Also tour guides tell tourists about the history of the place they are visiting, information which otherwise could hardly be obtained.

Second, group journeys are supposed to be previously organized. The travel agency makes the full program of the trip:
25 hotel reservations, transportation, food, and sightseeing. Furthermore, many services and museum taxes are cheaper for a whole group. In this way, tourists are much more comfortable, as they safe time and money, and are able to enjoy their vacation without worrying about anything.

Third, traveling in a group can provide people the opportunity to get to know with many other tourists who are from different backgrounds but are brought together by their common interest of the place they are visiting. Such group trips
30 are a great chance for making new friendships and eventually learning a lot about different people.

For all these reasons, I prefer to travel in a group with a tour guide, as it would guarantee a more convenient and enjoyable journey.

Topic 74 **Is it better to travel with a tour guide?**

When people are asked to list their hobbies, travel is among the most frequent words quoted. Some would choose to travel by themselves alone, some others prefer to traveling with a few close friends or family members; while still others, including myself, agree that the best way to travel is to join in a group led by a tour guide.

A good tour guide, who has professional knowledge and rich experiences about certain places, would make our journey more efficient and enjoyable. Traveling to new places is an important way to know our world in the perspectives of cultural diversity and geographic peculiarities. However, we often find ourselves confounded and do not know what to do
40 next when we are in a new place. A tour guide may help us to arrange the optimum itineraries and schedules. He leads the group around to show us unique tourist spots that we should not miss. His explanation on certain scenic spots is also useful for us to understand further about the new place.

Besides, a tour guide would ensure the maximal security of the group member. Tourists are always warned against the potential risks ant pitfall, since strangers are easily attacked. An experienced tour guide teaches his tourists some tips and
45 skills to guarantee the security. The tour guide is particularly indispensable in any emergencies, as he can make a timely response and right decisions.

A tour guide, besides his training and knowledge, is also a person with a good sense of humor. Far away from our friends and families, tourists often feel lonely sometimes during the journey, especially when on the way to a new destination. A good tour guide are skillful enough to relieve the loneliness by telling jokes and interesting stories, playing magic tricks,
50 and so on, which make the journey joyful and pleasant.

Topic 74 **Travel with a tour guide**

There are basically two ways of traveling: traveling in a group led by a tour guide, or traveling independently. There are advantages and disadvantages fir the both. By traveling in a group, you will enjoy the companionship, comfort and safety of group travel, and learn more information about the place from a tour guide; while traveling independently, you can maintain the freedom, flexibility and individualism. Some people say that for most people, the best way to travel is in a group led by a tour guide. I agree with this opinion.

5 Firstly, you will enjoy the companionship when traveling in a group. Usually a tour group consists of around 20 people. These people travel together, eat together and stay at the same hotel. During the trip, you can always find someone you like to talk with, and you will never feel lonely as when you are traveling alone.

Secondly, you will enjoy the comfort and safety of group travel. When traveling in a group, everything is pre-arranged by the travel service, and you do not have to worry about booking a ticket, finding a hotel, decide what places to visit, and so on. In the meantime, as you are not preoccupied with arranging the trip by yourself, you may find yourself concentrate
10 more on the trip itself and enjoy it more. In addition, it is much safer to travel within a group. What a relief when you know that your personal safety is always taken cared of by others.

Thirdly, you can learn more information about the place from a tour guide, and not worrying about missing an important spot. The tour guide will take you to each spot that should be visited, and give you detailed information about the place you visit. You never have to find information about the places you are going to through the Internet or buy a book from
15 the bookstore. Traveling in a group can save you time and money on information searching.

In conclusion, there are many advantages of traveling in a group. Although for young people, traveling alone is more advantages and stimulating, for most people, traveling in a group is the best choice.

Topic 74 **I prefer traveling alone**

Some people think is better to travel in a group that is lead by a guide. For my experience so far, I am inclined to believe that such a way of traveling has more disadvantages than advantages.

Although is better not to travel alone and a guidance is always welcome, traveling alone is sometimes more desirable. The group structure is, in my opinion, quite relevant for a pleasant vacation. It is important for me to travel with people that have the same interests as I do. Otherwise we might not agree on the spots we want to visit or the restaurants we want to eat at. Usually the most successful trips are together with my friends and not with a heterogeneous group of unknown
25 people. I would rather travel alone, or with just one friend, than with a group whose company I would not enjoy.

On one hand, if for instance, I plan to visit a foreign country, a place that I have never been before, a place where people most likely do not speak my language, I feel it is better to have someone to guide me and to help me with any situations I may encounter. It is safer not to travel alone. It is also pleasant to have a guide that provides background information and interesting facts about the places that I visit.

30 On another hand, especially if I am to visit a museum, an art gallery, or a historical city I prefer to buy a map and walk by myself rather than with a guide that would impose on me his/her impressions and knowledge. I do prefer to discover on my own, and to choose what I want to see and to decide how much time to spent in one place or another. I think that the success of traveling in a group depends mostly on factors as the organization of the group, the abilities of the guide, and the place of destination.

35 I enjoy traveling in groups, but only in small ones, and with people that I know. Otherwise I think is better to travel on my own, to see what I like, where I like, and whenever I like.

Topic 75 **Multiple subjects vs. one subject**

The whole point of my answer is that it is better for universities to require students to specialize in one subject. It is just what the majors are called for, even though there are a couple of the advantages for students to take classes in many subjects.

It is a more sensible decision that universities require students to specialize in one subject. They must have known that the depth of a certain subject is infinite, and both the students' energy and time are limited. Only when a student specializes in one subject, can he focus on it. Thus it ensures the students to become proficient in a subject when they are conferred the degrees. That is just the purpose of education.

It does not mean that students do not have many classes to attend even if they just specialize one subject. There are a lot
45 of sub-subjects or divisions of a main subject. The science of journalism, for example, can include the theories of journalism, the histories of journalism (both domestic and international), the news writing skills, the interview courses and the editorials writing and so on. The students have to study all of these above course in journalism major. It means a lot of work to do even if students just specialize in one subject.

I do not deny that there are a couple of advantages for universities to offer students the option to take many subjects.
50 One thing, the work places require multi-disciplined personnel today. Students who take many subjects may meet that request. Another advantage is that other subjects that students take can help their main subject. Whatever the benefit it will be, however, the other subjects that students take should not interfere with their main targets.

In the whole, if students' time and energy allowed, universities could allow students to take as many subjects as possible.

However, I think that possibility is small. So I have to say that it is better for universities to urge students to specialize in one subject. After all, the main subject already needs a lot of work to cope with, considering the depth and width of one subject.

Topic 75 Multiple subjects vs. one subject

Some universities require students to choose a variety of subjects; others only require students to specialize in one subject. I deem the first one as the premier choice. Among countless factors, there are three conspicuous aspects as follows.

The main reason that students should take classes in many subjects is that they can make full use of the abundant resources that a university has to offer. A university has plenty of educational and research resources. It is a very good idea to make full use of these valuable assets while studying at the university. The best way to achieve this
10 is to take a variety of subjects as much as possible. Through learning these courses, a student can get access to knowledge and resources in different areas. On the contrary, if a student only specializes in one subject, he will not have a chance to get access to other resources offered by the university.

Another reason is that by choosing many subjects students can broaden their scope of knowledge and make a solid foundation for their future concentrated study. Whatever the student will concentrate on in his senior years in college, it is
15 necessary that he choose a wide range of subjects to build the knowledge foundation. Take the field of Business Management for example, the student has to acquire knowledge in writing, accounting, economics and human resource management before he can successfully start his major concentration study.

The argument I support in the first paragraph is also in a position of advantage because students can be more adaptable in their future career if they choose a variety of subjects during their university study. It is obvious that the development
20 of modern society requires people with inter-disciplinary and comprehensive knowledge. If a student chooses a variety of subjects in his university study, and gained a breath and width of knowledge, he will be more adaptable to the requirement of the society, and be able to easily adjust to many kinds of jobs. This will benefit his future career.

In a word, taking into account of all these factors, we may reach the conclusion that students should take classes in many subjects in a university.

Topic 76 Should children start learning a foreign language early?

Nowadays, some may hold the opinion that children should begin learning a foreign language as soon as they start school, but others have a negative attitude that learning a foreign language early will pose too much pressure on kids and will affect their mother-tongue learning. As far as I am concerned, I agree that bilingual education should start as early as possible. My arguments for this point are listed as follows.

30 I agree with the statement without reservation since children learn second languages quickly than adults. As we have observed, children can learn languages faster than adults; immigrant children translate for their parents. Child learners speak without a foreign accent, whereas this is impossible for adult learners. Therefore the earlier kids learn a second language, the less difficulties they would meet when they grow up and have to face a foreign language-speaking environment.

35 Another reason why I agree with the above statement is that I believe that bilingual education can be fun and stimulate children's learning interest. Many parents and teachers know how to teach kids a second language in an interesting way. One of my students told me that, when he was in kindergarten, every day his mum taught him a few native language characters as well as their meaning in English. As time passed, the kid became keen to learn English. Sometimes he gave his mum and dad a quiz by speaking some English words and asking them what the meanings are.

40 Bilingual education will not affect the mother-tongue study of children. As we are living in an environment of pure native language conversations and traditional culture, it is impossible for us to give up our culture and language. Teachers also are trying to arrange the curriculum in a appropriate way. For instance, they create an English-speaking environment for children in the morning, and a native language-speaking environment in the afternoon.

Bilingual education has become a trend. No matter we like it or not, future educational undertakings will become more
45 international, and exchanges between schools throughout the world will increase. Given this, speaking a common language is important and, to this purpose, bilingual teaching is an inevitable way.

Topic 76 Should children start learning a foreign language early?

Considering the existing educational system, some people argue that learning a foreign language in an early age is unnecessary and it may give the young children too much burden. However, they may neglect that learning a foreign language can be an enjoyable experience for children and it is necessary to catch up the worldwide trend. In my opinion, learning a foreign language, such as English, as soon as they start school has so many advantages. With globalization and communications among different countries, the world is becoming smaller and smaller. Therefore we cannot deny the importance of a second or third foreign language.

In fact, we should begin to learn a foreign language as early as possible. There are three reasons about it.

First, a child has a very passionate interest to study. Everyone should agree with it, for we all have the same experience that a child always asks you about something with full of interests. He or she always try to understand things around him/her and would be eager to seek answers about their questions. On the contrary, when a child grows up, he or she will gradually lose interests on new things.

5 Second, compared with adults, children have greater abilities to study a foreign language. Many studies indicate that a child can study a language more easily and quickly, meanwhile he or she has a good memory to remember new words, and can distinguish the subtle difference between two words that sound similar.

Third, studying a language is not an easy job, which need a long term and continuous effort. Language is not only a tool, but also part of a culture. If we want to be proficient with a language, we must spend a lot of time studying it.

10 In a word, children should start learning a foreign language early. As I far as I know, in my country many elementary schools have given English lessons, which will surly beneficial to the future of our country.

Topic 77 **Separate schools?**

Nowadays, some people may hold the opinion that boys and girls should attend separate schools, while others have a negative attitude. As far as I am concerned, I agree that boys and girls should go to separate schools. My arguments for this point are listed as follows.

15 Single-sex education provides an environment for boys and girls to concentrate on their study. Research shows that a single-sex school environment can eliminate the distraction from members of the opposite sex, and therefore is academically beneficial to students. Girls in an all-female school can establish self-esteem, and avoid the situation faced by young women in co-ed schools such as struggle to survive emotionally. They will be able to focus more on their academic curriculum, sometimes specifically designed, and prepare for their future education and career. The single-sex setting
20 eliminates social distractions and allows for better concentration on academics.

Another reason why I agree with the above statement is that traditional gender stereotypes are often reinforced in single-sex academies. Boys tended to be taught in more regimented, traditional and individualistic fashion and girls in more nurturing, cooperative and open environments. This will develop their virtue and prepare them for their future roles in the society.

25 Taking into account of all these factors, we may reach the conclusion that boys and girls should attend separate schools. Of course, there are also disadvantages of single-gender education, and simply separating boys and girls does not always improve the quality of education. A lot of efforts should be made to ensure that a single-gender education system be successful implemented.

Topic 77 **Should boys and girls go to separate schools?**

Should boys and girls attend separate schools? This question is very arguable. Before rendering my opinion, let's consider the advantages for boys and girls to attend separate schools. Since boys and girls are different in many ways, they have different hobbies and the ways to learn new things. If they attend separate schools, the education can be more efficient because the school can teach them differently according to their personalities. But the disadvantages are greater. While boys and girls attend separate schools, there're few chances for them to
35 communicate with opposite sexes, which will become a handicap for them to communicate with each other in their future.

As far as I concerned, boys and girls should not attend separate schools. The first and foremost reason is that people should have experience with the opposite sex when they are at school, because the society consists of both male and female members, and people have to learn how to communicate with the opposite sex.

Moreover, people have to learn from the opposite sex. For example, while females should learn braveness from males,
40 males should learn carefulness from females. In addition, in a family, to learn from the opposite sex becomes more important to keep the family harmonious. In addition, the knowledge of the opposite sex is also important. Without such knowledge, dealing with the opposite sex in a relationship becomes extremely difficult.

Finally, as we can see, it's definitely important for boys and girls to attend schools together, so that they can learn from each other, communicate with each other and they can understand each other well, which is very valuable for their future.

Topic 78 **Teamwork vs. independent work**

Some people like to work independently, while others would prefer to work in a team. Is it more important to be able to work with a group of people in a team or to work independently? Depending on different personal traits and working environments, people will have different answer to this question. I think being able to work in a team is more important for me.

First, the modern society and industry is a complicated system that requires teamwork, communication and cooperation
50 among companies and individuals. Take a computer system for example, it comprises of hardware, operating system and software, which are manufactured separately by different companies. Not one single company can accomplish a computer system without using products and technologies from other companies. Similarly, in a company, communication and teamwork is more and more important among workers because a worker cannot do his/her work properly without

interacting with his supervisor and colleagues.

Second, there are many advantages of working in a group than working alone. Teamwork provides a worker with a cooperative, friendly and enjoyable work environment. The team can also be helpful in responding to a worker's questions and problems, therefore increase the work efficiency. Teamwork can also challenge a worker's abilities and he/she can
5   acquire valuable experiences from it.

Third, the ability of working independently does not contradict with the ability to work in a team. For example, in a team environment, I enjoyed being a major contributor to my team. The fact that others depended on my work made me feel like I was doing worthwhile things. For example, I was in charge of the front end for the GUI. This was very valuable experience, because I know how important it is to work in a team.

10   Inclusion, I think the most important quality in a work environment is the ability to work with others in a team.

| *Topic 78* **Teamwork vs. independent work** | There are many ways in which people can complete their works. Some prefer to work with a group of people on a team. Others prefer to work independently. To work with others can inspire their spirit and produce twice the result with half the effort. In my opinion, working on a team is more important. |

15   In business, people who are able to work with a group of people on a team tend to communicate well with others. In order to complete a sophisticated task, individuals must work together, each sharing a part of the whole task, in order to achieve the results. The team must interchange their ideas during each process in the forms of meetings and discussions. Each one tries his/her best to give a better idea to make the process more time-efficient.

In addition, we cannot live in a society independently and we need to communicate with each other, so communication
20   skills are very important to this society. Through teamwork, we can develop and improve this ability.

Although one can complete a work independently with one's innovation and sometimes can accomplish a perfect work with great compliments, many reasons show that throughout teamwork really can achieve more than we may think of. No wonder, in the F1 race, team order is the most important thing that every member in the team must obey.

| *Topic 79* **Who would you choose to build a statue for?** | If the City Government of my town - Moscow asked me to choose a person whose statue will be built, I would choose no one. And here I can explain my point of view. |

In my opinion there are already statues of many famous people who merit a statue. Right in the center of Moscow there is a great statue of Jury Dolgirukiy. He founded the Moscow City in 1447. He is also famous as a great defender of his people. If you look at this statue, you will see a very strong man riding a horse with a spear in his arms and the injured dragon lying on
30   the ground. In my view it symbolizes the meaning of his deeds and people's remembrance and respect to him.

Another statue in Moscow is that of Alexander Pushkin. He was one of the most famous Russian poets. He has made an important contribution to the worlds literature. His poems are realistic. They answered to questions asked so many years ago, and they can still answer today's questions. His statue looks so natural as if he is alive. His statue is standing in the middle of the Pushkin Square. With a book in his arms, he looks very calm and contemplative.

35   Another monument that I consider impressive is the monument for people who died during the Second World War. I cannot describe it because there are no proper words to express the emotions I feel when looking at this statue. I just feel painful and sad for their death and as people cannot bring them back to life, they can only try to prevent future wars.

In conclusion since there are already enough statues for famous historic figures in Moscow, I would like to say that I prefer to see modern art sculptures in the streets of this historic city. I would allow young modern sculptors to exhibit
40   their works in the streets.

| *Topic 80* **Describe a custom from your country** | Who took care of you before you are eligible to go to the daycare? That grandparents taking care of their baby grandchildren is a tradition in my country. I would like people from other countries to adopt this tradition. |

At first thought, this tradition seems to be unimaginable to people who are accustomed to the
45   "parents-children breeding" model. However, did you notice that swarm of young mothers are roaming in the department stores with their babies during working hours? Young ladies quit their jobs and sacrifice their careers to look after their offspring. How many women can really keep up with their professional work after several years' absence from their positions in such a fast pace society? A babysitter may help you, but do they really care your baby as his grandma does? The answer is No. Grandparents ensure the love, care, health and education of your kids.

50   On the other hand, senior citizens gain more happiness through this day to day caring of their young grandchildren. Old people are sad about the aging and loss of work. When they spend their time with young kids, when the fun and loveliness filled in their soul, all unhappiness disappears. The moments they spent together with the babies are so sweet they can improve seniors' mental and physical health.

It is undeniable that the relationships of different generations will be tightened. Needless to say, kids will be tied with their grandparents in this process. I was brought up by my grandparents who are in their nineties now. I still call them quite often and buy gifts for them. I feel the strong connection among us.

From above analysis, I highly recommend our custom of grandparents give their hand to cultivate future generation.

Topic 81 **Has technology made the world a better place to live?**

With the development of technology, there have been a lot of changes to our life. Admittedly, some of these changes are bad, causing many environmental and social problems. However, most of these changes contribute to making our life more convenient, more comfortable and more wonderful.

10 First of all, due to the improvement of technology, people can enjoy more conveniences than ever. For example, it only takes travelers or businessmen several hours to go to another countries by jet planes, which makes the world seem to be much smaller. With the help of the Internet, people at different corners of the world can communicate with each other at a significantly high speed and low cost. It is technology that has cleared away the barriers that once prevented people from leading a convenient life.

15 Secondly, technology has made our life as comfortable as we can imagine. Sitting in air-conditioned rooms, people do not have to suffer the extremely cold or hot weather any more. Whatever vegetable or fruit we want to eat, we can always find it in a supermarket regardless of the season. We can also go to work in a place far away from our homes by using automobiles or public transportation tools.

In addition, technology provides us many choices to spend our spare time. Listening to music by using an MD, MP3 or Walkman, surfing the Internet or watching digital movies, all of these entertainments make our life wonderful.

20 In conclusion, although technology has brought about some problems, such as air pollution caused by increasing number of automobiles, and ethnic problems caused by cloning human beings, the benefits of technology far outweigh its bad influences. So it is safe to say that technology has made the world a better place to live.

Topic 81 **Has technology made the world a better place to live?**

A great many achievements have been accomplished in recent decades in almost every area of technology, such as in computer science, manufacture, and medicine. But there have always existed two opposite attitudes towards technological development. Some people agree that these new technologies have made the world a better place to live, while others hold the opinion that technology has caused many problems to the world. As far as I am concerned, I agree with the first opinion that our world is becoming better for living with technology progress. Several persuasive reasons go as follow.

30 Firstly, technology developments have greatly improved people's living conditions, making our life more convenient and efficient. We have elevators taking us to the top of a skyscraper in just a few seconds; we have air conditioners to keep the indoor temperature comfortable; and we even have household robots now to help to take care of the trivial housework.

Secondly, technology developments have also made communications much easier, and thus helped to enhance relationships among people. The wide use of pagers, mobile phones, and wireless Internet has greatly facilitated the way 35 of daily communication. They can bring people so close even though they may actually be thousands of miles apart.

Thirdly, developments in technology can provide better medical access to make people live a healthier and happier life. By taking advantages of the most recent developments in biotechnology, such as genetic engineering, I am convinced that people will have a promising prospect in treating all kinds of human diseases, including AIDS and SARS.

It is true that technological developments have also brought some serious problems. One of them is that some 40 technological developments have done harm to the environment. For example, too much emission of waste gases, mainly carbon dioxide, has increased the global temperature significantly. However, people can reduce and finally eliminate these harmful effects by improving the technology itself or finding a more advanced and reliable technology.

I believe that with the new technologies appropriately adopted for good purposes, our world would be made an even better place to live.

Topic 81 **Has technology made the world a better place to live?**

Since the end of the last century, when technology started to make a full impact, debates have sprung up among people worldwide as to whether this technology has made the world a better place to live or not. In my perspective, the new developments have indeed improved our lives.

One striking example of how Man's new inventions have helped us to lead a better life is the whole set of time-saving electrical appliances and tools, ranging from washing machines to 50 microwave ovens. No longer do we need to go down to the river to wash our clothes on rocks or to heat our food with wood and charcoal for never-ending hours. Nowadays, our daily chores are merely simple tasks, needing only very little efforts on our part. It is the machines that do all the boring and tiring work.

Consequently, we are left with much more leisure time to spend at our free will. Technology has exerted a great influence on the ways people relax themselves today. It has transformed our previously boring leisure time into long hours of excitement, enjoyment and fun. For instance, nobody can deny that video, computer and PlayStation games have added spice to our lives, especially those of children. The home cinema, recently available on the market, has made many happy families around the world.

5 Technology has not done good deeds only in those areas. It has gone even further by improving considerably communication among countries. Owing to new technology such as the Internet, fax and mobile phones, barriers among nations have started to disappearing, thus turning the world into a 'global village'. In our modern era, it is even possible to be living in a poor country while studying with the top professors in England via the Web by enrolling in an online degree.

We have therefore seen how technology has made the world a better place to live in some ways. However, just as the
10 English proverb goes, "Every coin has two sides", technology has also had a few negative effects on our society. Thus, the same timesaving devices that save us so much trouble have quickened so much the pace of life. Nowadays everyone is stressed and is always preoccupied. Moreover, overexposure to video games and the television has been proved to be harmful to people's health, creating eye and back problems. In addition, new technology like the Internet has allowed the brewing of new types of crime and criminals such as hackers and viruses.

15 In today's world, technology is having a deep influence on the way people do things. But the issue of whether this technology has made the world a better place to live in will continue to be a controversial topic.

Topic 81 Has technology made the world a better place to live?

Being modern human beings, people nowadays have enjoyed so much from the highly developed technology. The improvements of technology have changed people's life styles significantly. Admittedly, sometimes, technology worsens the condition. However, compared to its advantages, the bad impacts are so tiny.

In the modern world, we lead a much better life than our ancestors. We no longer need to be on guard all day to prevent us from being attacked by wild animals; we no longer live in rock caves which are dangerous and not comfortable; we can no longer put all of our hope to the God to pray a mild weather which will bring us a harvest. We can utilize technology to increase the quality and quantity of plants. Moreover, modern
25 technology of medical treatment helps us cure the number of terrible diseases that will deprive the life of human.

Besides, technology provides us many unimaginable tools that benefit our life. We can travel from one place to another by plane only in few hours, while it would take our ancestors several months or even years in the ancient time. We use computer and robot to help us with hard and routine works. Computers also improve the efficiency of our work.

However, technology not only brings us gold but also rubbish. Pollution is one of the most terrible problems. The excess
30 use of technology brings disasters to people and the world. The rivers and oceans are not as clear as before; the wild animals are disappearing. In order to save the world and also ourselves, people should limit their demand from nature and use technology in a sustainable way.

All in all, technology itself is neutral thing. Whether it will benefit people or do harm to people depends on the people who use it. Fortunately, most of the time we have utilized technology in the right way, therefore, the technology benefit
35 our life much more than its harm.

Topic 81 Has technology made the world a better place to live?

Standing at the turn of the new century, we observe the twentieth century as a great advance in technology. With those advances, human lives have changed dramatically. In some ways, life is worse, but mostly, it is better. So personally speaking, I am, and probably will always be, one of those who agree with the idea that technology has made the world a better place to live.

First of all, technology has brought with it a more comfortable life. Not only do we use air-conditioners and heating systems during summer and winter, but also do we experience many changes in food preparation methods to prepare delicious food. Due to the development of architectural technology, our living conditions are greatly improved.

Besides, traveling and communication are much more convenient nowadays. We can travel around by airplanes and railway
45 networks. We can talk to each other through telephones. Twenty years ago, it was a dream that we could obtain information as well as shopping via the Internet.

The last but not the least, through the process of technology improvement, people begin to realize the fact that only reconciling with the nature can we maintain a sustainable development. That is why we today pay so much attention to environmental protection. Many factories have achieved economic growth without polluting the environment by utilizing
50 certain new technology.

Instances of the same sort can be multiplied indefinitely. When taking into account all these merits we may safely arrive at the conclusion that advantages of technology outweigh any disadvantages it may bring to our lives. Though I must admit that people sometimes invent some things that threaten the lives of themselves, no one can ignore the additional conveniences and satisfaction offered by technology, and just with such experiences the human being forge ahead swiftly to the future.

Topic 81 Has technology made the world a better place to live?

Many people take the view that technology has made the world a better place to live. As far as I am concerned, I share the common view with them. Because I could pick up examples here and there around us and I would here explore a few of the most important ones.

The main reason is that if we look around, we may find that technology makes for us a better place to live. Take our house for example, without architectural technology, we could only live in the open wild. Thanks for those architects and engineers, we can live in a warm comfort house that protects us not only from the rain and wind, but also from the coldness of the winter, and the hotness of the summer.

10 Another reason is that we could communicate with our relatives or friends without the need of meeting them face-to-face. Information technology helps us a lot in communication. For instance, telephones and cellular phones help us talk with others no matter where they are; computer networks connecting the whole world offer us another alternative of communication. By email, our messages can reach the destination in just a few seconds.

Furthermore, transportation technology realizes the dream of people who want to travel around the world or to the space. 15 We all can imagine that without car, bus or bicycles, how could most of us manage to get to work everyday?

In a word, technology has changed the world in a better way for us to live in terms of housing, communication, transportation and many other aspects. Taking into account of all factors mentioned above, we might reach the conclusion that technology has made the world a better place to live.

Topic 82 Can advertising tell about a country?

Nowadays some may hold the opinion that advertising can tell you a lot about a country. As far as I am concerned, I agree with this statement. My arguments for this point are listed as follows.

One of the primary causes is that advertising is always a reflection of a country's culture and customs. Advertising varies from country to country, depending on the country's particular conventions. For example, a Japanese advertisement may feature a Japanese lady with a traditional kimono, while an American advertisement may 25 feature a western cowboy with a hat and riding a horse. Through advertisements, we can have a general understanding of what people from other countries look like, what they wear during their daily life, what they eat, what kind of transportation they use, and what they do during their spare time. We can always learn different cultures of different countries through these culture specific advertisements.

A further more subtle point we must consider is that we can understand a country by its products. When we see a Toyota 30 or a SONY advertisement on TV, we realize that Japanese people see quality as a vital aspect of their products, and we know that how these people are always trying their best in high technology development, and ensure the best quality in their products. When we have gained a deeper understanding of a product, we can also gain a deeper understanding of that country and people.

What is more, when we become curious about the culture and customs of a country through advertisement, we are willing 35 to spend more time on reading about the country, explore more deeply about it, and even someday travel to a country we like to visit. All these might have started with a small advertisement on TV! Is that amazing?

In short, advertising can really tell you a lot about a country's culture and customs.

Topic 82 Can advertising tell about a country?

Advertising plays an important role in modern society. Advertisements covering every aspect of social life can tell a lot about a country by the marriage of substantial information and colorful expressive forms. Although many disagree with the title statement, I believe that we can learn a lot about a country's economy, culture and beauty spots simply by advertising.

Advertising offers a great amount of economic information about a country. Take commercial advertisements for example, they unveil many direct and useful economic messages: major commodities, service level, living conditions, and so on. Undoubtedly, politicians, businessmen and citizens will all take advantage of these helpful advertisements.

45 Advertising also reveals greatly distinctive traditional culture about a country. It can easily be attained by observing advertisements associated to art, literature, custom, and social ritual, which have been deeply rooted in a country's unique history. For example, advertisements for some articles used in a Chinese wedding reflect their way of thinking, an appreciation of harmony, and a peculiar taste for wedding clothes. Advertisements of those kinds can thus show plenty of cultural heritages boasted in a country.

50 Furthermore, advertising helps people learn more about a country's beautiful scenery. Advertisements about travel serve this purpose perfectly. Information and knowledge about various resorts might be obtained by happening to see a photo advertisement posted on a wall by some travel agency. Advertisements on television, on the contrary, frequently provide us many opportunities to watch all kinds of unusual beautiful places we may never have thought of before.

All the above evidence supports the undeniable fact that advertising can tell a lot about a country. I must admit, however, some advertisements become more or less homogenous around the world due to the tendency of globalization. Some even fail to signify any special characteristics that are essential for a country when they need to do so. But all in all, no one can ignore the abundant and useful information about a country afforded by advertising.

Topic 83 **Is modern technology creating a single world culture?**

I strongly agree with the statement that modern technology is creating a single world culture. Modern technology like computers and the Internet is bringing people together, and making the world smaller.

First of all, with the development of modern technologies such as computers, English is becoming the most important language in the world, and the importance of other languages is
10   getting weaker and weaker. Admit or not, the most common language used today on the Internet is English, and this makes English becomes the one and only most important language in the world. On the other hand, computers can cross the barriers of human language. No matter where people are, and no matter which language people speak, they always use computers the same way, and basically they are using the same kind of software packages, like the Windows Operating Systems and word processing software packages. The computer language is also a universal
15   language. Programmers from different part of the world can work in the Silicon Valley together. Although they might have difficulties in communicating in English, they have no problem at all writing programs with Java, or C++.

Besides, the development of the Internet is unifying people's life style. Internet is being used in almost every corner of the world. People are doing almost everything with the Internet, like getting all sorts of information, shopping online, paying for their bills and checking their balances in the online bank. Over 90 per cent of people in the world use the same kind
20   of Internet browser - the Internet Explorer, and the interfaces of almost every Internet page looks like the same, although they use different language and design. People from all over the world are doing the same thing each day on the Internet, and their living habit is becoming closer and closer with each passing day.

In addition, modern technology has facilitated the communications among people from all over the world, and therefore has resulted a single world culture. For instance, people can chat with a friend or a stranger who lives abroad over the
25   phone, or the Internet, and they can also see and listen to him/her through a camera and a microphone attached to the computer. The ease of communication helps one culture learns from other culture, and brings the world together. Before people can see each other through TV, they used to wear their local costumes; nowadays T-shirt and blue jeans have become a universal custom for people. This is a concrete example that modern development is creating a single world culture.

30   Based on the points discussed above, we can see why I agree with that modern technology is creating a single world culture.

Topic 83 **Is modern technology creating a single world culture?**

When we look back to the history of human being in recent 200 years, we will be surprising what a huge change modern technology has brought us. Trains and planes connect people everywhere. Radios and televisions enable us to keep with every news happened around the world. More and more chances of communication influence different cultures deeply.

To discuss the impact that modern technology has given on different cultures, most people would agree that nowhere in history has the issue been more visible that people in different countries are getting more and more alike. Most of the time, you cannot tell which country a person is from only by his/her clothes. Young people all over the world can enjoy McDonald's and other western food the same way as
40   Americans enjoy. A pop music singer can have her fans in every corner of our planet. People around the world share news from newspapers and TV and express concerns on the same topic.

"The world is getting smaller!." How often we hear such words! But that is only part of the truth. Not everything in a country's culture can be changed. Something developed from thousands of years ago and has already been a part of a nation's spirit cannot be wiped off easily. For example, the family concept of our country has never changed. We still
45   prefer a big family that all generations live together. That is the definition of happiness in our value system. We still appreciate the thinking of Confucius and take it as guideline of our daily life. At the same time, many countries make great efforts to preserve their culture heritages. People around the world take more and more pride in their own cultures, and try to cherish them.

Certainly, modern technology make possible for cultures to communicate with each other. But I don't think it is creating a
50   single world culture. Communication brought by modern technology can be an instrument for improving and learning, but not a tool for erasing individualities. And it is the cultural diversity that makes our world more beautiful and interesting.

Topic 84 **Has the Internet provided a lot of valuable information?**

The Internet...is it a boon or a curse? This is a very debatable topic. We would need to look at the pros and cons of it and then draw conclusions. Even then it would not be possible to totally answer yes or no to the question. It would depend upon individual personalities as well as the situation that we are in. In my opinion, the Internet is definitely a valuable source of information, but as with all forms of technology one must know how to make the best use of it.

Let's step back a few years from now. We were totally dependent on books, the experience of other people or data stored in other forms for getting information of any sort. The problems with those kind of information sources is that it is time consuming, inconvenient and often times even misleading. The concept of weeding out data from old reports and books
10 was a time consuming and painful process and would itself deter people from trying to get new information.

But today with a touch of a button we can get any information available, sitting in the comfort of our homes. We are more knowledgeable and aware of things happening around us. Technology has given us the greatest power at our fingertips...the power of knowledge!

Lets take an example. Suppose someone wants to start off a business venture. He can get all information regarding other
15 companies in the same line of business, he can do a cost benefit analysis, gather corroborating data, make new contacts, and so on, thanks to the internet. He is now well informed. If he has to discuss this with other potential partners he is armed with a wealth of information.

On the other hand the Internet does supply an overload of information. Hence if you give a topic in a search engine such as Google, you will get a number of sites that would cater to the information required. Now if one were unable to decide
20 what information to cull out and what to leave, it would be a painful experience rather than an enjoyment.

So in conclusion, it really depends on how you use a particular technology - used in moderation and in an intelligent manner it could be the greatest tool. Otherwise an enemy that steals time and waylays and deters a person from achieving his ultimate goal.

Topic 84 **The Internet**

Nowadays, no one can deny the importance of the Internet. Sitting in front of a computer, clicking a mouse three times, you can get access to the information highway, which provides you numerous valuable sources of information. Thanks to the Internet, people can quickly sell, advertise and share knowledge, idea, and personal feelings.

Because we are easy to access to so much information, it can create some problems to us. Children are easily suffering from inappropriate information on the Internet, since it is very hard to control information from the Internet. More and
30 more porn pages are quickly emerging and continuously sending emails to children's account. With their curiosity, children click on these links that lead to these pages, and see things that they should not have seen. They do not realize that they are unconsciously affected because their parents cannot examine all the content they view.

Consequently, children are now becoming the number one victims of sex abuse and criminals in America where it is very easy to access bad websites such as porn sites and sex forums. It is the Internet that probably causes problems to children
35 if parents do not pay much attention to them.

Although the Internet offers us large amount of information, its reliability is dubious because many untrue news stories can be posted to it and cause confusions to many people. It is very difficult for us to find out what websites are reliable and what are not. My teacher, for example, is advocating her students to use books to study, research, or write a report instead of using the information on the Internet.

40 In conclusion, the Internet causes trouble to people, especially young people and children. Although people can get access to up-to-date knowledge and information, problems caused by using information from the Internet are inevitable. Therefore, while the Internet can provide a lot of useful information, its hard cannot be underestimated.

Topic 85 **A one-day-visit to your country**

If you attend a conference in China, and would like to take a one-day-visit on site seeing and shopping, there are three factors you might consider: this place must have special tourist features which can represent China, and this place must be close to the place where the meeting is held, therefore you do not have to spend too much time on traveling.

If you are in northern part of China, the best place that you should visit is the city of Beijing, although spending one day in Beijing is too short of a period to fully explore the splendors of the city. Nevertheless, for those of you without the luxury of time, make sure you don't miss a few key points of interest--the Summer Palace, the Forbidden Palace, the
50 Forbidden City, and the Great Wall of China.

The Summer Palace is a royal retreat located on the bank of a large lake. Visitors can walk along a waterfront promenade that leads to a concrete ship docked at the far end of the walk. At the concrete ship, you can take a ferry back to the entrance of the palace. Something you may want to do while at the Summer Palace is going into the gift shop, get dressed in traditional Chinese clothing, and pose for a souvenir photograph.

The Forbidden Palace is absolutely breathtaking. There are a series of gates that lead to the main palace grounds. Pay particular attention to the stairwells in the palace courtyards. There are slabs carved with intricate dragon designs, which the emperor was suspended over in a caravan whenever he left the palace grounds. It would be a good idea to get a local guide to lead you around the palace and explain the significance of various buildings.

5 Finally, don't miss the Great Wall. It's located outside of the city and it takes up most of the day, but it's well worth it. When you ascend the Great Wall, there are two paths--one veering to the left and the one veering to the right. The path on the right is less steep and an easier climb. However, if you take the path to the left, you can see the remains of the original wall, and there is a cable car you can take down to the parking area.

Shopping in Beijing is becoming more convenient by the day. The Silk Market at Xiushui Street is favorites among tourists,
10 experts and locals alike. There you can bargain with the shop owners and buy good quality clothes with a very low price, you can even see plenty of pirated software- ironically, within sight of the US Embassy.

So, there you have it. I encourage anyone to spend at least a few days in Beijing, because there is so much to see.

Topic 86 **A time and a place in the past**	One of the most exciting events of the last century was the end of World War II. By defeating the German army, U. S and British forces stopped the tyrant Hitler in his way to conquer the rest of the world. All over Europe, the day that ended the war resembled a new era. Thus, it would be fascinating to witness how things changed dramatically from war and death to peace and bloom.

The end of the biggest war mankind has ever known also ended the Holocaust. Hitler and his administration decided that they should kill all the Jews in Europe. Thus, under the mask of "working camps" they planned to build special prisons,
20 where they can deliver the Jews in order to murder them in various ways. This evil plan caused the biggest massive murder in the history of mankind. The day the war ended, reflects also the end of this evil murder, which followed by the recreation of the Jewish nation.

After the end of the war, nations started to rebuild themselves; big countries in Europe like Germany, France and England signed peace agreements that influenced the future of the whole region. Without borders between countries and
25 with free marketing system, Europe gradually forgot the sorrow of the deathly war. At that time, Europe countries were famous due to the amazing achievements in sport, art, and fashion. For example, Picasso, one of the world greatest artists, inspired by this era and reflected his feelings in his works. Gradually, the situation of the economy changed, and Europe became one of the best places to live and to invest in.

"History repeats itself" is a famous and practical sentence; being a witness to this kind of amazing change is experience
30 that takes place once in a life time, thus this specific segment of history is extremely interesting and important, and if I would have the opportunity to choose time and place in the past - this is what I would choose.

Topic 86 **A time and a place in the past**	The topic makes me recollect my childhood, the happiest time that I had in my hometown. It is a remote village on the Qinghai-Tibet Plateau full of imagination and intrigue. My childhood there was cheerful and unforgettable.

It used to be a very small village, surrounded with high mountains; the melted snow water from the top of the mountains formed many clear brooks and went through the village. The crystal water moistened the grass and crops in the village and also provided the village people with all sorts of fish and shrimps. The appearance of the mountainsides varied as the seasons change - yellow in spring, green in summer, red in autumn and white in winter. The top of the mountains was always covered with snow, shining under the sun. When you were in the village, you would
40 feel you were touching the sky and you will feel a sense of holiness around your body.

My childhood friends and I enjoyed our life in the village so much. We liked to swim in the water freely and catch the fish on fine days. We grazed the animals in the grassland after school. The sheeps on the grassland are like stars on a vast velvet green carpet. We played games in the pasture, we sang folk songs on the hill, and we climbed trees in the forests. We were always so happy that we often forgot to go home or go to school. I boast it was the most beautiful place in the world,
45 although full of impoverishment. The villagers were so poor and they barely have enough food at that time, but they were so optimistic. They kept working hard with little return without any hesitation or complain. It was since childhood that I learned how to face hardships and failures in my life.

My childhood days were innocent and worry free. I left my hometown for a better educational opportunity when I grew up, but I always miss that wonderful homeland. I take every opportunity to visit it. The pictures of the place and the life
50 there will always live in my mind.

Topic 86 **A time and a place in the past**	If I were afforded the opportunity to go back to a specific time and place in the past, I would venture back to ancient Greece. During the 5th century B. C., the Greeks were in the process of developing and reforming a wide range of cultural, social, and scientific pursuits that still

have a significant impact on the world today.

In the arts, Greece excelled in many fields, particularly dramatic literature. The works of Sophocles, Euripides and Aristophanes have had a tremendous influence not only on western literature, but also western thought in general. The works of these playwrights are still performed on stages around the world today, and many of them have been adapted to
5   movies. Still, it would be a rare and exciting opportunity to see these plays performed for the first time.

The ancient Greeks also excelled in the social sciences. Perhaps their greatest contribution in this area came in the form of democracy. The Greek words "Demo" and "Crazy" mean "People" and "Rule" respectively. Today, many of the world's great nations have adopted, and to a certain extent, modified the ancient Greek system. Yet, it originated from ancient Greece.

10   Academic subjects such as Philosophy, Astronomy, Physics and Biology also received a great deal of attention in the ancient Greek world. The philosophical writings of Herbalists, Plato, and Aristotle have had a profound influence on western scholarship for well over two thousand years. The Mathematical theories of Pythagoras and Euclid, combined with theories from other great ancient civilizations, provided a foundation upon which later mathematicians such as Newton and Einstein based their work.

15   The world of the Ancient Greeks would most certainly be an exciting and stimulating place to go back to. Politics, Drama, Physics, and a number of other subjects were still in their infancy, and all were being fiercely debated and examined. It would undoubtedly be and enriching experience to observe and take part in such a fascinating civilization.

Topic 86 A time and a place in the past

Till now, there is only one thing that makes me feel repentant of. My girlfriend died in Japan, and at that time I was doing my TOEFL test. If I could go back to some time and place in the past, I choose to go back to January 19th 2002...

My girlfriend's name was Christina. Her father is a Japanese, and her mother is a Chinese. She looks as beautiful as an angel. During last winter vacation, I started to prepare for the TOEFL test. Of course, I did not spend enough time with her as usual. I only saw her once every two weeks. The night before the TOEFL test, she came to my house. I enjoyed her cooking, and everything looked fine as usual. The next morning, she cooked the breakfast for me.

25   Before I left, she kissed me and said "Jackey, good luck. I love you!" I replied: "Thanks, honey! I love you, too. " The test went fine. After the test, my cell phone rang as I turned it on. It is one of my best friends, Moon. He said "Jackey, Christina went back to Japan. She is very ill. Now she is in the hospital and she is in the dangerous period. You have to come to Japan right now. We will see you in Japan!"

Christina is ill! How come I did not know this! When I finally obtained the visa and arrived at the hospital in Japan,
30   Christina said, "I think your business is more important than me. I do not think you need me any more! Goodbye, forever." She went forever. If I could go back, I will stay with her and spend much more time with her. I could even drop my test for her.

In fact, it is impossible to go back! Christina has died. There is no another Christina for me, but the TOEFL test will still be held four times per year!

Topic 86 A time and a place in the past

If I could go back to some time and place in the past, I would choose my childhood and my hometown. There it was full of my child's happy days. Especially nowadays, I live in a metro city full of chaos, traffic and pollution.

I would never forget the clear stream in my hometown. My friends and I used to swim and fish in the water, and play on the grass nearby. Currently I am still looking for such a nice place for my child, but I cannot find
40   it anymore.

I have lost contact with my close friends in my childhood for nearly twenty years. Their appearances are still kept in my memory. Their honesty, naive and helpful characters taught me what is real friendship. Perhaps they were all married and even have children, perhaps they have achieved their childhood dreams one way or the other, and perhaps they are struggling for living just like me. I wish we could get together sometime like our childhood years, free from worries about
45   the future.

I still remember my hometown in New Year times. Every child was dressed well, and got more freedom from their parents than other days in the year. Everyone in my hometown was happily talking about their harvests and their plans in the next year. Needless to say, us children can enjoy lots of delicious foods in such days.

During my childhood days, I lived happily and healthily in a beautiful environment, and I had very close friends. I wish I
50   could go back to enjoy my cherished memories again.

Topic 86 Visiting modern times

As a student in art history, my interest had always been on modern art. If I could travel back in time and space, I would pick Paris at the verge of twentieth century, the place and time of modern art development, without hesitation.

I believe that living during the period of the avant-garde art in Paris would be something quite exciting. I could go to experience the Eiffel Tower's opening, or visit the first Cubist exhibition. I would also be enthusiastic to attend Bergson or Poincare's lectures at College de France, or read articles in the newspapers of the time. I have always curious how people
5   felt when they saw for the first time an automobile or an airplane.

Moreover, I think it would be exciting to see how long distance communication became a reality, and how people perceived the introduction of the Greenwich Universal Time. This was an age in which incredible changes took place in the way people saw the world, in the way they perceived and understood time and space. It was the time when Einstein published his first studies about relativity. It was, as far as I am concerned, a time that it is worth taking a look at. I believe
10   that Paris at the end of the 19th century and the beginning of the 20th would be something fascinating.

If I were to return from the past back to our own times, I would be much more confident in my researches about that time, and my contribution to the study of art history would be a quite substantial one. Till now I can only read books and articles about it, and just imagine the wonderful time Paris had been just before the war!

Topic 87 **What is an important discovery in the last 100 years?**

I think the most important discovery that has been the most beneficial for people in my country is the invention of the Internet. So far as I can tell, the Internet has been beneficial to people around the globe. My view is a commonsense one, based on the fact that the Web is a vast storehouse of information and opinions, which can be of science, literature, politics, sports or even, sex. Anyone with access to a computer and a dialup connection can unlock the door and trawl through its offerings.

20   The Internet can be used as a broad base of knowledge that contributes to the educational system. Students and teachers benefit from the use of the Internet, as well as administrators and others outside of formal education. Students benefit because the Internet provides a resource to supplemental information for any subject. Educators benefit because the Internet provides a vast knowledge base to prepare for teaching topics. People are not only learning from the Internet, they are contributing and sharing knowledge through networked communities. The Internet is the advancement of
25   education for all its users.

The Internet is changing the way we do business. The Internet can deliver better customer services to people. Using Internet broadcasting, we are able to target the right audience, prepare and present a technical presentation on a popular topic, interact with new customers, and collect hundreds of highly qualified leads. As Internet companies continue to find innovative ways to leverage the capabilities of the Internet for businesses, the more we will learn how to provide optimal
30   solutions for customers. Which in turn, will greatly benefit people.

The Internet today is a way to transfer and share information. On the whole, it is a benefit to individuals of all kinds. We do have problems surrounding the Internet that need to be solved, but as with all new technologies there are debates and opinions. Since the Internet technology is spreading, it will soon become as popular as all other forms of communication. If you have not tried it, do so.

Topic 87 **What is an important discovery in the last 100 years?**

There are many important discoveries in the last century. Some of them had fundamental influences on the development of my country - China. However, I believe that one of the most important discoveries is the Cross-feeding method of rice discovered by a pioneering crop scientist Mr. Weiming Yuan in the early 1980's.

China has a long history of agriculture. Chinese people have been relying on agriculture for
40   more than 2,000 years. Moreover, China is still basically an agricultural country now and will continue to be it in the next 20 to 30 years, even though its industry is undergoing revolutionary development. One of the most important agriculture products - rice, is essential to the people of China. Since Yuan's discovery has dramatically increased the production of rice in China, we can say that Yuan's discovery is beneficial for the people of China.

More importantly, rice is the major food of people in Southern China, where half of Chinese population lives there.
45   People in the South eat rice everyday. So the consumption of rice is tremendous. As Yuan's cross-feeding rice seeds and raising methods provided 1.5 to 2 times more production of rice, people could effectively relieve the food supply crisis - a crisis that have caused millions of people to die in the 1960's.

When Chinese population exploded in the 1970's and 1980's, the effect of this discovery became much more significant. Yuan's discovery also corresponds to China's current government policy that China takes agriculture as its first industry.
50   This is because China has over 80% of farmers, and it's not realistic for it to become an industrialized country in a short period of time. Thus rice growing is still a crucial part of China's economic.

Overall, since most farmers in China are utilizing Yuan's discovery to increase rice production, and agriculture plays the most important role in China, I can firmly say that Yuan's discovery has been most beneficial to people in my country in the last 100 years.

Topic 88 **Has telephone made communication less personal?**

Since the beginning of humankind people need to communicate with each other. After the development of languages and thanks to the incredible ability of mankind to advance, nowadays we enjoy the use of many different types of communication. Letters, the Internet, or telephone allows us to communicate freely with the rest of the world.

In spite of above mentioned, I agree with the statement that new types of communications have made contacts between people less personal.

Unfortunately, the technology age we live in forces us to adopt the contemporary way of communication, which is almost impersonal. While hurrying to work more and more, chasing our aims, or focusing only on money making, practically we have forgotten that one of our primary social needs is to communicate face-to-face. To save time we often prefer to send an email or to make a phone call than to have a simple face-to-face talk with our friends or parents, for example.

Furthermore, those types of impersonal communications will sooner or later place us into isolation. Nowadays, we are often afraid to make new acquaintances; we have troubles to express ourselves when we communicate face-to-face; or we experience difficulties to hold an informal conversation. What is more, we find much easier to communicate with other people by email and phone.

Not only do we forget about our simple role as social members but we also do not enjoy it as we did before. Modern technology has made connections between people so impersonal that we are at the threshold of a new single world culture. This fact gives the answer to the question why so many people of our generation are victims of the illness called loneliness.

Although telephones and the Internet have made contacts between people much more easier, our virtual friends will remain virtual and a simple call will not substitute the hours we can spend with our families. Therefore, I truly believe that nothing can replace personal, face-to-face communication between people.

Topic 89 **What person in history you would like to meet?**

If I were granted an opportunity to travel back in time, the first person I would like to visit is Buddha. I hope to learn from such a wise and benevolent figure on my own. And I want to ask him for advice on the predicament we human beings are in.

Buddha is a symbol of humanity, a symbol of wisdom, leniency, tolerance and virtue. Millions of people over the world respect him. Sometimes it occurs to me rather difficult to understand that why a person of two thousands years ago can affect human spirit so much. If I had the opportunity, I really want to stand beside him, touch him, and perceive his strength.

When I visit him, I would ask him about the idea of tolerance non-violence. What I want to ask him is that how people, in an era full of violence, can restore the trust among each other and learn to negotiate peacefully. I would ask him if we still have any possibility to stop the war in Iraq, to calm the violence in Palestine, to return peace back to Afghan, to cure the terrible nightmare of Sept. 11 catastrophe in New York.

When I visit him, I would also ask him about diversity and co-existence. What would he think of Jesus Christ, Allah, Confucius, whether we have only one path to final happy or we would have different choices? Will Muslims, Christians, Buddhists, Communists, Green Peace Warriors and any other groups of people co-exist in this tiny global village? I would ask him about Hitler, Stalin, and Ben Laden, whether he thinks human beings should tolerate them or not? I would also ask him if he could give any advice for ordinary people like me, how to access happy, and how to access peace.

Buddha is Buddha, and he would not disappoint me. I am sure!

Topic 89 **What person in history you would like to meet?**

There are many famous people in the history of human beings. And I want to meet almost all of them if possible. But if only one choice is available for me, I will choose the great thinker Confucius without hesitation. The reason for my decision goes as follow.

In the first place, from my point of view, Confucius had a great influence on the culture and history from ancient time to present society in China and almost no one could be comparable with him in this respect. At the earliest of human society, Confucius firstly advocated education and civilization and taught Chinese people how to build a civilianized relationship among people. There is no doubt that this idea benefited the development of the Chinese society. It is the result of education that makes Chinese people create abundant culture from one generation to the next. Therefore, Confucius had a significant influence on Chinese history.

In the second place, Confucius encouraged people to respect their parents, treat their friends honestly and have a loyal heart to their emperors. At that time, only when people accepted these ideas could they really understand their own responsibilities for family and the society. Without these Confucius thinking, people may not know what is supposed to be the correct behaviors when they live with family or survive in the society. It is Confucius's idea that gave them a clear guidance. Until now, these ideas still have great effects to the behavior of present people.

Last but not least, Confucius has broad knowledge in many areas, such as literature, astronomy and geography etc. It is this knowledge that helped him complete many famous works. Experts from all over the world have paid great attention on the research of these famous books because many useful ideas in the books are still beneficial to our society. For example, Confucius advocated that humans should live in harmony with nature. In the present society, people destroy
5   forests in some areas, so living environment of human being has been damaged seriously. If we had observed Confucius ideas, this would not have happened.

In conclusion, Confucius is a great and famous thinker in the history of China. He provided us with the basic idea of education and civilization in human society, created the guidance of behavior for families and the society, and left us with abundant spiritual works. Therefore, he is the one who I want to meet most. I really hope that someday time could go
10   back, so that I would meet him in the actual world.

Topic 89 **What person in history you would like to meet?**

If I could travel back in time to meet a famous person from history, I would like to meet Christopher Columbus. Without a doubt he was one of the greatest people who have ever lived. I choose him not only because he found America in 1492, but also because he had all the qualities that can define a successful person to me: brave, adventure spirit, attic faith, determination and perseverance.

First of all, I am strongly impressed with his daring and adventurous spirit. What he wanted to do, in the eyes of the public at that time, was a risk. Risking his life, in addition to a number of ships and other people's lives. But he had great courage and had success.

Secondly, his attic faith in the scientific theory that the earth was round had also led him to success. Despite the fact that
20   most people still adhered to the belief that the earth was flat and that ships would fall off the edge, if they sailed too far in any direction. Columbus trusted the scientific theory, which was accepted only by few intellectual elites. It was his voyage that proved it.

Another great attribute from Columbus is his strong will and perseverance. If I could meet him, I would ask him how, after having his idea---voyage to India by a daring new route, namely, westward---rejected by the English, French and
25   Portuguese courts, he still found the courage to ask yet another monarch to support him. I would like to hear what Columbus said to the King and Queen of Spain to convince them that this plan would be profitable for them, when they knew that he had been turned down by three other monarchs and any amount of money, supplies, or men with which they provided him could potentially be a total loss. Columbus was so determined that he finally convinced them.

If I could have a chance, meeting Columbus would be my first choice. In my eyes I see Columbus as a man "...more
30   stupendous than those which Heaven has permitted..." no matter what anyone says.

Topic 90 **What famous athlete you would like to meet?**

If I have the opportunity to meet a famous entertainer or athlete, I would like to meet Michael Jordan.

Jordan was neither tall nor strong in his childhood, but he never gave up playing basketball. He has huge success today as a legendary guy in the basketball history, and is a god for all the basketball fans all around the world. I think the reason of his success is because his diligence, courage and his strong inner desire to win. All these are what I admire most of him.

Jordan won six championships of NBA. That was the heydays of Jordan. Six rings! That is every NBA player's dream. Someone spent many years in order to get a ring but failed, like Carl Malone, and King Baylor. Jordan got six! His last ring was won by his exciting shoot, which was once considered the last and perfect moment in his life and a best end for his
40   history of playing basketball.

Jordan's name was linked with "perfect" when people mentioned Jordan. A great deal of courage is needed for one to break off the word "perfect" which he used years to establish, but Jordan did it. He came back again, not as a god, but as a common basketball player. He was no longer young and could not act has what he did when his young. There are even some fans that opposed him to come back; they did not want to see their god beaten by the youth. In the opposite, Jordan
45   did quite well, though not as good as before, but better than what we all imagined. He, a nearly forty-year-old man with two injured knees, led Wizards get much better marks than it did last year. He could still sometimes score more than forty points. What support him is the steadfast belief he had and the strong love of basketball. This gave him the unbelievable strength.

If I saw him, I wanted to ask him how he managed to gain the desire and where does this love come from, maybe Jordan
50   would just give me a smile and say, "I love this game!"

Topic 90 **What famous entertainer you would like to meet?**

Everyone dreams to be handsome, rich and happy. Famous actors and actresses, pop stars or athletes are so popular because they realized the dreams many ordinary people have. If I could meet a famous entertainer or athlete, this person will be Julia Roberts.

Julia Roberts is a very talented actress. She can play many characters and each one is new and different. She seems to become the person she is portraying and gives a 100% to the performance. Pretty Women is my favorite because it was the first Julia movie that I saw and it was her big break. I still watch the movie to this day and enjoy it. Steel Magnolias is 2nd. Julia was in the company of a very talented cast and held her own. It's a classic, something you always enjoy watching.

5   I loved Notting Hill because the movie was full of many emotions. It made you feel happy after seeing it. I enjoy all of her movies. I see them even if the critics dish the movie. If she is in a movie I know her performance will be worth seeing. Her Oscar was very worthy of her as she was of it. Her Oscar was a long time coming. I am sure we can all look forward to many more great films to come and her always Oscar winning performance. Julia Roberts is not only beautiful, but she executes the characters she plays so well, that she can almost bring us to tears almost.

10   If I had a chance to meet Julia, I would also thank her for always thinking of the poor and the needed. After the disaster in New York and Pennsylvania, her face looked the sincerest of all of the stars. Also, I heard on the news that Julia gave $2 million as a tribute. Recently, you pleaded at US congress for money on a children's disease. Thank Julia for helping with such a kind heart especially during a time when so many have lost so much! I know that they appreciate your support and thoughtfulness, Julia.

15   Such is Julia Roberts, a pretty woman and America's sweet heart, and she is the star that I definitely want to meet the most.

Topic 90 **What famous entertainer you would like to meet?**	Many people dream to meet a famous entertainer or athlete. If I could meet such a person I would like that it be Bulgarian entertainer Slavi Trifonov, who presents evening show, "Slavi's show" on BTV channel, because of the following.
	First of all it would be interesting for me to meet the man, who had very big influence over the audience. Resent sociological researches show that more than two million people (the population of Bulgaria is around seven million people) watch his show every evening.

Furthermore you could hear discussions about his show or jokes, which he told during the show, almost everywhere, in a public transportation, on a street or even at work.

25   The second reason for which I would like to meet Slavi Trifonov is that in my opinion he is very brave man. He does not afraid to ridicule those Bulgarian politicians, who abuse their power for personal purposes, despite of personal threats, which he received several times. For example, a few months ago, he received a threat for making a hidden camera for a member of Bulgarian Parliament who did not want to pay a penalty for parking on an inappropriate place and who also offended a policeman.

Last but not least, I would like to meet Slavi Trifonov, because he took in the past a leading role as one of the organizers
30   of throwing down Gan Videnov's socialist government. Some days after the show "KU-KU" (in which he participated at that time and presented his political jokes and songs) was watched, the students' demonstrations against poverty, unemployment and high inflation rate began. Thanks to that the government resigned and new elections started a few months later.

To sum up, I would like to meet the famous Bulgarian entertainer Slavi Trifonov, because he has a big influence over many
35   Bulgarians, he is very brave and he was the organizer of an important historic event in modern history of my country.

Topic 91 **What question you will ask a famous person?**	If I had the opportunity to sit down and meet one of my idols or heroes, I could come up with hundreds of questions to find out what they did to get where they are, but in particular I like to have asked Helen Keller, what would she have made of the technology available today to blind and deaf blind individuals?
	When Helen Keller was nineteen months old, a serious illness almost took her life. She survived the disease had left her both blind and deaf. Her education contributed to her first

teacher, Anne Sullivan. Anne taught Helen to finger spell, and manage to let her understand the meaning of words. Imagine how hard it is for a person both blind and deaf to relate words with real world objects, although she never had a chance to see those objects!

45   Another teacher Mary Swift Lamson who over the coming year was to try and teach Helen to speak. This was something that Helen desperately wanted and although she learned to understand what somebody else was saying by touching their lips and throat, her efforts to speak herself proved to be unsuccessful. However, Helen moved on to the Cambridge School for Young Ladies and later entered Radcliff College, becoming the first deaf blind person to have ever enrolled at an institution of higher learning.

50   After World War Two, Helen spent years traveling the world fundraising for the American Foundation for the Overseas Blind. They visited Japan, Australia, South America, Europe and Africa. Her hard work and achievements was widely recognized throughout the world, and she was acknowledged as "the Miracle Worker."

If Helen Keller were born today her life would undoubtedly have been completely different. Her life long dream was to be able to talk, something that she was never really able to master. Today the teaching methods exist that would have helped

Helen to realize this dream. What would Helen have made of the technology available today to blind and deaf blind individuals? Technology of today has enabled blind and deaf blind people, like Helen, to communicate directly, and independently, with anybody in the world.

Topic 92 **One-season or four-season climate**

There is no denying the fact that whether to choose a place that have the same weather all year long, or a place where the weather changes several times a year is a popular topic which is much talked about. Although it seems that normally we cannot tell which one outweigh the other between these two kinds of places, they deserve some close examination.

If three criteria were taken into account, I would prefer living in areas where the weather changes several times a year. There are no less than three advantages in this as rendered below.

10 First, varied weather or climate broadens the range of our pastimes. For example, we can go swimming in summer and go skiing in winter. If the place we live in has only hot weather all year long, like Singapore, most of us can never have a chance to go skiing.

Secondly, the change of climate gives us opportunities to wear many kinds of clothes. Some say it is a waste of money to buy clothes depending on seasons. However, wearing various clothes, looking at others' fashion, and feeling the change of
15 seasons is very interesting for me.

Thirdly, changing of seasons is good for our health. When winter comes our body's metabolism slows down, and when summer comes it speeds up, so that our body can maintain a good rhythm. Also snows in the winter can kill a lot of bacteria and bad insects, so that in spring our chance of being infected with a disease such as flu is decreased and we can enjoy nice atmosphere and sceneries.

20 For these reasons, I prefer to live in areas that have several changes of weather. Only these three reasons can make a person draw the conclusion that living in areas that have season changes is better.

Topic 92 **One-season or four-season climate**

The South of Spain or the South of Antarctica? The Northern United States of the Northern Maldives? Where we live - the climate that surrounds us - has a tremendous effect on how we live our lives. In many cases, our emotional well-being depends on the climate we live in. Even more important than the general climate is the change in climate. I strongly believe that a four-season climate is better for us psychologically and physically. For this reason, I prefer to live somewhere where the weather changes several times a year.

There are great psychological benefits of living in a varied climate. Take my hometown, Cleveland, Ohio, for example. Winter in Cleveland can be quite depressing. The sky is often gray and snow and wet rain dominates the weather forecast.
30 It's not all bad, though. This is a great time to do snow skiing, sled riding and enjoy a cold weekend afternoon in front of the fire. While the outside elements can sometimes bring you down, most Clevelanders would tell you they prefer a snowy winter and a white Christmas. It's what makes the holiday season more special. Even more is the excitement when we see the first glimpse of springtime-the daffodils start to spring up and the days become warmer. This time often coincides with Easter. What would Easter be without a soggy egg-hunt in the back year? Then, of course, there are the progressions
35 from spring to summer and summer to winter. The long summer days do something for our spirits-late nights on the porch watching the fire flies at dusk make us all feel a little bit younger. The warm days and cool nights of autumn are not far behind, either. Those Indian Summers, as we call them, are reminders of how the seasons have whisked by us in a fury.

In addition to the psychological effects of weather change, we also experience a great physical benefit. Winter weather brings many outdoor sports in Cleveland like ice skating, cross-country skiing, downhill skiing and much more. The first
40 signs of spring get us out the door hitting the pavement to shed our winter weight gain. And summer? What a beautiful time in northeast Ohio as we venture to the metro parks for long walks, to Lake Erie for a dip her warm waters, to the garden where we tend to our flowers and foliage. Autumn serves as a reminder that those warm days are slipping away. What better physical benefit than raking leaves, mowing the lawn for the last few times before winter and preparing the house for the cold weather?

45 Some people prefer places like Florida where it's hot and hotter. I suppose it means a smaller wardrobe and a more predictable lifestyle. For me, nothing beats the traditional four seasons I experienced growing up. It has shaped the way I view each holiday respectively. It has carried many fond memories of an active youth. Now that I live in a country with very little weather changes, I long for a White Christmas, a wet Easter, a hot yet breezy 4th of July, and a crisp yellow and orange Halloween.

Topic 93 **What are important qualities of a good roommate?**

At first glance it seems very difficult for us to define what are the important qualities of a good roommate. However, after serious considerations we can see that under most circumstances, a good roommate should at least have the following three qualities.

First of all, a good roommate should be open and willing to communicate. There are always issues regarding rent, bills, food and household duties, guests, privacy, noises, sharing and borrowing, to name a few, and interests and hobbies of roommates are not always the identical. There will always be conflicts among roommates. When problems or conflicts arise, roommates must openly discuss the issue and reach a solution to the problem. In addition, a successful roommate relationship requires good communication. Take time to talk frequently to each other; chatting with each other helps keep up the basic relationship that can provide the underpinning

5   for a harmonious relationship. Therefore open and willing to communicate is the first important quality of a good roommate.

Secondly, an important quality of a good roommate is considerate and understanding. A good roommate understands what you need; He is a good friend and a good listener, and offer you help when you need it. Of course, you should not depend on your roommate to satisfy all your social needs. Make other friends and get involved in activities is also

10 important, and could leave more private time for your roommate.

The third important quality of a good roommate is that he should be a hard worker, and have the desire to do better. As we know, roommates will always influence each other in some ways. As an old Chinese proverb, one who mixes with vermilion will turn red; one who touches pitch shall be defiled therewith. So like choosing a friend, it is very important to choose a roommate who has good qualities.

15 Of course, some roommates eat and socialize separately and barely get to know each other. They never become friends. Still, if your roommate possesses the above-mentioned qualities, your residential life will be peaceful and enjoyable.

Topic 93 **What are important qualities of a good roommate?**

Each of us, when attending a university, might live with one or more roommates. During that period of campus yeas, we spend a lot of time with them. Thus, the relationship with a roommate affects not only our life but also our study results. I would prefer to have a roommate who is friendly and helpful.

A roommate is a person who lives closest to us during university time. Every day we meet and talk to him. Therefore, it is very important that he is friendly. Imaging, after some stressful hours in your class or library, you come back to your dorm room where your roommate is in. He gives you nice smile and ask you how thing are going. I am sure that you will feel relieve all strains and this circumstance brings you the feeling of

25 being home.

Being helpful is also an essential characteristic of a good roommate. I would say that, most of the students who live in university hostel are far from their home. That means, if some accidents such as being ill or injured happen, you cannot rely on your parents or close relatives. In this scenario, the roommate is very helpful. He could call an ambulance or drive you to the hospital.

30 Let me conclude by saying that, in our life, we may encounter many difficulties or stress, but we should make our own lives more meaningful by being friendly and helpful to other people. In this sense, being a good roommate is also being a good person.

Topic 94 **Does dancing play an important role in a culture?**

I cannot imagine that there is a person who would disagree with the statement that dancing plays an important role in a culture. Every culture, that I have known, has its own specific dance. In addition, dancing has not only an important role in a culture but it also is an inseparable part of it.

Since the beginning of humankind dances have played am important role in every culture because while dancing people can express different moods and feelings, or they can practice various religious and cultural rituals. In the modern society, dancing still remains the most significant part of the cultural

40 life of all primitive tribes such as Bushmen in Africa, Aborigines in Australia or Indians in North America.

If we take a deeper look at the cultural life of modern society we will see that dancing have played an extremely important role for many generations of people. Dancing has marked people as the Jazz generation, the Rock-and-roll generation, the Disco generation, the Techno generation, or the Rap generation. Actually, every Dancing generation has been characterized by specific moral and ethic rules, and cultural traditions have been changing to a certain extend.

45 Anthropologists give a definition to the word 'culture' as common ideas, traditions, religion and customs that are shared by a particular group of people or a particular society. As dancing have always been means for people to show their belongings to a certain society, it has become an important part of the culture of any community or nation. In conclusion I would say that if people manage to protect their national dancing from oblivion, I am sure that they will keep the spirit of their predecessors alive for good.

Topic 94 **The role of dancing**

Dancing is an important art form, and also plays an important role in a culture. Some dance spontaneously happens at celebrations as an expression of emotion or some happen in a more structured manner at ceremonies.

Dancing plays an important role in ceremonial events in many cultures. For example, during the Pukumani ceremony the dances performed reflect the relationship to the deceased. In Lebanon, the classical belly dancing still plays an important part at weddings, representing the transition from virgin bride to sensual woman, and is also popular in nightclubs. On the other hand, residents of the Greenland believe that the dancing and drum can be used as a tool to dissolve conflicts between people.

5   As we may see from the above examples, dancing is an integral part of many cultures. Of course, dancing does not have the same functions in our modern life, but many people in our society still find dancing an enjoyable form of entertainment and art. Young people go to disco with their friends to release their energies, and they find dancing a good way to relax and make friends. Older people dance together as a social event and a good means of exercise.

In addition, many people go to theatres to enjoy performances of ballet and modern dances. Enjoying those beautiful
10   dancing, music and costumes in a dance performance, can give us a wonderful experience, and help us develop appreciation of art, and enrich our after work life.

In conclusion, no one can deny that dancing plays an important role in a culture.

Topic 95 Should government spend money exploring outer space?

The word "Space adventure" has captured a large number of people's heart. Many men have been attracted by the unknown world and have desired to live in space at some future time. The universe is the last and infinite un-explored region for human beings. However, space researches do not accomplish only by yearning. These researches cost hugely. Another way to express this is that spending money always has its opportunity cost. In other words, money spent on some venture could have been used for financing some other alternative venture.

Some people believe that money spent on space research benefits all of humanity. Other people believe that there are
20   better opportunities for spending this fund.

This first group of people claims that space researches have helped all of humanity's lives extremely. They point out that researches on space have informed us about much environmental damage which we have caused to our planet. Similarly, they declare that the present satellite system is due to the researches done in the past in space. There are also numerous new materials and inventions that can be traced directly to space researches. These people hope to spend more money on
25   researches, visit all the planets, and build space colonies.

On the other hand, there are people who assert that money spent on space is a complete waste because it does not have sufficiently direct benefit to all the humanity. For instance, there is a sizable portion of the humanity does not have any access to food, education, sanitation, health care and especially peace.

Personally, I find that I cannot align myself completely with either group. I have some reservations about both positions.
30   No one can deny that weather satellites and communication satellites are useful investments. But unrealistic researches like exploring Mars or Venus does not have any good bearing on most peoples' development at the present. Some scientists may be interested in the composition of those planets, but the opportunity cost is extraordinary. In my opinion, it may cause lack of social infrastructures, if states inject immense funds into space researches in the limited budget.

Topic 95 Should government spend money exploring outer space?

Managing the government spending properly has always been a concern for all countries in the world. Some nations spend a lot of money on outer space explorations, while others focus on providing the basic needs for their people. As far as I am concerned, I believe that governments should spend more money on social benefits, education and health care rather than wasting money in other aspects.

Of course, exploring the outer space and traveling to planets such as the Moon are surely very
40   important to the human society. It increases our knowledge and understanding about the space and the universe as a whole. However, this should be a secondary matter for the governments. Spending too much money would be a waste of money. Governments' top priority should always be satisfying the basic needs of their people.

All countries in the world ought to provide enough financial resources for schools. If there is no investment from the government, children will not be well educated and they may not have an opportunity to go to a university. Therefore, it is
45   important to ensure that everyone will be able to pursue and fulfill his or her own educational goals. Universities should have the latest collection of books and up-to-date sources of information. All schools should build new classrooms and other facilities.

Another point that we must consider is making sure that the government will have enough spending for social benefits and the health care. We should construct more hospitals and rehabilitation centers both in the cities and in the countryside.
50   We ought to generate more money to guarantee the life of old people and disabled people. The government should also provide free health and medical care for all the population. They have the responsibility to assist the poor people who do not have basic resources to survive. The state government should also help unemployed and underemployed individuals. The society itself will benefit from the expenditures of the government toward social benefits. Furthermore, it will promote the economic growth and the development of all the countries.

In conclusion, governments should spend less money on explorations of the outer space because it is less urgent. Instead, state governments have to concentrate their attention on social benefits as well as education for future generations. Financing social programs is no doubt their primary duty.

Topic 96 **The best way of reducing stress**

They say that "Life is a big headache on a long noisy road." This statement truly explains life nowadays. Life in the twenty first century is full of stress. From dawn to dusk, everyone has to go through a rigorous schedule. Even children are not exempt from this rush. Everyday there are deadlines to meet, reports to write, bills to pay, meetings to attend, papers to submit, etc.,. Life is a never-ending race to most people. The everyday grind builds up stress and fatigue.

10 Stress Reduction has become a priority with individuals as well as organizations. People have different ways of escaping the stress and difficulties of modern life. In my opinion the best ways of reducing stress are meditation, exercise and reading books.

Meditation is an effective way to overcome stress. Meditation not only soothes the mind from tension but also regulates heartbeat and blood pressures. It helps an individual in attaining inner peace and equilibrium. Meditation helps in tapping a person's inner potential and opens his mind to the universal spirit.

15 Exercise is another way to reduce stress. Exercising not only promotes health but also improves thinking. When a person exercises the muscles in the body get a workout that in turn burn fat. The burning of fat releases stored energy and the person has an exhilarating feeling. This feeling helps the person to overcome stress. Thus Exercise is very useful tool in stress reduction.

Reading also has a beneficial effect on individuals in stress. Reading a great book is very therapeutic to a person with stress.
20 Reading helps the mind to look at other things and reduces the focus on the person's difficulties. Elegant poetry and beautiful prose can soothe a person's mind and help him reduce stress in his life.

In conclusion, Meditation, Exercise and reading are the best ways to reduce stress.

Topic 97 **Teachers' pay**

Education is one of the holiest occupations in my view. I disagree with that teachers should be paid according to how much their students learn. Although teachers are important for students, the most important part for learning knowledge is students themselves.

Different teachers has different style, so it is hard to evaluate how well each teacher teaches according to how much students learn. As nobody would have the same character, teachers also have their own teaching styles such as humorous, gentle, strict, to name a few. Maybe some students like humorous teachers, while others prefer a gentle one. But probably the students of a strict teacher could give good results in their study, even though these teachers teach the same thing. We
30 could not say that the strict teacher should be paid higher than the gentle teacher, since we know that the students have learned more because they were afraid.

On the other hand, how much or how well students learn depends on students themselves. In a school, it is easy to see that some students are with high marks, while some others have lower marks. A teacher is a person who direct students how to learn. Students should do much more works. The more attention students pay, the more knowledge they learn.
35 The hard-workers probably get higher scores. Students' learning results depend on individual students' intellectual abilities and the time and energy that they put into learning. Sometimes it has nothing to do what how well the teachers taught. In addition, knowledge that students learn not only comes from the teachers, but also from many sources. Family influence, extracurricular reading and out-class teaching are some of the sources that can provide students with knowledge.

In sum, although teachers are important in students' education and learning, there are many other factors that decide how
40 well students' learn. So it is unfair that teachers are paid according to how much their students learn.

Topic 98 **Stuff to represent your country**

If I can send one thing to represent my own country - China to an international exhibition, I would choose a book that has graphical illustrations besides each context.

The main reason is that paper was invented by one of our ancestors and it is essential to our everyday life. Were it not for the paper, many documents would not have been passed down
45 for centuries. In addition, with the written language being used, many famous people and great things about my country can be recorded in this book. For example, it can explain the educative theories of Confucius, one of the greatest educators in our country.

On the other hand, with the universal language of graph, people around the world can understand more easily with the help of the vivid presentation. In this way, even a young child who does not read will learn what I want to tell them.

50 In a word, people attending the exhibition will know that Chinese people discovered paper, and Confucius was one of the greatest educators in China. Besides, this book also reminds us how clever our ancestors are and what we need to do to keep up. With these wisdoms, we can invent more convenient equipments or make important discoveries to better our lives for the future.

In conclusion, if I have the opportunity to introduce one thing to people in the world, I would bring a book that documents all the traditional inventions and people of my own country. In that way, the world will understand more about my country.

Topic 99 Would you rather choose your own roommate?

Some students do not prefer to have the university choose their roommate. However, as far as I am concerned, this is part of the university experience. Therefore, I would rather have the university assign a roommate to share a room with me. I base my views on the following reasons.

First of all, even though the university will assign, it is actually not totally a matter of chance. For instance, we all filled out information sheets. The school knows what we are majoring in, what our interests are, and our study habits and our goals.
10 I think they are probably very good at matching roommates using this information. Besides, if a mistake is made, I can change my room assignment next semester.

Secondly, it is a lot of work to choose your own roommate. For example, if I did want to choose my own roommate, I would first pick some candidates from the list supplied by the university. Then I would write to them and they would write back. Through our letters, we would find out if we shared common interests, such as sports or movies. Because of my
15 investigation, I would probably get someone compatible with me. However, it takes time and labor to go through, though. Besides, the process of finding similar interests is not all that different from what the university does.

Finally, trying to predict whom I am going to get along with is not a science. I might choose someone who sounds just like me and still find that the two of us just do not get along as roommates.

Besides, I think it would be boring to room with somebody who is just the same as me. I would rather be with someone
20 who has different interests and likes to do different things. Maybe I would even get a roommate from another culture.

In conclusion, having the university choose a student to share a room is a far better choice for me. Assigning roommate in body may suit some students. However, I think it is always important to meet new people when we enter a university. Besides, another reason I am going to the university is to be exposed to a lot of new experiences. These new things would allow me mature in character.

Topic 100 Computer technology or basic needs?

Some people think that governments should spend as much money as possible on developing computer technology or buying computers, while others think that governments should spend money on the basic needs of their people. As far as I am concerned, this money should be spent on some more basic needs, such as protecting the environment and improving public services.

30 In the first place, pollution of the environment has become the biggest problem in today's society. People will not find clean water to drink if they do not do some work to keep the water clean. There would be no fresh air if every one in the city drives a car to work. More and more wild animals are facing the danger of extinction because of the shortage of habitats. There would be no more wild animals if people continue to destroy forests. Therefore, there are more basic things that governments should do such as keeping the water clean, keeping the air fresh,
35 and keeping the forests intact.

In the second place, there are many problems with the public transportation system in big cities. The buses during the rush hour are overcrowded; some people cannot get to work on time because they spent too much time on the buses or trains. Consequently, government should spend more money to improve public transportation systems, which will benefit the people and the business in their cities.

40 From what I have discussed above, everyone can see that there are more things a government should do than buying computers, such as protecting the environment and improving public services. Therefore, I think governments should spend more money on the basic needs of the people instead of spending a lot of money developing computer technology or buying computers.

Topic 100 Computer technology or basic needs?

Many people believe that governments should spend as much money as possible on developing or buying computer technologies, while others think that governments should spend money on more basic needs. While both spending on computer technologies and on basic needs of the society are important, I think that government should concentrate on the latter. Computer technologies are not very good investments from the point of view of society as a whole, while investments in essentials have a much higher rate of return.

50 Investment in areas related to computer software, networks and hardware are not very profitable and will not improve life of ordinary citizens. Several years ago many people believed that by investing in computer-related fields we can improve performance across the board, but the reality has not been what we have thought about. Most of Internet companies and dot-coms went bankrupt. Although huge money was poured into those companies, many of them cannot stay in business anymore. The promise of improved performance has never come true.

Even in the United States, the most powerful and prosperous country in the world, there are still more than 20 million people who live below the poverty line. More than third of the earth population live on less than one dollar a day - the official threshold of poverty declared by United Nations. We can greatly improve the life of those people by investing in public education, organizing loan agencies or other projects that can help to alleviate poverty. What's more, computers can 5 actually make this problem worse, because with the application of computer technology, more and more people are losing their jobs - thus making most of the world's uneducated population obsolete and without means to sustain themselves.

Analysts expect that in several decades more than third of the population on the Earth will not have access to clean water. This can result in famine, deteriorate public health and other disasters. Some argue that we might have wars for the access to clean water. To prevent this scenario we need to invest a large amount of money in projects that will help to save clean 10 water on our planet.

In conclusion I want to say, that investments in computers will not solve a single problem of our society. Computers will not prevent famines, which are so usual today, or help poor people. On the contrary, computers can make poor blue-collar workers out of work and money to support their families. So governments around the world should spend all available money on basic necessities of our society, not on some dream projects.

Topic 101 **Doing work by hand vs. by machine**	In general, there are two ways of making products, one is by hand and the other is by machine. It is undeniable that products can be manufactured easily and efficiently by machine. But for me, I prefer hand-made items for their features of individualism and flexibility.

First of all, hand-made products are more unique and personal. Take birthday cards as an example, instead of same pictures on the printed cards available in the market, well-chosen images such as our own 20 photos printed on a self-made card can surely distinguish the card from others. Owing to its uniqueness, the self-designed card will be of greater value for the person who receives it.

What's more, garments made by hand are fitter than machine made ones. Although men's suits and lady's dresses can easily be found in shops that sell machine-made clothes, many people go for tailor-made clothing simply because tailors can make those clothes precisely according to individual customer's measurement and styles. Obviously, the fitness of 25 clothing is what those people care about most.

Finally, producing items by hand is more flexible. It releases people from being confined by modes that are necessary for machine-made manufacturing. For example, in hand-made pottery making, people can create new designs at any time. While in machine manufacturing, however, modes have to be made in advance, and afterward all finished products are based on the same modes and have completely the same looks. If a different look is needed, people must re-produce the 30 modes first. Moreover, there are still some items that cannot be produced by machine because there are no matched modes.

In conclusion, it is easy to get the conclusion that doing work by hand is more flexible than by machine in most cases, so I prefer products that are made by hand.

Topic 102 **Should students evaluate their teachers?**	I am always amazed when I hear people saying that students have no rights to evaluate their teachers, and that if they do so, they should be regarded as dishonest. Even one did not know from concrete examples that schools should ask students to voice what they think of their teachers, one can deduce it from general principals.

It is true that a young man, one of the students, may be conceited, ill-mannered, presumptuous or fatuous, but no one will have the ability to make sure that all teachers are not behaving like this. When a student has some fault, it is the teacher's 40 duty to tell him what he should do; on the other hand, when a teacher does wrong, others, including his students, are bound to let him know.

It is as if, sometimes, that what many teachers have done are devoid of any mistake, however, the way they taught still deserve improvements. In schools, students try to develop abilities and skills, and prepare for their careers in the future. It is true that what they get from schools may be perfectly adapted to the society during a certain period of time, but the 45 world is not still; it is changing all the time. What is learned today may become outdated tomorrow. As a result, teachers, who are bound to make improvements of what they teach according to the reflections of the society, should be evaluated by their students.

Furthermore, giving students the right to evaluate their teachers help create the air of freedom in schools. This is especially important to inspire students' thought, and to encourage them to think. If students are not allowed to voice 50 what they think of their teacher, they will have to do what the teachers tell them exactly, only to become robots that can to do nothing other than following instructions.

Taking into account of all these factors, we may reach the conclusion that it is significantly necessary to ask students to express what they think of their teachers, and this does good to the students, to the teachers, and to the society as a whole.

Topic 103 **What characteristic makes people successful?**

In my point of view, a sense of humor is as important as, if not more important than, other characteristics that a person can have to be successful in life. This I support with the following reasons.

Firstly, humor helps us to maintain a correct sense of values. It is because that we are always reminded that tragedy is not really far from comedy, and then we never get a lop-sided view of things. A small example could get some light on this point. Once I failed an assignment again, and I told myself that God was on vacation these days. I did not feel frustrated, and I succeeded the third time. So, if we can see the funny side, we never make the mistake of taking ourselves too seriously. It is helpful for us to keep self-confident.

10 In addition, the sense of humor is associated with happiness, and happiness will influence people around us. Those who bring happiness to others probably have a good relationship with people surrounding them, which is essential to a successful life. We all have the experience that we are inclined to talk and cooperate with humorous people. We may treat such experience as an enjoyment instead of a rigid work.

However, to be a successful people is a tough thing. We need intelligence, honesty, determination, a sense of humor and 15 so on. Without intelligence, we could not find the keys to solve all the intricate problems. Without honesty, no one would trust us and we could achieve nothing alone. Without determination we would easily bend for difficulty.

Even so, I still think of humor as the most important part. A sense of humor supports an active attitude towards life. And it is such attitude that encourages intelligence, honest and other characteristics in you. To summon up, a sense of humor is the most important characteristic. If happiness is one of the great goals of life, then it is the sense of humor that 20 provides the key.

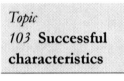

Topic 103 **Successful characteristics**

Many people believe that one can be successful if he/she is committed, honest, faithful or intelligence. But the foundation of each of these qualities lies in believing the power the person has, and working accordingly to achieve the goal. There are many people, who are honest, beautiful, good and soft spoken, intelligent and even faithful, but only some are 25 successful in achieving their goals. While all of these characteristics are equally important and act as the medium for success, the most important is the power to cope with circumstances and keep our spirit goes on in the most difficult situations.

It is well said that we cannot direct the wind but we can adjust the sail. Similarly, on the way to our destination, we will come across a lot of obstacles, but we need to find the way to come across that situation. This is where success lies. No 30 matter how low we fall, what matters is how high we bounce back.

Success can be measured by what we have and how much power we are using to achieve our goals. For example, while in playing games, it is sure that one team will win and another will lose, but the spirit is not just in winning but also in learning new techniques and improving team sprit and cooperation skills. A winner team cannot always be successful, but the successful team is the one that has improved a lot with respect to its earlier performances.

35 Though the person is honest, intelligent, faithful and committed, it is not sure that he will be successful. The most important character rather than these is efficiency, , which is to understand the environment and the need, and to implement best of the best ideas and actions. No matter how smaller step it can be, but it can bring great changes. As Shiva Khera once said, "Winners do not do different things but they do things differently", which better explains the meaning of being successful.

40 Success is not just winning, but also is how much we are satisfied with whatever we are doing. So, all qualities like honesty, intelligence, and faithfulness are directly proportional to success. The definition of success for each of us may vary. Some may think the reason for success is honesty while others may think it is the commitment. But, in my opinion, where there is will there is power, so each of us should know our strength, and work accordingly to be successful. And we should measure our success not with others but with what we have and what we have achieved.

Topic 104 **Contributions of artists vs. scientists**

Science and art are two main streams of knowledge accumulated from ancient times by human beings. They have their own characteristics and provide to the society their contributions, which benefit the world in which we live. Some people think that the contributions of scientists are higher than that of the artists. Before I give my opinion, I want to see the two sides first.

50 Science is defined mostly as the knowledge related to the natural world. I think most of its domains are involved in material things, such as food, housing, clothing, transport, etc. It is usually easy for people to feel the existence and progress of science, because it is usually taking place around us they are apparent. In the past and present, science has changed our life a great deal, and I believe in future, it will continue to improve the world we live in.

Art is more related to our spiritual world. It has a long history, too. It has developed coincided with science. Art helps us to appreciate the beauty that exists in life. Many people admit that art can nourish their minds and refine their spiritual world. In this respect, art is a good complement to science.

I can hardly tell which one has more weight in terms of the contributions to the society. They are both indispensable in this world. The history of human has proven this. So I do not think it is wise and safe to say that one of them is more
5 important than the other. As far as I am concerned, I think they both weigh profoundly with regard to the contributions to the society.

**Topic
104 Contributions of artists vs. scientists**

Social benefit, I think, can be defined as the profit that people who live in the society can share and appreciate. When we compare the contributions of artists and scientists, it is quiet difficult to outweigh one of which. However, it is because we tend to easily find the contributions of scientists to our daily life that I am on the side of those who contribute to the society in a tangible way. Now I would like to illustrate some examples that support my opinion.

First of all, all the appliances such as televisions, personal computers and microwaves ovens that we use in our daily life are contributed by the scientists' efforts and aspirations. Nowadays, we can barely survive without those products that always help with our daily tasks. Most of those are the great invention that is developed in the
15 past 50 years. Almost all people in the society can share those contributions. Scientists' contributions are more than just inventing those appliances. Thanks to their tremendous perspiration, our mental and physical health is ensured and protected in many ways. Newly developed technologies help physicians to practice operations. A number of medicines relieve and alleviate our illnesses. Those improvements in the medical field can easily make people to admire scientists' contributions.

20 On the other hand, artists' contributions are sometimes difficult to appreciate. There are a variety of buildings with artistic forms that are designed by artists. However ordinary people cannot truly appreciate those great works. In view of social benefits, those contributions are less important to people in the society. Therefore, artists' contributions to the society are unfortunately less attractive for me.

With the illustrations above, I definitely believe that scientists contribute more to our society. Although life without artists'
25 works is dull and meaningless, we cannot survive with the contributions of scientists for sure.

Topic 105 University housing vs. apartment

In dorms, students can learn to improve their communication skills and to live with others harmoniously. Roommates must adjust their eating and sleeping habits regarding to each other's needs. Each one must adjust his free time in such way that he does not bother others while they are studying. The environment of dorms is likely the environment of formal offices
30 where everyone must find solution to various problems and cooperate with others.
Consequently, by adapting to conditions of living in dorms, students can actually prepare themselves for their future jobs. The environment of a dormitory is friendly and understanding, because it consists of students who have same goals and interests. For example, if one failed to understand his lecture, he can ask others for help. Furthermore, students can find that it is easier to find topics to chat or conduct activities together because they have so much in common.

35 Apartments have quietly different surroundings. Students usually have fewer neighbors and roommates so that they have less distraction. Thus, students can concentrate better on their schoolwork. As a result, their grades could be better. Moreover, living in apartments maintains students' privacy. One has his secrets that he does not want anyone to know and sometimes needs to spend his time alone to think about his problem. Another advantage is that people who live around apartments are diverse. Thus, students learn to contact with ordinary peoples and are not confined to the academic
40 community. Therefore, students are offered a wide variety of experiences that will be useful in the future.

If I were in a situation to choose whether I would live in a dorm or have a separate apartment, I would choose to live in a separate apartment. It could be argued that living in an apartment limit the contact of a student with his fellow students. This argument goes on to assert that such students are deprived from social environments and therefore remain aloof and introvert. However, it is a fact that students can make enough friends even if they live outside of the university, especially,
45 in the cases where students live with their friends.

Furthermore, students can visit each other as often as they need to. They can maintain a good relationship with their fellow students in a way that does not affect their school performance. Alternatively, students who live in academic dormitories are constantly surrounded with familiar people so they cannot avoid excessive socializing even if they don't want to. As a result, they do no have enough time for studying and the get low grades.

Topic 105 University housing vs. apartment

Accommodation is one of the basic needs of people in today's society. The choice of living in dormitories on campus or finding an apartment off campus depends upon the student's preferences.

A student living in an apartment may seem to hold this view that he can share his room with other people who would reduce a great burden on paying off a huge amount of rent. While living in a dormitory one cannot have this type of advantage. On the other hand, a student who prefers to live in a dormitory may hold his view that one does not have to worry about getting up early and to rush for a bus or any other means of transport to attend one's class.

5 The strong view presented by a student living in an apartment is that he does not have to abide by the rules, e.g. the main terms and regulations for a student living in a dormitory. Whereas, a student who chooses to live in a dormitory may strongly condemn this view: he express his view stating that a student living in an apartment also has to follow the rules of maintaining the room properly, such as to clean the rooms and make it neat and tidy, wash the bathroom properly etc.

A student in a dormitory holds this view that everything has been provided to them. All the facilities are provided in a university dormitory; while living in an apartment one may not gain this advantage. On the contrary, a student living in an 10 apartment hold the view that a dormitory student is restricted to certain things such as they are not allowed to go out of the university beyond given times. While living in an apartment, there won't be such problems, and one is free of time restrictions.

In my view, I prefer living in an apartment because I hold my opinion that if I do not have enough money to afford a living in dormitory, then certainly I would live in an apartment where I can share my rent with other people. Every thing 15 has its advantages and disadvantages, and it is up to a student to decide what he chooses and how to make use of his choice.

| *Topic 106* **Means of transportation** | Advances in science have thrown before us a number of options for covering distances, either long or short. |

The type of transport to be used for covering distances depends upon a range of factors like 20 distance between the and starting point and the destination, time and money constraint for traveling, availability of different mode of transports, time taken for travel, safety considerations and the number of persons traveling.

To cover a distance of 40 miles, for instance, the options I can think of are on foot, by bicycle, by motorcycle, by car, or by bus. The longest time taken for traveling this far will be on foot while the shortest time will be by car or motorcycle, but again since the number of persons traveling is one which is me, a car will not be a feasible option as it will be 25 underutilized and will prove to be costly because of high fuel consumption and initial cost.

A bicycle will be cheaper in terms of initial cost and there is no fuel consumption. But it will take much longer time to travel, and it may cause physical fatigue. Therefore, this option is ruled out. A bus will prove to be a cheaper mode but the flexibility is limited regarding timing of arrival and departure. A motorcycle will be economical but will not be safe to drive on highways.

30 Therefore considering all modes of transportation available and taking into account various factors mentioned above, I will prefer to take a bus as it will be safe and economical, although it is less flexibility in terms of departure and arrival times.

| *Topic 106* **Means of transportation** | The 40 miles distance is not very long for me. There are three kinds of transportation tools I could use to travel 40 miles from my home. They are driving a car, taking a train, and riding a bike. |

It seems very difficult to prefer one to another because all of them have their advantages and disadvantages to the extent that it is hard to distinguish. Yet that does not mean they are of the same to me. To be frank, I would prefer riding a bike. I like it because riding a bike is one of the best physical exercises. During my early high school years, I used public transportation to go to school, therefore I often got sick. Ever since I started riding a bike to school, I had never been sick 40 again. Bike riding makes me strong.

Bike riding is also a flexible means of travel. I do not need to worry about the bus or train schedule. I do not need to care about the parking problem; I can leave my bike almost anywhere. In addition, I can go to some places where automobiles and trains cannot reach, such as rural areas. Once I rode a bike in France. Along the wine road, we biked from Strasbourg to Colmar, stopped at each small village every 2-3 miles, tasted the fresh homemade wine, and enjoyed the medieval 45 architectures in those villages. It was absolutely a romantic trip!

Although driving a car or taking a train is faster than riding a bike, and save your concerns about the weather, they have a lot of disadvantages. Driving a car can cause parking and environmental problems, and taking a train is limited by the train schedule. Both of these means are expensive. One needs to pay for the gasoline or train tickets. No wonder, I prefer riding a bike!

| *Topic 107* **Should higher education be available to all?** | Some people hold the opinion that university education should be available to all students, while others believe that higher education should be available only to good students. I deem the first one as the premier choice. |

The main reason is that providing all students with the opportunity to obtain higher education

is highly beneficial to the development of modern society. More and more people will be able to obtain knowledge and become professionals if higher education is available to all students. Since there are not only a lot of excellent professors who have significant experiences of teaching and research but also plenty of advanced facilities such as laboratories and libraries at the universities, students have much better opportunities to acquire knowledge and skills. If everyone in a
5 society is highly educated, there will be no doubt that the society will be able to develop at a great speed.

The second reason is that it is obviously not fair to a lot of students if a university education is available only to some students. I am convinced that everyone in the world should have the same right to acquire knowledge no matter what his intellectual ability or financial status is. There is no reason for people to judge students merely based on their academic performances and decide if they should be granted with higher education. It is only fair that everyone has the right to
10 obtain a university education.

Last but not least, people are able to obtain better jobs since universities can better prepare students for their future careers. At universities, there are a lot of opportunities for students to participate in co-op programs. By participating in co-op programs, students cannot only learn how to write resumes but also practice their interviewing skills. All these skills gained at universities will be highly conducive for students to quickly obtain job offers after graduating from universities.

15 To sum up, taking into account of all these factors, we may safely reach the conclusion that higher education should be available to every student.

Topic 107 **Should higher education be available to all?**

While higher education should be available to all students, I am sorry to say I strongly believe that the higher education of better quality should be available only to better students because this is a simple resource management issue although it would hurt many people's feeling.

It is given that colleges and universities cannot possibly be built equally with the same quality of facility, faculty, curriculum, etc., which resulted in different school reputation. Therefore, certain schools must be more competitive than others. Then the question is who should be selected to attend the better schools.

In California universities, there used to be a quota system ensuring students' race distribution does not deviate too much from that of the entire state. However, students in different ethnic groups do score very differently in the standard SAT
25 and ACT exams. As a result, the minimum admission scores were quite different for different ethnic groups. The local newspapers called it reverse race discrimination and California state government reportedly cancelled the quota system few years ago.

As a matter of fact, Germany has been administering an exam at the end of primary school for years to divide their students into two categories. One for higher education and the other for vocational training. A system like this would
30 make sure that limited educational resources are used in the most effective ways.

As for China, late Chairman Mao did make all the universities in China open to public, which lasted as long as 10 years! The result? These students were criticized as having college student's title, using high-school textbooks and staying at primary school level. Not only the society refused to recognize them as college students, even the government called them college trainee instead of college student!

35 Again, it would hurt some people's feeling, but the policy is strongly supported by early genetic research. My education psychology textbook described tracking investigation on twins from the same egg, but growing up in different families for whatever reasons. If all babies were born equal in their future physical and mental abilities, there would be much less correlation between the twins than that between the twin and his/her sibling in the foster family. Unfortunately, statistics is science from God. The conclusion in the textbook is that the babies' future physical and mental abilities are 75% related
40 to genes and 25% to the post-born environment and personal effort.

The truth is obviously there, but to be politically correct is something I admit very necessary. This is why every country is sending better students to better schools, but keeping the issue low-key.

Topic 108 **The best way of learning**

When it comes to the issue of understand of life, some people suggest that the best way to learn about life is getting others' opinions, while other people maintain that the best way of learning is through person experience. In my point of view, the latter opinion carries more weight.

In the first place, learning from previous successful experiences is beneficial for people. For instance, a student who is preparing for an important exam can think of the past exams that he did very well, and he can review more effectively if he learns from these exam experiences. Moreover, the student can acquire the lesson from life that people who work
50 effectively can be successful.

In the second place, learning from past failures can help people to understand the meaning of life. An example is that, losing money because of unwise investments is part of many businessmen's experiences. When a businessman is planning to invest a big amount of money, he can look back at his experiences of the past and avoid pitfalls that may cause him to lose money again. As a result, he probably will seek advices from professional people and plan his investment more carefully this time. Learning from those failures can surely help people learn how to make wise decisions in life, and people can understand that avoiding mistakes is the keys to succeed in life.

In conclusion, although learning from one's personal experience may have a few drawbacks, its advantages far outweigh its disadvantages. Both good and bad experiences can help people understand life better.

Topic 108 **The best way of learning**

As life is rigorous and challenging for most of people (excluding children who have a silver spoon in their mouths right after they were born), everyone needs to take advices from others or accumulate experiences to face the life. However, people have different ways to learn about life. Some tend to learn by listening to advices of family and friends. Meanwhile, others prefer to learn through personal experiences. In this essay, I will discuss the advantages of these two different ways.

10 Some people like to understand life by listening to advices of people around them. This offers a good chance to gain knowledge and experiences from others who have already experienced hardships and tasted the bitterness of life. This method is much convenient and faster than the other one because there are a lot of experiences in life that have already been experienced by other people. Other people's opinions and advices simply offer us a shortcut to success.

On the other hand, young people, however, prefer to learn about life through their personal experiences. However, to
15 acquire these experiences, one has to pay a price. One must have to experience a lot of failures before he/she can savior the sweetness of success. It may also take a long time for someone to stand up from his failures. In addition, it requires a lot of time for people to accumulate these valuable experiences.

Comparing and contracting these two approaches, I personally prefer the way that of listening to the advice of family and friends. This is the best and easiest way for young people like me to start a real life.

Topic 109 **Follow the customs of the new country**

Nowadays it is quite common for people to move to other countries either for work or for study. When they move, some of them decide to follow the customs of the new country, while others prefer to keep their own customs. If I were forced to choose one of the two positions, my choice would be the former.

To illustrate my point, let us first take a look on why some people dislike the idea of following the new customs. First,
25 people who have a strong religious background that are different from that of the new country tend to stick to their own religious beliefs. Second, older people are usually accustomed to their own life styles, and it is very hard for them to change their ways of life and accept new ideas and cultures. Thirdly, some values and phenomena in western countries contradict eastern values, such as the use of drugs, alcohol and certain behaviors of young people. So when people move from a traditional eastern country to a western one, they find it very hard to accept the new customs.

30 Although I must admit that it is not always necessary to change our own customs, I believe that the advantages of adapting to a new culture are apparent. In the first place, by following the customs of the new country, we can learn more about the country and understand its people more quickly, and can become a real member of the country. To share the same custom means that having more things in common with local people, and it can pull people together. Furthermore, we have to adapt to customs of the new country, if they are written into the law. Take the country of Singapore for
35 example, for many decades the law had banned the consumption of chewing gums. A young man from the United States violated the law and was served with their caning punishment.

In addition, people who stick to their way of life may sometimes feel lonely and isolated. They tend to complain about the life in the new country and most of them eventually return to their home countries.

In conclusion, I believe that the advantages of following the customs of the new country are obvious because you can
40 easily learn about the new country and quickly adjust to the new life. What is more, you can live more comfortably and avoid troubles and misunderstandings in a foreign country if you think and behave the way other people do.

Topic 110 **Being alone vs. with friends**

There are many lovely things in our lives such as the fresh air on a winter day, the beauty of the country in autumn, learning of love and the growing of a friendship. Everyone has friends or desires friends in the pursuit of sharing emotions. Thus many people enjoy spending most of their time with friends, like me, while others prefer to remain alone.

There is no doubt one needs time for oneself. When I retreat to my dorm at the end of the workday there is no one to tell me what to do. I often write little secrets in my dairy, enjoy soothing music without being disturbed or read philosophy books. Being alone provides a time to reflect and ponder one's future life course, with a greater clarity and purpose. Accompanied by many friends from the dorm I would have no chance to relish such retreats.

50 On the other hand, spending time with friends is stimulating and provides a mental break from ones daily routine. Since I am a sociable and open person, I invariably feel happy and relaxed when I do things with my close friends. We can take part in all kinds of after-school activities such as playing volleyball, swimming or climbing. Some profound, or stimulating ideas often appear in my mind when I am with such friends while being alone often no such inspiration manifests.

When I come with friends I can always exchange views with them about study, society or love thereby obtaining some interesting information or knowledge. A group of people provides a means of testing one's ideas and learning from one another. When I confront serious problems and I am unsure of which course of action to pursue a close friend provides a means of reassurance that I am not alone in my way of thinking or chosen course of action.

5   Being with friends can be fun and aid one in overcoming the trying periods in life. Being happy in life means doing the things you enjoy and having someone to share the feeling with you. Being with friends most of time is an enjoyable aspect of life for me as it is a source of inspiration, satisfaction and ongoing education.

Topic 110 Being alone vs. with friends

Some people like to spend most of their time with their friends. Other people, however, just want to be alone in their spare time. As far as I am concerned, I belong to the latter kind of people.

In the first place, I feel comfortable if I am alone. This is not because I do not like friends, but because of my personal character, quiet and a bit shy. When I am with my friends, I always feel embarrassed since I am always a listener. Trying to find topics makes me very tired. On the contrary, staying alone does not bother me. I do not need to discuss with others about what I want to do. Go shopping, go to a movie, go swimming, just do it. The most 15 important thing is, I do not feel lonely when I am alone.

In the second place, I need to have more time to learn new knowledge. I am working in the field of computer programming. As we know, the development of the computer technology is amazingly fast. If a person has not been working in this field for more than five years, he would find that he has to study from scratch when he decides to pick up his old job. So it goes without saying that I have to update my computer knowledge frequently in order to keep up with 20 my career. Based on this, I do not have much spare time to fool around with friends.

In conclusion, I prefer to spend most of my time alone not only because I am not good at getting along with friends, but also because I have to spend most of time in studying new technology.

Topic 110 Life without friends?

There are people in this world that prefer to live on their own, to stay as far as possible for the company of other people, to enjoy the silence and comfort of being alone, without anyone to bother them. For my part, I cannot imagine my life to be like that. I really think that friends are very important in my life and I like to spend as much time as possible with my friends. It is hard for me to enjoy the splendors of life without having anyone to share my feelings with. I have too often been away from home, from my friends and family.

I have seen wonderful places and things that could make me incredibly happy. However, the true happiness came only at 30 the time when I could share my experiences with my friends. Everywhere I go I need to find at least one person that in the end I can call a friend. Going to a concert, to a movie or enjoying a party, it is inconceivable not to go with a friend. I do not recall ever going to a concert on my own. And I missed several occasions to go to events that I really wanted to attend just because my friends were unable to make it, and I could not go without them.

Moreover, friends can help each other. It is good to know that somewhere there is at least one person whom you can 35 depend on when you are in need. I also enjoy helping my friends. Doing something good for someone is a really rewarding experience. While with my friends, we can also have discussions and share opinions on our future plans, our ideas, our thoughts, and our problems.

Although there are arguments on the part of leading a life on your own, and not depending on other people, I strongly believe that friends, family, people around you are important part of our life. Life is so wonderful because the people 40 around you.

Topic 111 Spend time with one or two friends, or many friends?

I cannot imagine a person who hasn't enjoyed the company of a friend. Friends are very precious and therefore, we constantly love and cherish them. Spending time with friends has always been regarded as a wonderful thing to do with no doubt. However, one might choose to spend time either with one or two close friends or a number of friends.

Certainly, there is a difference between the enjoyment gained by spending time with our few close friends and the delight obtained by hanging out with many friends. When we are spending time with our close friends, we can feel a special closeness and bond with them. With the company of intimate friends, we can be more open and true to ourselves. Although with few people around the scope of our activities is limited, it is compensated by the satisfaction that we gained from the warm atmosphere.

50   If a person doesn't like the joy attained from the company of just few close friends and wants to extend his activities with more friends, he can choose to spend time with many friends. When a group of friends gather together they can engage in many group activities such as playing games and sports, and travel to new places. This enjoyment doesn't necessarily require close relations among the group members. Being sociable and outgoing is good enough to create a pleasant ambiance for everyone.

I'd rather choose to spend my time with one or two close friends than being with a number of friends. With my close friends around we don't really have to do anything in particular together. For us the significance lies in the fact that we are together, sharing our time. As the saying goes, "I can spend hours without uttering a single word with my friend and I'd have the best conversation ever."

Topic 112 How should children spend their time?

In our rapidly changing world people begin to understand more and more that nothing is so valuable but knowledge. Education has become an important part of people's life. Due to this some people think that children should begin their formal education at a very early age and should spend most of their time on school studies. But others believe that young children should spend most of their time playing. To my mind these two views should be balanced so
10 as not to go to the extremes.

The first point of view that children should start early on their studies make me assume that it can be harmful and damaging for a child's physical development and personality. As a teacher I have seen the result of beginning education too early. Children are deprived of the enjoyment of their childhood years and their intrinsic desire to play. Some children cannot concentrate on their study and keep playing at school. Besides, the children who are not allowed to play and are
15 forced to study can begin to detest the education process and the teachers. So, to force children to study at an early age can spoil the whole picture.

When facing the question of early education it is also important to note that children who begin to study at an early age are often overloaded by studying material and homework, which they are not ready to cope with. Besides some parents neglect their children and do not pay enough attention to the children's problems at school thinking that they are still
20 young.

The second opinion that children should play instead of study also has disadvantages. In this case children are not well prepared for their school life at all. They have no idea what he is going to do at school. In addition, research shows that early education can benefit children's brain development and prepare them better for the futures school education. The most important time for early education could be missed if parents do not send their children to school at an appropriate
25 age.

In conclusion I would like to point out that that early education and play should be well balanced so that their enjoyment of childhood that is once in a lifetime would not be deprived. It is quite important for governments to design and implement an appropriate primary education system so that young children can have chances to both learn and play at school.

Topic 112 How should children spend their time?

To play or to study, almost every child will face such a problem. For sure, most children would like to choose to play because playing is their nature. But parents would think it is better for them to study. Which way is better? Personally, I think children should play more in the early years, and gradually it is better for them to spend more time on books once they have reached their school age.

35 When we think of school study, we think of textbooks and exams. That is to say, children have to do a lot of homework to practice what they learn at school. They have to memorize a lot of knowledge in order to get good scores in exams. To those small children who are too young to go to school, learning may become a torture. And consequently their learning will not be efficient, and they even would hate learning.

On the other hand, playing is also a learning process. Needless to say, children are much creative than most of us grow-
40 ups. Part of the reasons is that they still have a blank and original mind. They just use their own eyes to watch the world, and use their ways to explore the world. While playing together with other kids, they can practically learn many things, such as how to cooperate with others, and to help others. While playing with pets, they will know how to take care of them, and learn to take care of other people as well. While playing with toys, out of curiosity, they will ask all kinds of questions. When parents can explain to them, the information may motivate them to learn more knowledge through
45 playing.

During the childhood, it is better to play with other kids or with toys, since they can get basic ideas about friendship, people and the world. Playing is a necessary phrase for children to be mentally and physically healthy. When children reach school age, it is better for them to go to school, and gradually start learning knowledge that is useful for their future.

Topic 113 A new university in the community

It is said that a new university will be established in our community. Some people think it is better for the community to have a university. But others do not think so. As far I am concerned, I think both sides have their own reasons. Let us get down to the arguments first before we take a side.

People who hold the opinion of supporting the government's plan may have their views as follows. For one thing, a university around here may provide people with more chances to pursue advanced education. People living near here can

go to the university library at their leisure time. There they can use the various resources of education, such as the book collection, and the computers. In addition, they can take some part-time continuing education course to improve their skills at work, or pursue a higher degree. The other advantage of establishing a university here is that it may bring the community an academic atmosphere. With so many educated people around town, the community makes you feel so
5   peaceful and in harmony.

People who take the opposite side may present some disadvantages of building a university near the community. Firstly, they feel that a university may occupy larger amount of land and use a lot of money which can be used for some other purposes: such as a shopping mall which can make people's life more convenient, or a factory which can employ a lot of people. The benefits that can be brought by those facilities are more obvious and tangible. Secondly, they think that the
10 students in the university are young people who may sometimes cause troubles such as drinking, speeding or having wild parties, which could probably destroy the quite atmosphere of the community.

All above seems reasonable from their own respective. Personally I support the idea to establish a university in the community because it can really give us more chance to improver ourselves.

Topic 114 **Who influence more, family or friends?**	Young adults may be influenced by many aspects in forming their characters and outlooks on the world. Some people believe that family is the most important influence on young adults. Others think that friends are the most important influence on them. Both views base on respective beliefs.

It is true that friends may exert great influence on young adults. They may study together in the same school and share similar experiences. They have much in common and may share their innermost secrets that they never let their parents
20 know. Young people are easier to make friends with each other and communicate without bothering about the so-called generation gap, which is nevertheless a common problem existing between young adults and their families.

However, it's also generally accepted that parents are the first teachers in the growing process of their children. Parents teach their children how to utter the first word in their life, help them to step out their first pace, witness their first love and give important suggestions when children need them. On the other hand, children follow their parents' examples and
25 even adore them when they are growing from little children to young adults. They are usually ready to turn to their parents who have more life experience than them for advice when they are faced with important decisions. Therefore, parents who witness most of the whole growing process of the young adults till they are mature enough are more important influence on them than their friends.

Although young adults may reap a lot from their communication with their friends of similar ages, the most important
30 influence to their life is always their families.

Topic 115 **Making plans for free time**	In my opinion it is always better to plan our free time because although it is considered leisure time but some people might need it to get certain things done that could not have been finished if they were left to be done another time.

Probably for most grown-ups free time is only during their weekends which is usually for one or two days only. It is
35 actually a very short period of time if you have lots of things to be done. For this reason planning for leisure time is very important because there are lots of things that needs to be done and not all of theses things are for fun.

For adults, leisure time is not only about waking up late, spending the whole day in bed or in front of the television and reading some magazines. In fact if it is well planned, free time can be used to meet our friends, go to a restaurant, go to the cinema, go shopping or even read a nice book. Others may use it to do more important things such as taking up a new
40 hobby or studying if they are students. Consequently their time needs to be organized very well in order to accomplish all the things they need to do compared to the short time they have.

On the other hand, if we do not keep a list or a schedule of the things that we should do, we may only finish a thing or two but time will never be enough for us to accomplish all the tasks we have. It seems to me that leisure time should not be left without planning because it is really important to many people.

Topic 115 **Making plans for free time**	In an era when the pace of people's life becomes more frantic and hasty than ever before, there is a growing concern among the general public about the way to arrange their own leisure time, carefully planning or no planning at all. As far as I am concerned, the former one

should be wiser.

First of all, in the modern time that people are hustling around all the day and have so little free time, a meticulous plan
50 should be provided in order not to make full use of it. Unlike the ones leading their lives in the last centenary or in the rural areas, contemporary people, especially those in major cities, have been bothered by the pressures from their bosses, colleges, and even the family members. Consequently, the free time for such people is shorter than ever. As a survey held in some large cities shows, many young people my age have to work form 9 am to 10 pm, Monday to Saturday, and only have some spare time on Sundays. Just as an old saying goes, how time flies! If there were no careful plans, people's free

time would elapse without any value.

In the second place, people would have enjoyed themselves more if they have thorough plans on how to allocate their private time. It is obvious that if the leisure time were well organized, even a short break would make people relaxed and ready for their next round of struggles on their jobs. What's more, according to a health report, people would benefit

5   more if they conduct various activities during weekends and holidays. A careful plan will make sure that people can accomplish what they want to do during their free time.

All in all, in such a time that people have less time to spend than ever, a careful plan is of vital importance for people to relax and fully rest. After all, efficiency is the most crucial factor in this crazy time.

Topic 116 Which methods of learning are best for you?

All of us have different learning styles. Some people are more visually oriented, and they are better able to absorb information if they read about it or see it presented in graphics or charts. Many people find that even if they are instructed about a given topic, they will not understand the information unless they put it to use by themselves. Still others need to process the information by analyzing it and discussing with others. I believe that we benefit most from different ways informational input.

15   I like to read about a topic and consult other visual learning tools such as video presentations, diagrams or charts. This is the type of informational input that is most suitable to me. I also like to keep notes on a topic so that I can refer to them later. While this form of learning works best for me, I find that it helps if the information is presented in a number of other ways as well.

Information can be absorbed better if we not only read about it, but also hear someone talk about the topic. This can

20   personalize a topic and also help to clear up confusing points. Being able to ask someone questions when something cannot easily be understood can really help with the learning process.

Some people find that they cannot absorb knowledge until they are actually able to put it to use. While I find this is helpful, it is not the most important learning tool for me in most cases. In some instances, though, it can really make general concepts and ideas more understandable. For example, when reading about how to surf the Internet, it is difficult

25   to grasp some of the ideas and instructions that are offered. Once you actually try it a few times, it becomes easier.

I learn best if I am able to hear a teacher or speaker discuss an issue, follow along by viewing diagrams and charts and also reading supporting material, and then, in some cases, putting that information to use by actually conducting activities or exercises related to the material.

Topic 116 Which methods of learning are best for you?

People have different ways to learn knowledge. Some people learn by doing things; other people learn by reading books; others learn by listening to people talk about things. As far as I am concerned, the first method - learning by doing is suitable for me. The reasons are as follows.

In the first place, I normally have a better understanding on the things that I learned by doing them. Ten years ago, after graduated from a university, I began working for an electronic

35   company, which manufactures color televisions. During the first several months, I just sat in my office to read the mechanisms of color television from books. Those theories seemed to be so abstract to me that I can only understand 30% of them. So I decided to go to the production floor to learn about them. After taking part in the procedure of manufacture, I was surprised that getting hold of those theories was no longer difficult to me. I was able to assemble and repair televisions shortly afterwards.

40   In the second place, I can remember well when I learn things by doing them. People always have such an experience: they can memorize something when picking up a book and forget it when putting down the book. Knowledge cannot become yours by reading until you practice it. Knowledge learned from books is RAM, e.g. erasable memory; while knowledge learned by doing things is written in our ROM, e.g. inerasable memory.

In conclusion, I prefer learning by doing things not only because this method can help me understand things easily, but

45   also because it can help me memorize things longer.

Topic 117 Different friends or similar friends?

Some people like friends who are different from them, while others like friends who are similar. If I have to make a choice, I prefer similar friends.

Admittedly, the idea of having different friends is not without advantages. On one hand, contacting with different friends gives one a broader outlook to life. Different friends can

50   enrich our experiences by their conducts and thoughts that are different from ours. In addition, they can help a person enjoy a variety of interests.

Nonetheless, I believe that similar friends have more advantages. We can feel confident and strong when we have a group of friends who share the same opinions. A person with a purpose in life - such as an artist or a politician - may feel a special need to surround himself with people who can assist and encourage him in his work.

In addition, similar friends mean the same way of thinking and doing things; therefore they are generally more compatible and easy to get along with. I can think of no better illustration of the idea than the example of my roommate and I who both like studying quietly and dislike loud music, so we can enjoy a quiet environment together and concentrate on our assignments. We both go to bed early so none of us would be bothered while sleeping. Furthermore, it is convenient for similar friends to communicate and enjoy their leisure time together. My roommate and I frequently have fun together because we have the same hobby - playing chess.

For the reasons given above, I would have to declare myself as one of those prefer similar friends to different friends.

Topic 118 **New experiences vs. usual habits**	If one has never experienced the storm, how could one enjoy the beauty of the rainbow? If one has never experienced the unknown, how could one enjoy the joys that life has to offer? Therefore I always welcome new experiences in my life.

Some people like their lives to stay the same, and they do not change their usual habits. So all their life, they do not have many new experiences. They live only one lifestyle. No matter what happens in the world, they just keep their life the same way. They will not try a new job with a higher salary. For years and years they just stay with their old jobs, and live in the same town or even in the same house forever. Although some of them may want to lead a better life, they are not willing to change. They just fear changes.

We all only have one life, in other words, life is limited for every one of us, so why not take advantage of our life as much as we could? The only way to experience more is to change our usual habits and lifestyles and to try new things. For example, I have always dreamed of traveling to different parts of the world to experience different cultures and customs, to meet different people, and to enjoy different views and scenic spots. I would even live in a foreign country for a few years. Then I would really feel that I have lived a wonderful life.

Some people may say that you would have confronted much more trouble and difficulties brought by the changes in life. Yes, but life should consist of sweetness and bitterness, tears and laughter, that's the way life should be! If I haven't tasted the bitterness, then how can I appreciate the sweetness? Different experiences may help me develop a profound insight into life itself, and then I could really get to understand the real happiness of life, and really appreciate the life that I have!

In a word, I always look forward to new experiences in life, so that I could enjoy my life fully.

Topic 119 **Do clothes make a man?**	Would a frenzy people become cool, after he wears a lab white cloth? Would a child become mature, after he dresses a tie? And would a prisoner become a hero, after he takes off his prisoner's suit? At this point, I consider that the crucial factor of a people's behavior is not relied on what he (she) is wearing. Instead, the character of a person determines which type of people he (she) belongs to.

First and foremost, although clothes play an important role in people's daily life, they are not the determining factor of their characters. As we can see, the appreciation of one's personality largely depends on his (her) behaviors, including the way he (she) talks, and the way he (she) does things. After all, the primary function of clothes is to keep us warm, and to prevent us from being naked like animals. As a proverb goes, "A beggar would not be someone; even if he wears a gold hat."

Secondly, as far as clothing is concerned, there are many people wearing the same clothes, but they can behave differently. Take uniforms for example, we could not deny that some doctors are impatient when they treat their patients, while others are very nice. Some soldiers are nice to their prisoners, while others treat their prisoners badly or even abuse them. So it is quite wrong to conclude that all policemen are helpful, and all government officials are trustworthy, only because they wear the government uniforms. After all, the uniforms are only used to distinguish one job from another.

Due to the above mentioned reasons, I can safely conclude that people would not behavior differently despite they wear different clothes.

Topic 119 **Do clothes make a man?**	I do strongly support the statement that people behave differently when they wear different clothes. In other words, different clothes influence the way people behave.

Some small examples may give some light to the point. I usually find that those who wear suits and tie behave invariably the same in general. They probably look self-confident, genteel and intelligent, although most of them do not really have these characteristics. So, what I want to emphasize here is that clothes work as a symbol today and people wear them would act like what the clothes impersonate without being aware of it. We all have the experience that when we wear a T-shirt and jeans we feel vigorous and act like a 16-yaer-old boy.

On the other hand, we tend to wear clothes that are appropriate for the environment. When people go for a job interview, men will usually wear nice suits and tie, while women will usually wear fine lady's garments. Because people understand that "clothes make a man", and nice clothes can increase their chances of getting that job.

To take this idea further, with the help of different clothes, we can behave a way that is different from what we usual look like. For example, when a serious person who has a frustrating job takes a picnic outdoors, he will dress casually in order to remind himself that he needs to relax for this occasion. Another interesting example is that we can sometimes see from movies that a serious woman who has a formal job in an office wearing a sexy underwear and dance like a stripper at night

5   in order to seduce her husband.

So, as we can see, people really behave differently when they wear different clothes. So why not slip into casual clothes and give yourself a break right now?

Topic 120 Are quick decisions always wrong?

I agree with the statements that the decisions that people make quickly are always wrong. Those quick decisions that people make are like bids in a gambling. Even if they have a chance to win, they are still losers theoretically.

People should never make quick decisions without fully considering the factors that are influencing their decisions and the consequences of different decisions.

When people make hasty decisions, they rarely care anything about the situation. Situation is a very important factor in making a right decision. Different decisions lead to different results, so it is very important to make a decision carefully.

15   People who make quick decisions do not have time to look around and carefully analyze the consequences resulted by different decisions.

Secondly, there is a popular belief that people should decide quickly in order to catch opportunities. Unfortunately, that notion is completely wrong. If you made a quick decision without thinking carefully, how could you be able to catch the opportunities? "Chance favors the prepared mind," as a famous saying goes. Only when you have fully prepared, can you

20   really grab a good opportunity when time come. Otherwise the chance that you take hastily may result in a failure.

Thirdly, even if you can quickly analyze the situation based on the facts that are provided to you at the time that you make a decision, since you do not have enough time to verify the validity of those information, the information could be wrong, which could leads to wrong decisions. Even the president of the United States can make this kind of mistake. Mr. Bush made a decision to start the War on Iraq based on the false information that his subordinates provided to him, which

25   claims that Iraq has dangerous biochemical weapons. Maybe someday history will prove that the decision to start the War was wrong.

Life is not a lottery. Life is a stock market. Only when you make careful decisions based on thorough analysis, can you win. If you make quick decisions, chances are that these decisions will happen to be wrong, and you may lose everything down to your underwear.

Topic 121 Can we trust first impressions?

In our daily life, we will always hear a wealth of such cases as a guy who has fallen into love with a girl at the first sight, one of your friends who impresses your mother deeply on his first visit to your house and then is treated exceptionally well by your hard-to-be-pleased mother, and even the applicant who attracts to the human resources manager immediately during the first interview is easily employed, to name just a few. All of the above-mentioned cases tell us

35   that many people in the world trust the first impressions of a person, his character, his conduct and his eloquence, etc., all of which he displays at their first meet. But is all that he displays, or all that you understand through what he displays correct, or it is just a blur image that needs to be proved in the later days?

Before we get the question to be treated, let's think of the most probable (not absolutely) results of the cases mentioned in the first paragraph:

40   The guy who has just experienced the above-said romance has to say goodbye to his newly-met girlfriend because later on he finds out that she is not as good as she looks; the friend of yours who has just won your hard-to-be-pleased mother's trust is criticized by your mother because of his great incoherency in his manners, and even the newly-employed employee is dismissed because he is not telling the truth in his resume. Till now, do you still think the first impressions are dependable?

45   Psychologically, we have a very perfect image of a person in our head, of course, which varies from one to another owing to individuals' specific experiences, education and family background, and his or her own opinion. When a person who we meet confirms with the image in our head, we will, to a great extent, overestimate or even exaggerate his merits, while omit his shortcomings, maybe due to human nature and psychological reasons.

Thus we can ourselves lead to the answer to the question above that the first impressions of a person are generally

50   incorrect. In a word, to judge a person needs time and the first-sight impression is unreliable.

Topic 121 First impressions

In our social life, we may meet different people in different occasions. Some of them we may meet once; others may be staying with us for a long time, such as our classmates, or our colleagues. Some people trust their first impressions because they believe these judgments are generally correct. While other people do not judge a person quickly because they think first impressions are often wrong. Before I give my opinion, I want analyze the two opinions first.

For those who trust first impressions, they may argue as follows. For one thing, before two people first meet, they have no ideas about what the other person is like, and then they may have no inclination to cater to each other by behaving
5   differently. At those circumstances, it is a little bit easy to get to know the person's real character because they may behave naturally. In addition, some mysterious factors such as instinct may involve in the first impression which usually is proved to be the right one with no reasonable account, as is especially occurred in many married couple's first meeting.

The other group of people who do not believe in first impression also have their reasons. First, people's characters are different and complex. It is very hard to get to know them at the first meeting. If you want to know a person, you have to
10   spend lot of time to talk to them, and observe their behaviors at different occasions, and all these cannot be accomplished just in a few hours. Second, many people do not behave naturally when they meet strangers, so the first meeting will not be a good chance to know a person.

We can see that both the two sides have their reasons. But I prefer not to judge people in our first meetings. Because to me, I'm not very good at judging people and my first impressions are usually unreliable.

Topic 122 **Unleash your desires!**

It is quite normal for people who live in the modern society to feel the necessity to acquire new things or achieve a certain status that they do not possess. This behavior is due to human nature and continuous changes in the society, especially the emergence of novel products that most people find attractive.

The process by which people develop new products is mainly by looking at what people need. When there is a need, there
20   is a market. Although this could seem an acceptance of desire as a normal human behavior, I think desire is far better than what it is being think of, since this is the driving force for people to invent new products and discover ways to improve our life.

It is normal for people to attract to what they do not have, and it contributes to human's own process of development. History cannot evolve if human do not have desire. Everyone wants to achieve a better status in the society, and after the
25   desired status is achieved, a new desire appears and this becomes a never-ending process. The famous story by Alexander Pushkin, T*he Fisherman and the Goldfish*, depicted this human nature insightfully.

The desire of human being to lead a better life and use new products has pushed the technological advancement of our society. For instance, in 1980s, people desired to use personal computers to do word processing and desktop publishing. The necessity quickly converted to personal computer products that can accomplish that task. Afterwards, people were
30   not satisfied with computers doing work processing only. They need more powerful functions to process images, generate 3-D animations and play multi-media games. Today, the computers available in the markets are hundreds times faster than those of the 1980s, and we got bigger and much higher resolution screens. Obviously, it has been human desire and necessity that pushed the development of computer technology.

It is true that people never content with what they already have. Due to this dissatisfaction, this society is fast evolving.
35   Perhaps we may use words such as "wish" and "dream" to replace "desire". There will be more and more new products and services that are more comfortable and easier to use, in order to satisfy people's dreams. So, unleash your desires! Our wishes and dreams can make our life better.

Topic 122 **Should people satisfy with what they have?**

In contemporary society, there are new things coming up almost every day. Some people have to face such a fact that you can never buy a real new product, because the new one always appears after you have bought one. As a result, some of them are never satisfied with what have and they want to get something newer or something different. To some extent, it is a good way to keep up with the ceaselessly changing world. However, in my opinion, it is not always good not to satisfy what you already have.

For one thing, with the development of science and technology as well as the globalization, more and more brand new
45   things are produced every day, along with a variety of new findings, new lifestyles, and new types of services. If we ignore all the new things and always stay what we are, the only result may be that we will be obsolete in the society. In some degree, if we all stick with old things, there will be no new inventions and advancement of the world. The continuous needs in people's spirits can really push our society forward. Human beings live in a modern society after all, and we should have the desire to be in pursuit of a new life.

50   However, on the other hand, if we sought after material satisfactions without considering our financial reality, we could find ourselves in trouble. As we know, new products are manufactured and updated almost every day, so there is little possibility that you can always obtain the newest products. Moreover, every time a new comes into markets, the price is always much higher than older products. If you do not have a strong financial background to support your desire, how could you be able to afford them? For example, some people borrow money from their credit card for new and fancy
55   products without considering their affordability. In the end they get into financial crisis.

The purpose that we look for new and different things is to live better and happier. If your desires only get you into worries and troubles, it will be a better choice to learn to give up and be satisfied. In a word, living in a modern society, we must in pursuit of our life with a flexible attitude.

Topic 122 Should people satisfy with what they have?

Many of the world's religions share a belief that when a person is able to look at and confess his or her problems that person can begin to travel the on road to emotional recovery. A problem cannot be solved until it is clearly recognized. I agree with the above statement because I believe that dissatisfaction and suffering forces people to change.

10 History presents many examples of dissatisfaction and change. The history of China in this century might be seen as one of dissatisfaction and progress. Sun Yet San was discontented with the decaying imperial order, and so he created the "Revolution." Mao was dissatisfied with the course of events so he intensified the revolution; finally, Deng pushed the Chinese economy towards a free-market economy. Hence, China progressed towards its newfound "superpower" status.

In a not dissimilar way, during the eighteenth century many Americans became annoyed with the British regime and they start to fight for the freedom and independence. Hence the most powerful country in the world - the United States was created.

15 On a personal level, dissatisfaction can lead to changes within friendship and marriage. Perhaps it might even be said that true love cannot remain static. Matrimony and friendship are explorations of the higher emotions: they are pilgrimages towards the city of true values. If husband and wife are prepared to confront and discuss their problems, a blue period can give way to many years of happiness. Sometimes, for instance, a spouse may not recognize that the source of marital unhappiness is that the other partner has developed a need to have children. Whatever else may be said, most people
20 would agree that children change the lives of their parents.

The best method of utilizing dissatisfaction is to change things before they get out of hand. An intelligent man will constantly monitor his emotions; an intelligent politician will understand the mood of his people. Some people might suggest that the transition to independence for Canada and Australia was much smoother than that of the United States because Britain allowed those two dominions to evolve with time. To take the idea further, a good parent or an astute
25 politician will even anticipate potential dissatisfactions and therefore take precautions.

I agree with the above statement because, I believe that we are can grow up through dissatisfaction. Without the ability to recognize our discontent, we could collapse into illness. Suffering sharpens our senses.

Topic 123 Non-fictions vs. fictions

How could anyone suggest that people should only read about real events, real people, and established facts? For one thing, that means people would not be reading half of all the great books that have ever been written, not to mention the plays, short stories and poetries. For another, it would mean that people's imaginations would not develop and would remain uninspired throughout their lives.

Reading stories as a child helps develop our creativity since fictions teach us a lot about how to convert words into mental images. Fictions open our world up, exposing us to other times and different ways of living. Reading histories of those times would serve the same purpose, but histories are probably not as sharply and vivid as fictions. Reading an essay about
35 poverty in Victorian England is not the same thing as reading Charles Dickens' Oliver Twist. The image of a small boy being suffered in cold, poverty and hard labor are more horrifying than simply reading the statement, "Children were sold into labor". Reading fictions makes a more lasting impression in our minds and emotions about the past.

Besides, storytelling is an emotional need for human beings. From earliest times, humans have taught their children about life, not by telling them facts and figures, but by telling them stories. Some of these stories show what people are like
40 (human nature), and help us experience a wide range of feelings. Some tell us how we should act. Telling a child that it's wrong to lie will make little impression, but telling him the story of a little boy whose nose grows longer every time he tells a lie will make a much stronger impression.

Fiction is too important to our culture, our minds, and our emotions. How could we ever give it up!

Topic 124 Social science vs. natural science

The chances of receiving education are considered the most fundamental right of human beings in the 21st century. Naturally, the argument about what the students should acquire at schools has attracted many attentions from people of various walks of life. In considering the obligatory courses required at schools, people have different ideas. Some would hold the view that it is more important for students to study science and mathematics than it is for them to study history and literature.

50 I agree with this point of view completely. Although both social and natural science courses play an important role in the whole education system, natural science seems to have a greater impact on human progress. Our society is developing at a high speed quite unprecedented before. One cannot deny the fact that all of these results came directly from scientific discoveries. An example is that during the period of industrial revolution, it is science and mathematics that brought many inventions and discoveries such as assembly lines, mending machines and electric appliances which has freed the most of

people from manual labors once and for all.

The above reason I pointed out does not mean that literature and history cannot improve people's lives but they have few advantages to people's material life especially to those poor people who are still struggling for the essential needs of shelters and foods. Literature and history cannot be put into practice to some extent. Research and development of
5 science and mathematics on the contrary can be applied to our real life and improve our living standard. Take medical science for example, the new findings of treatments of certain diseases can save lives of many people. There still exist some fatal diseases that threaten people's lives. All this will depend on the development of medical science.

In short, all courses involving literature and history, science and mathematics are necessary and important to students. However, according to the reasons I discussed above, I want to make the judgment that science and mathematics course
10 are more useful.

Topic 125 **Should art and music be compulsory subjects?**

I totally agree with the statement that all students should be required to study art and music in secondary schools. It comes as a direct interpretation of the apothegm 'All work and no fun, makes Jack a dull boy'. The education of art and music is necessary to provide for that spice in life. The stress of life can be easily alleviated by the use of art or music, something that interests and titillates the individual. In secondary schools, students are like wet mud; they can be molded with the shapes one likes. Art and music are activities that bring out a softer, mature and a complete person. Without them, life tends to become dull and burdensome.

Students tend to get bored of pedantic learning, and need a break from regular classroom education in the forms of art and music. Providing good facilities to capable students enhances their talents in art and music. Moreover students can
20 develop their inter-personal skills when participating in extra co-curricular activities such as instrument, vocal and painting groups. The sense of honor will encourage them to improve their results on science courses.

Art and music are an integral part of a complete human being. They are one of the essential ingredients of life. So in order to develop students with full personalities, secondary schools should impart art and music knowledge to its students. On the other hand students should not be forced to take up some form of art or music. It should be entirely optional for
25 students to choose whatever forms of art or music that interest them.

It is art and music that differentiate humans from animals. The serenity and tranquility that music and arts provide only human can enjoy.

Topic 125 **Should art and music be compulsory subjects?**

Life cannot be full without understanding and appreciating the greatest culture inheritances from our earlier generations such as arts and music. Secondary school prepares us to enter into college and adult life. Therefore all students should be required to study art and music in secondary schools.

Arts are a part of our life. From antique cave drawings to African tribal crafts, from Indian totem poles to modern buildings, arts are everywhere. Not to mention those art exhibitions in art galleries and museums, which attract hundreds of millions of people to visit them each year. Even our home
35 equipments are made with a touch of art. Arts are ubiquitous.

Music is also an important cultural heritage of human being and remains a part of our present. It is common sense that music can relax our body and soul. For example, by listening to classical music that are played by traditional instruments, while gaining knowledge about the history and stories behind these music, students can really improve their knowledge, cultivate their spirits and broaden their views.

40 Studying arts and music in high school also allow students to take a break between those mentally demanding courses such as math and physics. These arts and music course can even help students improve their results in math and physics, because a good relaxation can help students concentrate more later on.

I am high school student myself and I believe that all students should be required to take arts and music courses during their secondary school years. It is not necessary for students to learn arts in order to become artists; but it is definitely
45 necessary for students to learn to appreciate arts.

Topic 125 **Should art and music be compulsory subjects?**

Art and music are the advanced products of civilizations. They have been developed through thousands of years and accompanied by the progress of science and knowledge. In this sense, some people think that all students should be required to study art and music in secondary school. In my opinion, I totally agree the statement for a number of reasons.

As is so often pointed out that art and music can broaden people's view of the world. The world that we live in is not only a material world, but also a spiritual world. The art and music that belong to the latter can benefit our souls and form our personalities. For instance, a piece of music often can bring us different feelings such as calm, happy, sad or sorrow. I would always like to listen to Tchaikovsky's *Pathetique* when I am in a bad mood; I always feel much better and ready to face challenges again after I hear it. I believe most of us have this kind of experience. Art and music education in high school can enrich students' life, even though they will not make them as a career at a later time.

In addition, the love for art and music can become a good hobby for a person who has this kind of education when
5   he/she is young. Many people have various hobbies that make their life meaningful and they may seldom feel bored during their spare time. Appreciating art and music is a great hobby. Many students acquire the hobby of appreciating art or listening to music after they took courses in art and music in high school.

Last but not least, for some students art and music can help with their career pursuit, because they can get inspirations from art and music to achieve in other fields. For example, the profession of architecture has a strong relationship with art
10 and music. "Buildings are frozen music." We can see that many buildings that were designed by architects were influence by some form of art. On the other hand, Albert Einstein, the Nobel Prize winner and the famous scientist, was also an excellent violinist and he admitted that music could refresh his mind and lead to more effective thinking. Moreover, some students pursue a career in art and music due to their art education in high school. They become artists or singers after they graduate.

15 Maybe we are not aware of it at first, but from the above arguments we could see that art and music education are very important for high school students. It will surely benefit their school life and life after.

Topic 126 Can young people teach older people?

Living at the start of the new millennium, in the most advanced technological era in history, one is confronted with a plethora of knowledge and information which itself continues to become outdated by the moment. While young people possess an ability to learn new concepts and absorb information faster and easier many now products or ideas could be taught to old people if they possessed the desire to learn.

The computer, for old people, has emerged as the first barrier and stigma. With a computer, one can work without paper and pencil, obtain useful searches on the Internet or make online purchases from ones home. However, many older people are not able to do these things since using a computer initially demands a modicum of
25 knowledge and skill. If one has time, there are rewards, however, to teaching our grandparents how to use a computer in order that they could discover the many benefits and pleasure of using a computer.

In addition to new technological products, ideas or concepts that have helped shape young people can be conveyed to old people. Many old people maintain that health, for example, suggests an absence of disease. Yet many of us have realized that the notion of being healthy contains emotional, social and physical health rather than simply living without illness.
30 Such scientific notions could be learned by old people from their children because young people may acquire such new ideas quickly. Why not learn something new from youngsters in order to adjust to a modern lifestyle and become healthier?

There is no doubt that there are many things we should learn from older people such as aspects of traditional culture or some valuable, life-teaching experience. But in modern society it is the young who, at the forefront of the era, possess updated knowledge, positioning old people to learn from those younger.

Topic 126 Can young people teach older people?

To my ear this statement sounds false and a little too fare-fetched. It is truth universally acknowledged that the old people have volumes of experience, while the young have the energy and lots of creative power. Therefore I think that it's not suitable to take sides in this situation. Because in my view there is no way to determine who is better - the old or the young.

Obviously, each of these groups has its own positives and negatives. I suppose they should co-
40 operate and be helpful to one another rather than try to rival. The exchange should be done for their own mutual benefits. Even though the old people possess a great deal of experience, it is sometimes not enough for surviving in the changing modern world. That's why they often get stuck with their dated information, without being able to break free from their own prejudice.

In many cases the old people are used to their old ways and, I imagine, it must be really hard for them to get adjusted to
45 the new environment. But one should always remember that, like it or not, only the fittest survive. Therefore, if the old people don't want to become extinct as dinosaurs did, they should rather learn some ways from the young. The thing is that the young people are way more flexible to all of the little changes happening in their everyday life. It is easier for them to get up-to-date and to face the fact that some old ways are no longer valid. For them it is not a difficult thing to come to terms with. I guess that this is something that could be of some use for the elder people as well. If they have lots
50 of experience to give, the young can teach them lots of flexibility in return.

In fact, I personally think that there are many things that the young can teach older people and flexibility is just one of them. But the problem is sometimes that the old are very unlikely to be willing to accept this kind of searching with their arms wide open. Most of the times they are conservative and prefer to stick to their old ways.

Topic 126 **Can young people teach older people?**

An English proverb goes, "You can't teach an old dog new tricks." With all due respect to this folk wisdom, I have to admit that it sounds somewhat dated to me. At the same time I agree that almost every saying has a grain of truth to it, and this one is no exception. Nor is another one? There is no fool like an old fool. As it can easily be seen, the two sayings contradict each other, which may seem terribly confusing. Nevertheless I would like to pursue the subject at some length and try to find out which one is in the right.

It goes without saying that the old dog has quite a lot of experience. During its lifetime it has learnt a lot of different tricks that now make it feel happy and content with itself. I believe it deserves all kind of respect and admiration, since it has done a pretty good job. But one should always remember that the kind of tricks it has been doing up to now are old-10 fashioned and not up-to-date anymore. There now exists a marvelous opportunity to do all of them over again in a better, more sophisticated way. It is not surprising that a young dog would be way more dexterous in performing those tricks.

Moreover, it can create some innovative, brand-new ways that an old dog has never even dreamed about. Therefore I suppose that the old dog should appreciate this never-ending source of energy and ideas, and maybe even pick up some of them. If the old dogs don't want to be considered off-the-shelf, they should rather be flexible and get with the times. 15 "You are never too old to learn" shrewdly reminds them another popular saying. But still there is no way for the mature dogs to humbly imitate their own puppies. It is advisable for them to share the accumulated knowledge with the young, to be more helpful and willing to co-operate.

At the same time, all of this will be accepted more easily if the old dogs don't try to impose their experience on the young. Then the latter would undoubtedly greet their teachings with their arms wide open. Both the old and the young should 20 never forget that they are living in the same world that belongs equally to the first group as to the second. Even though the modern world is changing all the time, there still are ways to get adjusted to it for both.

All metaphors aside, I guess that the young and the old must be very loyal to each other. They should exchange their experience and whatever else they have to give to each other. To get back to where I started? Nor the first nor the second saying is totally correct. As usual, the truth is somewhere in the middle.

Topic 127 **Reading fiction vs. watching movies**

Watching movies is a much better option compared to reading fiction. So I disagree that reading fiction is more enjoyable than watching movies. In fact movies provide a first hand experience with real emotions. Also movies can be watched with the company of others, thus making for healthy relationships.

Movies are generally much better received compared to novels or short stories. They tend to be much more exciting and 30 surely provide real-time first hand experience. Reading fiction, more often than not, gives only vicarious pleasure.

Also movies are a much better option for real emotions. The scenes, physiognomy of characters and background music all add up to a great experience. Howsoever good a piece of fiction is, it leaves much to be desired. The way movies exhibit a wide gamut of emotions and experiences are difficult to find in fiction books.

Another major reason for movies being more enjoyable is that one can watch movies in company of others. No such 35 sharing is possible in reading fiction. There is nothing like enjoying a movie with the person you love, or your family members, it provides the warmth to make for a pleasurable experience.

In conclusion, I derive much greater fun, joy and excitement from watching movies, than by reading fiction. According to me, movies will always hold the upper hand.

Topic 128 **Physical exercise vs. academic study**

I am surely of the opinion that physical exercise should be a required part of every school day. Even a small session of exercise, but a regular one, can go a long way to give a balanced body. The rest of the school day can take care of academic studies. The common saying 'All work and no play makes John a dull child' holds water here. Also a balanced body allows one to have a balanced mind on top of it. A small part of the day devoted to exercise can take a long way in preventing future health risks. Moreover in the age of fast-food getting rid of the couch potato image is essential for 45 today's young generation.

It can easily be reasoned that students have better concentration if they exercise regularly. The mind runs fresh only if the body supports it. Students always need a break from the daily tedious lectures, and exercise can provide it in the best way.

Another important reason to have daily physical exercise is its long-term benefits. Researchers have shown that daily dose of exercise can greatly reduce the risks of many diseases, especially heart problems. Physical exercise can act as a handy 50 weapon against the rising obesity at school students.

For maintaining good health, one always needs to do physical exercise daily. So why not do it in the discipline of the school? An entire day of academic studies can make life dull for students, and exercise can act as a pleasant escapade.

Topic 129 **Business research vs. agriculture research**

There are two kinds of opinions concerning the plan to develop a research center in our country. One is to develop a business research center and the other, a agriculture research center. Taking consideration of the current situation in China, I strongly recommend the former because it will help to solve the urgent problems in our country.

First of all, a business research center will help to develop the economy. At present, the global economy is slowing down and there is no evidence indicating that the recovery will come any time soon. Our biggest trading partners such as the United States and Japan fall into economic plight. As result, the exportations to those countries and direct investment from them are decreasing. The most important task is how to keep the economy growing healthily. The center will help to complete this task by exploring new business opportunities to
10 increase exporting and helping enterprises adjust themselves.

Secondly, a business research center will help to solve the problem of unemployment. With the reform of state owned enterprises, more and more workers employed by those enterprises lost their jobs. Our economic reform and adjustment is going through a vital stage. A business research center will help the enterprise figure out how to solve this problem and the unemployed people will have a chance to get jobs in new business fields.

15 Finally, it will help to solve China's rural problems. China has a big population, and nearly 70 percent of its population is farmers, namely, 700million farmers in China. Now the rural problem is focused on farmers who have been released from arable lands with the development of new technology can get their jobs. A business research center will help to develop rural economy in the industrial and service fields that can absorb the enormous number of farmers.

Based on the reasons I present above. I believe a business center will play a strong role at present than an agriculture
20 research center does. As result, I support the plan to develop a business research center in our country.

Topic 129 **Business research vs. agricultural research**

It is a well-established fact that science from the very beginning has aimed to serve the community. This has been in the form of taming the nature forces, alleviating some arduous problems, or improving the mundane life in one form or another. My country is a developing one, and is suffering from some economic problems. While agriculture has been the most pervasive hustle since the first Egyptian stepped into the Nile valley, nevertheless, I prefer the business center to be developed and hereinafter I will present and analyze this perspective.

Agriculture is responsible for providing the community with food and supporting some industries. For my country, there is no persistent conflict in providing food. Moreover, no conflict exists regarding the necessary water supply. Not denying that researches in agriculture will produce new generations of crops that consume less water, produce more nourishment,
30 resist diseases, or require fewer pesticides. However, in my perspective, we must provide more jobs to increase the income of families and hence supply them with adequate fund that will motivate the economy wheel. This attitude will result in more purchases and hence the necessity for increasing the agricultural production will arise. But first we must begin with research center that supports the economy.

To support the economy, provide more jobs, and increase the annual income per capita, we must focus on the most
35 lucrative activities. Agriculture is considered within the least profitable activities. While business fortifies all aspects of the economy, business research will improve sales of marketing centers, provide the industry with new ideas based on the requirements of the customers. Moreover, business will assert the economic side of management systems of factories and governmental facilities.

Ultimately, universities should provide the community with more researches and scientific potential in the field that
40 exclusively support the welfare of the community. Keeping this in mind, business centers will be the right choice.

Topic 129 **Business research vs. agricultural research**

Since the announcement of the University's plan to develop a new research center in our country, many people have showed their concern for the project and expressed their views of type of center it should be. It is now clear that the diversified views have converged to two: a business research center or an agriculture research center. Now that
45 we have to make a decision, I think we should choose the latter without hesitation.

As everybody knows, our country is an agricultural country whose farming produce is not enough to feed its own people. We have no way out but to develop our agriculture because agriculture is the foundation of our national economy and because it would be a disaster to the whole world if we rely on foreign food to feed the biggest population in the world.

To develop our agriculture, we cannot just call on the peasants to work harder because they have being working the
50 hardest from generation to generation. What we should do is to raise their educational level and provide them with better seeds, more fertilizers, advanced machinery and equipment, and up-to-date technical advice. In short, we have to rely on science and technology to develop our agriculture.

Some people would say that this couldn't be a convincing reason because science and technology are needed not only in agriculture but also in all other fields. My view is that our situation in agriculture is the most serious and the challenges are the greatest. Ours is a big country with widely different climates and soil conditions. If we are to assist the peasants, we have to study all types of crops and all the farming conditions in this land. With a research center, these problems can be studied and solved systematically. But so far, no agriculture research center worthy of the name has been set up while there is already a business center in the southern part of the country.

5 Because of the above reasons, I strongly recommend that we develop a research center for agriculture purpose and I also strongly recommend this center be well funded. If wee take this step and succeed in this endeavor, our agricultural produce will be greatly increased and our whole national economy will have a solid foundation.

Topic 130 Should children spend much time on sports?

Currently some young children spend a great amount of their time in practicing sports. Most parents feel quite happy because sports are good for their kids' development and team work spirit, however they are quite worried about some negative effects such as practicing sports occupies too much time, distracts their attentions on schoolwork and loses certain interests on other activities. In my opinion, everything has its good side and bad side. The important thing is to handle it properly.

Admittedly, practicing sports can help children's physical development, which makes them grow faster and stronger than
15 before. As we know, during children's development periods, especially from 10 to 16 years old, sports are really helpful for children to develop. Sports can create a strong body that reduces the possibility of contracting some diseases easily. Definitely we believe that children benefit from sports.

Another good thing is that sports teach us to learn how to corporate with other members in a team. Most sports are team work. If we want to play them well, we must master some skills to care about what our team members are thinking and
20 how to adapt each other to achieve a common goal. Sports are not an individual activity, it needs corporation and mutual understanding. This is not easy to master. Of course, for parents they are delightful to see their children to get this skill from sports.

On the other hand, practicing sports seem to occupy too much of children's spare time to concentrate their schoolwork. As a student, one's major task is to study hard and try to learn as much as possible, which needs students to devote much
25 time on study or their spare time. If children devote themselves in practicing sports, it is not denying that they cannot concentrate them on schoolwork at the same time. The consequence of practicing sports too much leads children to distract themselves, which influences their future.

Actually, besides sports, there are still many kinds of activities, such as drawing, collecting, good for their developments. If a child is too concentrated on sports, it is inevitable that he will lack of chances to explore other activities and lose some
30 happiness when engaged in different experiences.

Overall, on one hand, we should encourage our children to participate in sports activities; on the other hand, we must also remind them not to be too engaged because they should put study at the first place during their school time. There is a limit of doing everything.

Topic 131 Money and success

The notion of success holds different meanings for different people and groups. Such meanings have changed and evolved over time. Actually, many propose that possessing an abundance of money implies success. However, this view is rendered obsolete in the minds of those individuals who hold that one's success cannot be measured strictly by money.

Material possession has been traditionally accepted as the measurement of one's success or social status. When we initially refer to someone, we routinely mention how much money he owns and thereby believe this individual to be quite
40 successful if he is wealthy. In addition to this perpetuated concept, owning a lot of money is typically related to one's work ability and thus some people may simply consider money as a prime measurement of one's success.

However, this view has changed recently since many people have come to recognize that money in many cases cannot bring about happiness, health and success. A more precise, contemporaneous definition of success means doing the things one perceives are valuable to themselves and beneficial for others. The winner of the Nobel Prize for peace may think he
45 is has achieved success although he is rewarded little financial benefit. A person who loves animals and makes an effort to save animals that are on a path of extinction may think he has gained success although he may have expended all of his money on his career.

Another individual may define success as being able to make artistic masterpieces that can be accepted by public. As a composer, success is having his work praised by adoring fans and who help cause the work to be bought the world over.
50 Similarly, holding an exhibition in a famous art gallery may connote success for a painter.

People adhere to various concepts defining success. Money surely cannot be the only measurement of success. Acquiring true happiness in life and attaining success means having the freedom and capability of doing that which you enjoy and believing it to be valuable.

Topic 131 **Money and success**

Since people's criteria for success differ, there is much debate over whether only those who make a lot of money are successful. As far as I am concerned, in today's society that stresses on individual achievement, money provides the best evaluation of one's accomplishment.

To begin with, as a standardized measurement used for comparing values, money is objective rather than subjective, so it is considered an authentic reflection of one's achievement. As different people hold different understandings of success, assessing the amount of one's earnings has become universally accepted as a rule to measure one's success. Each year, Fortune Magazine publishes a special issue to rank the top 100 most successful people throughout the world according to their yearly income, because there are no other methods to rely on.

In addition, the amount of money one makes is the consequence of one's hard work and talent. To deny the accomplishment wealth brings is equal to deny the sources from which it springs. In the past, I only believed in spiritual values and then leapt rashly to the conclusion that the best thing in life involves no money at all. It is my uncle who showed me the significance of money and changed my opinion. He told me he respected money and made it a goal to strive for in his way towards success. Because he would have to pay a price for it in terms of time, thought and energy. Gradually, I came to realize it is the mental and physical labor he devotes in the process of making money that paves his way for self-accomplishment, and thus deserves appreciation and respect.

Finally, money is the most powerful possession in one's lifetime. As everyone knows, success is the ability to do whatever one wants to and to be satisfied with oneself. There is hardly anything that can be done without a certain amount of money. Indeed, with money, one can meet his or her material demand in life, such as taking effective medicines, living in magnificent houses, eating various delicious food, and so on. Also, with money, one can do a lot of meaningful things to benefit others, such as donations to poor people. All these will not only satisfy one's need for personal fulfillment, but also add grandness to one's success.

In conclusion, money serves as a measurement of one's achievement. But we should keep in mind that only those who obtain money by hardworking and use it to benefit the society are really successful.

Topic 132 **What new product would you develop?**

I live in a place where the environment is being degraded alarmingly and the desert is expanding rapidly. Subsequently, the people around here are suffering a lot from this vicious environmental vicissitude. So to change the current situation is a great challenge for the people living here. I believe to invent an electronic plant grower is significant to curb the environmental degradation.

Firstly, weather condition is too severe to grow any plants here. It is not efficient for us to afforest in such a vast area either. Furthermore, if the plants could not get the basic supplies like water, amicable weather conditions, it is almost impossible for plants to survive. The invention of electronic plant grower could be scientific enough, when it plants grass or trees, it will automatically put solid ice and other trace elements which could enhance the viability of plants. Thus, the newly planted plants could easily survive in it.

Secondly, the electronic plant grower could do a lot of onerous works in the field and tolerate unfavorable weather. It can extend to the most remote place to work where there are no residents at all, but could build up effective protection barrier to mitigate sandstorm. Furthermore, the electronic plant growers consume no water, which is precious resource in the desert. They can work day and night and take full time of planting season to plant as much as plants.

Thirdly, to afforest in such a vast and tough area, it needs numerous manpower for planting in short season and taking care of the plants. As an advanced robot, the invented electronic plant growers could reduce the pressure of manpower and keep the live human away from the life limit area.

To rehabilitate the environment is important more than anything else here, but the environmental rehabilitation could not do without some high-tech duplicate of human being like electronic plant grower. So I expect its birth with great hope.

Topic 132 **What new product would you develop?**

In most countries, people have to spend a lot of time learning a second language while at school. However, there're hundreds of different languages in the world, no one can learn them all. One of the most famous philosophers, Marx could speak more than ten different languages, which is already extraordinary for human beings. The difference between languages is a great handicap of communication between people from countries all over the world. A group of people planned to make a global language and ask everybody to learn, but finally the plan failed. Now there is a great need for an invention that can solve this problem.

If I could invent something new, I would develop an electronic translator. Unlike electronic dictionary, which can just translate a word into different languages, it can also translate a whole paragraph even a whole book into different languages. What's more, it can even translate the language you speak orally into other languages. For example, when you speak " Hello" in English, it will say "Nihau" in Chinese automatically when you switch it to Chinese.

It's obvious that this kind of invention is needed, and when it's invented, I believe it will spread out to everywhere in the world immediately. Then people will not have to waste a lot of time to learn foreign languages, and the communication between people from different countries will become much easier. Moreover, it will enhance the speed of globalization, which benefits everybody in the world.

5   For it to be invented, there's still a long way to go. But the science and technology is developing and more and more new things have been invented. In the future, the electronic translator will be invented, and it will bring people more convenience.

Topic 132 **What new product would you develop?**	People will normally invent something that they want very much in the real life if they had the ability. As a father of a two-year-old boy, I would make a baby sitter robot. The reasons are as follows.

In the first place, a baby-sitter robot can take care of my baby when I go to work. There will be a dilemma in front of parents when they have a child, who should stay at home and who should continue to work, mother or father? With a baby-sitter robot, they do not need to make a choice. Parents will no longer give up their jobs because of their child.

15 In the second place, a baby-sitter robot can make my baby stay away from danger. A person cannot concentrate on one thing 24 hours a day. It will be dangerous when he/she is taking care of a baby. A baby is so unpredictable that you never know what he/she will do in the next minute. For instance, the baby may swallow a coin or fall to the ground from the bed when you just do not look at him/her for a second.

However, a robot does not have such a problem because she is never tired. She can keep an eye on the baby all the time. Any potential dangerous action will be prevented. Even when the baby is sleeping, the robot can still watch the baby if 20 you want. In addition, a baby-sitter robot can entertain the baby. Songs and stories can be inputted in the robot's memory and replayed whenever the baby needs them. It is so easy to change them that the baby will never be bored on one song or story.

In conclusion, I would like to invent a baby-sitter robot not only because it can take care of my baby for me, but also because it can make my baby safe and happy.

Topic 133 **Are childhood years most important in one's life?**	It is about time somebody exploded that holy old myth about childhood being the most important years of our life. Childhood may certainly be important, but if we compared it with other period if life such as adolescence, I do not see any more importance.
	First of all, parents are absolutely dictators. Children do not have options, or if they do, nobody notices. Think of the years when you are a child. Who ever asked you an option? I

30 have no such experience, to say the least. Parents choose the clothes we wear, the books we read and even the friends we play with. We have to manipulate so as not to interfere too seriously with the lives of our elders.

Even so, it is only part of the reason. We have vague memory of most parts of our childhood. Many of the things we learnt, the happy hours we spent and troubles we suffered have no trace in our mind at all. Do you still remember every 35 quarrel you had with your little friends? Do you clearly remember every trip you had with your parents or other children? Most of you may probably say nay, I think.

However, we may learn a lot when we are children. All these may contain what we think of as the most important thing, but we are passive to learn them. Without independence, how can we say childhood is most important period of our life? So, as I see it, childhood is certainly not the moors important years of a person's life.

Topic 133 **Childhood years**	A person's childhood years are indeed the most important years of his life and I agree with this statement.
	The initial years of childhood are the time when a person learns a lot about himself and

his family and the society. A child's mind is impressionable and he imbibes values and behavior that he gets to see around him. So the role of his family and school is of utmost importance.

45 It has been seen that children who get the love and support of their parents and teachers in their childhood turn out be mature and emotionally balanced teenagers and adults. On the other hand, if we look at the childhood of criminals and other anti social elements, we will find that most of them have been through tough times as children. They were deprived of proper care and upbringing. Delinquents also have a history of abuse in their childhood many a times.

Children are always inquisitive and willing to learn. So if they are provided a stimulating environment in which they can 50 develop their talents and learn to enjoy their work, they become good citizens who are an asset to the nation. Family is the most important institution in a child's formative years because parents are role models for their children. Children develop their ethics, moral values and temperament in tune with what they see in their parents and elder siblings. The type of personality that a child develops is difficult to change later.

So I firmly believe that childhood is a vital part of a person's life that plays an important role in shaping his future.

Topic 134 Should children be required with household tasks?

When children grow up old enough to be able to help with some household tasks, some parents do insist that their children should take those kind of family works as early as they can, I do not think there is any in properties about the parents' conclusion.

As a complex activity for children, household tasks will do them good, both physically and mentally. When children are about the age of 4 or 5, some simple tasks such as wiping the kitchen floor or cleaning their own dishes after supper will urge them to balance their using of their forearms and wrists, fingers, and develop their brain power to control all those cooperating activity of arm muscles and their whole nerve system. When they grow up a little more, maybe parents could teach them to operate on washing machines or to use microwave-ovens, that kind of activity can make them learn the basic principles of auto machines, which no doubt will make them to face the outer world in a brand new way.

Helping in family works also can take children into more active communication with their families. When parents first teach children to use simple tools, children will learn how to understand the instructions clearly, and they may learn to communicate with other kids taking the same assignment to solve their own problems. So, family work is not just a kind of work assignment for children, it is more like a kind of learning process, they can learn not only how to finish those assignments but also learn how to communicate with each other.

After finishing those household works assigned to them, kids always get compliments from their family, this will encourage them to try different things in a more creative manner at home or at school the other day.

In a word, I think it is very beneficial for children to take the household tasks as early as they can, that will make them more active, more intelligent in communication and more happy in living with their families in harmony.

Topic 134 Should children be required with household tasks?

Should children be required to help with household tasks as soon as they are able to do so? People have different opinions. Some people think that parents can do all the household tasks without children's help, children are still too young to do house work and sometimes they even make things worse. Other people, however, argue that it is very useful for children to take part in the household work. As far as I am concerned, I agree with the second opinion.

In the first place, children may have the sense of contribution when they take part in household tasks. After a child was born, the parents are always the part that gives, such as feeding, changing clothes, and bathing the baby. Others help children because they are too young to do these tasks. When they grow up, they will gradually have the ability to do something, such as washing clothes for themselves, cleaning the room for themselves. If they are required to do what they can do, after finishing their jobs and looking at the result of their jobs, such the clean clothes and the clean room, children will have a strong sense of contribution and success, which will help them form a good personal character.

In the second place, participating the household tasks will teach children how to cooperate with other people. For instance, When doing a house cleaning, one person cannot finish it all by oneself. Different tasks should be divided among several people. For example, dad cleans the windows, mom cleans the kitchen, boys clean the floor and girls decorate the wall. Gradually, children will get to know that they need to cooperate with others to make things done better and faster.

In conclusion, I believe that it is very helpful for children to take part in household tasks not only because children can have the sense of contribution and success, but also because children can learn how to cooperate with others.

Topic 135 Should high school students wear uniforms?

I hate uniforms! It makes all the students look the same. When I am trying to find my friend from a group of student, I always make mistake because I cannot tell the difference among the girls who are all wearing the same clothes. Moreover, I am always nervous about my uniforms since I may not have another one to change into. The other one is still waiting to be washed or is still wet. After P. E., you cannot identify which coat is mine, so I just take one that looks like it. I am sure the coat I am wearing now is not the one I had first. That is my life with uniforms.

Because everyone is against it, my school revoked this rule. Then, we could wear everything we want to. But new problems came up. Everyone began to buy new, brand name, expensive clothes and the campus because a big stage in no time. At last, the uniforms came back to our lives.

Undoubtedly, everyone has the freedom to choose what to wear and, of course, everyone wants to make himself/herself good-looking. But when we are just students, study is our first important thing to do. Paying too much attention to attire can influence our study. Furthermore, we may spend too much money that is not earned by ourselves but come from our parents' hard working.

The reasons above cause more and more schools make a rule to forbid trendy dresses or make students wear uniforms. It is not a good way but an effective way to solve these problems.

If we want to get rid of uniforms forever, we must solve these problems by ourselves instead of the schools rule. We should earn school's trust by our behavior, then we can thoroughly say goodbye to uniforms!

Topic 135 **Should high school students wear uniforms?**

When asked about what to wear to school-uniforms or not, some people hold the opinion that to wear school uniforms is better than to wear other clothes one want to in many ways. Others, however, stand a very different ground. Personally, I prefer to wear school uniforms because it has more advantages.

There are numerous reasons for me to believe to wear uniforms are better and I would in here explain few important ones. The main reason is that to wear school uniforms can make the students more concentrate on study. It can be given a concrete example that students go to a school that requires them

10   wear their uniforms will surely have less trouble in picking clothes to wear every morning. And they will not pay their attention to the clothes others wear; this means they can be more concentrated on the study.

Another reason why I advocate the attitude of that wearing uniforms is better lies in the fact that the uniforms is specially designed for the students. I believe it suits for them very much and can do well to the students at school. On the contrary, some of the students do not know what is good for them, and will choose some clothes that do not suit them or even do

15   harm to them. All these demonstrate the undeniable fact that to wear uniforms at school is better.

Of course, choosing to decide what to wear to school also have advantages to some extend, this enable the students to develop the habit of making choice all by themselves, that is to make decision themselves. If all the factors are completed, the advantages of wearing uniforms carry more weight than that of not. From what we have discussed above, we may safely draw the conclusion that wearing uniform at school is better.

Topic 135 **Should high school students wear uniforms?**

My high schools required us a few years ago to wear school uniforms. Somehow this requirement is not mandatory anymore, therefore only a couple of students have decided to wear the uniform from time to time. Other high schools in my town never required such things as a uniform, so the decision of the principal brought a lot of contradictory discussions.

In my opinion, the fact that this requirement did not last is a confirmation of the fact that it

25   was not a good idea. First of all, I consider that what we wear expresses our personality. Our clothes tell a lot about the type of person we are, so an outfit established by others means a denial of expressing ourselves. It is also true that we cannot wear at school fancy clothes, like when we go out with our friends, for example. But even if some of us decide to wear extravagant clothes, I think this issue concerns only them. They establish an image of themselves and therefore they will be regarded as they wish to be regarded.

30   Teachers told us that we should be proud to wear the high school uniform when people recognize us on the streets, saying that we belong to the best high school in town. We were not exactly regarded as eminent students, especially by our colleagues from other schools. I believe that the way in which we behave and the way we think shows better what kind of an education we have than the fact that we are wearing gray clothes, which we do not even like. The schoolyard looked so strange when we were coming out from classes. All of us in dark uniforms, as if we were alike. We were not, and we

35   should also show that to people surrounding us.

It's my belief that requiring high school uniforms is an unnecessary thing. A prestigious high school is not a high school who likes to show off with its students, but one who lets the students express themselves freely.

Topic 135 **Should high school students wear uniforms?**

It is a confusing question to decide whether to wear regulative school uniforms or not. As far as I am concerned, although school uniforms will not make everyone satisfied, the advantages of wearing school uniforms outnumber those of the opposite views.

The first and the most important function of school uniforms is let young students focus on studying, not diverting to compete with other classmates' clothes. If school uniforms do not exist, being easily impressible, children will pay much attention to what their friends and stars on TV wear to show fashionable, fancy and stylistic pattern. It is reasonable to make the young people wear uniform to

45   prevent them from diversion of studying.

Furthermore, school uniforms save money for students' parents. Because of love, they hardly refuse to buy new clothes for their children even though they really do not need yet. The young consider little about money and have small resistance to the temptations of the fashionable T-shirts and jeans, and their parents usually spoil their children. So school uniforms can help students learn frugality, plainness and neatness are much more worthy than fashion.

50   The last but not the least reason for school uniform is to strength the spirits of students' organization and the obeying of regulations. That moral practice will benefit them to the preparation for future occupation and experience.

In short, school uniforms are in use of students' study distraction, frugality, and moral benefits. We can safely draw the conclusion that school uniforms are valuably recommended.

Topic 136 **Is winning the most important aspect of playing a game?**

To my way of thinking all the humanity is bit by bit losing the very important strain of enjoying life as a process not only gaining any profit. As it is happening with all life throughout, then it concerns the playing games as well. Of course some kind of award, at least wining, is very important to gain sense of complacence and self-confidence, but it should not be the main purpose of playing games. Therefore I strongly disagree with the opinion that playing game is fun only when you win. Here go my reasons:

First of all, the main purpose of the game is to enjoy the game as the process and through this process to communicate with other players you are playing with. This is extremely important both when you are keep playing with your family members, and with your friends. If playing with our family and friends were fun for us only when won, it would loose its main purpose of bringing joy of communicating with other people through the game; be it more serious games, for example Chess, or simple games with the ball. Therefore it is very important to teach people this kind of playing from early childhood.

Secondly, there exist games, especially popular in the western world, serious sport competitions, as basketball, tennis or football. In this case playing game brings joy only when it ends by winning, for they are supported by terms of money and recognition. Then, I think, games gain a strained meaning, because sometimes they more look like war actions, rather than competitive games. In this case is very important not to loose the human proprieties and game may be fascinating as well.

At the end I would say, that it is very important for people of different ages to learn to gain fun and joy from games without winning, just communicating and getting more acknowledge with other people through the game. Because, to my way of thinking, that is the main purpose of the game.

Topic 136 **Is winning the most important aspect of playing a game?**

The statement in the direction is a long-term consideration of many people including me. Many people will argue that playing a game is only fun when you win. I, however, after thinking about it on many occasions, decide to stand up against this view for the following reasons.

The first and the most important reason for my opposing the idea is that playing a game, no matter you win or lose, helps release a person from the heavy pressure, in most cases, resulted from intellectual activities. There is no better example than myself when I was trying so hard to enter the university. At that time, when I was too exhausted to memorize any single incident in the history book, a play of badminton would refill me with fresh energy to go back to my studies, though I hardly won any of these badminton games as my partner is an excellent player. Therefore, the biggest advantage of playing games lies in the fact that it helps people relaxed.

Another reason for my disagreement is that one will find out his or her capacity of making progress while playing a game. When learning a new game, if your opponent is a more mature player than you are, it is for sure that you will not win him or her at the beginning, but in the process of the game, if you are a conscientious player, you will definitely learn to grasp the basic skills of a certain game, which enable you to play better and better. Consequently, the awareness of your ability in learning new things is the best award you can find in game playing.

Therefore, I will conclude by saying that playing a game itself is worthwhile and to win or not to win is not a matter to concern since you could get rid of the feeling of exhaustion and confirm your confidence as a learning-capable being.

Topic 136 **Is winning the most important aspect of playing a game?**

Recently, many people argue as if it is a general truth that playing a game is fun only when you win. In various games and matches, the main aim of players from both sides seems to be winning. And winning is not only for the players themselves, but also for the honor of their team, and even for that of their nation. But to be frankly, I cannot agree with them. There are numerous reasons, and I would explore only a few primary ones here.

The main problem with this argument is that the real meaning of a game is to enjoy the process of the game; the result, whether it is win or lose, does not seem matter. Think of the original games of our ancestors, the goal is to show their love of sports, their physical strength and celebrating the hunting. And the true intention of their game is for relaxation and amusement. Another good example is that children enjoy playing games more than adults. When we watch children play, we can understand that they are more concentrate on the game itself, and do not care for the result. There are to young to realize the importance of winning the game, therefore they enjoy it more.

If the players play a game for winning, they will concentrate on scores too much, and forget to enjoy the game. In this society, everyone want to be winner, for they will not only win the honor, but also win fame, money, and so on. In the same way, the loser will lose everything. It seemed that playing a game become a way to get material comfort, but not fulfillment of spirit.

Furthermore, when players play a game for winning, they face the stress from the team, even for the nation, and they struggle to win. Sometimes, players do everything by fair means or foul in order to win. They may use illegal drugs, or bribe the judges. There are various scandals about athlete almost in every international game, and this thing become more and more serious. These are all because the results of games have been linked to money and the honor of a country.

General speaking, when you only want to win, you will lose the fun of playing a game. Taking into account of all these factors, we may reach the conclusion that, it is wiser to learn to enjoy playing without regard of the result of game.

Topic 137 **Should high schools allow students to choose subjects?**

There are lots of debates among parents, educators and students on the issue of whether or not to allow students to study the courses that students want to study. It seems to be reasonable to many people that allowing students to choose the course they want can inspire their learning interest and find their talents on certain subjects and pursue further development. But if we take a deeper consideration, it is not difficult to make the judgment that to ensure the students have a comprehensive knowledge domain is the main objective of high school education, therefore I disagree with the idea of allowing students to study any courses that they want to study.

10 As we all know, the main purpose of school education is to provide a systematic education to all students. In order to let students be educated in all aspects, the curriculums have to be researched and predefined by professional education institute. If we allow students to select course, we cannot guarantee all necessary courses to be covered in the regular class time. Moreover, both parents and educators believe that high school education shall provide each student a fundamental knowledge base that is essential to their future development in the society. It is the school's responsibility to enforce the
15 rule and make sure that all the necessary knowledge is to be taught.

On the other hand, we may consider introducing some optional courses to the high school curriculums so the students can choose some of the courses within the limitation of a big syllabus. For example, for an art classes, the school can offer music and painting courses and each student can choose either one of them according to his or her personal interest. But this is not to say that the students should have the freedom to choose any course.

20 In conclusion, high school education is a standardized process in which major courses shall be predefined and we need to make sure students are educated in all necessary fields and build a foundation for the development after high school.

Topic 138 **Member vs. leader**

I agree with the statement that being a member of a group is far better than being leader of the same due to that an individual can adapt certain qualities. Major among them are compromising abilities, sincerity and doing work perfectly free from external pressures.

25 Firstly being a member of a team acquires the ability to compromise and to cooperate with other members. Both of which are very helpful for an individual to cope with future life and to develop strong characters. Teamwork by itself increases social skills and develops friendly attitude among teammates. Every member freely mingles with each other and shares his responsibility in times of need. For example if a co-worker falls sick, he is taken good care and other members will share upon his duty.

30 Secondly comes sincerity, a member in team is always under strict control and supervision of the leader. As a result of which he is very careful not to make mistakes and performs his tasks accurately and attentively. For example, if a member in the group has to come to work at 9. 00am, he comes there well before time and never gives chance to anyone to comment that he arrived late.

Finally comes the quality of work that is always done perfectly by a member because he is free from external pressures,
35 unlike his team leader. Neither he need to worry about the outcome nor take the headaches of any failures in the future. So he does his best in doing work with complete satisfaction without worrying about the results. For example, many higher authorities and pressures of outcome of the game influence a captain in a baseball team. In doing so he may not perform up to the mark and may lose his concentration at the playground. On the other hand an ordinary player has no tensions and pressures and mostly he becomes the main person to win the game.

40 In order to build a strong character by acquiring qualities like compromising, sincerity, and doing work perfectly with free mind it is better to be a member in a group rather leading it.

Topic 138 **Member vs. leader**

According to my opinion, it is always better to be a leader than a follower. True leader show initiative. They take actions and they assume responsibilities. A leader makes a decision. Some followers may approve of the decision, others may complain about it. However, these
45 followers all chose to follow, not to lead. They chose not to make a decision. That's how I am different. I am not a follower. I want to make decisions.

A good leader will not react to events, but will anticipate them. A leader will start a plan of action and then will persuade others to follow. For example, a class president at a local college may feel that the relationship between the community and the campus is not a good one. The citizens may feel that the college kids make too much noise on the street, litter public
50 areas, and shop in other communities. A good class president will recognize that the community and the campus depend on one another. The president will ask the student body to keep noise down, help clean up the neighborhood, and work with businesses to attract students. A good leader takes the initiative.

Good leaders must be action-oriented. Having taken the initiative, they must see the job though. They have to take charge and lead the followers. They have to motivate and encourage the followers. The followers (in this example, the student body) must understand why good relations with the community are necessary. The followers must be persuaded to do something about it.

I enjoy taking the initiative, determining the direction, and being responsible for my actions. I do not want to suffer through other people's stupid decisions. If there are going to be stupid ways to do something, let them be mine. Would

5 not you agree?

Topic 138 **Member vs. leader**

One of the most frequently confronted situations of modern life is to be included in a group as a member or to strive for the leadership of a group. A member will have to follow the leader's order, an argument goes, but he will feel less pressure, thanks to fewer responsibilities.
I'm afraid I can hardly agree with this argument as far as it goes. For me, two advantages of the leadership stand out with

10 great force.

Firstly, common senses lead us to the conclusion: a leader is the core of a group or an organization and has the supreme power in it. Winner of the competitive elections, a leader meanwhile wins the authority of dealing with the affairs within the group in his own way. Generally speaking, everyone will hope that his personal point of views can be adopted to solve certain problems. When it comes to members of a group, they may feel free to propose an extraordinary variety of

15 suggestions. No matter how proper they may be, it depends on the leader to turn them into final decisions or just to deny it. A CEO, the head of a company, for example. No subordinate dare start a project or invest in a program without his permission. In contrast, the CEO will take risks in an unpredictable deal, providing he considers it worthwhile. Obviously, whether a leader or not would make a difference.

And secondly, a leader can make the best of his position to have his working abilities and social skills developed. Just recall

20 our personal experiences, which will support my statement about the second advantage, a more important one. As we grow from children into teenagers, we are proud of organizing a football match or being the key figure of a game; as we leave adolescence behind and enter adult life, we are eager to play a vital role in campus activities or clubs. But why? The very reason is that we believe it wonderful opportunity to prepare ourselves for future careers by communicating with the people in and out of the group and conquering the difficulties facing the group. And so is the fact. An example is my

25 uncle's success as a businessman. Enthusiastic about being the leader of any group he joined, say, monitor of his class, he was always more self-confident than his peers and his outstanding abilities in management won him good reputations.

I think that such a closer look at the subtle advantages of being a leader offers some startling surprises to those advocates of being a member of a group. Why do you still confine your attention to the temporary relaxed feeling of a member? Why not seek for the benefit in the long run as a leader? Please join us, and another prominent leader will probably come

30 into being among us.

Topic 138 **Member vs. leader**

Both a leader and members play crucial roles in a team. However, being a leader asks for much more talent and special ability in dealing with challenges and different types of people. The truth is that very few people have these qualities. Therefore, I think for majority of people, being a member is better, for that would be the position where one can make the most contribution and make one's life

35 worthwhile.

First of all, being a member does not mean being less significant in the success of a task. Often enough, people are amazed by the glory of a successful leader, who has to bear the extra pressure, responsibility and risks to achieve the supreme statue and to gain the power of authority. However, people overlook the vital contributions made by the group members and think them as less important. They also forget about the fact that the main body of a group is made up by

40 members who is the main driveling force that makes plans into reality. A captain of a ship is the leader who needs to give instruction on how he wants the ship to be driven. All other cruise members need to do their jobs well to ensure that the ship go into the right direction at suitable speed. Unlike most of the people would have argued that members just simply follow what have been told, I think members also have to think. It is only that they have to think specifically in the area of their job instead of think globally. Most people will work the best with a specific goal in the particular area that they are

45 most familiar with.

Secondly, being a member gain no less sense of satisfaction than being a leader. This, of course, depends a lot on one's perspective of success. In my point of view, success means being able to make the best of one's ability and to have achieved the self-motivated goal. Being a member makes no less chance to be successful. In fact, most people will perform better in this less stressful state, compared to the highly pressured nature of a leader's work. Knowing that his

50 accomplishment of the assigned task contribute to the overall success of the group, and the vital role he has played in supporting other members and the leader, one can appreciate the fruit of success.

Last but not least, being a member means more involvement with the actual process of the work and naturally leads to closer bond with other colleagues. Usually, after working closely together after a period of time in a project, a mutual understanding naturally develops between the members. This would take a leader great effort and maybe a long time to be

55 regarded as member of the party. There is famous Chinese traditional saying that goes, "one cannot stand the cold for being up there." It is a well reflection of the loneliness to be a leader. On the other hand, one can be embedded in a family

of coordinators who understand each other well and easily help and support each other.

All in all, besides the common opinion about more free time and more leisure lifestyle of being a member instead of leader, I think the above three points are strong enough to show that it is better to be a member for most of the people.

Topic 139 What is the most important room in a house?

Every room in a house plays a special role in our life. The living room mainly provides people with a place of entertainment, the dining room a place of having dinner, the storeroom a place of storing sundries, the study room the place of studying, and the bedroom a place of sleeping. In my opinion, among all these rooms, the bedroom is the most important room in a house. This point of view is based on the following reasons.

First of all, people commonly spend most of their life in bedrooms. Normal people spend 7-9
10 hours in the bedroom that is about one thirds of a whole day. If people pay enough attention to their bedroom, they will actually make most of their lifetime better. For example, if people have fresh air in their bedroom, that means they breathe fresh air in one third of their lifetime. As for other rooms, since people don not have to stay such a long time, their important are much less.

Secondly, bedrooms provide people a really private space. Different people have different tastes. In this private space,
15 people can assign the environment as their will. They can decide the color of the wall, the arrangement of the furniture and the little decoration in their own bedrooms. Furthermore, if they want to be completely alone for thinking independently or just for quiet, staying in their own bedroom will be the best choice. This is another reason why a bedroom is the most important room of a house.

Lastly, good bedrooms can always help people have a good sleep which can make people recover from the tire gained
20 from the daily work and well prepared for the following day. Suppose having not slept well for several days, people will be slow both in their thinking and action and they will even feel ill. On the contrary, with a good sleep, people will have a good mood and good energy. In the daytime, they will act effectively and they will probably do a good job. Thus their confidence will be increased. Therefore, bedrooms are the most important for it has big connection with the quality of the other time of people.

25 In conclusion, if you want to make most of your life time better, if you want to enjoy a really private space and if you want to get best prepared for the following days, give enough attention to your bedrooms. Bedrooms provide us the basic factors in our life. Therefore the bedroom is the most important one in a house.

Topic 139 What is the most important room in a house?

What do I consider the most important room in the house? Why is this room more important to me than any other rooms? As the questions pops up before me, so do the images of the various rooms in my house. I think that I consider the dining room to be the most important room of the house.

First of all, this is the room where all the members of the family sit down together, at least for dinner. This brings closeness among the various members of the family. It also gives each of the members an opportunity to relate his/her experiences during the day and share those of others. It is here where
35 tensions die down when mother cracks a joke or dad relates a humorous incident of his job.

Secondly, this is where we feed and nourish ourselves. It serves as a point where you stop, even for a minute(like morning rush hours),and grab your bread and milk. The dining room serves as a showroom of the kitchen bringing the not-so-good looking vegetables appear mouth-watering. This is where you take your food normally.

Thirdly it is the room to which you turn too when a large number of relatives arrive. Set up some more chairs and you are
40 ready to take care of all of them. Can you do this in the bedroom or the bedroom? Some will suggest outdoors as an alternative but do all people have the luxury of a lawn? And what if it's raining? Turn to the dinning room!

In concluding, I would like to say that the dining room seems to be the most important of all rooms in the house. It is a nourishment point, an expansion unit and a family hub, all combined into one. I consider it as the server of the modern home, networking all aspects into one entity.

Topic 140 Hand vs. machine

From my point of view, there are many factors affecting whether to choose an item made by hand or by machine. The main factor to make a judgment is whether we use the item for our daily life or for collection and decoration purposes.

For items used in our daily life, the choices we make depend on the following factors: function, form, and price. Function is the most important thing for us. If a product is beautiful, but it is not able to perform the function, it can only be called
50 a decoration, or a piece of garbage. For example, when we buy a TV, what we really care about first it is the quality of the picture and sound, how many stations it can receive, and whether it can be connected easily to the VCR and DVD player at home. The second factor that affects our choice of a product for daily use is its form. Is the TV too big, too small, or too ugly? Will it fit into the living room? Will it be compatible with the colors of other appliances and the furniture? The

third factor we may consider is the price. Even if we are very happy with the item, there is no meaning if we cannot afford it.

So, in our daily life, there is really no difference whether our clothes or furniture are made by hand or made by machine. It just doesn't matter as long as they can perform their function. For items for collection and decoration, it is a completely
5 different story. Ancient tools and historical artifacts have more market and educational value than modern day massively produced products, and traditional handicrafts make good tourist souvenirs and beautiful decoration for the house. Therefore, when it comes to items for collection and decoration, I would definitely choose items made by hand, because they are just so special.

In conclusion, depending on different items and different uses, I will make different choices.

Topic 140 **Hand vs. machine**

Although products such as furniture or clothes made by hand are detailed and unique pieces, I consider that is better to buy items made by machines. The main reasons to do that are, price, and warranty, as well as standardized methods to manufacture them.

The more automatic a production line, the lower the cost. When we buy a made-by-hand pure wool suit, we are buying a product with both more quality and more suited for our specific needs. Nevertheless, such kind of suit is often quite
15 expensive than a suit made in an automated manufacturing process. The same increase of price takes place with shoes, cars, sweaters, toys, or any other item built on a customized basis.

Another reason for me to choose an item generated by machines is the standard. I know when a buy a car from Ford Motor Company, that the parts of its engine compliant the requirements of Ford, and have less risk of failures caused by manufacturing mistakes. This is possible because most of the production phases were completed by machines such as
20 assembling robots, sensors, and computers. On the other hand, a Rolls Royce car, despite the fact I do not have the money to buy one, is made by hand, and such piece of detailed and beautiful work probably might have little manufacture defects that automation avoids.

Finally, because of the standardized methods used to manufacture some item, producers can offer more extended warranties to their products. A three hundred dollars watch probably can work properly for over ten years, and the
25 producer can offer a warranty longer than would offer a famous watch producer from Switzerland who makes all of his watches by hand.

Technology has extremely benefited our contemporary society. The use of machines on production processes increase quality, decrease prices, and continuously provides improvements to every product in the market. For that reason, I think that items made by machine are the best for me.

Topic 140 **Hand vs. machine**

There are many items that are either made by hand or by machine. For example, clothes are made both by hand and machine. My preference would be machine made clothing because the most merchants would carry it for sale during certain seasons and it is not as expensive. There may be one or two disadvantages to the clothes made by machine; however, I believe that there are for more advantages. The reasons for my view go as follows.

35 One of the minor disadvantages of a machine-made clothing is its quality. For instance, I would often purchase my clothing that is imported from Hong Kong or Korea, which has better quality than that made of my own country. In general, machine-made clothes are produced in large quantities according to season. When the season changes, another line of fashion will be on its way out for sale. Consequently, many businesses would not use higher-quality materials to produce its' line of clothing.

40 The main disadvantage of a machine-made clothing is the quality of the materials being used. But the advantages far out weight hand made clothing because clothes made by machines are produced faster. Due to the quicker production; people can have access to the latest styles and colors. For instance, swimsuits, pants, shirts, tops, etc... have different types of styles, colors, and cuts. Due to the seasonal trends, majority of the people does not worry about the quality of the clothes.

The second advantage of machine-made clothes is the price. Because these clothes are produced in larger numbers and
45 the quality is lower, the pricing will also be lower than hand made clothes. Due to the mass production of machine-made clothes, merchants will be able to purchase a certain line of fashion in larger quantities. With larger quantities of same fashion around, the prices will also be cheaper. This will be a positive situation for the consumers, whom would like to spend as little as they can, but still wants to remain in fashion.)

Although I agree that there is a disadvantage to machine-made clothes, I feel that the advantages are more important.
50 Machine-made clothes can bring the latest fashions from Japan and certain western countries. In addition, the price is lower. Therefore, in my opinion, these advantages play an important role in the consumers' decision to purchase clothes.

Topic 141 **Change about your school**

Talking of making an important change in my school, I'd like to suggest that our education system put more emphasis on the development of learning skills and applications of theories into practice instead of simply learning knowledge from books. The proposal is based on the reasons as follows.

For one thing, overemphasis on academic learning poses a threat because of confusing the purpose of learning. As school credit is usually considered the major criteria of academic learning, in a credit-driven school, one may try hard to learn simply for learning's sake. In other words, college students tend to blindly cram their brains with numerous texts and
5   formulas while do not have a clear idea of what they really want to learn, why they need to learn, not to mention how the things they are learning are useful to the reality. An example is way that common ESL students learn English: they may spend several years in reciting grammar rules, but can hardly utter an English word in front of a foreigner.

Another reason that causes me to make the suggestion is the requirement of today's ever-changing knowledge economy time. With the increasingly accelerated pace of information explosion, one can hardly depend on knowledge from books
10   that he or she has learned at school. Mastering learning skills and knowing how to apply the skills into practice are becoming indispensable than ever before. A recent survey conducted by educators shows that most students in our country lack the ability of using tools and solving problems compared with their counterparts in the United States. This informs us to take a serious look at our book-knowledge based education pattern.

In sum, it's high time for us to give a touch on our education pattern concerning the narrowness of book-knowledge
15   learning as well as the necessity of practical learning required by the contemporary world.

Topic 142 **What gift would you give to help a child develop?**

Children's development plays a crucial role in building their physical and mental characteristics. It is known that children are able to absorb all necessary information provided by their parents and other adults. Their unlimited curiosity for discovering new interesting facts could help their development, especially in their early ages. We know that nothing could raise children's interest and attention as high as various gifts we presented to them. Hence, every gift for a child should contain particular purposes to help in child's development. In my opinion, a perfect gift for a child could be Lego toys.

I strongly believe that Lego, known for its impressive building sets, acclaimed and praised by pediatricians worldwide, has its versatile capabilities to help children develop creative, logical and imaginative skills gained during playing with this
25   terrific invention. Children could create and construct many different objects, depending on their ideas and enthusiasm. They could spend hours and hours playing with this amazing toy, constructing from simple squares to intricate and complex objects such as electric automobiles, airplanes and spacecrafts.

The quite interesting fact of this toy is that parents could observe developing processes of their children in a short period of time. This advantageous aspect of Lego toys, in my opinion, could affect on significantly important increases of the
30   children's development. Such increases of logical and organizing skills could be accomplished faster than those of children, who do not have these toys. As a result, this advantage could provide much better results in children's future school classes, especially in Algebra and Geometry.

Generally, toy-building sets, such as the already mentioned Lego, could effectively develop many important skills and characteristics, beneficiating children's future abilities to think, organize and make correct decisions. Also, the most
35   important fact is that children's development could be achieved significantly during playing time with Lego toys rather than doing perplexedly complicated exercises, resulting in a slow progression. And as a result, this perfect gift could bring development, fun and enhanced imagination to children and their parents.

Topic 142 **What gift would you give to help a child develop?**

People enjoy endless excitement and joy of receiving gifts ever since they are very young. As reading this topic, I recalled the sweet memories of my birthdays, a little girl waiting beside the table expecting her gift from dear parents. In turn, if I am a parent who is choosing a gift for my deeply beloved child, what gift shall I give to my little girl? Undoubtedly, I want my gift to be meaningful and helpful on my child's way of life that is long and awaiting. A book will be my best option since this chooses is testified by my own experience.

Books give little children wings of imagination. I remember my first favorite books were a series of cartoons called
45   "Ddcat" in which a mighty cat comes from the world of future brings to a dumb little boy all the amazing inventions. I laughed for the funny endings caused by the boy's improper use of those inventions, and I cried for the separating of these two dearly friends, but I was mostly amazed by the wild imagination --- the ability that was later revealed to be gained in my own writings.

Books are children's windows to the world. My own little, limited world was so much extended by books, which would
50   take me to the North Pole of the Earth to visit the people who live in the world of ice, which would tell me the old tale from ancient time of how the beautiful princess found her love, which would show me the miracles of nature through the world of little ants. It was through books I first acknowledge such a world I live in.

Books teach children the principles of life. When I first cried for Snow White who was driven out into a wild forest by her evil stepmother, I learnt what was good and evil. When I went to my father to admit it was me who dropped the plate
55   after reading the tale that children who lied would have long noses, I learnt that lying was a shameful deed. When I was

touched by the wisdom and love in the book "The Greatest Salesman in he World", I learnt to pursuit the meaning of my life.

A good book can give children the access to the world of imagination, knowledge and truth. I believe that a book can contribute to a child's development much more than a soccer ball, a camera or an animal, which is convinced by my own
5 benefits from books. A book, with your love and care, may be a gift of life for you loving child.

Topic 142 **What gift would you give to help a child develop?**

Perhaps it is the happiest time for children when they get a gift from others. When picking out presents for children, probably different people tend to choose different items. In my opinion, a gift can always contribute to a child's development no matter it is a camera, a soccer ball or a toy animal. However, as far as I am concerned, I would choose fairy books to help him or her develop.

Firstly, fairy books can help a child improve his or her mind and then learn to tell the right from the wrong. As we all know, fairy stories are all written from an imaginative perspective, which beautify the good and uglify the evil to the full. So through reading fairy books, children will definitely get to know whether a thing is good or not as well as what they should do if they are caught in the similar situations as what the stories put in the books. And I
15 believe it will be more beneficial for them to learn a lesson from those vivid stories than just from the plain words of their parents or teachers.

Furthermore, fairy stories can stimulate a child's incentive to reading, which eventually will improve his or her communication skills. All knows it that the communication skills such as reading and writing ability are most important in our daily life. Excellent reading ability helps a child understand the reading materials better; in the meantime, superior
20 writing ability helps a child be understood by others better. Meanwhile, the attractive plots described in the fairy stories will always make a child concentrate on the books for long. Therefore, it is obvious that the children's reading and writing ability will get improvement gradually then.

Altogether, fairy stories or fairy books not only can help children improve their minds, but also can help them better their communication skills. And such is right the reason that I would choose fairy books as a gift to a child.

Topic 143 **A long vacation vs. several short vacations**

It is a hot topic among educational institutions, parents and students themselves about what kind of vacation students should have. Some people want several short vacations, while some others would like to have one long vacation each year. If let me to choose, I prefer the latter for at least three reasons.

For the first reason, to make use of a long vacation we can do something that needs a long time to finish. For instance,
30 traveling far to several different interesting places would be the favorite thing for many students with heavy daily study burden. However, it is completely impossible for students to do such things if time is limited. Perhaps some students need to learn some new knowledge that they are interested in as a hobby, such as going to a dancing class, this period of time just provides them the best chances.

For the second reason, with a long vacation, students might be able to find a relatively fixed part-time job to practice
35 themselves using the knowledge they gained in class which is beneficial for students' future careers as well as saving some extra money for expenditures of the new academic term.

The last but not least, long vacation means that the teaching time is concentrated within a limited period that will make the study more efficient. Such example is that whenever we come back to school from holidays, it always takes us quite a long time to get use to the study environment, which reduces the effects of teaching. So, it is reasonable to arrange the
40 class in a concentrated time.

All in all, from the analysis above, I hope that the government or education institutions can adopt one long vacation instead of several short ones each year.

Topic 143 **A long vacation vs. several short vacations**

If a student only has one vacation each year, even that is a long vacation, he or she will have to have a long boring school term after the vacation. I believe that students should have several short vacations throughout the year for several reasons.

The first reason is that several short vacations mean several short school terms. The schools can arrange all year's curricula in several short terms more clearly, more efficiently and more effectively. Every subject will have a clear start and end, and can be taught intensely. Otherwise, it will be very difficult to arrange so many subjects in one long term. Schools may have to split the long term to fit in different courses, or let all the subjects take turns in one
50 week. That really confuses the students.

Another reason is that several short vacations are also good for parents to arrange. It's easy to deal with a short vacation than a long vacation. Parents can send their children to short term holiday camps, or just have them travel around. But it is almost impossible to let them do those activities throughout a long vacation. Needless to say, it's much easier to find a short time baby sitter.

Furthermore, several short school terms can help to keep students' interest in study. Every time when they return to schools after a vacation, they will be refreshed and willing to learn. On the other hand, a long school term will make students feel bored and exhausted.

5   On the other hand, a long vacation may have some benefits. For example, students can attend an after school like a summer school to learn some extra courses, or high school and college students can find a part-time job to make some extra money. Nevertheless, for all the reasons I mention above, only one vacation will make school life boring. So I support that students should have several short vacations throughout the year.

Topic 144 A traditional house

Young people usually prefer living in a modern apartment building as they often take consideration of the fashionable things, while more experienced adults would rather live in a traditional house as they like the feel of family and the quiet atmosphere around the traditional house. For my part, I would like to live in a traditional house.

First of all, there must be a variety of old things in the traditional house, owing to many years it has passed by. In my opinion, every old thing has an old story. When you take an old book from the bookshelf which your grandfather has read,
15   when you use the broom your grandmother ever used to clean the house, when you sit on a chair where your mother ever sat to make a sweater for you, I am sure you will feel very warm from the bottom of your heart.

Second, traditional house is often in a quiet district where you can obtain a good chance to relax yourself and think quietly after your work or study. After the temporary relation, you will probably have more energy to put into your job or study.

Third, since it is a traditional house, there must be a good neighborhood around it. If you are in some trouble, the
20   neighbors would help you, and you will feel convenient and joyful living in the traditional house.

On the other hand, if you live in the modern apartment building, the relationship between your neighbor and you is so aloof that you certainly cannot find warm help as you do in the traditional house. Admittedly, living in a modern apartment building has a few positive factors, such as, it may be near your work place, you can save time and money on transportation, you would live closer to modern life, and so on. However, at the same time you will not feel the warmness
25   of the people's relationship. So if we take a careful consideration, it is not difficult to get he conclusion: living tin the traditional house is your sagacious choice!

Topic 144 A traditional house vs. a modern apartment

I know there are advantages to living in a modern apartment, but I'd prefer to live in a traditional house. My main reason is that I love traditional designs. They're graceful and warm and inviting. I think modern designs are very empty and sterile and not appealing. So, because of the way it looks, I'd choose a traditional house.

I recognize the fact that a modern apartment is going to be in much better shape. Being new probably means all the plumbing works, the roof is not going to leak, the windows are properly sealed, and the kitchen appliances are in working order. A traditional house cannot guarantee any of that. In fact, it's likely that things will break down or need replacement, simply because of age.

35   Still, if the appliances are old, so is the wood, and that's a big advantage as far as I am concerned. Very few new buildings have the kind of beautiful woods that were used years ago. It's something that cannot be copied.

Space is always important to me, too. I need a lot of room for my home office, my clothes, and to display all the knickknacks I have picked up in my travels. I also like to have interesting space. I do not want all the rooms and windows the same size or a boxy design. A modern apartment usually comes in one size and shape. A traditional house is going to
40   have a variety of spaces where I can put a little table or a window seat. And it will have lots of room, from basement to attic. These are all good reasons for me to prefer living in a traditional house.

Some people love modern design, but it's not for me. The space and beauty of a traditional home are more important to me than having everything new and perfect.

Topic 145 The role of advertisements

The issue of the role of advertising in our lives is a very controversial one. Some people think that advertising encourages us to buy things that we really do not need, because they claim that advertisements have the power to influence on our purchasing behavior. Nevertheless, my point of view is that advertisements are incredible source of information about new products that may improve our lives.

First of all, these advertisements can help us to choose things easier and also save our time. For example, as a result of such an advertisement, a few years ago I bought very useful tool to lose my weight. The only thing that I needed to do
50   was to attach it to any problem area of my body for twenty minutes a day. Thus I did not to have do heavy exercises to lose my weight. The additional advantage was that this tool also helped me save time for my favorite activities.

The second reason is that quite often advertisements tell us about new products that can save our money. Again as a result of such an advertisement I bought some special micro fiber cloths, which could help me to clean my apartment only by using water. Thanks to its specific characteristics and possibility of long-time usage, I do not need to buy any more different kinds of liquids or powders for house cleans. Therefore the advertisement of this kind of cloth saved my money.

Last but not least advertisements can tell us about new products, which bring us new ways to cook healthier food. Fore instance, after watching a television advertisement, a friend of mine bought a special pot, with which she can prepare meat and vegetables without using any water or oil. This pot uses only the natural hot steam to cook. Thus it helps to keep more vitamins and minerals in the food, and get rid of the fat.

In conclusion, advertisements of new products definitely improve our life, because they tell us about things that make our life easier, save our time and money, and even cook our food better.

Topic 145 Advertising

Advertisements, one of the symbols of the modern society, are prevailing in every part of the world. Widespread and influential, advertisements are capable of convincing people to purchase commodities that they do not need. Among various factors that contribute to the phenomenon is the temptation of seeming lower price, the influence of celebrities and, in some cases, the exaggerated functions of the products.

The foremost reason for the phenomenon is that hardly anyone is able to resistant to the tempting low price, which is a trick played by the sly and shrewd merchants. For example, there are always so many products on sale that few of us are able to be sensible and rational enough not to be lured by the huge price tags with "sale" on them. As a matter of fact, the buyers are hooked by the seeming discount. By frenetic and irrational shopping, people would stock up piles of items that they actually will not be in need of in the foreseeable future or even for the rest of their lives.

Another subtle explanation rests on the fact that celebrities, who have been paid a considerable sum of money, play an important role in the effect of advertisements. Some famous stars are so influential that companies focus their attention on them and make the best use of their fame. As a result, a group of loyal fans would rush into stores and go into rapture if they are fortunate enough to possess one. Consequently, both the stars and the sellers benefit from the commercial game, regardless of what the consumers obtained.

The third convincing reason I would like to mention is that the exaggeration made in the advertisements by the merchants is also deceitful. It is, undoubtedly, confusing and puzzling for ordinary consumers to distinguish the unqualified ones from millions of products presented in front of them. In addition, a majority part of the merchants, some of whom are inadequate and inferior, are in the disguise of appealing appearances. Consequently, if is of no wonder that consumers would buy products preached to be perfect, a considerable number of them are nothing but a waste of money. Naturally, it is probably too reckless to maintain that advertising is a matter of cheating since some accompanying merits also come along with it, such as the aesthetic values.

However, the minor advantages will never prevent us from concluding that advertisements attract consumers to purchase useless products, because of their so called discount, the effect of celebrities and the boastful description.

Topic 146 Outdoors vs. indoors

Have you ever dived into a pool in the mountains? Have you ever jogged through the quiet forest? Have you ever enjoyed the sunshine on the afternoon beach? If you do not have such exciting experiences in your leisure time, you may sure lose something valuable that your life can offer. That is why I prefer to be outside than to be inside for my leisure activities.

At first, outdoor activities give me opportunities to touch the nature. I can remember how I was impressed by the beauty of the summit, which only successful climbers can see. Standing on the top of the mountain, I could even reach the blue sky. Outdoor leisure activities help us appreciate the sights of nature, which is not available in our ordinary routines, or indoor activities.

Secondly, outdoors activities are also beneficial for our health. Plenty of oxygen will refresh our brains. The Fresh air, the sunshine and the soft breeze are the basic elements that contribute to a good health. There is no doubt that the only way that we can access these elements is through outdoor activities. After all, no one in the world tend to refuse a strong body, therefore no one has a reason to refuse outdoor activities.

Leisure activities outdoors provide both the chance of appreciating nature and the most practical way to stay healthy. Those indoor activities cannot compare with them. So I prefer to do my leisure activities in the nature. I act outdoors, therefore I exist.

Topic 146 Outdoors vs. indoors

People would show different preference to indoor activities and outdoor activities. Some may be interested in spending their leisure time indoors, while others may be fond of the latter. As far as I am concerned, I would always prefer to be outside for my leisure activities.

In the first place, outdoor activities can provide me a pure natural environment in which I will feel more relaxed and refreshing. For example, I can always feel regenerated only after one-hour jogging along a quiet street, with the fresh cool air and wind around. Moreover, it is a real fun to travel and enjoy so many wonderful sightseeing in different places.

During their vacation, most people would choose to travel to enjoy a period of leisure time so that they can refocus on their studies and businesses.

In the second place, participating in varied outdoor activities can help us increase knowledge through our own experience and widen our horizon. As a famous saying goes: to become wiser, you need to not only read ten thousand books but also
5 you need to travel ten thousand miles. It is true when we go out we have the chance to meet different people and different things, which cannot happen if you stay indoor. We chat with people and exchange ideas, we visit many places and learn different cultures, all of which can let us know more about a true world.

In conclusion, I personally prefer outdoor activities to indoor ones not only because I can enjoy the relaxation and refreshment in the nature but also through participating in varied out activities, I gain valuable opportunities to convert
10 theoretical knowledge from books into a kind of real experience.

Topic 147 **How should your school spend a gift of money?**

Our educational objective is not only to fill students with the knowledge, but also to improve their capacity and skills of analysis, which will benefit the students all their lifetime. So to achieve this ambitious objective, it is necessary that the school shall have all sorts of laboratories to facilitate various laboratory tests in the school. So naturally, when my school receives a gift of money, I think the best way for us to spend the money is to build basic laboratories for the students and teachers.

Firstly, our school is not well equipped with such a basic necessities. We have capable teachers and intelligent students in our school, which created a strong academic study atmosphere. But due to lack of necessary laboratories, the teaching is only limited in the class. Students learned a lot about the theory but no more practice, which detracts the understanding
20 of students and affects building up of their capacity to apply the knowledge into practice. Therefore, the educational quality is questionable. This has impaired the fame of the school. Consequently, brain drainage is a big problem in the school. The excellent teachers and intelligent students are desperately looking for well-equipped schools for their teaching and studying. So to curtail the loss, it is the high time to invest the fund to build up all these necessities.

Secondly, to spend the money on establishing laboratories will benefit the school for good in the long run. Parents assess
25 the school according to the educational facilities that the school possesses. Poor facilities will keep students away from the school. So from the point of view of attracting more students, building a first-class laboratory is the prime task of the school. Furthermore, the local education authority has also paid attention to the problem of poor educational facilities. If the situation maintains like that without any improving, I suspect our school will be closed down by the authorities.

Last but not at least, if our school use the money on building educational facilities, it will make the donators more
30 comfortable. By building a new laboratory, I believe it can attract more donators.

In sum, to spend the gift fund to build up the laboratory is a wise choice, which not only can satisfy the students and teachers in the school, but also can make the parents and the donators happy.

Topic 148 **Does playing games teach us about life?**

Playing games plays a significant role in people's daily life. You can always see children playing soccer or basket ball in parks, and adult enjoy themselves with the bridge game in clubs. Game may become more and more complex as we grow up, but our enjoyment has never changed. It give us lots fun, meanwhile teach us about life.

First of all, playing games teaches us about the strategies which we can apply in our real life. In fact, most games' original ideas come from real life. For instance, Chess imitate the battles between two countries. During the game of chess, we need to analyze what situation we face, evaluate our assets, guess
40 what our rivals would do in next steps and make the best choice from several possibilities. In real life, when we meet a challenge, we usually analysis the situation and estimate our ability and decide what to do next. Therefore, games are mirrors of real life.

Playing games also teaches us how to deal with other people. We learn about teamwork during the game, if the games are played in teams like soccer or basketball. Nobody can win the game by himself even though he is strong, and runs fast.
45 Everybody should communicate with his co-players. Also, in real life, no one can survive without other people's help and cooperation. A man who gets along well with his co-workers is likely to be successful in his career.

Meanwhile, playing games also help us focus our mind and energy to reach the goal, and teach us to divide a difficult problem into several relatively smaller and easier tasks and solve them one by one. Playing games also teach us to adjust our plan when situation changes. Finding a good job is always not easy, especially during an economic downturn, as we are
50 currently experiencing. At this moment, we may go to school to pursue a higher degree instead of job hunting. It is those games such as chess that teach us to adjust our strategies and pace in real life.

Life is not a game, but games surely teach us a lot about life.

Topic 149 How would you use a free gift of land?

If I have received some land to use as I wish, I would use this land to build a library. I like to use the following reasons to explain my choice.

The first and most important reason is that a library can bring plenty of knowledge to people. I remember the famous words that knowledge is power. Apparently, a library is the ideal place for people to attain knowledge. In a library, we can get all kinds of valuable information that we need, such as knowledge of geography, history, music and politic, and so on. We can imagine that it is so comfortable and enjoyable when we sit in a quiet library and immerse in the world of knowledge that we cherish.

Another equally important reason is that people can spend their spare time in a more meaningful way in a library. Now the life pace is faster and faster, so people, especially young people, like to go to see a movie, or to go to a disco party. In comparison with those places, I think that a library can provide a quiet and comfortable atmosphere for people who want to reduce the pressure of life.

Moving on to wider themes, a library is a good and safe place for children. Parents would rather let their children go to the library frequently than seeing their child spending lots of time in playing games or watching television. After all, a good book can provide children with enormous help to their future life.

From what has been discussed above, I may safely draw the conclusion that using this land to build the library for people will be my first choice.

Topic 149 How would you use a free gift of land?

Land is an invaluable asset and from time of immemorial it has been regarded with respect and perhaps envy by those who do not own any. Land is equivalent to money in a tangible form and the potential of undeveloped land has to be seen then to be believed. When it is given in the form of a gift its value is infinite, because this is something that is stolid and eternal. I can let my imagination run riot when I see the various uses it can be put to. As it is a gift I am assuming that the land extends into a few acres.

I have always wanted to live in a sprawling house surrounded by gardens that are bathed in a riot of color. I need space to breathe and the matchbox apartments of the city make me claustrophobic. Long verandahs with porticos must open into rooms where light and air reign supreme. Luxurious bedrooms unmatched in size and decor, lounges which exemplify what they stand for, salons, elegant drawing rooms, a huge library, a study, studios to pursue my hobbies and spiral staircase which lead to the upper floors are what I envision as an abode.

That however is just the tangent of my dreams that touches the periphery of the land. Moving out towards the gardens I find I require even more space than I did for the interior. I need a couple of summerhouses and small private cottages to enable me to get away when I want. A conservatory filled with plants and unusual flowers, a huge swimming pool, a small gym and a spa would be fitting as extensions.

It would perhaps be selfish to utilize all the land for myself. I would like to do something for the people around me. A free reading room and a circulating library is something that many people do not have access to. This I would like to construct for them. To culminate it all I would like to use part of the land to construct a public park and playground for the kids who do not have any such facilities.

Dreams are nice and they sound even nicer when put into words. If I get a piece of land as a gift these dreams can become realities. I enrich my life style and those of others too by bringing joy and spreading it too. I wish it came true.

Topic 150 Is watching TV bad for children?

Everything consists of goodness and badness. People cannot evaluate something only by its benefit or only by its harmfulness. This is why I disagree with the point that watching television is bad for children. I admit that if the children do not watch TV properly, such as watching television excessively or seeing something unfit for them in TV, watching TV would do harm. However, watching TV can benefits children if they make good use of it. Watching TV can help children learn a lot of knowledge in an interesting way, can be a good entertainment for children, and can help children manage their time. In those senses, watching TV is not bad for children.

First of all, most TV programs for children are designed in an interesting way, which is easier for children to understand. For example, a lovely presenter tells a beautiful story with attractive frames on TV and at the same time she introduces some knowledge to her young audience. Thus, children can get knowledge by listening to a story.

Secondly, watching TV can be a different form of various entertainments from what children are accustomed to. Most children like animated cartoons that give them charming images. Some children may enjoy their time in children entertainment TV programs and may also enjoy watching other children performing in TV. Hence, watching TV is another entertainment for children.

Lastly, watching TV can help children make good use of their time. Many TV programs have their certain times. Children always know the show times of their favorite programs. If they want to watch these programs on time, they should complete others things by that time. In other words, children have to be quicker in their other activities. Thus, watching

TV can be an active help when children plan their time.

I do admit that watching TV properly needs direction of the parents. Yet, we cannot doubt watching TV is good in some ways for its teaching knowledge to the children, for its entertaining the children and for its well effecting on children's time. I believe most adults today can still remember how their favorite children TV programs benefited them when they were children.

5

Topic 150 **Is watching TV bad for children?**

Television has increased the speed at which news travels and it can bring situations and images into our homes that previous generations would not have had the opportunity or regret to witness.

Television is commonly criticized as being bad for children that an important fact sometimes gets overlooked. In my personal opinion some types of television viewing may actually enhance children's intellectual development.

10

Television contains an enormous variety of forms and content. The effects of television viewing depend on program content and genre. According to a research, young children who spent a few hours a week watching educational programs such as Sesame Street, Mister Rogers' Neighborhood, Reading Rainbow, Captain Kangaroo, Mr. Wizard's World and 3-2-1 Contact had higher academic test scores 3 years later than those who didn't watch educational programs. On the other hand, children who watched many hours of entertainment programs and cartoons had lower test scores than those who watched fewer hours of such programs. Good educational programs can provide lasting benefits to children.

15

Children are most likely to become actively engaged with television content that is neither too easy nor too difficult to comprehend, that is, content that provides some challenges, but also allows a child to gain a sense of mastery. Just like our muscles, the brain gets stronger when it is used, and atrophies when it is not used. It seems that lack of use also leaves it vulnerable to degeneration later in life.

20

Of course, there are some bad sides for children to watch TV. Our TV-watching children increasingly view life as an entertainment extravaganza, in which they yearn to play a starring role, and here the nasty content of so much modern broadcasting comes into play. Besides, it is hard to watch an evening of TV without encountering unspeakable violence, whose perpetrators are celebrated. Again, the effects of television viewing depend on program content and genre, and parents should teach their children on choosing the right TV program to watch.

25

Topic 150 **Is watching TV bad for children?**

With the advancement of technology, the greatest difference between children now and in the past is that children now enjoy more luxurious usage of newly invented technologies. Nowadays, children virtually superfluously spend their after-school life on watching television programs, playing computer games and Internet chatting apart from completing their necessary homework. Though it is well debatable on if it is good or bad for children to watch television, however, I do think that watching appropriate amount of television programs is good for the development of a child.

First of all, television programs provide an extensive amount of information and knowledge for children to learn on their own. It is a well-known fact that, with audio and visual aid in a learning process, a child will pick up knowledge more easily rather than broadly absorbing whatever his teacher regardless of his interests delivers. For instance, the Discover Channel provides services of introductions to science and technology in a very comprehensive manner. In fact, TV programs provided by this channel convey knowledge by giving many detailed examples from the actual world, instead of producing the theoretical models. Watching television programs of this kind does no harm to the children, but in fact, provides more comprehensive education to them.

35

40

Further more, watching television widens a child's mindset. In order for a child to grow into a matured adult, he needs to have an astute brain to adapt to the society. Television programs provide a lot of up-to-date news and information on current affairs. By watching television, one is able to receive information in a relatively shorter period of time. Empirically, a better-informed child is more likely to mature earlier than his peers. This also enables him to gain pre-matured experiences for his future work as a member of the society. In light of this reason, watching television is definitely beneficial to children.

45

However, in order for a child to grow in the right direction, appropriate programs have to be selected for him to watch. Otherwise, he may end up watching programs that may misguide him in this global world. This may be very dangerous to the physical and mental health of a child, as a little bit of misbehavior may cause great harm to the child. A good example illustrating this point is a TV drama series where a princess demonstrated some dangerous actions to the audience. Unfortunately, most audience of this series is children. Due to their lack of mature mindset and appropriate parental guidance, they ended up having followed the action of the actors, and getting themselves into serious injuries, and some even died. Hence, it is inevitable to see that watching television programs without appropriate guidance from parents may result in serious troubles for children.

50

The advancement of technology has allowed children now to have a more enjoyable life compared to their parents. At the

55

same time, children are able to pick up knowledge from TV programs. However, parents need to pay close attention to the programs that their children watch to ensure that they are appropriate, so that their children will grow up healthily.

Topic 151 **What is the most important animal in your homeland?**

My homeland Taiwan is well known for its great and diverse possession of animals. However, among this great variety of animals, Taiwanese deer is the most important and unique animal. This beautiful animal saved my ancestors from starvation in their pioneer days, and what's more, it symbolizes the beauty of my homeland Taiwan.

When my ancestors first came to the Island of Taiwan, they had nothing except a few pieces of clothing and tools. As they were facing hunger, they caught the glimpse of a beautiful deer in silky beige fur and snow-white spots. Astonished at the sight of such a stunning creature, they appreciated God for
10 bestowing them such a precious gift. The deer saved my ancestors from starvation, and hence, my people worship it as the gift from God. Were it not for the Taiwanese deer, my ancestors would not have survived, and I also would not be sitting here writing this essay.

Moreover, Taiwanese deer symbolizes the dazzling beauty of my homeland---the Taiwan Island. Taiwan has been famous for the name "Formosa" which means "beautiful" given by a Portuguese explorer in the1600's. Its beauty is celebrated
15 worldwide. Moreover, the Taiwanese deer is widely recognized as one of the most beautiful kinds of deer. It acquires silky fur of the color of cedar, covered by little white spots that spread out like stars in the sky. In addition, I can proudly and positively say the only place on the Earth where you can find a Taiwanese deer is the Taiwan Island. Every characteristic of the deer matches my beautiful homeland perfectly, and the deer is the best representative of my homeland.

Overall, although there are various animals living in my homeland, Taiwanese deer is the most important one as it was the
20 food that saved my ancestors and it represents my homeland. Unfortunately, this incredible creature now is facing extinction. I genuinely hope by writing this essay my voice can be heard and people will try to save the Taiwanese deer.

Topic 152 **Why should forest be saved?**

Have you ever stopped other people when they were chopping down the trees? Have you ever felt painful when you saw a large piece of forests were burning down by the fire from the television? Have you ever shouted to those people when they were using woods to build their house? Maybe you have not. Just because human beings have not paid enough attention to those events, many parts of the world are losing the most important natural resources---forests. I strongly feel that it is important to save forests on the Earth. In the following discussion, I will reason and provide evidence to support my point of view.

In the first place, the most important reason to support my viewpoint is that the forest is the heart of the Earth. Just like
30 the heart of a human being that contributes to all of the circulations in a person, the Earth needs its heart to keep working. Everyday, forests take in the carbon dioxide, and by combining with the water, they produce the basic sugar -- glucose--for other living creatures and also release the most important gas to the Earth's atmosphere--oxygen. Without food, a person can remain alive for 5-10 days; without water, a person can survive for 1-2 days; but without oxygen, no body can keep alive after 10 minutes. When people are destroying the forests, they are trying to ruin their own lives.

35 In the second place, forests are the significant resources to hold the soil. The roots of the trees stretch into the Earth and tightly grab the soil. However, after losing the forests, during rain time, the soil will be easily brought down. For example, because of the expansion of the city, a large piece of forest was destroyed in the rural area near my hometown. One day, one of my old friends went to that place to do a research. However, just as the bus arrived to the foot of a hill on which the entire forest had just been brought down, suddenly, it was starting to rain. The water brought down a large amount of
40 soil and rushed down with unimaginable speed. Without a time for the bus driver to react, the bus was covered under the mud. The mud not only destroyed the bus, but also killed all the people in it. I cried when I heard the news, but no tears could bring my friend's life back.

To sum up, forests are the important natural resources for our human beings to preserve. In order to live a better life, every person needs to take care of the environment.

Topic 152 **Why should forest be saved?**

What is clear is that forests provide humans with many social, economic, and environmental benefits.

However, huge areas of the richest forests in the world have been cleared for wood fuel, timber products, agriculture, and cattle. If the current rate of deforestation, about 80,000 square kilometers per year, is kept, they may completely disappear by the year 2030. In Vietnam, our country, according to
50 the ministry of Natural Resources and Environment, 1,054 forest fires occurred last year, destroying 15,370 hectors of forest and causing damage worth US $ 9,8 million. Particularly, Upper U Minh, formerly a nature reserve, was mostly destroyed, just after being re-classified as a national park.

In fact, like Vietnam, the countries with the most tropical forests tend to be developing and overpopulated nations in the southern hemisphere. Due to poor economies, people resort to clearing the forest and planting crops in order to survive.

ToeflEssays.com

Therefore, the most effective conservation policies are to relieve poverty and expand access to education, healthcare, and the most important, alternative livelihoods. Allocating forests to farms and plantations is also a sound one. In addition, stricter laws should be issued to reduce the destruction of forests, which is caused mostly by logging interests.

5　All in all, nowadays, one of the greatest concerns worldwide is the loss of natural resources, particularly forests. Many solutions have been suggested to save forests from destruction. However, many forests in the world remain unprotected.

Topic 153 **Is a zoo useful?**

Every city has one or more zoos. For a while, people think that a zoo is no useful purpose. If I were faced with this issue, I would think that zoos are useful. In the following discussion, I would like to reason and provide evidence to support my viewpoint.

10　The first reason is that zoos are often used as places to preserve the endangered species, such as the giant pandas and tigers. It is the conservation of animals that is the most important function of a zoo. With the advances in reproductive technologies, which assist in breeding captive animals, the zoo has become the most important place for animal conservation. Thanks to zoos, certain species of animals have been saved from extinction. Such animals are bred in captivity and when they are ready to survive in the wild, are reintroduced to their original habitat - in the rain forests of Brazil, for instance.

15　In the second place, children can obtain direct knowledge about a variety of animals by visiting zoos. They can see what a tiger is like, hear various sounds of birds and tell one animal from another. If there is no such a place, how can they make contact with animals? They may never have a chance to see various animals even though they learn many from books. When I was a little girl, I liked animals very much, especially birds. But I could not feed them for myself, so the zoo which was located near my home was the place I went to most frequent. And I really love these places.

20　Finally, a zoo is a place for fun. In fact, this is why it is so good at educating the public about the importance of conserving wildlife and the environment: it puts fun into education. Seeing pictures is not the same as seeing animals at close up. What makes visiting a zoo so enjoyable is our close contact with them. Therefore a zoo not only attracts many tourists from other countries, it also allows us to see, without having to leave home, big cats and exotic animals of distant countries.

25　In summary, I believe that a zoo has some useful purposes to serve: to preserve the endangered species, to educate the public about wildlife, and for its visitors to have fun. So a zoo of course is a useful place for us and we should have them.

Topic 154 **Is it right to ban smoking?**

Smoking is highly injurious to health and its adverse effects on passive smokers is well established. I, therefore, strongly favor the ban imposed in many public places and office buildings in various countries.

30　Smoking in public places and office buildings irritates and causes discomfort to non-smokers. Moreover, the passive smokers are also highly susceptible to various diseases like cancer and other ailments based on the findings of various researches. As public places and office buildings are open to all the people especially office workers, no individual has any right to knowingly cause harm/injury to others health.

The health problems caused due to smoking in public places/offices would result in additional financial burden on the
35　exchequer to divert its resources in medical facilities to combat such problems. These avoidable health problems of the employees due to such few irresponsible smokers would result in increased absenteeism and economic loss to the companies. It is a common experience that offenders do not bother to follow any civic rule unless heavy penalty or strong rule is imposed by civic authority.

However, it would be prudent to provide some limited confined places in the public areas and in the office buildings
40　exclusively for the smokers. These rooms are required to be adequately provided with proper devices for removing obnoxious gases like CO_2, SO_2, CO, NO_2 etc from the smoke before being released to atmosphere. A nominal fee might be charged from the smokers to discourage their smoking habits.

Finally, I strongly support such rule to impose ban on smoking in public places in order to avoid detrimental effects on the health of common people knowingly.

Topic 154 **Is it right to ban smoking?**

There is no doubt that we human beings are social animals. Living in a society, we certainly cannot do whatever we like. Putting ourselves in other people's shoes is a key principal to live in a social group. Smoking in public will violate this basic rule. Therefore, I believe that people should not allow smoking in public places and office buildings.

It is widely believed that smoking is bad for people's health. Since not everyone likes smoking, the rule banning on public
50　smoking should be enforced. It goes without saying that public spaces such as office buildings, department stores or classrooms are places for everyone including adults and children. The second-hand smokes produced by smokers may be more harmful for the health of non-smokers according to the New England Medical Journal published several years ago.

Moreover, smoking is bad for the health of smokers. The rule might help the smokers who want to quit smoking. The rule can reduce the opportunities for smokers to smoke and gradually help chain smokers get rid of this bad habit. Smoking is a habit that is not easy to quit. The rule might use its legal power to assist the smokers to protect their own health.

5   Smoking in public spaces might be dangerous because there are a lot of careless smokers who forget to extinguish the sparkles after they smoke. The irresponsible action may lead to big fire and a great numbers of people will be hurt in the accident. Nevertheless, enforcing the rule can prevent the occurrence of accidents.

Some people might believe that it is their rights to smoke wherever they please. However, I would say that people who do not smoke have their rights not to inhale second-hand smokes and risk their life in dangerous places. Smokers still can smoke in their private places such as their bedrooms or living rooms as long as no other people's rights are not damaged.
10   After all, the rule is used to protect the personal liberty of everyone.

Topic 155 **What plant is important to the people in your country?**

There are many kinds of plants in Thailand since Thailand's land and climate are very suitable for agriculture. As soon as I am asked what the most important plant in my country is, I undoubtedly point out that rice is the most necessary plant in Thailand for several important reasons that I will detail in this essay.

Firstly, rice is the main kind of food in Thailand. Even though there is much more food here such as noodle or fast food, almost all Thai people still eat rice as their daily traditional dish because we have eaten rice for a long time from our ancestral age to the present time. Moreover, rice still provides substantial energy to our bodies, so we have enough energy to do our activities everyday. For foreigners, they can have breakfast only with hams and eggs. For me, if I have breakfast with no rice, I feel that I am still hungry.

20   Secondly, as a agricultural country, exporting rice is the main part of my country's revenue. Even though we sell several kinds of plants to other countries, rice still makes much more income to us than others. In addition, Thailand ranks first in rice exports in the world. I cannot imagine if we do not have rice as the vital economic product, how could our country survive. I absolutely see the significance of rice because even USA also eagerly tries to develop and cultivate rice by itself in order to defeat Thailand.

25   Obviously, no other plants can replace rice in terms of the important food and the vital economic values at present and in the future, even though several kinds of plants are also cultivated here.

Topic 156 **Which country would you like to visit?**

If I have the opportunity to visit a foreign country for two weeks, I would not hesitate to choose Gambia---a country lies in West Africa.

I began to notice this tiny country at the time I was reading the novel - *Roots*. It tells the story of an African-American family and a descendent finally found out his roots in Gambia. I was quite impressed by the characters, plots and interesting African life styles described in the novel. The book gives me a totally different view about Africa and it was my first time to take a close-up look into an individual African country.

In the past when I think of Africa I think of poverty, disease, and poor people, but never had I realized how amazing Gambia is until I finished reading this novel. They have lovely traditions. Every night, people from the same tribe would
35   gather together. Adults could talk about things happened in the daytime while kids enjoy the stories told by the elders. Teenagers go hunting every day and compete for the most harvest. They never write down their history, but the historians would take the responsibility of passing it down by telling the following historians these huge historical events. Everybody leads a happy and serene life and live in harmony with the nature. I can imagine the vast grass, wavy lake, cheerful herds; it is a fairyland far from conflict, controversy and war.

40   How can anyone be not attracted by Gambia after knowing a little bit about it? If Pushkin had had the chance to visit this fascinating country, he would probably say "Oh, Gambia! How violently its name plucks at everyone's heart!"

I have been dreaming to visit Gambia and joining those villagers, sitting under a big tree, listening to the stories, hunting the animals and being enlightened by the historians. How I wished to go there!

Topic 157 **Computers vs. traditional schools**

Different persons will have different opinions about studying at home or studying at school. I will prefer to go to traditional schools because schools provide disciplined learning, experienced teachers and good facilities.

Although learning from computer and television is comfortable, it is void of disciplined learning environment provided by schools. Schools provide balanced atmosphere where each subject is given equal importance and is taught on a regular basis. This leads to an overall development of children. This discipline is absent in
50   learning through computers and televisions at home. We are inclined to subjects which appeal us. Some children finds art and crafts as interesting and devote most of their time in them, while others find math and science more interesting and avoid reading books on social sciences. This erratic and unbalanced reading inhibits overall development. Moreover children are too young to decide what they should learn or should not. At this situation schools prove to be beneficial

where teachers knows their students and give individual attentions to improve their skills.

Not everybody can afford the best equipments and technology available in the market. At this juncture schools provide best-experienced teachers and best facilities available. Schools invest on these instruments that students can use while it is difficult to buy each and every piece individually by yourself if you are learning at home. Also there are instances where
5   students are required constant vigilance. For example while performing experiments in chemistry, which involves lots of dangerous chemicals, an experienced adult such as a teacher or a lab technician must present. In these labs children are in habit of messing with things. They try to experiment mixing every solution they can find. So regular vigilance is required on each student. Similarly while doing dissection of rats in biology labs, from time-to-time guidance is required by students to understand and complete the experiments successfully. No television or computer can give such attention to
10   each individual.

While studying at school, children get to know each other. They learn to work in team when they are given group assignment. They learn to distribute tasks among themselves according their strong points and complete their tasks. Therefore a feeling of compassion is developed among them, which is not possible in television learning.

Keeping all these benefits in mind, I would like to go to a traditional school for my learning.

Topic 158 **Are celebrities opinions right?**

Everyone is entitled to have an opinion. When it comes to opinions, though, there's a difference between the majority of people and celebrities like actors, athletes, and rock stars. If you're an average person, only your family and friends care about your opinion. If you're famous, the whole world listens, or so it seems sometimes. Is this the way if should be? I do not think so.

20   We shouldn't pay attention to famous people's opinions just because of who they are. Being a famous basketball player doesn't make someone an expert on environmental issues. However, that basketball player has a better opportunity to be heard than most people do. If that player feels very strongly about an issue, he can use his fame to draw attention to it and get other people involved. That way they can saw attention and needed dollars to that issue.

People who are rich put their money behind a cause. In the same way, famous people are using their most valuable asset.
25   In their case, it's not money. It's their name recognition. Should people pay attention to what they think just because of who they are? I don't think so. I also do not think we should discount what they think just because of who they are. They have a right to their opinion. If their name draws people to that cause, all the better for the cause.

I think too often we categories people and try to keep them in their place. Celebrities have brains and should be allowed to use them. When they're advocating a cause, their opinion should be just one of many factors we use to evaluate that
30   cause.

Topic 158 **Are celebrities opinions right?**

In today's commercial world, companies try to sell as much of their product as possible. In this scenario they try all means and methods to peddle their wares. One of their methods is eliciting the good offices of famous personalities such as actors, athletes and rock stars to endorse their products. But why would they resort to this? Past experience and research must
35   have indicated that this kind of propaganda does bear fruit and people are lured by the opinions of such high fliers. In my opinion blindly believing and following such opinions would be quite foolhardy. It would be more feasible if one analyzed the opinion using their own common sense and judgment and made an informed decision. Hence we should not totally disregard the opinions of these personalities but listen and act upon them in a sensible and discerning fashion. But blind faith without verification would not be advisable.

40   Depending on the situation and the product being sold or the message being propagated, we could choose to follow or opinion or disregard the same. It would also depend on the credibility of the person endorsing the product. Even in the situation where the person is a big wig with an impeccable reputation I would suggest corroborating the authenticity of his/her claims before believing the same. After all, we are thinking individuals vested with the power of intelligence and the ability to choose. We must not abuse this right. In some cases, we find famous people stating their opinions about a
45   social cause... In this case, they are being used to spread more and more awareness and influence people into the bettering the society they live in. For example, we find some of the big shots in the entertainment industry rallying for AIDS awareness... yet others who encourage people to donate their organs after death. These are social messages for the betterment of the society. One might choose to listen to these messages and act upon the same, or disregard them... but at least one can give it a thought.

50   On the other hand, lets take another example of an issue that is still being hotly debated and is in the eye of a major controversy. It has recently been revealed that aerated drinks with coke as their basic ingredient contain harmful chemicals & pesticides. As soon as this rumor began doing the rounds, the relevant companies roped in the top-notch film & sports personalities getting them to endorse their product via equivocal statements about the safety of their product. The Health board took umbrage to this fact as it had not yet been fully proven that these drinks were indeed devoid of pesticides.
55   They declared that the public was being intentionally misled. Thanks to the endorsements by the famous stars, most

people, a lot amongst them being youngsters, disregarded the health warnings of the Health board and continued consumption of these drinks.

This example should lay bare the capricious nature of opinions of these famous personalities. They may be driven by financial and publicity seeking goals.

5 Hence in conclusion I would like to say that it is best to hear out the opinions of famous personalities, but finally make an intelligent and informed choice based upon our own experience, information and intelligence.

| *Topic 159* **What change should be remembered?** | The past 20th century has been a century of advances and developments: the emergence of the Internet and web technology. When I think of the 21st century, I am afraid to say that nothing but only bad come to my mind: overspreading epidemics, increasing religion conflicts and resources overusing. |

The first thing that has hit my head is the overspreading diseases which modern medicine has nothing to overcome. For example, in Asia, there were hundreds of people who had a new disease called "SARS", a killer responsible for over one hundred people. In Hong Kong and Vietnam, the bird flu infected large numbers of poultry and caused children's death. In the United States, the west-Niles virus is feared among public since it transmits through mosquitoes. All of these
15 diseases are new to human because of their rare genetic structure. Such diseases challenge modern medicine. However, there are only prevention but not cure.

Another thing that on everyday news is the religion-related terrorists activities. Even now the American-Iraq war has been tensioned in spite of the last's cease-fire. Some people say that this is a war between Christianity and Islamic, others insist that this a war aimed to oil power. As a result, innocent children and the public are sacrificed for those so-called "cause",
20 meaning justice or security. It is hard for me to understand that how much human being have involved from animals, if we can only use force in this high technology time.

The last but not least thing that occurs to me is the concern of natural resources. Despite the fact that we are running out of available natural resources such as clean water, oil, and natural gas, our life is becoming more and more convenient, which means we will consume more energy than ever. This is also a vital problem for human's existing.

25 For the three factors I have mentioned above, I believe that there are some changes in this century, although I doubt whether those changes will lead us to happier future than now.

| *Topic 159* **What change should be remembered?** | Which invention was the greatest invention of the 20th century has been discussed many times. Different people have different views. Some think the greatest invention was television; some think it should be cars. But as far as I am concerned, the greatest invention of the 20th century would be computers. The reasons for my opinion are as follows. |

First of all, computers save a great deal of efforts people spend on calculating. Before computers were invented, people had to calculate manually. Sometimes it took scientists weeks, even months to have a result. Of course, they might make mistakes during their calculation. That affected the accuracy of data. But with the help of computers, people are freed from heavy calculation. If only takes seconds to have a result which used to take weeks in the past.

35 Second, computers can simulate different environments that cannot be created in real life. In the science research, sometimes scientist need to have a simulation environment to improve their theories or as a basis of further research. Without computers it's difficult to have accurate and reliable results. But computers can make everything easy. Just input programs and data everything will be done.

The reason I think is becoming more and more important nowadays. That is computer is the way of access to the Internet.
40 The Internet was developed based on the local area network (LAN) of computers. Today, the Internet has become the fastest developing medium in the world. You can find almost everything you need on the Internet, communicate with friends, read news, watch movies, listen to music etc. But you must do all the above things on a computer. Cannot log in the Internet means behind times today.

Although many other inventions of the 20th century brought great convenience to human or changed people's lives,
45 computers have the most valuable contribution to human, and it will have much more contribution in the future.

Topic *160* **Complain in writing vs. complain in person**	I would actually prefer not to complain at all, and in cases where it is really necessary to do so, I would most likely complain by phone.
	Although, in order to stay within the topic let us compare two given possibilities; complaining in writing and complaining in person.
	Complaining in person enables us to interact personally with a real person who represent the company where we purchased a product from. This method of complaining definitely gives certain advantages as opposed to complaining in writing. For instance, one can always ask to

speak with a manager if he would find a clerk's answer not good enough. And this approach also enables us to take the reason of complaining with us and actually demonstrate to the manufacturer or seller what is the actual problem is.

On the other hand, complaining in writing has its own advantages and could serve as a very powerful tool to a sophisticated complainer who knows how to fight for his rights. Firstly, words written on paper could serve as a latter proof in court, if, of course, the dispute would go that far. Also in some cases the company we purchased a product from 5 may not have live representatives available in your region, and therefore, complaining in writing could save you unnecessary long trip. Finally writing a letter with complains could save you a lot of aggravation that you always risk to get by complaining in person.

I personally prefer to complain as less as possible, although if I had to choose from two forms of complaining, I would choose to do it in writing.

Topic 161 Why people remember their gifts?

I have never met a person who does not enjoy receiving gifts or presents. In my opinion, the reason is that it makes us feel special and loved. Sometimes we appreciate more the attention of the person who gives us a present than the present itself. However, definite gifts mean much more than others; they have a great value for us and they become precious pieces of our memories.

15 There are many celebrations in one's lifetime when he receives presents - birthdays, anniversaries or any other happy occasions. Some of them he remembers as more special and important than others. Why is so?

One hand the reason could be that the present means something really significant. It may also be truly expensive. Moreover, the gift could be unique and invaluable for the one ho has received it.

On the other hand we remember some gifts as special ones because they have been given to us as a sign of endless love 20 and care. Furthermore, they could be given as signs of appreciation and respect. Sometimes even the trivial present given from somebody really special could become a treasure. What is more - it could be remembered as one of the most special gifts that we have ever received. In other cases some presents are thought to be special because they are given as a surprise without any occasion and remind us that we are still truly loved or not forgotten.

I consider that the answer to the question, why people remember special gifts or presents that they have received, is 25 absolutely simple. It is because they are…special. No matter what the reason is, every one I know remembers his or her special presents and gifts.

I remember mine. And I am sure, dear reader, that you remember yours, too.

Topic 162 Do starts deserve high salary?

Everyone needs money to support his family and enjoy life. I believe that is one of the most important reasons why people go to work. While an average person just earns basic salary, some famous athletes and entertainers earn millions of dollars every year. Why is that so? Do these people deserve such high salaries?

Before answering these questions, let me ask you another question, where did your salaries come from? From our employers. Right! Those famous athletes and entertainers made a lot of money for their own employers. Because their skills and achievements on some specific sports or entertainments, other people would like to pay money to watch them 35 playing games or acting in movies. This is part of the nature of human beings. From this aspect, they earned what they got. They deserve what they earned.

In addition, usually those athletes and movie stars have some special talents in a certain area. Athletes are experts at some specific sports such as baseball, basketball, football and so on. Movie stars are good at performance art. Average people cannot reach that level, no matter how hard they try. People who watch their games or movies can obtain happy 40 experiences and enjoyments, which can enrich people's life and benefit people's health. Without sports and movies, our life would be much boring and less pleasant.

Furthermore, those famous people sacrifice something to get what they have. For example, almost all athletes suffer from injuries because of heavy trainings and physical competitions to win the games. Movie stars have to face the fact that the average people are not only interested in their movies, but also interested in their personal lives. This is also integral part 45 of human beings.

Do not be jealous of those famous athletes or entertainers, although we all admire the millions of dollars they made. They have talents, they made us happy and they sacrificed something, either injury or privacy. They earned their own paycheck.

Topic 163 The importance of reading and writing

For ages, reading and writing has been vital aids to the intellectual, emotional and spiritual growth of mankind. With rapid changes in the society and scientific advancement of human race over the decades, the necessity and importance of reading and writing has increased remarkably. It has become a pivotal skill a person should learn to be successful.

Several reasons account for the lesser importance of reading and writing in the past. Firstly, education was restricted to certain sections of the society and not everyone benefited from its

advantages. Only the learned few enjoyed intellectual satisfaction. Knowledge was not shared freely due to lack of proper means of communication, thus preventing many from realizing the benefits of education and learning. Secondly, technology was not so advanced in the past. Hence the general pace of life was slower than it is now and people did not feel the need to keep themselves abreast of affairs around them. In other words, the need did not arise for mass awareness
5   and participation in efforts for intellectual enlightenment through reading and writing. Nevertheless, writing was a more popular than reading since it was the most common means of communication - in the form of letters.

However, at present the scenario has changed considerably. Innovation and change are integral parts of life. Now advancement in technology marks the day. To cope up with the rapidly evolving new ideas and concepts, reading has become more important now than ever before. Invention of high-tech gadgets and state-of-the-art information systems in
10   areas of communication, transport and general business demands more awareness about contemporary events and changes. With advancement in technology, man's eagerness to succeed has increased. Consequently the realization has dawned on him that such dreams can be materialized through intellectual advancement - a feat possible only through self-reading and personal research. With the invention of computer has commenced an age of electronic communication and online commerce.

15   Although writing letters has decreased considerably with the advent of electronic mail, it will take some time to make our varied businesses paperless. Thus though reduced, people still do some writing, wither in forms of documents, memorandums, business contracts or research papers. Education has made people more aware of his potential and reading and writing has become instrumental to man's success in today's competitive world.

Topic 164 What do you do for good health?

'Health is wealth' is very much true. One must try hard to remain healthy. If we are healthy, we can easily fight with other problems of life. But if we are unhealthy our most of life will go in fighting with health problems. It eventually leads us to failure.

People do many different things to remain healthy. Some go for a healthy diet, other recommend exercise, and the rest thinks that health awareness is important. But in my view one must not think and act only on one aspect. People must go for a healthy diet, exercise and health awareness.

25   A healthy diet is very important for one to remain healthy. People must take care of their diet. Diet should be balanced. Nowadays Americans are facing a very big problem of obesity. This is due to their unhealthy diet. Most American used to eat in fast-food restaurants. Obesity leads to many health problems like heart attack, blood pressure, cholesterol problem. Fat people can work less and with less efficiency. I sometime eat food for my tongue's taste too. But most of time I stick to my balance diet which contain fruits, green vegetable, and juices. I always take care not to intake more oily food or
30   sugary food. Sticking to healthy diet put me in great shape and healthy life.

Exercise is also important. Nowadays people make lots of excuses for not do exercise. Some have time problem, some have physical problem, some have space problem. But I think these all are excuses. One can find little tome for his or her self for healthy life. Everybody nowadays is busy but taking few minutes out of this busy schedule make lots of difference. I personally prefer Yoga. Yoga not only gives physical exercise but also mental relaxation. Meditation is my favorite. This
35   helps me in concentrating in my work as well as relaxing out of this stress full life. Few minutes of exercise can make lot difference.

Health awareness is a factor why people are living more. Nowadays life span of people is increased. People are living longer. This is because of health awareness. Regular medical checkup, clean –tidy life style, nutritious foods are few examples. Previously people eat what they found. But nowadays people read ingredients of food product as well as how
40   many vitamins it contains. I personally select food product according to my needs of vitamins, minerals etc. I also schedule appointment with my physician once in a six month. And also take care of go to dentist once in three months. In total I would love to remain healthy and for that I'll work what ever it takes. I also urge other people to stick healthy lifestyle by taking healthy food, exercise and regular medical checkup. I believe in 'prevention is better than cure.'

Topic 165 What is one thing to improve your community?

Volunteering a few hours each week to some community activity is an important way of investing in the future of our society. I chose to spend my time working with elementary school children helping them to learn to read. Developing good reading skills will help these students keep up with their classmates, open new worlds to them, and help them succeed in life.

Students who are not good readers cannot keep up with their studies. They will not understand
50   the lessons; they will come to school unprepared; they will not be able to perform. By learning to read, students will be on equal footing with their classmates. They will be active participants in class.

Books on different lifestyles, occupations, cultures, or governments will open new doors to students. Students who cannot read will only know what they see around them. Students who can read will be able to travel to new worlds and experience new ideas without ever leaving their classrooms.

55   Today, a person who cannot read is severely handicapped. A non-reader will have to work at the most menial jobs. Readers,

especially good readers, have the whole universe open to them. They will have the possibility to learn any job that interests them.

By volunteering to help an elementary school child learn to read, I am helping him or her not only today, but also for the rest of his or her life. I am helping them keep pace with their peers and explore the world and themselves through books.

Topic 166 What events make a person an adult?

The difference between children and adults are very easy to tell from their physical outlooks: children and small, weak, have a poor judgment, and have to depend on adults. On the contrary, adults are big, strong, and more independent. Every child will grow up to become an adult. What events make a person an adult? In my personal opinion, there are a lot of events that mark the turning point for a person to become adult.

10 In many countries, when a child becomes eighteen years old, he or she legally becomes an adult. There will be a big celebration and many best wishes from relatives and friends; the young person may also have a great longing for a bright future in his adult life. He may move out from his parents' house and live alone; he may start dating and doing activities which only adults can do, such as going to a pub.

Graduation from college is another big turning point for a person to become adult. In college the young person may reply
15 fully or partially on his parents for financial support, but after he graduates, he must find a job for himself, and live on his own. Graduating from college and joining the work force can also make a person an adult.

Marriage is also a big event to a person. Once become husband or wife, the young person starts to take care of others, and take responsibility for the family. Once the young person becomes a parent, he or she should also take care of the baby.

20 I believe that getting married and have children is the most important event that turns a person into an adult. Only after one gets married, does he or she take on the responsibility to the family and the society.

Topic 166 What events make a person an adult?

People recognize a difference between children and adults. There are usually some certain experiences or ceremonies that make a person an adult. Some children are in a rush to become adults and it seems to be running away from it. The child can make others believe him as an adult, by acting like one.

In most countries attaining puberty is a big step toward becoming an adult, therefore many people celebrate it. For Moslems, puberty is very important, because from that point of time the child must say his prayers. Age is another important thing for adults to accept a child as an adult. That is way we celebrate our birthdays, reaching a certain age that might differ in different countries, but it usually is the same age as a child can vote.

30 There are many events that help a child act more like an adult. For example, working and earning money is a good way for those how to become adults sooner. It gives the child confidence to be independent. For example being able to leave their parents and stay on their own can make a difference. And of course being ready to accept responsibility changes the opinion of others about a child.

So there are many ways to that even when a child dose not want to become an adult will be known as one, sooner o later.
35 And for sure for dose how are in a hurry there are lots of ways that they can prove to adults that they deserve being one earlier than they are expected to be.

Topic 166 What events make a person an adult?

What are the differences between children and adults? After a short while staying with a couple of children and adults, one may discover the answer in several aspects such as the language skills, the analyzing skills and the ability to get along with other people. Obviously an adult acts much better in solving problems and working with other people than a child does. But what events make a person an adult? As far as I am concerned, two main events are vital to the process of growing up: the experience of education and the experience of social activities.

Firstly, the most remarkable differences between children and adults are the language skills and the analyzing skills. Education is the most efficient channel to help children develop all these abilities. In grammar lessons, children have the
45 opportunity to master the rules of language gradually until they are able to understand the ideas of others completely and can fully express themselves. Through training in the lessons of reading comprehension, they learn to grasp the main idea, the structure and the organization of an article effectively, which enables them to absorb knowledge through reading in the rest of their lives. Also, the lessons in sciences like mathematics and logics contribute much to sharpen their ability of analysis. This ability is potentially a powerful device in solving all kinds of problems not only in their future careers but
50 also their daily lives as adults.

On the other hand, to get along well with other people is a highly required skill for an adult. Children often encounter obstacles with their friends in occasions like distribution of toys. They frequently show insufficient care about others and lack the strategy of compromise. Such poor performances will be improved only by continual social activities during which children will gain the precious idea of team spirit and learn how to cooperate with each other step by step, until eventually they become competent group members, which is an essential demand of adults.

Taking into account all the descriptions above, with the two major experiences, as in education and in social activities, children would turn into qualified social members, namely adults.

Topic 167 Should the school purchase computers or books?

The problem that whether school should choose to buy books or computers can be controversial nowadays because people often think that computers can replace books soon. However, I would like to be on the side of people who suggest that schools should books instead of computers. There are several reasons of it and I will discuss two main causes.

First, even though students can access the information they want more easily, they often recognize that most of the information in computers is apt to be inaccurate. Due to the fact that many people send their information by the Internet or email in order to get their own interests such as money and fame, in this case, their information are often distorted and biased.

Second, students who study their special area cannot get a deep and wide knowledge through computers because the knowledge from computers is inclined to be shallow and introductive. If possible, students have to print them out to study with long time and write something related on it.

School's essential purpose, I believe, is getting student to have a deep and wide knowledge to prepare for their future lives in society. In this perspective, books are more suitable to achieve this quintessence duty of schools than computers. Therefore schools should choose to buy books.

Topic 168 Why study abroad?

Nowadays, more and more students choose to attend schools or universities outside their home countries. Then why studying abroad is so attractive to people even though it often means greater expense and more difficulties? Because those students are bound to benefit considerably from their foreign study experience.

The modern world needs people to have comprehensive knowledge and experiences. The world is no longer a separated one in which each part can afford to be totally independent. The communication and interchange in fields of culture, business, finance and other human activities are so unprecedently frequent and vigorous that the general or specific knowledge of other members of the global village turns to be most important to the prosperity of countries, or the success of peoples. This kind of knowledge is usually better achieved if pursued abroad.

Furthermore, foreign experiences improve one's willpower and ability of adjusting to a new environment, and one's capability to overcome various hardships and setbacks. Young people are considered aggressive and ambitious. Their success is not based on comfort or easiness, but on their incessant painstakingly efforts and their never-ending willingness to surpass themselves. In a foreign country they are confronted with greater challenges, more unsteadiness and less help from their families and friends. All these undoubtedly lead to an independent, self-supporting, resourceful person who will also be sympathetic and generous to other people around.

With these advantages, we may conclude that the foreign study experience enlarges a student's view of the world, as well as improves one's personality and character, which will guarantee a more splendid future in his life and career.

Topic 169 Why is music important to many people?

Obviously music has inspired a seemingly endless stream of fantastic productions such as CD, MTV, broadcasting, concerts and so on, which we just cannot live without. Today music is not just something for fun at all. It springs out general human feelings, needs and desires at every level.

Music can brings us information about cultures, history, science, and religion all over the world. It is like the vase that can collect every little dew in every corner in the world and then pure it to irrigate people's hearts and allow people to understand each other better regardless of different languages, ages, and races.

Music provides an opportunity to reduce stress and help us walk fearlessly towards difficulties. "Never give up never give in. There can be miracles when you believe through hope is fragile it is hard to kill. " In this rush world it is inevitably that we sometimes feel so tired and frustrated and even are going to lose our hope. When our favorite tunes start playing filled with magic and power, they are like the catalyst to refresh our heart and to enable us to think on the right track In stead of beaten by adversities, we can feel so optimistic that we will continue being the truth seekers and rule our domain whatever how hard it is.

Answered without hesitation, music is an exploration of our deepest feelings and motivations and one of the greatest of human treasure. Not only is it hard to measure how much those musicians' masterpieces bring into our society but also it is also difficult to imagine how long they will continue to influence us. In conclusion, as music can function as the roll to bring the world peace and beauty, and bring people happiness and enjoyment, it is self-evident that music is so important to us.

Topic 169 **Why is music important to many people?**

Music plays a very important role in our life. We can almost hear music anywhere. Different music serves different functions in our life. Why is music important to many people? The reasons are presented below.

Music is a very important form of art. Like other arts, music is ubiquitous and has become a part of our life. The whole lifetime of most people is accompanied by music. A baby falls in sleep in the music of a lullaby; a young student may learn to play a musical instrument and listen to music from the radio, TV and a Walkman. There is music for birthdays, for weddings, for Christmas, and for New Year's Day. There is music for every single occasion in our life.

We are surrounded by various kinds of music since we were born and music has become an integral part of our life. Interesting enough, music often serves as an important part to other art forms, such as music in dancing, drama and movies. As a matter of fact, many famous music pieces come from dancing and movies, such as the theme from "Love Story".

Music is part of the history. The history of music is almost as long as the history of human civilizations. Music from old times has become the great culture heritage to us. One of the examples is classic music of Beethoven and Tchaikovsky. People enjoy their music from generation to generation.

Listening to music is one of the most popular forms of entertainment. There are so many kinds of music that can suit tastes of different people. Young people like pop music and Rock-and-Roll and older people may enjoy classical music and opera. Whether we are happy or sad, there will always be music that we can listen to.

People can express their feelings and emotions through music. Lovers often play soft love songs to show their love and devotion to each other.

For the reasons presented above, we can see how important music is to our life. It is hard to imagine a history without music, and a life without music.

Topic 169 **Why is music important to many people?**

"Music hath charms to soothe the savage breast."

English literature is full of references of music. Literatures of different eras reflect the likes, dislikes and nature of people belonging to that era. If you read music-related phrases or poems of any era, you will find that these phrases or poems reflect the same reasons people listened to music years back, as they do today.

Music is, and has always been a part of mankind. Walk into any IT company today, and you will see people working with their headphones on. Stroll into the reception of any Multinational company, you will be greeted with a pleasant music playing at a low volume from the speakers. Most people say that music helps them work better and creates a relaxing ambience. Any great occasion is incomplete without music. Be it Valentine's Day, friendship day, someone's birthday, or a party. On Valentine's Day, love songs hit the top charts; special cassettes are complied as valentine day's specials. On parties and birthdays, people like to celebrate with loud music.

Can you imagine any type of dance without music? Dance steps are created according to the rhythm and beats of different types of music. Operas, plays and musicals all revolve around music. While watching different dance forms and musicals, you also enjoy the music that is a part of it.

You will find that music is your best companion. If you are feeling low, there will be peppy songs to cheer you. If you are in a philosophical mood there will be different types of music to add to your reflective mood. Different people have different preferences towards music during different moods.

There is an endless variety of music available - instrumental, blues, jazz, rock, pop, reggae and lots more. Every type of music has a different impact on people. Some people prefer to begin their day with soft instrumental music. Some prefer hard rock playing in their cars as they drive to work. Different people like to end their day listening to different types of music.

So, music is an inherent part of human life. Even nature has it's own music. Bird's chirping in the morning, water gushing down rivers, and breeze blowing through trees are all a part of nature's own music. Life without music would be still and meaningless. That's the reason people listen to music for different reasons and at different times.

Topic 170 **Why are groups or organizations important to people?**

Human beings are social animals. One cannot live a good life, if totally without others. Although people sometimes may prefer staying alone to think and do their things, generally, they have to join social activities. Obviously, group activities are an important part of people's lives.

Since the ancient times, people learned to live together. Compared with the cruel natural environment, human beings seemed too weak and helpless. Wild animals posed a threat to their lives all the time. If, instead of fighting with the severe nature together, by living alone, few could be successful to survive. People at that time had to take part in-group activities.

Even in today's modern society, with the help of highly developed science and technology, people do not need to struggle for survive and life becomes no longer as dangerous and hard as before, group activities are still a necessary in many aspects. In my opinion the following are some important arguments.

5   First, group activities help people to reach their goals. As we all know, one piece of chopstick is easy to be broken, but when ten pieces of chopstick are bound together, it will be a tough job to break them. Suppose building a house, one person may spend years to finish, but when groups of people take part in, the building will be accomplished more quickly.

Besides, group activities can help people when difficulties arise. It is hard to imagine when a person, who never joins in group activities, suddenly got sick, what he will feel if nobody comes to help and take care of him.

10   The most important of all, group activities make life more colorful. This can be testified in our daily life. It is fantastic to take part in signing, dancing, or traveling groups, after tight-stringed workdays. But all this activities will lose their attractions and meaning if done by a person alone. Suppose a very sociable person may be surrounded by applause and respect. Absolutely this will boost up his self-confidence, and therefore makes his life more enjoyable.

Group activities have already become an indispensable part of people's life. So how can you shun other people? Go out
15   and meet them!

Topic 171 **What one thing would you take for a trip?**

Whenever I prepare for a long trip, I remember that there is always one thing which I will remind myself to take with me every single time, that is a photo of my whole family, with my mom and dad and me in it. I know that one will be enough for me, and I tell myself at the bottom of my heart that this one photo will be my best companion through the entire trip. It
20   constantly brings me back the warm feeling of home and it helps me overcome those difficulties on my way.

Wherever I go, one family photo always tends to provide me the familiar feeling of home and a sense of belonging. For any person, especially a sensitive girl like me, the biggest enemy is nothing but loneliness and fear. Immersed by that wordless isolation and fear of the brand-new environment you have to deal with. There are no friends by your sides to
25   talk to and there is no one or place you can rely on. What do you need the most at this moment? I may say a photo of your family, of all your very dearest family members in it, your mom, dad and your brothers and sisters. They are the biggest comfort one can feel so directly and immediately. Their sincere smiles and their soft and emotional eye-expressions soon remind you again that familiar feeling of home and the power to assure you that no matter where you are, you are not a rambler in this cold world and you are not all alone by yourself, you belong to them and to that home.

30   Also, a family photo helps one get through one's difficulties when they are on a trip. What do we think of the most when we are in trouble or in those tough situations that we have to deal with? Is it not our own families? What are we longing to see and hear the most? Is it not their loving faces and their caring words? Well, why not take a look at your photo in hand when they are not around at those particular moments? For it has a incredibly invisible power which can restore your inspiration and your faith at that very instant when your eyes make contact with your mom and dad. You feel as if you can
35   see through their eyes and hear their genuine suggestions.

Relief you from that desperate loneliness and comfort you when without anyone around but those hardest times come into life; that is what a family photo can do--forever be a very best companion of you on your way of that endless trip...

Topic 171 **What one thing would you take for a trip?**

When you see a beautiful view of rising sun, when you see a spectacular waterfall, when you enjoy the moment you travel with your friends, at this time, what do you especially want? I believe the answer is a camera. It is also what I would take in addition to clothing and personal care items when I plan to have a long trip.

The main reason for taking a camera is that a camera will record everything that happens during a trip. If you see a beautiful scenery, you can take a picture of it. If you meet a humorous and nice person on the way, you can have someone taken a picture for you and the new friend. If you meet a girl you fall in love in the trip, why not ask your friend to take a
45   picture when you give a rose to her? Let's imagine how disappointed it is if you do not have a camera with you at that time.

Another reason is that each picture is a memory. Maybe a person will take many trips in his life, if you take many pictures in each trip, you will find it is just like a novel about your own life. When you are old, you will always recall many things that happened long before. At that time, you will take out the albums and look at them with happy tears. You also can find how you loved the life and what a pleasant life that god gave you.

50   Above the two reasons, you can find it is very important to take a camera with your trip. And that is my choice when I am preparing for a trip.

Topic 171 What one thing would you take for a trip?

If there were just one other thing I could take with me on a trip, it would most probably have to be my copy of *Hitchhiker's Guide to the Galaxy*, my favorite novel by Douglas Adams.

This might seem to be a strange choice to many people, most of whom would generally prefer instead, to take something of more practical value, like a cell-phone or a camera. I however, do have reasons for my decision.

For one thing, I am a book-worm. I adore reading books, and cannot imagine a world without them. Books relieve boredom, dissipation, and listlessness. To me, books are the perfect antidote to counter depression and loneliness, feelings that one is bound to experience if one is going to stay away from home for such a long period. *The Hitchhikers Guide to the Galaxy* is a book that is calculated to enliven any mood, and any situation.

Another reason for my choice is that a trip generally entails a lot of traveling. I am not excessively fond of traveling, but I happen to be one of those people who can read while traveling, and so find it a most delightful way to spend journeys that otherwise tend to be rather tedious. The book has made bearable many a boring journey in the past and I anticipate that it will stand me in good stead during this trip too.

The hitchhiker's guide to the Galaxy has been my favorite book for a long time now. I have read it several times, and look forward to reading it again and again. It has brought laughter and humor into my life, and I cannot remember a page in the book that I did not enjoy. It has been an admirable travel companion to me in the past, and I would definitely take it with me on my trip for the simple reason that it is one of my most prized possessions.

Topic 171 A picture

If I were supposed to leave my home for one year, I will take surely with me, besides clothing and personal care items, the picture of my girlfriend.

I will take my girlfriend's picture with me, mainly because she is the most important person in my life. Also to be able to see her all days and finally to remember that there is something important to return my home.

My girlfriend is the love of my life. During all the time I have spent with her, I have realized that she is the only woman I want to be for the rest of my life. She brings me both peace and security. Furthermore she gives me a reason to keep enjoying this party called "the life." No matter how, I will always try to be with her. That is why, carrying a picture of her can be a way to see her during all this long year. I could see her anytime I wanted to, no matter what time it is. In the mornings I would receive all her blessing thoughts just by looking to the picture. This would give me the strength to start the day with happiness. In the afternoons I could buy some food and eat in front of her to feel that we are eating together. Finally during the nights I could talk to the picture, pretending that she is there in the same place with me, and tell her all the experiences I got through the day, so that would help me to go to the bed not feeling alone but full of peace.

The picture would help me to remember that there is someone in other place who loves me and who cares about me. It would remind me that I have her to support me and give me all the confidence I need to be a better man in my life. In conclusion, If I have to choose one thing to take with me in a one year trip, that will be without a doubt my girlfriend's picture. Basically I would feel that she is with me all the time, I would remember that someone else loves me and that I love her too, and finally the picture would bring me the strength and will to be a better person and return eagerly to my home.

Topic 172 How can schools help new students with their problems?

Students always face problems when they move to a new school. It might take a long time for them to get familiar with the new neighborhood and the new environment. And it is undoubtedly the responsibility of the schools to help them out.

The most urgent task is to settle the newcomers down and make them acquainted with the neighborhood. In some public schools, the school-owned apartment is far from adequate, therefore the schools may do something to help the students find apartments, as well as provide them with temporary accommodations. There is also little time for students to learn where the laundry, the post office, the supermarket, etc., are. Thus, it is helpful and convenient of the school to provide information as above for the new students.

Students do study. So it is also important for new students to be familiar with the academic stuffs of the new school. I believe it is the academic departments' responsibility to provider the students with such information. Introductory seminars help students be aware of how do the faculties to in their research work such that they can choose their research field and advisor rationally.

What is more, it is also necessary for the newcomers to be fully involved with the traditions of the new school. It is well known than different schools have different traditions, and these traditions should be a precious experience of the students. Then it is always reasonable that the schools provider some opportunities, for instance, holding lectures.

To sum up, the schools may take various measures to help the new students become acquainted with their new neighborhood, and to give the new students adequate information about the school, for example, academic information and traditions. These make the students familiar with the new schools as soon as possible.

Topic 173 Does borrowing money from friends harm friendship?

It is claimed that developing a real friendship is a long and complicated process. Maybe the reason is that firstly people have to know each other very well. And after that they begin to trust each other and to prove themselves as real friends.

Unfortunately, it is as difficult to develop a friendship, as it is easy to ruin one. One of the things that can test friendship is borrowing money from a friend. I do agree that sometimes it could harm or damage the friendship. Money can destroy almost everything, in fact.

Borrowing and lending money can be considered as signs of mutual trust. And if the money is not given back in time or not given back at all it will embarrass both parties. Thus series of misunderstandings begin which could actually ruin the 10 friendship.

Borrowing money is often comprehended as a simple act of help and favor. But when the faith in the reliability of a friend is lost it will harm and damage the friendship for sure.

Friendship resembles a contract between two people, although its rules remain unwritten. And when one of the friends does not play by the rules the other one simply quits the game called friendship. The result is a bitter recollection from a 15 damaged friendship. In conclusion-we have a few real friends in our lifetime and it would be a shame to lose some of them because of such banal problem as money. In my opinion, money does not worth as much as our friends do. And if we cause harm to any of them and if we ruin something so important and invaluable as real friendship because of money, it will be one of the biggest mistakes in our lives.

So let's be wiser and never make a friend go because of money.

Topic 174 How is your generation different from your parents'?

Everybody talks about a conflict between generations. This is a well-known expression, used as an explanation for misunderstandings between people of different ages. Although sometimes this is an excuse for not recognizing who is wrong or right, it is certain that every generation of people is different in important ways.

Even though everybody probably thinks this way, the differences between my generation and 25 my parents' generation are striking. The technological progress is a certain cause for these differences. My parents did not have access to information as teenagers nowadays have. Television, for example, was a luxury that not many people could have afforded, and even if they could, the television programs were very poor. I remember my mother mentioning how eager they were to watch TV series like "Samantha" or "The Giants' Planet." Those films seem so trivial these days.

30 Another important difference between our generations is caused by the type of political power that governed the country. My parents grew up under a communist regime whose main characteristic was censure. This censure prohibited them to speak up their mind in public. Strict rules must have been obeyed; otherwise they could have been seriously punished. Nowadays, we live in a democratic environment that cannot possibly be compared with the pressure of a communist government. This means that people are encouraged to think for themselves and not to fear to express their true opinion. 35 Of course, this leads sometimes to violent acts from people who misunderstand the role of the democracy.

Differences between generations have always existed and it is natural for them to exist. Progress leads to differences of opinions and points of view. It is true that my generation and my parents' generation are different, but this does not mean that one is significantly better than the other one. I think we all should remember that before starting to judge one another.

Topic 175 Should students do some of the talking on classes?

There is a growing public concern over education methods, and the speaker in the title above advocates that education will be truly effective only when it is specifically designed to meet the individual needs and interests of each student. By contrast, some people may argue that the traditional teacher-centered way is more suitable for education. On balance, I would like to side with the former opinion.

First of all, the traditional teacher-centered education ignores the individual needs and 45 interests of each student, which proves counterproductive. For centuries, we place too much emphasis on the importance of teachers in education, and take it for granted that it is the teachers' duty to determine what and how to teach, meanwhile, the students should accept what are provided to them. But recent study committed by many experts of psychology and education reveals that this traditional single-side education method has low efficiency, because this way of teaching puts students in almost a passive position. As our society progresses every minute, old concept of education 50 should be transformed, from teacher-centered to student-centered, which will help to achieve more quickly and effective teaching and learning.

As a matter of fact, only earnest communication and interactions lead to better effects of study, and they should base on the acknowledgment of the differences from on student to another. Since teaching is a process full of interaction, a mutual understand helps teachers to adjust the way of teaching and to let students represent their reactions at the same time. Furthermore, every student is a unique individual. They may differ from each other in regards to reading, writing, comprehension, etc. Consequently, when teaching the classes, a teacher takes diversity of students into account is more likely to pass knowledge to students than a teacher who ignores the difference.

In addition, student-centered education can most effectively involve individual student in the learning process. When
5   student-centered education is introduced, students will feel that they are be focused on, which may help them to participate in the learning process, and this proactive condition will contribute to effective learning. Not only do the students benefit from this method, teachers will soon discover that teaching is becoming a joyful thing, not dull any longer. Another reason to advocate student-centered education is the relationship between students and teachers, or learning and teaching, which was considered two separate things, are in fact two sides of a coin. Once the harmony between these two
10 things is established, effective education will become reality.

However, when we suggest student-centered method, winking at students' unreasonable desired would only result in chaos in education. Like any method else, student-centered education may also have some side effects, if we do not make some rules to control students' behavior, teaching will a tough job and leaning will like playing games. Since these images are not supposed, appropriate management should be introduced with student-centered education.

15 In sum, it is very likely that people will never be able to come to the same conclusion on this controversial issue due to their different experiences and conflicting values, public awareness of the various dimensions of the issue discussed in the above argument will certainly contribute to the thorough understanding of the problem. Though different views exist, I insist than student-centered education with effective management will enrich our education.

| Topic 176 **What holiday would you create?** | If I could create a new holiday, it would be a holiday that honors the freedom and progress of the Afghan women. I would established the holiday to multiply efforts of the Feminist Majority Foundation with the Campaign to help Afghan Women and young girls to ensure that women's rights are fully and permanently restored after the fall of the Taliban regime, which symbolized the brutality against the women in Afghanistan in the past years. |

When the Taliban took control in 1996, they instituted a gender apartheid for the women where they imposed strict edicts
25 such as banished women from the work force, closed school to girls, expelled women from universities, prohibited women from leaving their home unless accompanied by a close male relative, forced women to use the burga or chadari, paint windows of women's houses black, prohibited women from being examined by male physicians, while at the same time prohibited most female doctors and nurses from practicing.

The reality for the women during Taliban control shows a lot of horrors against the women who defied the rules of the
30 Taliban and were severely punished. For example some girls were killed in front of their families because they run to the schools; some women were brutally heated because their ankle was accidentally showed from underneath their burga. Two women accused of prostitution were publicly hanged in the stadium.

Today, after the fall of Taliban, women can leave their homes without the escort of a male family member. They no longer have to cram into the back of buses and give up their seats to men. They can get their hair and nails done in beauty salons
35 that have opened up all over Kabul. Girls can go to school, and young women to universities, where they sometimes even share classrooms with men. Being a woman can sometimes be an advantage in the job market. In Kabul, Indian models are admired for their fashion, but many Afghan women still wear the traditional burqa.

I would like that the people celebrate the new holiday by publishing the advances of the campaign through web sites, organizing some lectures about the progress of the afghan women, promoting scholarships for women to study, and
40 encouraging the women from all over the world to maintain the faith to pursue the dreams.

The reason why I would create an international holiday for the Afghan women is because the international community must now act to ensure that women's rights are fully and permanently restored, to reestablish a constitutional democracy in Afghanistan that is representative of women and ethnic minorities, and to show an example to women of the world of how can we solve difficulties in this way.

| Topic 176 **What holiday would you create?** | People remember the memorable events and great deeds or achievements of great people of a country by celebrating specific holidays as a mark of respect and honor. If I have the opportunity to create a new holiday in my country India, I would like to add 27th August, as one of the national holidays to honor the birth day of noble laureate Mother Teresa to remind all of us about her selfless devotion to the poor, destitute and unwanted sections of our |
50 society.

Mother Teresa left her country, Macedonia at a tender age of eighteen and embraced the city of joy, Calcutta, to serve the poor. She initially taught in the Christian missionary school and later she was moved by the pathetic conditions of the homeless people mostly living in the slums. She gave up her teaching profession and started working with her meager savings for the uplift for the causes of the poor.

Initially she had to face the trouble weather from various sections of society. Her continued selfless devotion and love for such unwanted and neglected sections of people was widely acclaimed later on by majority sections of the society and generous financial grants poured in from various agencies. She had further extended her "mission of Charity" for the lepers, orphans etc with the support of over 1000 volunteers working beyond the geographical boundaries of India.

5   Her love and selfless social service is unparalleled and needs to be reminded on this 27th-August each year by different like-minded groups in the society to walk to different slums with the poor, lepers, orphans or people sufferings from various incurable diseases and bestow their love and affection. They should provide them with clothes, foods, gifts, and financial assistance and take them out in the heart of the city through a procession.

This would help the weaker sections of the society to join the mainstreams of the society and they will not feel neglected
10   and uncared for. Moreover, such love and affection would avert the increasing trend of crimes in the society.

In the present day everyone is on a retrace for his or her material comfort and the human value is on the decline. The remembrance of Mother Teresa's teachings would motivate people for contributing towards a great cause of the society and make this world a better place to live.

Topic 177 **A vacation or a car?**

On the question of whether it is better to use one's savings to buy a car or go on traveling, I, more often than not, prefer to the latter decision.

It is true that having a car has a variety of advantages; I must confess that I myself enjoy the fun of driving and the strong sense of freedom gained from owing a car. Superior as it is, nevertheless, it brings its own problems. For one thing, private car burdens the traffic that has already been over loaded. Every one of us must have experienced the miserable feeling of being stuck at tollgate on our way to office; only at this moment do most people
20   realize how bad the result of uncontrolled increase in private vehicles can be. For another, it worsens the problem of environmental pollution. The fun of driving is one thing, while how to deal with the consequence of air pollution is another. It is estimated that every year the government of China spends well over 12% of its fiscal income to tackle the environmental damage caused by automobiles.

As a matter of fact, the advantages of going traveling outweigh any benefit we gain from having a car. First of all, studies
25   show that traveling is amongst the most desirable alternatives of social activities. It is obvious that a person fund of traveling must be healthier that one 'dwelling' in his car. Hiking, mountain climbing, camping, skiing, canoeing and all other tourism related exercises force us to use our muscles, stretch our bodies and deepen our breath. More over, the overwhelming joy of conquering a mountain peak or lingering in one of the most famous Middle East bazaars is surely out of reach in your car. In addition, traveling fans hardly have to suffer from the torture of sleepless which has long been
30   bothering the 'white collars'. Still, the enchanting beauty of various landscapes and folk cultures helps broaden your eyesight and provides you with a brand new insight into the mysterious planet.

From what has been discussed above, we may safely draw the conclusion that it is not only wise but also socially desirable for us to spend our money on tourism rather than buying a car.

Topic 177 **A vacation or a car?**

The development of technologies and industries has brought us many conveniences. With the help of modern conveniences such as cars, buses, trains and planes, one can travel a great distance in a short period of time. One of my friends has received a gift of money. He is thinking about using this money to buy a new car or go on a vacation. Personally I would suggest that my friend buy a car.

The first and most important reason is that a car can bring him convenience. Undoubtedly, nowadays people rely on cars for transportation more than ever before. For example, when he drives a car to go shopping, he may feel more convenient
40   and can pick up more groceries than before because he can put groceries in the car trunk instead of carrying them by hands. Furthermore, when he wants to pick somebody up, or travel to a scenic spot, a car will make him feel convenient.

Another great reason why I encourage my friend to buy a car is that my friend will not spend much time on commuting anymore. Everyday we waste too much time on waiting for a bus or riding a bicycle to work. We all experienced the frustration of taking a bus. After having their own cars, such the problems will disappear automatically.

45   Of course, if my friend decides to use his money to go on a vacation, I think that there are some advantages also. For example a vacation may increase his personal experience and knowledge, and may even reduce many troubles that are related to a car. But if all the factors are contemplated, I think that the advantages of buying the car will carry more weight than those of going on vacation.

From what has been discussed above, I may safely draw the conclusion that buying a car will be a right choice for my
50   friend.

Topic 178 **Changes in the 21st century**

About a decade ago, people were eagerly looking forward to ushering the new century-the 21st century with the hope of seeing a fresh beginning of human civilization. There is no denying that with the development of the IT industry and numerous other industries, people's life is getting more and more convenient. However, I have to act as a wet blanket here, unwilling though I am, to point out that the blind "progressiveness" of human beings have caused an irretrievable disaster that is revealing its monstrous face in the new century.

5   The first sign of damaged nature appeared much earlier without being noticed by us. As a result, nature continues to be abused. My grandmother lives in the countryside. Years ago, when I was still a little girl, there was endless woods and crystal clear streams and rivers there, but now, what you can possibly find are chopped down wasteland and yellow-colored brooks. The environment is deteriorating in spite of a few people's awareness of the danger.

Consequently, the deteriorated environment breeds a far more moody climate than before. My hometown is a beautiful seaside city. Living here for more than two decades, I didn't see any sandstorm until this spring. I could hardly breathe or
10   see things clearly in the yellowish air. I was in shock. Another example comes from a city afar near the Mediterranean. Floods devastate the summerhouses along the coast, aborting people's plans for the summer and causing enormous damage to the economy of those countries.

Therefore, I want to say when you are surfing on line, browsing the messages sent through your cell phones and busy in doing biotechnological experiments, do not be overwhelmed by the benefits of the new century, instead, you should think
15   more about how to protect the environment and thus improve the climate, which is indeed the biggest change brought by the new century.

Topic 178 Changes in the 21st century

With the advent of the 21st century, the world is facing many changes. There are incredible advancements in science and technology fields. In my point of view, these breakthroughs will bring more conveniences to people and make our life easier.

20   First of all, one of the most significant changes is the use of computers and robots. Using of such computers and robots in industries can bring an increase in output and accuracy. Also, these computer parts and robots are being made so tiny that they can be built into both personal and industrial equipments.

Moreover, there will be more innovations, inventions and researches in different areas of science and technology, such as more advanced telecommunication with a new generation of satellites, faster means of transportations, newer engines for
25   planes, and quicker diagnosis of diseases by using advanced auto analyzers.

On the other hand, a few disadvantages such as air and water pollution, decreasing of natural resources cannot be underestimated. Although these negative aspects are almost negligible in comparison with great advancements of this new century, most scientists believe that these negative effects are not overrated.

In conclusion, it can be concluded that not only does the new century brings us many great advantages, but also it brings a
30   few disadvantages in which people have to deal with.

Topic 179 What are qualities of a good parent?

Parents play an important role in the child's upbringing. However, it is not easy to be a good parent, much to the surprise of those who think dealing with young children is a piece of cake. In my view, to be a good parent you have to meet certain requirements that I am going to discuss further in the following paragraphs.

35   You should spend time with your child. Please do not mistake me. By that I am not saying you must resign from your job and stay at home with your baby all day; instead, I am referring to quality time. To be a good parent you need to know your child well; if you do not even have the minimum amount of time to start with, how on earth are you going to know your child? No matter how busy you are, be you a businessman or a police officer, you must get some time off work to be with your child. Knowing how impressionable a child at his tender age is, you cannot expect him to feel close to someone
40   he barely see everyday, much less play the role of a good parent. However, I am not talking about large amount of time that busy as you are, you may not be able to afford. Remember, it is quality time, not quantity time. You can be a CEO and still be a good parent if you make good use of the limited amount of time you spend with your child. A small talk after dinner or a little story before bed may well perform the magic.

In order to be a good parent, you also have to be strict; it is for the child's own good. He may not like it of course, who
45   will? However, it is from strict parent that a child learns discipline. Under certain circumstances I even agree with the use of force. A good beating or a severe scolding is far easier to remember for a little child than a patient persuasion. He is too young for you to reason with; but you can make him learn his lesson the hard way if the little sweet talk fails. Though I think the use of force is the last resort a parent should turn to, it is nonetheless rather effective.

A good parent should be caring and loving. A strong bond is formed between the parent and the child if there is love.
50   This is something magical and inexplicable but both the parent and the child feel it. What makes a parent so special and important is the unconditional love he/she gives to his/her child. A loving and caring environment is very crucial in a child's growth. Statistics have shown that those from happy families have a more optimistic view of the world and generally live happy lives, while those from broken families or families where both parents quarrel often are more irritable and peevish. A child's character is easily shaped by the surroundings so it is a parent's responsibility to provide a loving

environment to his/her child.

A good parent should also be a good role model for the child to look up to. A child learns many of his habits from his parents and it is all up to a parent to choose what kind of habits he/she wants his/her child to inherit. For example, a parent should immediately quit smoking if he/she notices his/her child has the tendency to pick up this bad habit. All in

5 all, a good parent should behave himself in order to set good examples to his child. To be a good parent is hard but not impossible; in fact I believe all those who really put in a great deal of effort should find themselves doing well in this job. After all what is more important is the attitude; if one wants to be a good parent, he can do it.

Topic 180 Why movies are so popular?

There is no denying that movies have inspired a seemingly endless stream of fantastic and exciting issues that we just cannot live without. In fact, the dizzying emergence of movie production can create everything we can imagine on screens and what's more they continue bringing us the most wonderful stars and classic stories that will be always remembered by us. Movies have not only been a kind of entertainment we can enjoy, they but have also helped build up an important part of our society.

15 With the high-tech development of electronic tools it is possible to make everything we are eager to see, especially something that people are always curious about such as dinosaurs, spaceships and even something very scary, unbelievable or gorgeous. For example, directed by an impressive well-known story, The Lord Of The Rings brings us to a supernatural world filled with miracles and imaginations that impressed people a lot.

Based on nicely written stories perhaps the most important thing is that movies introduce us those amazing actors. Not
20 only are they so pretty and handsome but they also are the best artists that contribute to our world in many ways. Because of all the celebrated characters they personated, they are considered as the symbol of brave, optimistic, strong-willed and pure-hearted people who are dare to walk fearlessly towards the challenges. Encouraged by them, we become more and more confident and make our minds to be the truth seekers that will insist on overcoming every difficulty to stop being mundane and mediocre.

25 Even some stars were gone long ago they are still our irreplaceable spirit's leaders such as Clark Gable, Audrey Hepburn, and others. Movies are always not just be appreciated by their dramatic pictures, they are deeply analyzed by worthiness, humanity, ideology and the complex influence they will bring into people's mind. In conclusion, with gorgeous ornamentation and very valuable themes it is no surprising that movies are extremely popular overall the world. Known as the epitome of our realistic society, movies can always dominate its place and continue to bring us what we want to see in
30 sight and what we want to feel in heart.

Topic 181 Should lands be developed?

Just as our human beings came from nature, we would return to nature sooner or later. It is self-evident that losing our natural condition means that we are building up a sepulcher for ourselves.

Nature is the original source of our food, house utilities and industries. So we cannot live
35 without her. Sucked the nutrition from nature, we created a wonderful world. She is our mother who we always turn back on. Wise and resourceful are people to try their best to keep nature prosperous and abounded.

Many people may hold the wrong opinion that spending money in preserving nature is a big waste of money. Even though, it is true that we cannot see much of the returns in the near future, it is worthy in the long run. What is more, nature itself can make money. The beautiful landscape of nature that was saved will attract many visitors. We also have
40 many different famous places for people who came from all over the world. In fact, it is a high-profit business and will contribute to our economic in the days coming.

Taking a look at our country's qoe-state, our agrarian land is diminishing quickly. Nature areas are vanishing year by year. We are just facing a thorny way that needs us to take measurements on immediately. Thus, there is no reason to neglect the fact that there is more need for land to be left in its natural condition.

45 Burdening the great historical task, we cannot use up the limited source to fulfill our unbounded desires. Housing and industry but make us live a bit more comfortable now. They cannot lead us go further. We should leave what we have inherited from our ascendants to the descendants.

Topic 182 Is human relationship with pets useful?

Human has a long history of feeding pets. With the development of human society more and more people have pets in their families. They love to be accompanied by their pets and they look them as their family members. They eat with their pets, stroll with their pets, and even sleep with their pets. And I think having a close relationship with pets is very good for people, the reasons why I say so as follows.

First, having a pet is very good for children. Children always need someone to play with them, take care of them, but their parents cannot do it all the time. When children have a pet, for example, a dog, they will be attracted by it and spend most of their time playing with it. The children will not feel lonely when their parents cannot take care of them. Besides, that also makes parents have their own time to do something they need.

Second, pets are also good for adults, especially those works under pressure. Now many people work so hard everyday
5 that they do not have time to relax and talk with friends. If they have pets, whenever they get to home they can talk to them, look them as persons, tell them what they are anxious about. This would help people to reduce their pressure and make them have a better mood.

Third, most of the owners of pets are senior citizens. That's not a coincidence. Because youngsters leave home for their new lives. They do not have much time to spend with their parents. The old people feel so lonely when they facing the
10 empty rooms. Pets can reduce their loneliness. Old people can take care of them, feed them, talk to them just like taking care of their own children. And the medical research shows that patting pets, such as cats and dogs can reduce the blood pressure, this is also very important to old people.

Although sometimes pets make your room a mess, break your favorite vase, even some time they bite you, the advantages of having a close relationship with pets overweight the disadvantages. Have a pet if you like and enjoy it.

Topic 182 **Is human relationship with pets useful?**	Many pets are said to be men's best friends. Though being only an animal or a bird, still they are considered to be a part of the family. They share a special bonding with the members of the family. I definitely believe that these relationships are good. There are many reasons to it.

We see many families today with dogs or cats as their pets. We get a variety of pets' food.
These families feed their pets with these foods available in the market and raise their pets like their own family members.
20 Today the expenses for raising a child and a pet are the same. Though an animal cannot talk it can understand well and the same as what human beings do. Many pets provide emotional support to the family that they just do it by their mere existence.

Dogs are said to be the best caretakers. They bark upon strangers and welcome known people. In this way it helps his family by guarding them against any dangers. There have been many cases in the past were animals have actually helped in
25 preventing robbery or any other unknown dangers.

These animals do feel the same as humans do. When the family to which he belongs to is not there at home he becomes sad and stops eating. In fact these animals show different signs when they are happy. For example, dogs wag their tail when they see their owners or any of the family members. Since they have the same quality what humans have they are bound to get close to family they belong to and it's the same with the family too. They are provided medication if not well,
30 taken to veterans and treated in the same manner in the way any other family member would have treated if unwell.

Animals are said to be their best friends since they do not stab the family they are in. There are movies that show different relationships, which an animal shares with his owner. These movies actually depict the real cases or the real emotion of the animals as well as the family towards them. They expect love and care, which their family gives. Also in a family, when a child grows up he goes to high school and then college. He no longer stays with his parents. But the pet of the family is
35 still there in that family caring and being cared by the family.

Thus because of the human quality of kindness, emotional and well being animals form an important part of the family they belong to and the family treats them as one amongst them.

Topic 182 **Is human relationship with pets useful?**	Pets have always been a part of human life structure. Thus, each and every human culture contains different morals and regulations on treating the pets. For my part, I must argue in favor of treating pets almost like family members. I am going to mention two reasons to support the slightly altered idea.

First of all, I'd like to mention the fact, that no matter human, animal or plant a living thing has needs and feelings, which if not fulfilled, could have serious effects on its physical and mental (or spiritual) health. Thus, although one may criticize owning and keeping a pet, does not bring as much responsibility as raising a child, the concept of responsibility and caring
45 remains the same in both situations. Consequently I believe the owners should be blamed in case they do not realize and accept the pet's rights, and history of binding in the loving and caring natural environment, which fulfilled all its needs, and in case they keep and treat it as it were a mere source of entertainment or labor. As I mentioned before, a pet is almost comparable with a child. Taking the responsibility to pet an animal requires determined commitment to fulfill its needs and replacing the loving environment it could have in nature, with another loving one. Therefore, if accepted in the
50 social culture as a member of the family, the pet is more likely to receive what it deserves.

In addition to the necessity of the sensational bindings and mutual relationships between the pet and its owners, which makes it like a member of the family, there is a disadvantage to this highly sensational binding. First, they owners should always keep in mind to prioritize emotional and financial needs of the human family members. Secondly, most domestic animals have shorter life than human beings, therefore the owners -in other word, human family members- usually encounter its death during their lifetime. As a result, I believe that the owners must always keep this fact in mind in order to prevent deep sensational damages. Consequently, although taking care of the pet's health, the owners should be able to control their emotional reliance on the pet. However, the unsafe and corrupted human communication in our modern world makes lots of owners so bound to their pets, that they find living difficult after their loss.

5 A question has been raised on whether pets should be treated as members of the family or not. The needs of pets and the responsibility of the owners as well as the fact that pets usually die before their owners and that human family members must have higher priorities, make me agree with the idea in case the word almost could be added to the main question.

Topic 182 Is human relationship with pets useful?

I think that having close relationship with pets is good as long as you do not over do it. Pets are friendly and loving. Let me explain my point of view.

Pets can be our friends. Especially in old age when our children go away from home to study we feel lonely, then we can keep a pet. Pets could keep us busy and lessen the feeling of loneliness. We can spend most of the time with pets like feeding them, and taking them a walk. Pets are healthy to keep if they could take our mind off of the troubles of day. But on the other hand, if we worry unnecessarily about the items

15 such as food, clothes etc. and behavior of pet, then it's not healthy for us.

Some animals like cats, parrots, and rabbit are very loving. We can easily love these animals. But emotional involvement with animals is not very good. Some people treat pets as part of their family. They take pets to their own bedrooms and give them place to sleep on their bed. They give them seat on couch or take them in the lap. I do not think all this is very healthy for us. We should have separate utensils and space for pets. A few people try to teach pets eating with spoon and

20 forks, they are happy if pets learn easily. Expecting pets to behave like humans might not be good for pets, after all they are animals.

There are many store who sell all kind of stuff related to pets such as pet food, pet clothes, pet toys, and pet homes. Buying nutritious food and separate homes for pets is necessary. We should even buy a few toys for entertainment of our pet. Now a day's pet owners spend hundreds of dollars on buying special types of pet food, costly toys, and expensive pet

25 homes. They try to get luxurious things for their pets. I think these people should donate some of that money to child food banks, since many children in our country do not have food to eat. I think spending extra money on pets is waste of money.

According to me, pets can be friendly and feeling close to them can be healthy, if we do not worry much about them.

Topic 183 What have you learned about a country from its movies?

I believe that every film contains a lot of information about the county where it was made. Usually films show us the great variety of cultural peculiarities about country where they came from. Personally, I have learnt many new things about different countries and their people from watching their movies.

I remember, as a child I used to enjoy watching Indian films. It was very exciting experience

35 for a young girl who was fond of Indian songs and the national clothes. From Indian movies I learnt that the Indian culture is very rich and colorful. I found out that they are mostly romantic people who love to sing and dance. Also, it was interesting to know that there are different religions and a plethora of ethnic groups in India.

I would say that I learnt a lot not only about Indian traditions and culture from watching its films. To tell the truth, Russian movies were very educational for me too. If you watch them carefully, you will probably notice that they contain a

40 great amount of information about Russian people and their culture. For example, I realized that Russians are incredibly honest people who like to celebrate many events with a lot of food, and of course with vodka. I learnt from Russian films about their hostility and willingness to great and meet other people. Russian movies show that all that is a big part of their traditions.

To summarize, I would say that from watching international films we are able to learn many new things about different

45 nations. Moreover, films educate us about cultural and traditional varieties of many countries.

Topic 183 What have you learned about a country from its movies?

Movies are an important part of the culture of a country where they are made. Watching a film, like listening to music or reading a book can tell one a lot about things that people value and the way they interact. In this essay I would like to share my perception about the United States that I gained by watching American movies.

My first observation is that the USA is a very rich country. This is reflected in the types of average people shown in the movies, most of whom are home-owners with a car and a full-time job. They usually can afford to dine in fine restaurants and travel around the world. For example, in the recent movie "Just Married", a young couple from America stayed in nice hotels and traveled all around Europe for their honeymoon.

US movies are also high-budget movies with a lot of special effects and excellent sound and picture quality. This is another reflection of the amount of wealth in the country that can produce movies such as "Troy", "Titanic" or "Gladiator" that featured both multi-million budgets and collections from the theaters around the world.

5   Another observation is that Americans are very individualistic and independent people. Children leave the family after the high school, since when they often do not receive support from their parents and have to rely on themselves to maintain their living. Many young movie characters (such as in the movie "Bartender" have to support themselves or their education by low-prestige jobs such as waiting even if their parents are very wealthy.)

The last feature of America that I observed from US movies is that Americans are very direct in dealing with other people. They quickly speak their mind regardless of the other person's title or the social status.

10 I am well aware that movies may exaggerate some of the features characteristic of the country they were made in. Nevertheless I believe that in general they give a fairly good picture of the country's traditions, norms and values. I think that by watching American movies I gained a good understanding of the Unites States, its society and its people.

Topic 183 What have you learned about a country from its movies?

As my number one hobby, movies take me to different eras, atmospheres, feelings and nations, all the before mentioned is in hand thanks to the technology available nowadays.

The film industry can be observed and digested by many angles, entertainment, documentary, science fiction, comedy or drama. The magic of taking the time to observe rather to watch a film produces a mind trip to every way the camera was filming.

Issues such as costumes, politics, ignorance, and fear need no passport while being filmed, the human condition as well as its surroundings can be captured in the memory thanks to filming and its up braking industry.

20 Simple daily basis activities, such as public transport, or main social principals or prejudices such as apartheid or racism, can be shown all over the world not only on a printed basis such as a newspaper, book or magazine, but by the whole image of it, not withstanding that images do say more than words, but often help to diversify the truth or the real facts of information. Close related to the before mentioned idea, stands the interpretation that producers, directors, actors and viewers make a truth of their own, but isn't that the way that the world is known?

25 Definitely since the beginning of the film industry, the movies have showed the existence of the different, the opposed, the distant, but far away from it, movies can help to break trough intellectual, political, and cultural barriers, in order to know better our world.

Topic 183 What have you learned about a country from its movies?

Since its birth, films always function as the main media depicting the environments and people in details. Pondering the specific aspects in the filmmaker and country, we can achieve valuable and wealthy information.

The first treasure we can dig is some social problems in the country reflected by the film. Hollywood, the largest dream makers' cradle, prefers to support some movies revealing some serious current social problems confronting in the United Stated society. Take the Oscar-winning Film in 2001, The American Beauty, as an example. That film received lots of admiration and compliments. We

35 can learn from the film that in the most advanced economy, the normal American people's life still have some dilemma such as marriage dissatisfaction, family cracking, and moral suspicion.

On the other hand, we can learn from a film about the country's history. Take the best foreign film, Crouching Tiger, Hidden Dragon, for example, we can appreciate the Chinese ancient melodious music, exotic costumes and magic martial arts. A movie from a country with its own history and tradition that totally different from those in the western movies not

40 only tells a romantic story but teach something beyond as well.

Finally, the country's own culture will be revealed in their films naturally. For example, another foreign film, Life is Beautiful, made in Italy, tells a Jewish tragedy happened in the Germany concentration camp in the Second World War. Instead of using the sorrowful way to express the plot, the inspirited filmmakers use obviously humorous and romantic ways which probably are rooted in the Italian culture. Culture usually expresses itself in the film spontaneously.

45 All in all, we can achieve some current social context, or specific historical tradition, or culture in the films. These are the aims that directors, cinematographers, and actors have been working for, and the most important, those are factors why we go to the cinemas.

Topic 183 What have you learned about a country from its movies?

Films are a mirror of a country. It depicts the life of common people in a country at a given period in history. This can be exemplified by taking a review of period films like "Elizabeth - the Last Emperor" and "Gandhi", etc. These movies have not only portrayed the lives of famous individuals of their period, but they also give coverage of the people around them, the events that shaped up their personality thus giving us insight of the life style in that particular period.

They not only depict the period in history but also in present. Globally many countries have undergone so many changes recently that we can divide the time period in cluster of 10 years each. The films arrived in each decade portrays the life style of the people in that decade. Thus proving a hallmark of changes in nations thinking, economy, and fashion.

5 Films reflect the attitude of the particular nations citizens. For example once I had seen one Japanese movie about a woman in transition phase during her divorce. It exemplifies the reaction and outlook of man/woman/child and society in total, towards the painful episode like divorce. I have also came across a movie in my country on same topic. The reactions of people to divorce in this movie are totally different than the one I saw in Japanese movie. This can be a classic example of the difference in the cultures of two countries.

Thus the movies can tell us much more than expected about the country's culture, people. They also make us aware of the
10 current issues in country, the trend, and the fashion prevailing in country.

Topic

184 Individual learning vs. group learning

Some students prefer to study alone, while others prefer to study with friends. Although studying with friends has its advantages, in my point of view, I would like to study alone. The reasons are as follows.

When you study, especially when you study some subjects that are hard to understand, such as math and physics you need to concentrate on them. That requires a quiet environment without distractions. Studying alone can provide that, and you can read your books and think of questions without being disturbed. It will help you to understand the knowledge better and to remember the knowledge better.

Furthermore, studying alone has another advantage that studying with friends does not have. That is it forces you to think.
20 When you face some questions hard to solve, and there is no other students around you, you have to think of the questions hard and try you best to solve them. This gives you an opportunity to improve your ability to deal with problems by yourself. Obviously, studying with friends cannot give you these. Because when you meet some questions, you probably turn to friends for help.

The third advantage of studying alone is also the most important reason. It can make you think independently and have
25 your own opinions. You have to think independently when you study alone. No one can give you interference or suggestions. You will not be affected by other people's opinions. That can help you create your own thoughts, not to become a parrot. After all, the best parrots still live in cages.

Though studying with friends has some advantages, for instance, it can help you to solve your questions faster and improve your friendship, however I think the advantages of studying alone overweight these of studying with friends. My
30 preference would be to study alone.

Topic

184 Individual learning vs. group learning

We as human beings have different qualities, strengths, and weaknesses. Same goes for studying. Every individual has a different way of studying, where one finds it easier to understand and comprehend the matter he/she is studying in his or her own way of learning. However, methods of studying can be classified into two major categories, namely, individual studying, and group studying.

Some people prefer group studying, because for them group studying provides them with diverse information, that is to say, that each member in the group participates and is able to provide different information on one subject.

Another reason is that if any member finds difficulty in the subject, he/she can easily discuss the problem with other
40 group members, who will be most ready to help each other. Then there is also the aspect of division of work. For example, if students are given an assignment to complete, and if each person in a group is responsible for a different topic, then the load of work is divided among the members of the group and will eventually not burden any one person. On the contrary, many students prefer studying alone, mainly because they want to do their work on their own. Doing so really helps them, because they alone are responsible for what they are studying, and therefore are responsible for their own
45 grades, this evolves a sense of responsibility in the student. Also, since there is no one to share their work with, they have to do all their work on their own, which again is an advantage. For example, a student who studies alone, when given an assignment, does it entirely by himself/herself. Doing so, each and every topic is familiar to the student and the entire work is a product of his/her own effort. So, if he/she gets a grade on such an assignment, the student would know what his potentials, what his strengths and weaknesses are.

50 I prefer to study alone, since in that way I get the proper sense of what my weaknesses are and what my strengths are. I get to improve my weaknesses. Although if I find any difficulty I cannot take help from any other person unlike students who study in groups, but then I can always ask for help from a teacher. But I believe studying on one's own is important because anyone can study in groups but when it comes to individual studying it becomes tough. And in the real world an individual is confronted with situations that a person is responsible individually. And a person can acquire such a sense of
55 responsibility only through working on his or her own.

Thus, it can be concluded that studying alone is more effective than studying in groups. Although, the different methods of studying mostly depend on what works better for the student.

Topic 185 A house or a business?

Faced with the question whether to buy a house or a business if I had the money, I came to the conclusion that basically the two investments have a major difference that radically influences my choice. I believe that spending the money for developing a business, despite being somewhat risky, is the more reasonable choice as it could bring with it not only eventual profits but also valuable knowledge and experiences to the person involved. In contrast, buying a real estate such as a house can only lead to future troubles and expenses.

Some people prefer to invest their money on things like houses or automobiles because they like the sense of secure and comfort that brought by such assets. But are they really as secure as they seem to be at first glance? First of all, rarely can anyone pay the whole sum for a house at once. In most cases it requires monthly payments for years as well as taxation. In addition keeping a house in a proper condition also costs a lot no matter whether it is used by the proprietors or tenants.

Second, in today's active world where people often move from place to place in search of new experiences or better career opportunities, it has become common for many young people to perceive the place where they live as a temporary hotel where one returns only for eating and sleeping. So it is enough for it to be convenient and affordable.

Investing in a business, on the other hand, is a very serious initiative and a great challenge as well. Deciding to start one's own business requires a certain sense of risk and a strong desire to succeed by improving one's skills. Specialized knowledge in the business field is very essential too. Certainly, however, no one can do all the work by him/herself. So a person who starts his/her own business will have to learn more not only about accounting or management but also learn how to hire the right professionals to manage some of the business affairs for him/her. Furthermore, in spite of the fact that it may take many years and numerous unsuccessful attempts, a business could bring very profitable results as it could grow and develop.

For all the reasons that I mentioned above, I believe that by investing my money in a business I will find many new opportunities for self-improvement and have the chance to be financially independent. Then maybe one day, when I am old and tired, I will buy my own house too.

Topic 185 A house or a business?

If I have enough money to purchase either a house or a business, I will choose to buy a house. Having a house is good for living, for children and even for a business.

Having my own house, my family can move out of the apartment where we are living now. I can decorate it just as what I want. I can fill my own house with furniture and appliances that I want. Everyday after I come back home, I can lie down in the white sofa I bought and watch a movie using the home theater system. But if I still live in an apartment, I will not be able to buy all the furniture that I want, because I know I only live there temporarily and there is not enough space for new furniture.

A new house is also good for the children. I can buy a house within a good school district, so my children can go to those prestigious schools now. And all I have to pay is just the property tax and some insurance fee. No rent for living anymore. No tuition for private schools anymore. Needless to say, Children can invite their friends over and have their party in the backyard. A house will win my children's big smile.

After purchasing a house, I still can do my business. With my own house, I can use it as a collateral to get a business loan. Now I can purchase that business. Maybe I am lucky and talented enough to run the business well and get some extra money to payoff the entire loan, and then I get both a house and a business. Maybe I am good in this business and can only pay off the loan after I sell the business, then I still get a house. Maybe I lose too much money in the business and the loaner take my house, and then nothing is different if I first chose to buy a business, because at last, I will own nothing for that bad luck.

Purchasing a house has a lot of benefits. Though buying a business can get me into business sooner, I think I do not need be so hurry because I like to enjoy the life first. So I will use the money to buy a house.

Topic 185 A house or a business?

If I were to choose to buy either a house or a business, I would definitely select to purchase a house because of three different reasons. First, my current house is too small to fit all of our family members. Second, buying a house is a good investment because its price tends to increase over time. Lastly, I am not keen on doing my own business.

To begin with, my family is considered one of the extended family. We currently have ten people live under the same roof. Although there are enough rooms to fit all of us in the same house now, it seems to be a problem in the future since my brother is going to have a baby. Therefore, it is a good reason for me to buy a new house to accommodate our family members.

Next, a house is always a good investment since its price usually increases over time. For example, my house in Bangkok cost around 500,000 bahts ten years ago. Its price unsurprisingly doubled. In other words, it costs around 1,000,000 bahts to buy my house presently. Therefore, buying a house is a sure bet to a good investment.

Lastly, as I grew up, I realized that I was not keen on business. When taking classes in business, I usually did not feel confident. For example, when practicing a case study on running a business, I did not want to take risks. Thus, the
5   business I ran failed. As a result, I am not sure that if I were to buy a business, it would be successful.

In conclusion, since a house would give me benefits such as providing more places for my expanding family and being a good investment, I, a person who is not keen on business, would rather buy a house rather than a business provided that I have enough money.

Topic 185 A house or a business?

If someone were generous enough to give me sufficient amount of capital to do one of the two things, I would probably go in for purchasing a house. To me, a house is one of the best securities one can have. Besides, I would not describe myself as being particularly business-minded, so given a choice between buying a house or starting a business, a home would be more appealing to me.

I have several reasons for this choice. All my life, I have lived in rented apartments, and am aware of the difficulties that my parents had faced. The constant insecurity of being asked to move out at short notice is one problem. I have watched
15   my parents hunt around for houses, the worry and tension that has caused to them, and finally, the relief and gradual sense of peace that settled in, when we finally managed to buy a place of our own.

Buying a house is an excellent investment, if done properly, and at the right time with respect to the market situation. Having a decent bit of property on one's hands is advantageous when there is a need for a loan during emergencies. Banks generally ask for securities, the most of common of which are houses and jewelry.

20   Also, a house is a source of ready money, since the market today is more often than a seller's market. If a respectable builder builds the house or building in a convenient locality, it generally fetches a good price, since these are the first two points that are considered by the buyers.

On the other hand, in today's world, with rising prices, inflation, an unstable economy, one can no longer be absolutely certain of a success in business, unless one has a sharp acumen, a sense of risk, and a true entrepreneurial spirit. A
25   business venture cannot be started half-heartedly, just because of availability of capital. A lot of hard work and enterprise is necessary to make a success out of a business in this world of cut-throat competition. I genuinely do not believe that I am cut out for it. My field of study is science, and I am more inclined towards a career that involves research.

Finally, I would like to say that it has always been my ardent wish to have a home that I can call my own, which I can come back to after a day's work, and this thought alone is sufficient to allow me to make my decision.

Topic 185 A house or a business?

Nowadays the only thing people seem to be interested is earning more and more money. Many people spend their entire lives doing business and neglect their family and friends. I do not want to be one of them. If I have to choose between earning money and spending time with my family I would choose my family. Therefore, if a have to choose between buying a nice big house for my family and me and a business that would take up all my free time I would choose the house.

35   The business can make you a lot of money, however, it cannot make you happy. The house, on the other hand, can be a dream that have come true. It can be the best place in the world for you where you can feel safe, calm, and free. The place where you keep all the things that you love and more importantly where the people you love most live. It is also the place where you will spend the happiest moments in your life.

Another reason to choose to buy a house is that it gives you security. The business may fail, but the house will always
40   remain yours. You know that no matter what happens you will always have a place to live. And if you cannot earn enough money to make your living you may let off some of the rooms.

Last but not least, I believe that a house is more valuable heritage than a business. A house can always be sold for its real price while selling a business can be quite difficult and even impossible if it has not been profitable for the past few years.

All things considered, there is no doubt that buying a house is the best choice for me. But a house cannot make me happy
45   if I live there alone. When I picture my dream house I always see my future children playing in it.

Find additional essays and updates at ToeflEssays.com

人群不同: children, adult, older.

CPSIA information can be obtained at www.ICGtesting.com
Printed in the USA
LVOW091109300113

317896LV00003B/25/A